ANALYTIC TECHNIQUES FOR ENERGY PLANNING

mo

ANALYTIC TECHNIQUES FOR ENERGY PLANNING

Proceedings of the First Symposium,
Organized by
The Operations Research Society of America Special Interest Group on Energy, Natural Resources and the Environment

Edited by

Benjamin LEV
Temple University
Philadelphia
Pennsylvania
U.S.A.

Jeremy A. BLOOM
General Public Utilities Services Corp.
Parsippany
New Jersey
U.S.A.

Frederic H. MURPHY
Temple University
Philadelphia
Pennsylvania
U.S.A.

Alan S. GLEIT
Versar, Inc.
Springfield
Virginia
U.S.A.

1984

NORTH-HOLLAND
AMSTERDAM · NEW YORK · OXFORD

ISBN: 0 444 86884 4

Published by:
ELSEVIER SCIENCE PUBLISHERS B.V.
P.O. Box 1991
1000 BZ Amsterdam
The Netherlands

Sole distributors for the U.S.A. and Canada:
ELSEVIER SCIENCE PUBLISHING COMPANY, INC.
52 Vanderbilt Avenue
New York, N.Y. 10017
U.S.A.

Library of Congress Cataloging in Publication Data

Main entry under title:

Analytic techniques for energy planning.

Bibliography: p.
1. Energy industries--Planning--Congresses.
2. Energy industries--Mathematical models--Congresses.
I. Lev, Benjamin. II. Operations Research Society of America. Special Interest Group on Energy, Natural Resources, and the Environment.
HD9502.A2A56 1984 333.79 84-1610
ISBN 0-444-86884-4

PRINTED IN THE NETHERLANDS

INTRODUCTION

The papers in this book are from the first of what is intended to be a continuing series of conferences organized by the Operations Research Society of America Special Interest Group on Energy, Natural Resources and the Environment (ORSA-SIG). The regular meetings of ORSA are designed for the sharing of ideas among operations research/management science professionals. The SIG meeting, held on June 7–8, 1983, had another purpose in mind, the bringing together of people from the institutions involved with energy issues and members of the OR/MS community interested in applying OR techniques to energy. The members of the institutions described their needs, interests and activities, and the operations researchers described energy-related projects on which they had worked. Often the presenters belonged to both groups, highlighting the role of operations research in contributing to energy analysis and planning.

The conference was sponsored by five institutions: The Texas Energy and Natural Resources Advisory Council, Battelle Pacific Northwest Laboratories, the Electric Power Research Institute, and Statistics Canada. The conference host was the Energy Information Administration of the U.S. Department of Energy. Representatives of TENRAC described their modeling, forecasting and planning activities, with particular emphasis on their on-going model-development effort. Speakers from Battelle described a number of studies utilizing energy demand modeling, supply analyses and large-scale aggregate models. Statistics Canada presented its Socio-Economic Resource Framework, which permits analysis of flows of materials and energy from the natural resource base required to meet Canadian and international needs. Representatives of the gas industry invited by GRI discussed their views on developing and implementing strategic planning processes. Members of EPRI discussed the activities and analytical needs of their departments. EIA described several new modeling efforts to improve their forecasting capabilities.

In addition, twenty speakers contributed papers to special topic sessions dealing with electric power, fossil energy and industrial energy use. The papers in this volume have been grouped into five subject areas reflecting the interests of the presenters. The first group of papers describe work in the area of fossil energy. The papers range from a description of how operations research helped in litigation over violations of the oil pricing regulations to comparisons of different coal supply models. The second group focuses on electric power supply modeling. These papers illustrate the diversity of modeling issues in electric power. They cover such topics as modeling the operations of a hydropower system, environmental issues, and using small models to understand larger, more complex models. The theme of the third group of papers is on energy use. Modeling the consumption of energy involves a different set of issues from modeling the various sources of supply. The multitude of ways that energy is consumed overwhelms the available sources of data and allows for only the most approximate structural models. The papers in this section illustrate how one deals with extracting as much as possible from available information in estimating consumption or the economic opportunities of a new technology. Modeling the interrelationships among the connected sectors in the energy system involves large-scale data management, modeling and computational issues. The fourth group of papers range from a description of the large socio-economic system built by Statistics Canada to market equilibrium models of the United States and Israel. The fifth group of papers illustrate how one combines a collection of models for analyzing selected policy issues. These papers describe the policy modeling activities of TENRAC on issues related to natural oil and gas.

This conference and proceedings was made possible by the generous support of our sponsors: the Texas Energy and Natural Resources Advisory Council, Battelle Pacific Northwest Laboratories, the Electric Power Research Institute, the Gas Research Institute, and Statistics Canada, and we gratefully acknowledge their contributions. We also want to thank the individuals at these institutions who coordinated their involvement: Robert Kieschnick of TENRAC, John Franke of Battelle, Dennis Fromholzer of EPRI, Richard Hilt of GRI and Robert Hoffman of Statistics Canada. The Energy Information Administration of U.S. Department of Energy graciously provided the facilities for our meeting, and we thank them and Susan Shaw of EIA who acted as coordinator.

Also to be recognized are efforts of the individual members of the organizing committee which brought the conference into being. Alan S. Gleit of Versar, Inc. served as general chairman arranging the sponsorship. Jeremy A. Bloom of General Public Utilities Service Corporation organized the program. Frederic H. Murphy of Temple University did the original planning for the conference and handled the publicity and liason. Benjamin Lev of Temple University arranged for publication of the conference Proceedings.

Finally, we wish to acknowledge the invaluable help we received from many individuals. Janet Sellman of GPU Services Corporation deserves special recognition for handling correspondence and the composition of the program. Catherine Swengel of Temple University served as Technical Editor and coordinated the production of the Proceedings. She deserves many thanks for her thorough and independent work on this project. The book itself was typed (more than once!) at the Temple University Manuscript Center with endless patience by Pamela Bennett, Shelah Burgess, Janet Evans and Ernestine Hopson.

January 1984

CONTENTS

POLICY MODELING BY TENRAC

LIST OF CONTRIBUTORS

R.C. Adams
Pacific Northwest Laboratory
Richland, Washington 99352
U.S.A.

Nils Andersson
Krangede AB
Stockholm, Sweden

J.C. Ammons
Georgia Institute of Technology
Atlanta, Georgia 30332
U.S.A.

Robert E. Brooks
RBA Consultants
4209 Santa Monica Blvd. Ste. 201
Los Angeles, California 90029
U.S.A.

Janis A. Bubenko, Sr.
Royal Institute of Technology
Stockholm, Sweden

Robert Ciliano
Mathtech, Inc.
P.O. Box 2392
Princeton, New Jersey 08055
U.S.A.

John Conti
Department of Energy
Washington, D.C. 20585
U.S.A.

J.L. Eisenhauer
Pacific Northwest Laboratory
Richland, Washington 99352
U.S.A.

Kristin Graves
E.H. Pechan & Associates, Inc.
5537 Hempstead Way
Springfield, Virginia 22151
U.S.A.

Hooshang Habibollahzadeh
Royal Institute of Technology
Stockholm, Sweden

K.E. Hamilton
Structural Analysis Division
Statistics Canada
Ottawa, Canada K1A0T6

Joan Heinkel
Energy Information Administration
Washington, D.C. 20585
U.S.A.

William Hery
Mathtech, Inc.
P.O. Box 2392
Princeton, New Jersey 08055
U.S.A.

Benjamin F. Hobbs
Energy Division
Oak Ridge National Laboratory
Oak Ridge, Tennessee 37830
U.S.A.

R.B. Hoffman
Structural Analysis Division
Statistics Canada
Ottawa, Canada K1A0T6

Lambert Joel
Energy Information Administration
Washington, D.C. 20585
U.S.A.

Robert L. Kieschnick, Jr.
Texas Energy and Natural Resources
Advisory Council
200 East 18th St.
Austin, Texas 78701
U.S.A.

J.C. King
Battelle, Pacific Northwest Laboratory
Richland, Washington 99352
U.S.A.

Michael J. King
Battelle, Pacific Northwest Laboratory
Richland, Washington, 99352
U.S.A.

William G. Kurator
Energy Information Administration
Washington, D.C. 20585
U.S.A.

Vicky C. Langston
7700 Old Springhouse Rd.
McLean, Virginia 22102
U.S.A.

Gunnar Larsson
Krangede AB
Stockholm, Sweden

Nissan Levin
Tel Aviv University
Tel Aviv, Israel

R.J. Moe
Pacific Northwest Laboratory
Richland, Washington 99352
U.S.A.

Frederic H. Murphy
Temple University
Philadelphia, Pennsylvania 19122
U.S.A.

Charles Mylander
Energy Information Administration
Washington, D.C. 20585
U.S.A.

Richard P. O'Neill
Energy Information Administration
Washington, D.C. 20585
U.S.A.

Edward H. Pechan
E.H. Pechan & Associates, Inc.
5537 Hempstead Way
Springfield, Virginia 22151
U.S.A.

Jeffrey P. Price
Resource Dynamics Corporation
1340 Old Chain Bridge Road
McLean, Virginia 22101
U.S.A.

J.S. Rogers
University of Toronto
Toronto, Canada M5S1A4

Douglas A. Samuelson
3443 Skyview Terrace
Falls Church, Virginia
U.S.A.

G.T. Sande
Structural Analysis Division
Statistics Canada
Ottawa, Canada K1A0T6

Reginald Sanders
Department of Energy
Washington, D.C. 20585
U.S.A.

Patsy Saunders
Energy Information Administration
Washington, D.C. 20585
U.S.A.

Michael J. Scott
Battelle, Pacific Northwest Laboratory
Richland, Washington 99352
U.S.A.

T.J. Secrest
Pacific Northwest Laboratory
Richland, Washington 99352
U.S.A.

Barry Sedlik
Dames & Moore
7101 Wisconsin Ave., Ste. 700
Bethesda, Maryland 20814
U.S.A.

Susan Shaw
Department of Energy
Washington, D.C. 20585
U.S.A.

Denis Sjelvgren
Swedish State Power Board
Stockholm, Sweden

William R. Stewart
College of William & Mary
Williamsburg, Virginia
U.S.A.

Ruth Stokes
Energy Information Administration
Washington, D.C. 20585
U.S.A.

David Strom
Office of Technology Assessment
U.S. Congress
Washington, D.C. 20585
U.S.A.

Asher Tishler
Tel Aviv University
Tel Aviv, Israel

Roger L. Tobin
Argonne National Laboratory
Argonne, Illinois 60439
U.S.A.

William A. Trapmann
Energy Information Administration
Washington, D.C. 20585
U.S.A.

Barbara Mariner-Volpe
Energy Information Administration
Washington, D.C. 20585
U.S.A.

Christoph Witzgall
Energy Information Administration
Washington, D.C. 20585
U.S.A.

Jacob Zahavi
University of California, on leave from
The Faculty of Management
Tel Aviv University
Tel Aviv, Israel

FOSSIL ENERGY

Analytic Techniques for Energy Planning
B. Lev, F.H. Murphy, J.A. Bloom & A.S. Gleit (Editors)

COAL SUPPLY MODELS: THE STATE OF THE ART*

Jeffrey P. Price
Resource Dynamics Corporation
1340 Old Chain Bridge Road
McLean, VA 22101

The state-of-the-art of coal supply modeling has advanced considerably over the last ten years and is continuing to evolve. A number of very different models have been developed to address coal supply issues. The diversity among the models reflect the varied objectives, backgrounds, and analytical resources of the different modeling organizations as well as differing views about the characteristics and behavior of the coal industry. There are also significant problems related to data quality and modeling techniques which constrain the ability of the models to address coal supply issues. Approaches to overcoming these problems differ.

1. INTRODUCTION

The future supply of coal -- in terms of production and price -- is affected by a range of factors. These include resource availability, coal mining practices and costs, coal market conditions, and an evolving array of government regulations and policies. In order to evaluate coal supply issues, forecasts of the effects of alternative conditions, regulations and policies on coal supply are required. The analytical considerations involved are complex and have been addressed by the development of computer models. Several coal supply models currently exist; results from these models frequently enter discussions of coal policy. Each model is based on different assumptions and, predictably, they each yield different results.

The Fossil Energy Program of the Department of Energy (DOE) and other concerned parties must frequently comment on energy policy proposals with coal supply implications and evaluate and compare outputs from various models. It is important for users of model results to understand the basis for the results as well as any potential limitations. Where model results may be different, it is also important to understand the reasons for such divergence.

1.1 Objectives and Approach

The objectives of this effort are to critically review and compare several widely-used coal supply models. A large number of models were considered for review. Seven models were selected:

- National Coal Model,
- ICF Coal and Electric Utilities Model,

---

*Prepared for Department of Energy. Full report published as DOE/FE-0031 and available from NTIS (Document DE 83-002088) under title "A Review of Coal Supply

- Los Alamos Coal and Utility Modeling System,
- Argonne Coal Market Model,
- DRI-Zimmerman Coal Model,
- Newcomb Coal Price Index-Quadratic Programming Model, and
- Utility Simulation Model

This review concentrates primarily on the coal supply and transportation components of these models. This is the component which deals with coal production, price or availability. Other model components are treated in the review primarily as they affect the functioning of the coal supply component.

The analysis was conducted in two phases. The first identified the relevant coal industry issues and modeling from the point of view of long term R&D planning. The second evaluated the usefulness of the various models in evaluating these issues. The purpose of the first phase was to set the stage for the second by providing a perspective on what the models are describing and by evaluating the opportunities and constraints posed by available modeling techniques and data sources.

2. MODELING ISSUES

Coal supply models must address a broad range of coal industry conditions. Choices made by the modelers about which coal industry conditions to address, modeling techniques and data use are the primary determinants of the quality of model results.

2.1 Coal Industry Conditions

Several factors have a significant impact on the determination of coal price, production and related measures of coal industry activity:

- Industry segmentation means that different conditions and prices may prevail in different markets for coal. There are four determinants of coal market segmentation:
  - -- coal quality,
  - -- geography,
  - -- type of customer, and
  - -- type of sale.
- Coal demand is determined primarily by electric utility capacity expansion and dispatch decisions and, secondarily, by non-utility coal demand.
- The production of coal depends on the available resources, and the costs of mining and preparation.
- Regulation of coal producers, carriers, and consumers affects both the costs of coal production and use and competition among the sources of supply. Air quality regulations further segment the market, cause price premiums to be paid for some coals, and limit the utilization of specific coals. Mine safety and reclamation regulations increase costs for the types of mines affected.

- The balance between supply and demand is through the transportation industry. Thus, transportation costs play a significant role in interregional competition among producers.
- Economic rents may be realized by various parties in specific market segments when the prevailing price of coal is above the cost of production.
- Inflation and resource depletion cause long-run trends to higher prices. Inflation changes prices in real terms to the extent that the components of production and transportation costs increase at a rate different from general inflation. Depletion, in an economic sense, may be defined as the removal of reserves from those available for future incremental production.
- Different pricing mechanisms are available for coal purchase transactions. The most basic distinction is between the long-term commitments of reserves and "spot" sales of near-term production. The "price" of coal for a specific transaction represents a set of unique conditions.

Coal supply models must explicitly or implicitly account for all of these factors.

2.2 Modeling Techniques

Four key decisions about modeling techniques must be addressed by coal supply modelers:

- Overall Approach. Model builders have a choice of several techniques. These include: econometric approaches, which apply statistical techniques and use large amounts of data; structural techniques, which develop relationships through engineering and economic judgment; simulation techniques which use judgment to develop feedback relationships; and simple accounting models, which manipulate assumptions external to the model. All of these techniques, individually and in combination, have been used in various coal supply models.
- Nature of the Coal Marketplace. Modelers make different assumptions about the nature of the coal industry. Choices facing modelers include: which market segments are to be addressed, the way that each segment is to be treated, which coal industry functions are to be modeled, the treatment of time, the type of competition to be assumed within the coal industry, and whether and how a market equilibrium solution is to be derived.
- Response of Coal Supply to Price. Most models (other than simple accounting models) develop "supply curves" which relate the quantity of coal produced to the price. These supply curves use various techniques to transform resource estimates into estimates of annual production. There are two types of supply curves which are differentiated by their treatment of resource depletion. Cumulative supply curves define depletion only in terms of cumulative production. Incremental supply curves define depletion in terms of both the commitment of reserves to future production and cumulative production. Given the same resource and other economic assumptions, incremental supply curves result in faster price rises in response to increased demand or cumulative production.

- Treatment of Coal Transportation. Coal transportation is, in itself, a complex modeling issue. Modelers must address issues such as the level of route and modal detail, methods of estimating future rates and the impact, if any, of capacity constraints. Limited modeling resources and techniques lead most modelers of coal supply issues to use relatively simplified transportation components within a much larger overall coal supply model. A number of models which focus on freight transportation (which can address coal transportation in detail) have been developed, but independently of models of coal supply.

All coal supply models are abstractions from the reality of the coal industry. They are attempts to identify and use the basic relationships which are assumed to underly the economic activity of the industry. Inevitably, this involves simplifications and idealizations of what is actually happening. The results depend entirely on the reasonableness and appropriateness of the assumed relationships, simplifications and idealizations.

Various problems must be addressed to develop a useful model. Different modelers approach these problems in different ways.

2.3 Information Availability

The availability and quality of information about the coal industry is a major determinant of the design of coal supply models. Where information is available and modelers are confident about meaningfulness, these data are to be used to estimate model parameters. Where there is little information or data which are suspect, modelers resort to assumptions or estimate relationships which are less robust.

There is an abundance of data about the coal industry, but there are limitations which influence coal supply modeling. The adequacy of information for modeling coal supply issues depends on the type of data required. In general:

- Coal Resource data are poor relative to the needs of coal supply modelers. The primary source of such information is the Demonstrated Reserve Base. For some models, this may be supplemented by data from other sources or by various manipulations. In any event, the bulk of the available data is out of date and inconsistent.

- Coal Accessibility data are nearly non-existent. Modelers must make *ad-hoc* guesses.

- Mining and Preparation Practices data is available from a variety of sources. These data, however, are only adequate to portray a broad-brush picture of these practices. The detail which would allow cost and productivity-relationships to be unambiguously identified does not exist. Modelers are forced to use or estimate engineering process models of coal mining and preparation.

- Industry Structure data is required to identify market and coal company financial structure. This data is generally adequate for modeling purposes.

- External Influences data primarily consists of information about the laws and regulations which affect the coal industry. While the laws may be readily identified, regulations are in a constant state of flux. Further, the impacts of these regulations may, in some cases, be identified only through extensive case-study analyses or by making broad assumptions.

- Economic Relationship data include information about general economic conditions, inflation, coal prices and coal contracts. Data about general economic conditions and inflation are generally adequate for coal supply modeling. Data about coal prices and contracts are available, but lack much of the explanatory detail that would make it most useful to modelers.

3. COAL SUPPLY MODELS

The seven models which are reviewed were designed primarily to address coal market issues. Some may integrate consideration of both coal supply and demand; others focus solely on coal supply issues.

3.1 Structural Models

Four structural models were reviewed. All share a common origin in the Project Independence Evaluation System (PIES) coal supply component. These models also utilize incremental supply curves.

National Coal Model (NCM). The current National Coal Model (NCM) is derived from a 1978 version of ICF's Coal and Electric Utilities Model (see below). NCM is currently being operated and regularly enhanced by the Energy Information Administration of the U.S. Department of Energy.
NCM is a linear programming model that minimizes the costs of coal mining, cleaning and transportation and the costs of electricity generation and transmission in five-year periods (e.g., 1985, 1990, and 1995). Utility coal demand is projected endogenously based on an exogenous forecast of electricity demand. Non-utility coal demand is an exogenous input. There are forty-four coal demand regions in NCM.

Coal resources and prices are presented by multi-step supply curves. There are thirty-one coal supply regions and forty distinct coal types in NCM.

Coal and Electric Utilities Model (CEUM). The Coal and Electric Utilities Model (CEUM) was developed by ICF, Inc. to analyze coal-related policy issues. It is a successor to the original National Coal Model developed by ICF, Inc. for the Federal Energy Administration in 1976.

CEUM is a linear programming model. The objective function minimizes costs for the sum of utility plus non-utility coal demands. For the utility sector these costs are the sum of coal mining, cleaning and transportation costs and electric generation and transmission costs. For non-utility sectors, total delivered costs are minimized. The linear program is generally solved for five-year increments (e.g., 1985, 1990, 1995). Multi-step coal supply curves characterize mine-mouth prices and reserves for fifty distinct coal types (including lignite and anthracite) in forty supply regions. CEUM forecasts utility coal demand endogenously from an exogenous projection of electricity demand. Non-utility coal demand is an exogenous input. There are forty-seven coal demand regions in CEUM.

Los Alamos Coal and Utility Modeling System (LACUMS). The Los Alamos Coal and Utility Modeling System (LACUMS) was developed by the Los Alamos Scientific Laboratory to evaluate the effects of government regulations on coal-related industries. LACUMS is a linear programming model with multiple data bases and a 1985-2005 time horizon. The model also has a non-linear programming option intended to aid in the modeling of utility dispatch on the demand side.

Utility coal demand is estimated endogenously. Non-utility coal demand is an exogenous input. Coal supplies are represented by multi-step supply curves. LACUMS is a derivative of the National Coal Model with more flexible input data base options, as well as water supply curves and explicit treatment of ambient air quality regulations.

Argonne Coal Market Model (ACM). The Argonne Coal Market Model was developed by the Argonne National Laboratory to forecast long-term regional coal production in five-year intervals. It is a quadratic programming model which minimizes the total cost of delivered steam coal (including environmental control costs). All coal demand is an exogenous input. There are fifty-two demand regions in ACM. The coal supply curves are linear approximations of multi-step functions developed in 1976 for the Project Independence Evaluation System (PIES) Model. There are nine coal supply regions with fourteen total coal types.

3.2 Econometric Models

Two models are reviewed whose parameters are estimated using primarily econometric estimation techniques. These two models, however, are quite different in approach.

DRI/Zimmerman Coal Model. The DRI/Zimmerman Coal Model forecasts coal production and prices annually to 2010 and is maintained by Data Resources, Inc. (DRI) as part of the DRI Coal Service. The Model incorporates cumulative coal supply curves for six major coal supply regions and six sulfur content categories. Coal supplies are allocated by a linear programming technique to meet an exogenous forecast of coal demand. The model can be run iteratively with the DRI Energy Model such that coal demand from the DRI Energy Model in year t is a function of coal prices in year t - 1 from the Coal Model. There are thirteen demand regions in the Coal Model.

Newcomb Coal Price Index-Quadratic Programming Model. The cornerstone of this model is an index which ranks major Appalachian coal seams which are currently mined underground. This index is a weighted average of coal characteristics. The index is transformed into a cost (mine-mouth supply price) and is used to create part of a long-run piecewise linear supply curve. Newcomb, now at the University of Arizona, is extending the index to midwestern and western coal fields.

Newcomb's index combines elements of structural and econometric approaches in an attempt to incorporate more information than other models on mining and cleaning costs. This approach was developed as a means of addressing problems perceived by Newcomb in prior models. Newcomb, for example, criticizes the use of point estimates of mining costs in the model mines of structural coal supply models because clearly defined statistical relations were not demonstrated between seam thickness and depth and mining and cleaning costs. Calculation of the error of estimation is thus impossible.

3.3 Simple Accounting Model

One simple accounting model is reviewed.

Utility Simulation Model. The Utility Simulation Model (USM) is used for some of the same applications as the coal supply models. However, USM is not really a coal supply model. USM forecasts coal prices using exogenous growth rates and does not characterize coal reserves with a supply curve.

USM projects investment and operating decisions made by electric utilities in each year over a 1976-2010 time horizon. The model projects the utility industry's response to energy and environmental policies, technology choices, projected electricity demand levels and economic conditions. The model outputs include forecasts of capacity expansion, electricity generation, fuel consumption and pollutant production for individual steam generating units or for county, state, regional and national aggregations. In addition, various measures of financial costs and statistics at the state level are projected.

4. GENERAL CONCLUSIONS

The state-of-the-art of coal supply modeling has advanced considerably over the last ten years and is continuing to evolve. A number of very different models have been developed to address coal supply issues. The diversity among the models reflects the varied objectives, backgrounds, and analytical resources of the different modeling organizations as well as differing views about the characteristics and behavior of the coal industry. There are also significant problems related to data quality and modeling techniques which constrain the ability of the models to address coal supply issues. Approaches to overcoming these problems differ.

In general, considerable uncertainty must be imputed to the numerical results of all of these models. All results--coal price, production, distribution, environmental residuals -- are the end product of numerous modeling assumptions and decisions based, in large part, on judgment.

- Coal prices represent different things in each of the models. The prices projected are not directly comparable among models. They represent different modelers' idealizations about coal sales transactions or the costs of production and transportation of coal. Prices do not necessarily correspond to any specific price of an actual transaction in the real world. Price stability in the models results from cost minimization algorithms which shift other factors (e.g., production and distribution) around in order to keep projected utilization costs from rising.

- Coal production and distribution, in the national aggregate, is usually projected to meet demand. Projections of regional patterns may be volatile, reflecting both the cost minimization solution techniques and uncertainty in the marketplace.

- Environmental residuals reflect the uncertainties in all the other model assumptions and data.

The value of coal supply models lies not in the absolute values of the forecasts but in the differences among alternatives and in future changes from the present. The issue is not which model is "right" or "wrong," but whether any model is explanatory. Models should be regarded as tools for conceptualization and analysis rather than as a principle yielding the "correct" solution.

Model understandability is important so that model users can have confidence in the model. Knowing why a model reaches its results is crucial to providing insights into the coal industry. Having "bottom line" results with no understanding of how and why these results were obtained is, given the inherent uncertainties, virtually useless. If the model is a "black box," this reduces the ability of the model to be explanatory.

4.1 Improving the State-of-the-Art

Several conditions would foster advances in the state-of-the-art:

1. Continued competition among modeling groups. No one model or approach has a monopoly on insight into the coal industry. Competition among modeling organizations is healthy and should be encouraged. A constructive skepticism from the user community is the surest spur to model improvement.

2. Recognition and identification of the inherent uncertainties. Both model operators and model users need to develop and use tools which allow for an explicit characterization of risk and uncertainty. The development of alternative scenarios is one approach which is widely used. While helpful, scenarios do not place bounds on uncertainty. Incremental improvements in the estimation of relationships may increase the apparent sensitivity of the models. All the models reviewed are continually undergoing such improvements. The issue, however, is not just model sensitivity. Rather, it is how to account for the inherent uncertainty of future conditions.

3. Better integration of coal transportation components. Coal transportation rates and capabilities are a major determinant of interrregional competition. Yet, the treatment of coal transportation in the models is usually the most simplified component. Development of more sophisticated transportation components has been limited by the complexity of coal transportation issues and by limitations in the state-of-the-art for addressing the formation of prices for transportation services (rates) that are not cost based. Further development of coal transportation components of the coal supply models would have a relatively high payoff in the quality of results, but would require an analytic "breakthrough" to address the key issues.

4. Improved data. Constraints on the quality of data about coal resources, resource accessibility and mining methods, in particular, have limited the ability of modelers to address these issues. In some cases, however, improving the data may be costly and many of the inherent uncertainties would remain.

4.2 Comparison of Model Capabilities

Coal supply models are used to project coal industry conditions such as coal production, distribution, price and environmental residuals. These models also project differences in conditions given alternative assumptions. Each alternative set of assumptions is usually termed a "scenario." Some assumptions may be about uncontrollable or uncertain conditions (e.g., oil price increase, electricity demand growth). Other assumptions may be about conditions affected by government policies. Coal-industry impacts of proposed government policies may be evaluated by different scenario assumptions which represent alternative policies. As an example, the effects of a proposed increase in black lung benefits may be projected by using scenarios with and without the assumed costs of the increased benefits.

Each model has its own view of the coal industry. To the extent that results of different models vary, there is an opportunity for the user to probe and, by explaining these differences, understand the issues that drive the coal markets. To the extent that results of different models are identical, the user of the results may take some comfort that different viewpoints yield the same bottom line. Yet, the same results could well be reached for the wrong reasons.

The basic relationships which determine broad model results at the national level are well understood and, given the requisite scenario assumptions, do not require a complex model for order-of-magnitude estimates (e.g., the relationship of coal production to utility load growth and nuclear capacity). It is the detail on which policies and decisions are often based (e.g., regional shifts in production). This detail requires more sophisticated models. Models provide an understanding of the sensitivity to key factors which affect the industry.

The capability of a model to assess the factors which affect the coal industry depends on the ability of the model to represent the coal industry in general and the impacts of the factors to be addressed. The usefulness of coal supply models lies in their ability to identify industry trends and to represent sensitivities. Model users may thus identify future conditions of concern or the consequences of actions.

Tables 1 and 2 present a list of factors which affect coal supply and demand and summarize how each of the models reviewed in detail addresses the impacts of each factor. Several models have a large number of exogenous input parameters which can be modified to perform sensitivity analyses. Other models do not explicitly represent some coal industry characteristics. These tables also show the way which factors must be specified by the model users in order for the model to be useful. If a model user wants the effects of a key factor, Tables 1 and 2 summarize whether the model modification is a structural change (S), an internal parameter change (I), or an endogenous calculation (E). If the required modification is an endogenous calculation, it may not be possible to "control" the parameter for analysis purposes.

5. CONCLUSIONS ABOUT SPECIFIC MODELS

Model assumptions have significant implications to projections of the price, production and distribution of coal, as well as to those for environmental residuals.

5.1 Structural Models

Structural models use explicit geological, engineering and accounting relationships to develop "building blocks" describing the coal industry. Typically, structural coal supply models are based on partial equilibrium algorithms which may require user specification of all or some of the projected level of coal demand. These models forecast the "optimal" mix of coal production by supply region and coal type, the transportation patterns, and marginal mine-mouth and delivered coal prices.

Four structural coal supply models were reviewed:

- the National Coal Model (NCM);
- the Coal and Electric Utilities Model (CEUM);
- the Los Alamos Coal and Utility Modeling System (LACUMS); and
- the Argonne Coal Market (ACM) model.

Price. Structural model coal supply curves are based on estimating real annuity new contract minemouth prices for blocks of coal reserves. As such, they are "incremental" supply curves. The prices they project are the minimum acceptable selling prices necessary to open a new mine for a particular coal type in a supply region. These prices represent expected production expenses plus the minimum return on invested capital required for a producer to open a mine. As annuities, they are the price which would be paid in real terms if the same prices were paid every year over the life of the mine.

Price outputs are the real annuities (not current year prices) for the last mine selected by the model to be opened. This formulation assumes that the marginal coal producer in each region sets the minemouth coal prices. Prices increase over time due to depletion, the opening of new mines to extract coal from less attractive, more expensive-to-mine seams as already producing reserves are exhausted.

The representation of minimum acceptable selling prices as real annuities is designed to provide a simple, easy-to-understand measure of the economic worth of the mining investment to both producer and consumer. The stream of actual prices paid over the term of the contract by the consumer may be different depending upon the contract negotiations, but for the minimum acceptable return to be earned by the producer, the present value should be the same as that for the annuity price. The structural coal supply models assume that the coal supplies will come from the mines with the lowest levelized, minimum acceptable, selling prices (all other factors--transportation costs, pollution control costs--being equal).

The coal prices projected by each of these models are a function of the assumptions used to develop and operate the models. These assumptions are necessarily simplifications and are based on highly uncertain primary data. Despite the deterministic formulation, there are wide bounds of uncertainty around the point estimates of coal prices (and other measures of coal market activity).

Price outputs do not represent any "average" projected prices that can be compared with a historical average annual price series. Contracts signed in earlier years may have lower prices because their capital costs had not increased to prevailing values and depletion had not been as advanced. Coal purchases under long-term commitments may not have price escalators or other terms which correspond to those assumed to calculate the marginal real annuity prices. Contract terms are a function of the relative negotiating strengths of coal producers and consumers, not modelers' assumptions about the marginal regional producer. Some commitments will incorporate economic rents. Spot-purchases may be at substantially different prices than the real annuity prices because of the market balance for a particular coal type. NCM, CEUM and LACUMS assume that the life of a new mine is also the length of the commitment between seller and buyers. Frequently, this is not the case, especially in the East. In this region, contracts of 3 to 5 years duration are common. Renegotiations at the end of the contract periods allow coal producers to realize economic rents.

Price outputs thus do not represent average contract or spot-purchase prices. They represent only estimates of prices for marginal balanced-market, long-term reserve commitments expressed in terms of an annuity. These models thus do not provide average price forecasts of prices that may be realized on specific actual contracts.

Coal price outputs in the linear programming models are relatively stable. The optimization technique, with its national cost minimization objective function, shifts production to less-expensive reserves when prices of one coal type increase. This acts to limit price increases. Many supply curves are not steep because of the distribution of favorable mining conditions (mine sizes, seam conditions). In addition, the transportation cost growth rates (in real terms) are generally low. As a result, marginal minimum selling prices increase slowly in real terms for any specific coal type.

The usefulness of the models for policy analyses depend not just on the absolute values projected for coal prices, but also on the sensitivity of these models to scenarios which may perturb the coal markets. In general, price shifts for the models most extensively reviewed (NCM and CEUM) appear to be in directions which one would expect. The magnitude of these shifts usually appears to be in a reasonable "ballpark" range, but given the inherent uncertainties, what is "reasonable" is necessarily a subjective assessment.

Production/Distribution. A major focus of structural coal supply models is where the coal is expected to be produced and what is the type (e.g., rank, sulfur content). For example, will Midwest coal demands be met by local high sulfur coal supplies or by medium/low sulfur supplies from Appalachia or the West.

Projections of where coal will be produced and how it will be distributed are functions of 1) the assumptions leading to the development of coal supply curves, 2) coal transportation costs, 3) the determination of demand and 4) the method of solution of the model.

Coal production and distribution by region are more sensitive to scenario specifications than are coal prices. This effect occurs because the optimization algorithms in the models are designed to minimize costs, in part, by shifting the sources of coal among the supply regions. This can lead to sudden shifts of production from one region to another as the total costs of burning coal change. Both linear programming and quadratic programming formulations have these "knife-edge" effects. In both, transitions to different lowest-costs regions occur at specific points. The supply and demand regions which are most affected are those in the Midwest located between several competing production regions. To some extent, the instabilities in these regions are masked by reporting on an aggregated basis.

Environmental Residuals. NCM and CEUM project aggregate particulate matter and nitrogen oxides emissions as well as sulfur dioxide emissions. CEUM has also been used by EPA to calculate cost-effectiveness ratios (e.g., changes in annualized costs per ton of sulfur removed) for alternative air emissions standards.

State Implementation Plan (SIP) sulfur dioxide emissions regulations are incorporated by regional averages for each demand region. In addition, Federal New Source Performance Standards (NSPS) are modeled.

Scrubber capital and operating costs have also been estimated to model the trade-off between purchasing a complying coal type or scrubbing a non-complying coal type to meet the applicable emission regulation. This feature has been expanded in NCM and CEUM to include partial and full scrubbing and wet and dry systems. The scrubber cost estimates are important because, for new utility coal-fired power plants required to scrub by NSPS, the scrubber costs determine whether it is less expensive to fully scrub high sulfur coal types or partially scrub medium sulfur coal types. The total amount of FGD sludge produced is also an output feature of CEUM.

LACUMS can project water consumption (surface and purchased) for energy conversion facilities (powerplant cooling and synthetic fuels plants) by region in the western U.S. LACUMS projects total regional sulfur emissions from all types of coal conversion (including coal-based electricity generation). LACUMS also has the capability of modeling regulations on ambient SO_2 concentrations.

ACM does not forecast any environmental residuals.

Mining residuals are not calculated by any of the models.

Summary. The four structural models have diverged significantly since their common origin in the PIES coal supply curves. NCM and CEUM provide the greatest flexibility to handle alternative coal production scenario assumptions because their operators have full control over the generation of supply curves. The addition of water supply and PSD increments to LACUMS allows the flexibility to address some demand-side issues which may be important in the West. LACUMS may also be somewhat more flexible in treating demand-side scenarios because of the ease with which alternate data bases may be defined. ACM's reliance on the old PIES supply curves makes this model obsolete. The linear approximation of nonlinear supply curves, the limited number of supply curves, and the lack of a coal demand sector reduces the sensitivity of ACM when compared to the other models.

5.2 DRI/Zimmerman Coal Model, An Econometric Model

The DRI/Zimmerman Coal Model uses a cumulative supply curve, which means that for a specific coal, all reserves with the same costs (including minimum producer's return) are produced simultaneously. Full costs equal marginal price for all production. By contrast, production from the incremental supply curves of the structural models may be from reserves with full costs in a range varying up to the marginal price. Marginal price equals full price only for the marginal mine. All other mines earn implicit economic rents.

Coal demand is an exogenous input to the DRI/Zimmerman Coal Model (except to the extent that it, if desired, can be run iteratively with the DRI Energy Model). This formulation clearly reduces the model's robustness compared to others which solve for both supply and demand simultaneously. It is the feedback between the supply and demand sectors which provides some of the more interesting insights about the behavior of the coal markets.

The use of the lognormal statistical distribution to categorize coal reserves is one of the more controversial aspects of the DRI/Zimmerman model. This was an attempt to cope with problems of the poor quality of data. Since there is no conclusive information on the true distribution of resources, this approach appears to be as reasonable as any other. The problem is that there is inadequate published information to prove -- or disprove -- any specific distribution.

Price DRI annualizes new mine capital costs for each type of equipment on an after-tax basis and adds current-year labor, materials and supplies estimates to estimate coal prices. This coal price is a current-year price, not a levelized price. This would be equivalent to a levelized price if it were assumed that labor materials and supply costs would not increase in real terms.

Marginal mine-mouth coal prices, marginal delivered coal prices including scrubbing costs and marginal delivered prices excluding scrubbing costs are output features. Coal prices rise slowly because of the degree of interregional substitution, limits on substantial annual production increases, and constraints on switching coal types imposed using data related to utility coal purchase contracts.

The DRI/Zimmerman Coal Model projections of coal prices are not comparable with any historical coal price series. They do not represent average long-term contract prices or an average of contract and spot-market coal prices over the entire coal market.

Coal prices are stated to represent the marginal full costs of production in the various market segments defined by the model. These full costs include operating and maintenance costs plus capital charges. Capital charges are calculated by annualizing new mine capital costs for each type of equipment over equipment lifetimes. Reserves at a price corresponding to a specific mine type are consumed at a pace independent of either the investment or the equipment lifetimes. Zimmerman and others state that the price represented in the Zimmerman model is that of a "variable-length contract".

There is a significant consequence of the investment lifetime being undefined relative to production lifetime. Zimmerman assigns a fixed price (which can be adjusted annually for real cost increases) to entire reserve blocks. This price is calculated based on an assumed rate of return over the life of the equipment. If the period in production, as chosen by the model, is less than the equipment lifetime, a higher present value of the revenues would occur. If the period of production chosen by the model is longer than the equipment lifetime, a lower present value of revenues would occur. Since price never varies, there is no control over the rate of return. As the production pattern may vary for portions of reserves at the same price, different rates of return for the same types of reserves may occur in model results.

The problem is that in the real world, investments yield production capacity, not production per se. Zimmerman makes this link when he develops mine costs because he calculates a specific mine size -- but he loses the relationship when cumulative supply curves are developed. The required rate of return is not assured by allowing the mine to produce at capacity for its expected investment lifetime or by changing the price with different production lifetimes.

There is another problem with having no mine lifetime and "variable-length contract" prices. What is the transaction that is being represented? Coal contracts with terms longer than a few months are commitments of reserves for future production. Most coal today is sold under the terms of such commitments. Producers can generally only obtain financing for new capacity if they have long-term commitments. Such commitments are an inherent part of operating a mine. Without in some way relating the coal price to the nature of the commitment made, no sales transaction has been defined.

The modeling of commitments is also important because models may have to deal with the breaking of commitments. Consider a scenario in which, for some reason (e.g., changing emissions limitations), the annual demand for coal from a supply region declines between periods. It is reasonable to expect that the prices should fall. Only mines whose variable costs of operation are below the lower prevailing price would remain open. If unused commitments of reserves are modeled, these may be "broken". Unused reserves can be allocated for future commitments and only lower-priced commitments kept. With a cumulative supply curve, there are no unused, committed reserves which can be made available for the future. Price rises will continue to be forecast despite the decrease in demand.

<u>Production/Distribution</u>. Regional production costs and coal flows are output features. The regional distribution of coal production between surface and underground mining is also an output feature. These model results are relatively stable because the model incorporates estimates of long-term contracts and limits on annual production increases/decreases. The lack of feedback from a demand-side in some model runs also contributes to stability -- and a lack of robustness because key demand-side determinants of production are unaccounted for.

Environmental Residuals. Aggregate air emissions are not an output feature of the DRI/Zimmerman Coal Model. Scrubbing costs and sulfur emissions standards are model parameters. The scrubber cost algorithm is a function of the required sulfur percentage removal and the average percent sulfur content. The scrubber cost estimates are based on data from 21 coal-fired power plants and are expressed as $/million Btu.

The structural coal supply models account for sulfur emissions regulations with average demand region/State Implementation Plan sulfur emission limits. The DRI/Zimmerman Coal Model does not use current State standards until 1985. Estimates are made of 1977 sulfur emission levels per million Btu of coal burned in coal-fired power plants (adjusted for power plants subject to New Source Performance Standards). These "current" emissions levels are decreased annually so that by 1985 all demand regions are in compliance with the law.

5.3 Newcomb Coal Price Index-Quadratic Programming Model, An Econometric Model

Price. Coal prices are not represented as marginal production costs. For underground reserves, the coal prices are represented as a value premium based on an index. For strippable reserves, the coal prices are historical 1973 values.

Long-term contracts are not modeled. Therefore, this approach represents the utility sector as purchasing all coal demand in a balanced spot market.

Production/Distribution. This model does present results purporting to be the distribution of coal production by supply district and the distribution pattern. Details by sulfur content and mining method are not available. Such results, however, may be biased by the assumptions enumerated above.

Environmental Residuals. This model does not calculate air emissions or ash and scrubber sludge disposal requirements. The amount of coal required to be scrubbed is also not determined. Coal is distributed on the basis of least cost without respect to the applicable sulfur emissions standard.

5.4 Utility Stimulation Model, A Simple Accounting Model

The utility simulation model is not a coal supply model in the sense of making explicit assumptions about many of the factors which affect coal supply. Projections of key coal supply parameters (e.g., price, production, distribution, and environmental residuals), however, are made by this model.

Price. Coal prices in USM are base-year prevailing minemouth coal prices for individual coal generating units, escalated by exogenous growth rates plus estimates of projected transportation costs. Average supply region minemouth or average state delivered coal prices are not output features of USM. Weighted regional average coal prices (first year and/or levelized) could be calculated. As noted, regional minemouth coal prices are exogenous model inputs. Output results for coal prices can only be an average of the simultated utilities' choices from the menus of coal types presented by the modelers and will only be as good as the coal alternatives input by the modelers.

Production/Distribution. USM does output utility coal production by supply region, distribution from supply region to demand region and coal consumption by demand region. In essence, these outputs reflect the simple accounting model structure - summations by regions of the model generating unit fuel choices from the exogenous menu of available coals. Details on mining method are not available, because mining activity, as such, is not modeled.

USM does not forecast non-utility coal demand, but it does provide annual forecasts of utility coal demand at a very disaggregated level - the electricity generation unit. Although the model time horizon extends to the year 2010, the reliability of long-term model results at disaggregated levels (e.g., counties) is weak for several reasons:

- announced unsited and hypothesized unit capacity additions are sited by county randomly based on siting weights and,
- the capacity mix of new additions by fuel type is fixed and does not vary with scenario assumptions (e.g., coal minemouth price and/or transportation cost growth rates, scrubber costs, oil or gas price forecasts).

Environmental Residuals. Emissions outputs from utility combustion sources by region include:

- SO_2, NO_x and particulate matter emissions,
- ash,
- FGD sludge,
- trace metals, and
- radioactive emissions from coal.

Again, emissions outputs can only be as good as the choices from the input menu of coal types.

TABLE 1

FACTORS AFFECTING COAL SUPPLY[a]

Market Conditions Affected	Factors Which Cause Change	NCM/CEUM LACUMS/ACM	DRI/ Zimmerman	Newcomb Index/QP
Availability of coal	Improved resource knowledge	1 - revise reserves data	1 - revise reserves data	1 - revise reserves data
	Depletion	E	E	E
	Resource accessability	1 - revise regional estimates	1 -revise regional recoverability factors for deep and surface mines	1 -revise national recoverability factors for deep and surface mines
	Mining recoverability	1 - revise national recoverability factors for deep and surface mines	1 - revise regional recoverability factor for deep and surface mines	1 - revise national recoverability factors for deep and surface mines
	Federal leasing policies	1 - revise national recoverability factors for deep and surface mines	1 - revise regional recoverability factors deep and surface mines	1 - revise national recoverability factors for deep and surface mines
Production costs	Mining Productivity	NCM/LACUMS/ACM: S - labor is fixed and not a variable; new cost estimates for model mines would need to be derived. CEUM: 1 - revise regional productivity factors by mine-type	E - function of seam thickness or overburden ratio; Productivity annual rates of change: 1 - by supply region and deep v.surface	Surface mines: S - not a model parameter; Deep mines: 1 - revise estimates.
	Wages	NCM/LACUMS/ACM: S - labor is fixed and not a variable; new cost estimates for model mines would need to be derived. CEUM: 1 - revise national wage rates for deep v.surface mines	S - base year labor rates are fixed; new cost estimates for model mines would need to be derived. Annual rates of change in wages: 1 - revise national estimate.	S - not a model parameter
	Coal producer real return on equity	1 - 15 percent nominal; 9 percent real	1 - 10 percent real	S - not a model parameter
	Mine life	NCM/CEUM/LACUMS: Annual production rate and annualized costs 1 - 30 years; ACM: Annual production rate: 1 - 20 years	Annual production rate: E; Levelized capital costs: 1 - 5, 10 or 20 years depending on expected equipment lives	Annual production rates 1 - 30 years; Annualized costs S - not a model parameter
	Tax law (ITC, income tax rate, depreciation)	1 - revise capital recovery factors	1 - revise capital recovery factors	S - not a model parameter

Table 1 (Continued)

FACTORS AFFECTING COAL SUPPLY[a]

Market Condition Affected	Factors Which Cause Change	NCM/CEUM LACUMS/ACM	DRI/ Zimmerman	Newcomb Index/QP
	Reclamation fees	1 - revise national estimates	1 - revise regional estimates	S - not a model parameter
	Federal/State taxes, royalties	1 - revise regional estimates	1 - revise regional estimates	1 - revise regional estimates
	Mine size distribution	1 - revise regional estimates(deep v surface)	E - "minimum efficient mine size"	S - not a model parameter
	Bounds on changes in production levels	1 - add constraints	1 - revise regional estimates	1 - add constraints
	Cleaning Costs	1 - revise estimates	S - not a current model feature	Surface mines S - not model parameter; Deep mines: 1 - revise index
	Mix of mining technologies	CEUM/ACM: S - fixed, not a model parameter; NCM/LACUMS: 1 - revise assignment of model mines to mine types by region.	S - fixed, not a model parameter	S - not a model parameter
	Black lung insurance tax	1 - revise estimates	1 - revise estimates	S - not a model parameter
	UMW welfare fund	1 - revise estimates	1 - revise estimates	S - not a model parameter
Distribution costs	Transportation costs	1 - revise estimates	1 - revise estimates	1 - revise estimates
	Intermodal competition	S - currently exogenous, one mode per link is input (e.g. unit train or barge); only one route is input for each pair of coal supply and demand regions LACUMS: E -allows rail/barge competition	S - currently exogenous one mode per link is input (e.g. unit train or barge); only one route is input for each pair of coal supply and demand regions	S - currently exogenous one mode per link is input (e.g. unit train); only one route is input for each pair of coal supply and demand regions
	Capacity constraints on specific routes	1 - add constraints on coal flows between supply and demand regions	Add constraints on coal flows between supply and demand regions	Add constraints on coal flows between supply and demand regions.

a S - Structural change,
1 - Internal parameter change,
E - Endogenous calculation.

Table 2

FACTORS AFFECTING COAL DEMAND[a]

Market Condition Affected	Factor Which Causes Change	NCM/CEUM/LACUMS	ACM	DRI/ Zimmerman	Newcomb Index/QP	USM
Total coal demand	Electricity demand	1 - revise regional estimates	S - not a model parameter	S - not a model parameter	S - not a model parameter	1 - revise regional estimates
	Utility coal demand	E	1 - revise regional estimate	1 - revise regional estimates	1 - revise regional estimates	E
	- changing load factors	1 - revise estimates	S - not a model parameter	S - not a model parameter	S - not a model parameter	1 - revise estimates
	- new nuclear capacity constraints	1 - revise estimates	S - not a model parameter	S - not a model parameter	S - not a model parameter	1 - revise estimates
	- changing relative generation costs	1 - revise estimates	S - not a model parameter	S - not a model parameter	S - not a model parameter	1 - revise estimates
	- oil/gas prices	1 - revise regional estimates	S - not a model parameter	S - not a model parameter	S - not a model parameter	1 - revise estimates
	- fuel use regulations	1 - revise estimates	S - not a model parameter	S - not a model parameter	S - not a model parameter	1 - revise estimates
	Industrial stream coal demand	1 - revise regional estimates	1 - revise regional estimates	1 - revise regional estimates	S - not a model parameter	S - not a model parameter
	Metallurgical coal demand	1 - revise regional estimates	S - not a model parameter	1 - revise regional estimates	S - not a model parameter	S - not a model parameter
	Coal export demand	1 - revise regional estimates	1 - revise regional estimates	1 - revise regional estimates	S -not a model parameter	S - not a model parameter
	Synthetic fuel plant coal demand	1 - revise regional estimates	1 - revise regional estimates	1 - revise regional estimates estimates	S - not a model parameter	S - not a model parameter
Coal type	Sulfur dioxide emission regulations	1 - revise regional estimates LACUMS: E - PSD ambient concentrations	1 - revise regional estimates	1 - revise regional estimates	S - not a model parameter	1 - revise regional estimates
	Pollution control costs	1 - revise scrubber and cleaning cost estimates	1 - revise scrubber cost estimates	1 - revise scrubber and cleaning cost estimates	S - not a model parameter	S - revise scrubber and cleaning cost estimates

a S - Structural change
1 - Internal change
E - Endogenous calculation

Analytic Techniques for Energy Planning
B. Lev, F.H. Murphy, J.A. Bloom & A.S. Gleit (Editors)

A NETWORK PROGRAMMING SYSTEM FOR STUDYING COAL TRANSPORTATION

Roger L. Tobin
Argonne National Laboratory
Argonne, IL 60439

This paper describes a network programming/data management system developed for the study of coal transportation. At the heart of the system is a freight transportation model that considers the decisions of both the shippers (e.g., coal buyers) and the carriers (rail and barge operators). This model functions primarily in a predictive mode, selecting appropriate coal sources, transportation modes, and transportation routes that minimize the delivered price of coal to each coal user. Congestion at locks and on rail lines can be predicted because the model can also account for the movements of all other commodities on the rail and waterway system.

The system framework is flexible in that it includes software and data bases that allow the user to easily define study regions of any size (sub-state to whole nation) and to specify different levels of transportation network detail within the study region. This allows for a completely detailed transportation network in the region of interest while modeling important movements into and out of the region on an aggregate network. This keeps the network programming problems to a reasonable size without sacrificing detail where needed.

The system was conceived as a management decision tool for the Office of Fuels Conversion, Economic Regulatory Administration, U.S. Department of Energy. It has been used to study the cumulative transportation impacts of switching 42 powerplants in the northeastern United States from oil or natural gas to coal and in a similar study of switching 14 powerplants in Florida from oil to coal.

1. INTRODUCTION

The Power Plant and Industrial Fuel Use Act of 1978 (Pub. L. 95-620), known by the acronym FUA, empowered the U.S. Department of Energy (DOE) to prohibit the use of oil and natural gas in powerplants and major fuel-burning installations. Based on this authority, DOE has identified 42 powerplants in the Northeast as candidates for prohibition orders that would require conversion to coal or exemptions on the basis of environmental or fuel-availability considerations. More recently, DOE assessed the cessation of the use of oil and natural gas in 14 powerplants in the state of Florida. Such region-wide conversions to the use of coal raise the question of whether the existing transportation system possesses sufficient capacity to deal with the expected increase in coal haulage. Such increases may create excessive congestion and delays or "bottlenecks" that will impact the freight transportation system. The potential for deleterious impacts can only be determined through a careful analysis of the intermodal freight network.

Such a network analysis is complicated by the large size of the networks encountered in practice (thousands of arcs and hundreds of nodes), by the presence of congestion, which introduces nonlinearities to a network model, and by the hierarchy of decision-makers involved in freight transportation. This hierarchy exists because the transport of any commodity depends on the decisions of shippers who require quantities of commodities at specified destinations, and the decisions of carriers who provide the transportation services needed by the shippers. Generally, shippers and carriers are distinct decision-making entities.

The need for a regional coal transportation impact analysis for the 42 conversion candidates in the Northeast motivated the development of a freight transportation model that could address this problem. The resulting model--the Freight Network Equilibrium Model (FNEM)--is a predictive, multi-modal, multi-commodity network freight model that accounts for the decisions of both shippers and carriers (Friesz et al. [3]). Use of the model for analyzing coal movements in the Northeast led to the development of improved data bases and data handling software to simplify updating, modifying, outputting, and graphically displaying the data. The network for the Northeast study was custom-built to provide detail where needed, to provide for coal movements at a national scale, and to be of a size that would allow for reasonable computation times. Rather than building another custom network for studying coal conversions in Florida (Tobin et al. [6]), software was developed that automatically builds networks with the desired properties, using several compatible network data bases. This software also generates supply and demand files for the network from basic data files.

The total system consists of compatible supply, demand, and network data bases; flexible network definition software; preprocessors and postprocessors; shipper and carrier freight models; and efficient nonlinear network optimization methods. This system significantly simplifies the process of conducting regional coal transportation analyses.

The center of the system, the Freight Network Equilibrium Model (FNEM) developed by the University of Pennsylvania and Argonne National Laboratory, is presented in the next section and its formulation and solution method are discussed. The data requirements of the model and the preprocessors developed to simplify handling these data are discussed in the following sections. The flexible region definition software and associated data bases are then described using examples from the Florida study. Finally, output from the model is discussed.

2. MODEL DESCRIPTION

The model is divided into two submodels that are applied sequentially (see also Friesz et al. [3] and Gottfried [5]). The first--the shipper submodel--is a simultaneous generation, distribution, modal split, and traffic assignment model; it is used to determine a user-optimized flow pattern in which shippers selfishly and noncooperatively minimize their delivered price of commodities. The results are a set of origin-destination (O-D) demands and a general routing pattern by mode and carrier which are then used as inputs to the carrier submodel. The carrier submodel determines a system-optimized flow pattern for each carrier in which individual carriers minimize their total operating costs while satisfying shipper demands.

2.1 The Shipper Submodel

The shipper submodel routes traffic over an aggregate abstract representation of the freight transportation network. This aggregate network need only include the nodes that might realistically be considered by a shipper. Although the aggregate network varies from application to application, its nodes include all potential origins, destinations, transshipment sites, and intercarrier transfer points (interline points). In addition, major points of transportation activity that might be of special interest can be added. An aggregate network is used instead of the real detailed network because it is this representation of the transportation system that the shippers actually "see" when making routing choices. Shippers are concerned with and have the power to determine the O-D pairs, mode(s), location of transshipments/interlines (if any), and, to some extent, a general routing pattern. Unless private carriage is used, shippers have neither information about nor control over the detailed routing choices with which the carriers are faced.

In the shipper submodel, it is assumed that the extent of commodity demand is known throughout the network and is given by the fixed numbers D_j^r which stand for the demand for commodity r at destination j. As noted previously, it is assumed that each shipper is separately and noncooperatively seeking to minimize the final delivered price of the commodity it is purchasing. The final delivered price to the shipper of a commodity r transported between O-D pair w on path p by mode s is

$$DP_{wp}^{rs} = q_r t_p^{rs} + m_i^r(o_i^r) + z_w^{rs} + \varepsilon c_p^{rs} \qquad (1)$$

where

q_r	is the value of time for commodity r;
t_p^{rs}	is the delay experienced by commodity r when transported by mode s over path p;
$m_i^r(o_i^r)$	is the price of commodity r at origin i of O-D pair w for supply level o_i^r;
z_w^{rs}	is the transportation rate for commodity r when transported between O-D pair w by mode s;
ε	is the permeability factor (see below); and
c_p^{rs}	is the unit cost to carriers of transporting commodity r over path p by mode s.

Note that in Equation (1), the actual monetary expenditure for transportation is expressed by the third and fourth terms only. This amount is equal to some base rate plus some specified percentage (ε , the permeability) of the carriers' actual cost. The z_w^{rs} may be considered the posted tariff between O-D pair w for commodity r moved by mode s; ε may then be adjusted to represent the degree of freedom that the carrier is permitted in deviating from this tariff based on the costs it is incurring in providing service. If an unregulated market situation exists, the ε term may be reinterpreted as a profit multiplier and the z_w^{rs} term deleted. If the market is highly regulated, the ε term may be set to zero and the z_w^{rs} term retained.

Because of the assumption of separate, noncooperative minimization of delivered price by shippers, the shipper submodel finds user-optimal flows. The resulting flow pattern obeys Wardrop's First Principle stated in terms of delivered price--i.e., no shipper can obtain a better delivered price by changing coal source, delivery mode, or carrier (Fernandez and Friesz [2]).

Origin-destination transportation demand functions may also be specified for each application of the model. These are especially useful for aggregate commodities or aggregate shippers where components of delivered price, such as value of time, may vary between individual commodities or individual shippers. A well-known function and the one used in FNEM for non-coal commodities is the negative exponential function (Wilson [7]),

$$T_w^{rs} = A_i^r \, B_j^r \, O_i^r \, D_j^r \exp(-\theta^r \, DP_{wp}^{rs}) \tag{2}$$

where T_w^{rs} is the demand for transportation of commodity r between O-D pair w = (i,j) by mode s; and A_i^r, B_j^r, and θ^r are parameters that must be calibrated.

A shipper flow pattern must also satisfy flow conservation, trip production, trip attraction, and nonnegativity constraints. Let f_a^{rs} denote the flow of commodity r by mode s on arc a of the shipper network, and let the arc-path incidence matrix be comprised of elements

$$\delta_{ap}^{rs} = \begin{cases} 1 \text{ if arc a is on path p and carries commodity r by mode s} \\ 0 \text{ otherwise} \end{cases}$$

Also, let P_w^{rs} be the set of all paths connecting O-D pair w and carrying commodity r by mode s. Thus, the constraints may be stated as:

$$f_a^{rs} = \sum_p \delta_{ap}^{rs} \, h_p^{rs} \text{ for all a,r,s (definitional)} \tag{3}$$

$$G_w^{rs} = T_w^{rs} \sum_{p \varepsilon P_w^{rs}} h_p^{rs} = 0 \text{ for all w,r,s (flow conservation)} \tag{4}$$

$$E_i^r = \Sigma_s \Sigma_j T_w^{rs} - O_i^r = 0 \text{ for all w = (i,j),r,s (trip production)} \tag{5}$$

$$F_j^r = \sum_s \sum_i T_w^{rs} - D_j^r = 0 \text{ for all w = (i,j),r,s (trip attraction)} \tag{6}$$

$$T_w^{rs} > 0 \text{ for all w,r,s (nonnegativity)} \tag{7}$$

$$h_p^{rs} > 0 \text{ for all p,r,s (nonnegativity)} \tag{8}$$

The set of all flows and demands satisfying these constraints will be referred to as Ω; that is,

$$\Omega = \{f,h,T\text{: Equations (3) through (8) are satisfied}\} \tag{9}$$

where f, h, and T are respectively vectors of arc flow, path flow, and O-D travel demand variables.

It can be shown (Gottfried [5]) that a user-optimized shipper flow pattern can be

Sulfur Category 1: 0.0-0.64%

NODE CODE	NODE PLACE NAME		MOVEMENT	ARCS	MILES	HOURS	DELAY $	TRAVEL $	TOTAL $
BEA051	Chattanooga	TN	Origin - Supply Zone Centroid						39.04
2365060D	DALTON	GA	Supply Access - Rail	1	27	1.1	0.00	1.07	1.08
2545010D	Marcy	FL	CSX Corp.	34	704	18.4	0.02	23.76	23.78
251PP085MAR	MARTIN		Individual Demand Access - Rail	1	0	0.0	0.0	0.0	0.0
			Trip Totals	36	731	19.5	0.02	24.83	63.89
BEA052	Johnson City	TN	Origin - Supply Zone Centroid						36.96
2155010D	JOHNSON CITY	TN	Supply Access - Rail	1	31	1.2	0.00	1.22	1.22
2545010D	Marcy	FL	CSX Corp.	34	806	22.1	0.02	27.20	27.22
251PP085MAR	MARTIN		Individual Demand Access - Rail	1	0	0.0	0.0	0.0	0.0
			Trip Totals	36	837	23.3	0.02	28.43	65.41

Sulfur Category 2: 0.65-1.04%

NODE CODE	NODE PLACE NAME		MOVEMENT	ARCS	MILES	HOURS	DELAY $	TRAVEL $	TOTAL $
BEA014	Williamsport	PA	Origin - Supply Zone Centroid						31.89
0741560E	LOCK HAVEN	PA	Supply Access - Rail	1	10	0.4	0.00	0.44	0.44
0877010E	Baltimore	MD	Conrail	3	174	4.1	0.00	5.87	5.88
T-PE3240	BALTIMORE	MD	Rail to Deep Draft	1	0	74.0	0.07	0.76	0.83
T-FWW	OFFSHORE	XX	Deep Draft Line Haul	6	1491	81.0	0.08	14.21	14.29
251PP101ANC	ANCLOTE		Individual Demand Access - Water	1	0	0.0	0.0	0.0	0.0
			Trip Totals	12	1675	159.5	0.16	21.29	53.34
BEA016	Pittsburgh	PA	Origin - Supply Zone Centroid						30.88
0885110D	CUMBERLAND	MD	Supply Access - Rail	1	51	2.0	0.00	1.97	1.97
0877010D	Baltimore	MD	CSX Corp.	3	185	6.2	0.01	6.24	6.25
T-PE3240	BALTIMORE	MD	Rail to Deep Draft	1	0	74.0	0.07	0.76	0.83
T-PE3050	PORT EVERGLADES	FL	Deep Draft Line Haul	5	1054	93.2	0.09	10.76	10.85
258PP011PEV	PORT EVERGLADES		Individual Demand Access - Water	1	0	0.0	0.0	0.0	0.0
			Trip Totals	11	1290	175.4	0.18	19.73	50.79
BEA049	Birmingham	AL	Origin - Supply Zone Centroid						45.50
P2130	BANKHEAD POOL	AL	Supply Access - Inland Water	1	20	0.8	0.00	0.74	0.74
P2620	MOBILE HARBOR	AL	Inland Water Line Haul	10	346	83.2	0.08	3.79	3.87
T-PE2620	MOBILE	AL	Deep Draft/Water, Selected Ports	1	0	60.0	0.06	4.25	4.31
T-FWW	OFFSHORE	XX	Deep Draft Line Haul	1	435	23.6	0.02	4.15	4.17
251PP017CRR	CRYSTAL RIVER		Individual Demand Access - Water	1	0	0.0	0.0	0.0	0.0
			Trip Totals	14	801	167.6	0.17	12.92	58.59

Figure 1. Example Output from Shipper Model.

obtained by solving an appropriately defined optimization problem. In particular, if $t_a^{rs}(f_a^{rs})$ and $c_a^{rs}(f_z^{rs})$ are the delay and operating cost functions, respectively, on arc a of the shipper network for commodity r transported by mode s, that optimization problem is:

minimize

$$Z = \sum_a \sum_r \sum_s \int_0^{f_a^{rs}} [q_r t_a^{rs}(y) + c_a^{rs}(y)]dy + \sum_i \sum_r \int_0^{o_i^r} m_i^r(x_i^r)dx_i^r + \sum_w \sum_{p \varepsilon P_w} z_w^{rs} h_p^{rs} + \sum_w \sum_r \sum_s (\theta^r)^{-1} T_w^{rs} (\ell n T_w^{rs} -1) \quad (10A)$$

subject to

$$f,h,t \;\varepsilon\; \Omega \quad (10B)$$

When $t_a^{rs}(f_a^{rs})$, $c_a^{rs}(f_a^{rs})$, and $m_i^r(o_i^r)$ are strictly increasing functions, the solution of Equation (10) is unique.

2.2 The Carrier Submodel

Based on the values of flow and demand (f_a^{rs}, T_w^{rs}) produced by the shipper submodel, the carrier submodel predicts the detailed routing assignments made by the carriers. As such, it uses the detailed description of the transportation network. For modes that control their own right-of-way, such as railroads, the model treats each carrier individually. For a mode that operates on rights-of-way it does not control, such as barges on inland waterways and trucks on highways, all carriers operating by that mode can be treated as a single carrier that controls that portion of the network, or each shipment by that mode can be treated as an individual carrier.

In order to predict the individual carrier's traffic assignments, it is required that the O-D demands be known for that portion of the network controlled by each carrier. The shipper submodel gives the transportation demand from original production origin to ultimate destination, the set of paths that will be used between each O-D pair, and how much of the demand will flow on each path. Therefore, all that is needed is to decompose these paths into the portions used by each carrier. The decomposition, a simple bookkeeping operation described in detail in Friesz et al. [3], yields numbers $\hat{T}_w^{rk}$, the fixed demand for transportation of commodity r between O-D pair w of the kth carrier's subnetwork.

Let A_k denote the set of arcs of the detailed network controlled by carrier k. Also assume that routing is system-optimized in the sense that total operating cost is minimized, i.e., routing is based on Wardrop's Second Principle. Let f_a^{rk} and h_p^{rk} refer to the arc and path flows, respectively, of commodity r on the portion of detailed network controlled by carrier k. These flows must satisfy the constraints

$$f_a^{rk} = \sum \Delta_{ap}^{rk} h_p^{rk} \text{ for all a,r,k, (definitional)} \quad (11)$$

where the meaning of Δ_{ap}^{rk} is analogous to that of δ_{ap}^{rs}, and

$$\sum_{p \varepsilon P_w^{rs}} h_p^{rk} = \hat{T}_w^{rk} \text{ for all } w,r,k \text{ (flow conservation)} \tag{12}$$

$$h_p^{rk} \geqslant 0 \text{ for all } p,r,k \text{ (nonnegativity)} \tag{13}$$

Define

$$\Lambda = \{f,h: \text{ Equations (11), (12), and (13) are satisfied}\} \tag{14}$$

The behavior of carrier k is therefore described by the following optimization problem:

$$\text{minimize } J_k = \sum_r \sum_{a \varepsilon A_k} c_a^{rk}(f_a^{rk}) f_a^{rk} \tag{15A}$$

subject to

$$f,h \ \varepsilon \ \Lambda \tag{15B}$$

One such optimization problem is solved for each carrier k comprising the freight system. Observe that when the arc cost functions $c_a^{rk}(f_a^{rk})$ are convex, Equation (15) yields a unique solution.

2.3 Solution Method

The solution methods developed for both the shipper submodel (Equation 10) and the carrier submodel (Equation 15) are based on the well-known Frank-Wolfe feasible direction algorithm (Gartner [4]; Friesz et al. [3]). This algorithm is very efficient for problems with this type of constraint set because the linear programming subproblems are shortest-path problems. Note that this algorithm is capable of finding local optima and, hence, solutions when the objective functions A and J_k in Equations (10) and (15) are not convex. This can be accomplished by using a line search procedure that treats nonconvex functions in the Frank-Wolfe algorithm.

The solution software has undergone a series of improvements in both speed and storage requirements. The current version, FNEM4, is the result of the experience and knowledge gained in the application of three previous versions of the model.

2.4 Model Validation

The model has been calibrated and validated three times in three different stages of development. Each new version showed improved predictive capability over the previous version. For a complete discussion of the calibration and validation procedures and additional results, see Gottfried [5]. In the first, rail link loadings were validated for the Northeast only, and all movements were treated as a single commodity. The network consisted of 5 separate rail carriers and 3 types of water movements. The second was national in scope for rail only, with movements separated into 15 commodity groups. However, at that time, the national rail network had to be treated as a single carrier. The third was national in scope for both rail and water with 17 rail carriers, 3 types of water movement, and 15 commodity groups. Only the last validation begins to reflect the full capability of the model.

For the purpose of model validation, FRA historical data were compared to the computed flow levels produced by the three validation runs of FNEM and to results from another large-scale multi-commodity freight movement model, the Multimodal Network Model (MNM) (Bronzini [1]). The historical usage is derived from the following density code assigned to rail links by the U.S. Federal Railway Administration (FRA):

FRA Density Code	Annual Gross Tons (millions)
1	0 - 1
2	1 - 5
3	5 - 10
4	10 - 20
5	20 - 30
6	30 - +

The MNM used an aggregate version of the FRA network with 7 density codes (in that application, the network density code 6 represents 30-40 million tons and density code 7 represents greater than 40 million tons).

Results of the model validations (Table 1) are very encouraging. The first validation of FNEM for the Northeast predicted almost half of the link loadings correctly and nearly three-fourths within one density code difference. This is substantially better than the results produced by MNM. Separating the movements by commodity group brought about a substantial improvement in the National model, and separating the rail network by carriers in the Full National model brought about considerable further improvement.

Table 1. Differences Between Predicted Railroad Link Traffic Densities and FRA Estimates

	Cumulative % of Links			
		FNEM Runs*		
Density Code Difference	MNM	Northeast	National	Full National
0	21	43	56	63
1	55	74	76	80
2	76	84	92	93
3	90	92	97	97
4	97	96	98	99
5	99	100	100	100
6	100	---	100	---

* See text for description of the FNEM runs.

3. DATA REQUIREMENTS

FNEM4 has the capability to model the freight transportation system in great detail. To do this, of course, requires massive amounts of data to capture the complexity of the system. Inputs to the shipper model include: parameters to specify various modeling options available; fixed O-D flows (contract coal); data on cartypes for other commodities being considered along with coal; definition of commodity classes being considered (e.g., sulfur content, Btu content, etc., for coal); data on arcs (connectors) in the network including rail, water, transhipment, network access, and interline connections between rail carriers; definition of supply and demand zones; zonal supplies for each commodity, zonal demands for each commodity; zonal supply functions for each commodity; individual point demands (utility plants); zonal O-D pairs; zone to individual point demand O-D pairs; and node data including yards, locks, ports and other connections. The shipper submodel generates a solution file that is read by the carrier submodel. In addition, the carrier submodel requires input parameters specifying options and carrier-specific network data (nodes and arcs).

The first application of FNEM indicated the need for preprocessors to simplify the preparation of input data. The input data files to FNEM are designed for efficient processing. However, this format did not allow for easy updating and modification. Software was developed to easily translate basic data files, which are in a format for easy maintenance and modification, into the format required by FNEM. The basic data files contain all of the information required for an FNEM run. The preprocessors sort the data files and convert them to a format designed for efficient processing and to minimize core storage requirements. In this format, the order of the data is very important, because FNEM relies on the location of data in sequence. Arcs, nodes, zones, and O-D pairs are all identified by FNEM by their position in sequence.

This software has greatly reduced the amount of time needed to prepare the numerous input data files for FNEM4. Without the preprocessors, any change in the network data required major editing of the FNEM input data files. Thus, it was time-consuming and inconvenient to create more than one case of input data files, especially network files, to use with FNEM. The preprocessor software enables the user to create the required input data files quickly and with relative ease, making comparison of alternatives and sensitivity analyses feasible.

4. DATA BASES AND FLEXIBLE REGION DEFINITION

An important aspect of the network programming system is a large support data base characterizing the rail and waterway systems, the coal sources, and the movements of non-coal commodities on the transportation networks. The rail data base includes three representations of the U.S. rail network, each at a different level of detail. The waterway system includes a complete network designed for studying coal shipments and support data giving details of locks, dams, piers, and ports. The data on coal sources include Btu, sulfur and ash content, ash fusion temperature, and production functions that relate mine-mouth price to production.

The flexible-region software package allows the user to automatically define study regions of any size (county to multi-state) and to use different levels of transportation network detail within each region. This allows the user to model a completely detailed transportation network in the regions of most interest while modeling movements to and from these regions on an aggregate network in the surrounding regions. Because of this flexibility and the numerous support data bases, the model is easily adapted to a new region.

The initial task required for using the software for flexible-region definition is specification of the levels of detail to be used in each part of the country. This includes the size of supply and demand zones as well as the level of detail for the rail network. The water network is sufficiently sparse that it can be used in full detail for the whole country. The trade-off to be considered in designing a network is between the level of detail of information required and the size of the data base required. Theoretically, full detail in the rail network with supply and demand zones at the county level could be used over the entire continental United States. However, the problem to be solved would have on the order of 10 million O-D pairs with a network containing approximately 40,000 separate links. This would be very expensive to solve and would require a very large computer.

For example, in the network developed to study coal movements into Florida, complete detail is required for the rail network in the southeastern region and a quite detailed rail network is required in the coal supply regions likely to serve as major sources for Florida utilities. For the northeastern and western United States, only mainlines are needed to represent movements into and out of the more detailed regions. Supply and demand zones should be of a size compatible with the level of network detail. The zones in the state of Florida are essentially at the county level. The zones in the rest of the southeastern part of the country are at the level of Bureau of Economic Affairs (BEA) economic areas, and those in the Northeast and West are, in general, aggregations of BEA areas. In the major coal-producing regions of the West, the zones are single BEA areas rather than aggregations so that any predicted western coal movements can be more closely identified. BEA areas were chosen as a basis for flexible definition because they are collections of counties economically tied to a single metropolitan center. These metropolitan centers usually are transportation centers, so that the BEA areas are compatible with the transportation network.

Three national rail networks provide three different levels of detail for developing a rail network. The most detailed level (18,382 links) is based on the data base developed by the Federal Railroad Administration (FRA). It has been improved by the addition of interline points and yards, and has been updated to reflect the latest mergers and abandonments. The middle level of network detail (1767 links) is based on a network developed by the Transportation Systems Center (TSC) of the U.S. Department of Transportation. This network has been improved by the addition of carrier designations, interline points, and yards and has been made compatible and consistent with the FRA-level network. The least detailed network (269 links) contains mainlines only and was developed for use with the flexible-network software.

The compatibility of network detail with supply/demand zone detail is given in Table 2; an X indicates compatibility of network detail (as indicated in the rows) with zone detail (as indicated in the columns). Default specifications are the diagonal entries in Table 2. The off-diagonal specifications are useful to obtain better transition from a less detailed network to a more detailed network.

Table 2. Compatibility of Zone Sizes and Network Detail

Network/Zone	County	BEA	Multi-BEA
ANL/FRA	X	X	
ANL/TSC		X	X
Mainline			X

For example, BEA areas in Georgia, South Carolina, and Alabama were specified to have the most detailed level of rail network to obtain accurate rail movements into Florida without increasing the number of supply/demand zones at the county level. The BEA area containing Chicago, which is in a Multi-BEA Zone, was specified to have the middle level of network detail to obtain good distribution of traffic out of Chicago through the coal-producing regions of Illinois.

The water transportation network includes transshipment links representing ports and other transfer facilities between rail and water. The network-generating software also generates "access" links that allow the zonal supplies and demands to enter and leave both rail and water networks at designated access points.

5. OUTPUT

Because of the complexity of the model, large amounts of information are generated by the model. The shipper submodel generates the O-D pairs for all commodities being considered, the amount of each commodity moving between each origin and destination, the modes and carriers used between each origin and destination, and the delivered price at the destination. The carrier submodel generates detailed routings over the network and total flow levels by commodity on each segment of the network. A sample page of output from the shipper submodel is presented in Figure 1.

For most studies, commodity flows other than coal are modeled to identify potential bottlenecks, but specific information about those flows is not required. In a case where only coal transported to a particular set of point demands is of interest, the other coal movements are modeled only to account for competition for coal supplies and coal transportation facilities, and detailed output on these movements is also not required. The total results of a model run are written to a disk file, and report writing and computer graphic post-processors are used to select the required information.

6. CONCLUSIONS

The network programming system developed for regional coal transportation studies greatly simplifies all aspects of conducting a detailed, large-scale study of coal transportation. In particular it provides the following benefits:

1. Only master data bases need be maintained. If significant changes have occurred in the master data bases, new study networks and supplies and demands reflecting these changes can easily be generated.

2. The ease of generation and modification of networks and supplies and demands greatly simplifies studying multiple scenarios and conducting sensitivity analyses.

3. The capability of easily generating a specially tailored network for a region allows for optimizing the trade-off between level of detail of results and computational requirements.

4. The multi-modal, multi-commodity model framework that considers the decisions of both shippers and carriers increases the accuracy of predictions.

REFERENCES

[1] Bronzini, M.S., "Evolution of A Multimodal Freight Transportation Network Model", Working paper, University of Tennessee, 1980.

[2] Fernandez, J.E., and Friesz, T.L., "Travel market equilibration: The state of the art", Transportation Research, 17B(2), 1983.

[3] Friesz, T.L., Gottfried, J., Brooks, R.E., Zielen, A.J., Tobin, R.L., and Meleski, S.A., "Theory, Validation and Application of A Freight Network Equilibrium Model", Argonne National Laboratory Report ANL/ES-120, Argonne, Illinois, 1981.

[4] Gartner, N., "Analysis and control of transportation networks by Frank-Wolfe decomposition", Proc. Seventh International Symposium on Transportation and Traffic Theory, Kyoto, Japan, 1977 .

[5] Gottfried, J.A., "Predictive Network Equilibrium Model for Application to Regional and National Freight Transportation Systems", Unpublished Ph.D. Dissertation, University of Pennsylvania, Philadelphia, 1983.

[6] Tobin, R.L., Jastrow, J.D., Meleski, S.A., and Zielen, A.J., "Florida Coal Conversion Regional Impact Study: Coal Transportation Analysis", draft, Prepared by the Environmental Research Division, Argonne National Laboratory, Argonne, Il, 1983.

[7] Wilson, A.G., Entropy in Urban and Regional Modeling, (Pion, New York), 1979.

Analytic Techniques for Energy Planning
B. Lev, F.H. Murphy, J.A. Bloom & A.S. Gleit (Editors)

COMPARATIVE ANALYSIS OF COAL-BASED ELECTRIC ENERGY DELIVERY SYSTEMS*

J.L. Eisenhauer

Pacific Northwest Laboratory
Richland, Washington 99352

Battelle, Pacific Northwest Laboratory has developed an integrated system assessment methodology and supporting data base to facilitate comparisons of selected technical, cost, environmental, and resource consumption characteristics of alternate large-scale electric energy supply systems. The purpose of this work is to provide a general purpose system assessment and planning tool for examining alternate energy conversion, transport, and transmission technologies. In this paper, I demonstrate how energy planners may use this model.

1. INTRODUCTION

The coal resources of the Northern Great Plains comprise one of this country's principal resources for generation of electric power. These resources, however, are at considerable distances from major electrical load centers. For example, the vast coal reserves found in eastern Wyoming and Montana are 600 to 1000 air miles from major Midwest population centers. Energy transportation is a major factor that must be considered when contemplating development of these remote coal fields.

Several possibilities exist for long-distance transportation of energy. Options include rail transport of coal, pipeline transport of coal slurry, pipeline transport of fuel gas derived from coal, and transmission of electric power by alternating or direct current. Variations within each of these transportation alternatives combined with a number of power generation technologies provide planners with many technically feasible system configurations. Selection of an appropriate system requires consideration of several important factors including technical performance, cost, and environmental and socioeconomic effects.

While several studies have examined the relative economics of rail transport and coal slurry pipelines (see [4], [5], [6], [11], [12]), no concensus has been reached on which transport mode offers the lowest cost. This is largely due to differences in the many technical and economic assumptions that are made and the complexity of the energy systems being examined. Because of the complexity of these systems and the interrelationships of their elements, it is desirable to perform an integrated system assessment that accounts for every link in the fuel cycle beginning with coal mining and ending with delivery of power to the load center.

Pacific Northwest Laboratory (PNL) has developed such an integrated system assessment methodology and supporting data base to facilitate comparisons of

*Work supported by The U.S. Department of Energy Under Contract DE-AC06-76RLO-1830.

selected technical, cost, environmental, and resource consumption characteristics of alternate large-scale electric energy supply systems. The purpose of this work, sponsored by the U.S. Department of Energy, is to provide a general-purpose system assessment and planning tool for examining alternate energy conversion, transport, and transmission technologies.

Using this methodology, energy planners can easily alter a large number of economic and technical assumptions and system configurations to assess the impact on delivered power costs, thereby overcoming some of the limitations of previous studies.

In this paper we estimate and compare the private costs of alternative electric energy delivery systems. Although the model is flexible enough to handle several different fuel-based energy systems, we limit our assessment to five generic coal-based systems. We show how energy system planners can use the model to determine the minimum private cost of electric power and to evaluate the effect of changes in key economic and technical parameters on the selection of a least-cost system.

The first section of this paper provides an overview of the model and outlines assumptions, limitations and the economic assessment methodology. An application of the model to a number of coal-based electric energy delivery systems is demonstrated in the second section including sensitivity analyses of key variables. The final section of the paper presents our conclusions and suggested extensions to our analysis.

2. THE ELECTRIC ENERGY SYSTEM SYSTEMS MODEL DESCRIPTION

In this section we provide a brief overview of the EES model, outline capabilities, describe the model structure and the cost assessment methodology, and highlight the model's current limitations.

2.1 Model Overview

The Electric Energy Systems (EES) model was developed for the Division of Electric Energy Systems of the U.S. Department of Energy to provide a general-purpose systems assessment and research planning tool. The model provides a means to evaluate existing and emerging electric transmission technologies against coal transportation alternatives. With the model's substantial data base and assessment methodology, it is designed to help direct research efforts for promising technologies.

As the model evolved, it developed into a general-purpose assessment tool for large-scale, coal-based energy systems. That is, in addition to evaluating emerging transmission and transportation technologies, it is capable of assessing emerging and existing coal-fired generation and gasification technologies. The model is designed to accept additional extraction, generation, and conversion technologies based on other fuel sources provided that appropriate data and technical relationships are available.

The model evaluates candidate energy systems using four main criteria:

. Cost performance,

. Technical performance,

. Environmental effects,

. Resource requirements.

These criteria can be used to evaluate individual technologies or entire energy systems. While the model provides detailed and summary information on energy systems, it does not select or rank preferred systems; it has no multicriteria decision-making capability. Ranking of competing energy systems for the purpose of selecting a preferred system must be performed by the energy planner using model output information and informed judgments on energy planning issues. The model does, however, provide substantial technical and cost information that can be used to help make planning decisions.

2.2 Model Capabilities

The EES model is an interactive, computer-based assessment tool that allows energy planners to simulate the technical, cost, resource and environmental aspects of candidate energy generation and delivery systems. The model allows flexible and timely evaluation of selected systems and permits access and changes to the data files to allow detailed analysis of energy systems. The model is easy to run and provides easy-to-read output in detailed or summary form.

The model can perform a variety of analytical functions. Some of the ways the model may be used for energy system assessments include:

- Comparison of the relative lifecycle costs of competing energy transport technologies including electric transmission, rail transportation, coal slurry pipelines, and coal-derived gas pipelines;
- Comparison of the relative lifecycle costs of complete energy systems comprised of extraction, transportation, conversion, generation and transmission technologies;
- Assessment of resource requirements, environmental emissions and effluents, and energy conversion efficiencies of candidate energy systems and their component technologies;
- Comparison of capital requirements and annual operating and fuel expenses for candidate energy systems;
- Analysis of the effects that change in costs and financial structure (e.g., interest rates, tax credits and depreciation schedules) will have on the overall economic competitiveness of candidate systems.

Energy planners and policy makers can use the results of these comparisons to:

- Provide a screening method for candidate energy systems prior to detailed site-specific or engineering cost analysis;
- Identify technical and economic problem areas within a technology that, if solved, would improve the cost competitiveness of the technology;
- Identify constraints to energy development for specific candidate systems (e.g., environmental, resource, and cost constraints);
- Determine which energy systems are most cost competitive under a variety of economic conditions (i.e., periods of high and low inflation and cost escalation).

The EES model offers several key advantages over other energy system planning tools. Due to the complexity and interrelationships of elements in a comprehensive energy delivery system, it is beneficial to perform an integrated assessment of all links in an energy system in order to capture all technical and cost effects. For example, when comparing the costs of electric transmission with coal transportation, the cost of the related electric power generation facilities will differ due to different coal storage capacities, coal unloading facilities, regional cost differences, and different cooling and emission control options. The EES model accounts for these factors when energy system assessments are performed.

Another key feature of the model is the ability to perform sensitivity analysis on a number of technical and financial variables. The effects of different depreciation schedules, interest rates, power plant efficiencies, cooling systems and other variables on total system cost can be easily and quickly analyzed using the EES model.

2.3 Model Structure

The model consists of a network of interconnected technology modules consisting of coal extraction, solid coal transporation, gasification, gas transport, electric power generation, and electric power transmission technologies. Each technology has a file that contains technical and economic relationships and a separate data file that contains supporting technical, cost and financial data. Specific technologies that were investigated by PNL and the network structure of the EES model are illustrated in Figure 1.

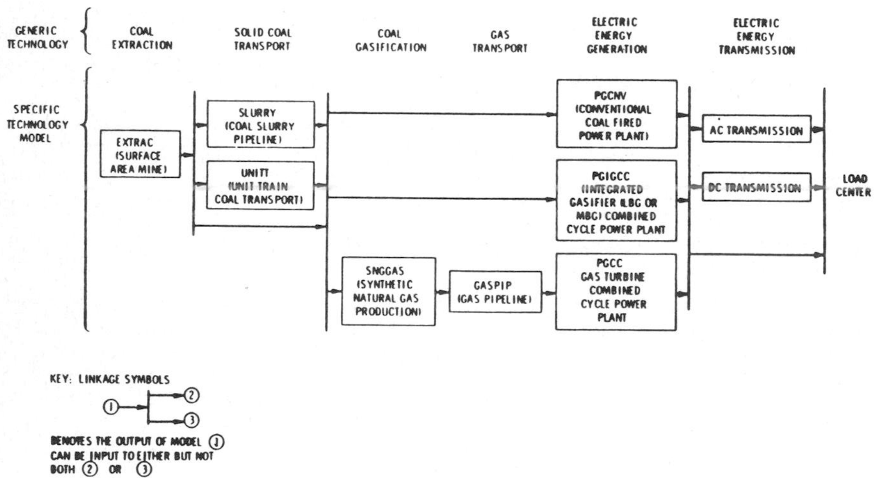

Figure 1. EES Technology Network Structure

The model reports the technical, economic, environmental, and resource characteristics of energy delivery systems by simulating the construction and operation of the system. In this manner costs, environmental releases, and resource requirements are calculated for the entire system for both construction and operational phases. Annual requirements for each of these factors are stored in vectors and subsequently used to calculate lifecycle requirements and levelized costs. Simulation includes likely assumptions about system features but does not currently involve any probabilistic modeling using random events.

In order to standardize our parameters and assumptions in line with those used by energy planners, we relied heavily on the Technical Assessment Guide published by the Electric Power Research Institute [3]. We deviate from the EPRI assumptions only when more detailed, case-specific information was available. Data sources are referenced in the data files along with the name of the user who entered it and the date of entry.

On a typical model run, the model prompts the user to construct a candidate energy system, in which he specifies the technologies being considered, total system capacity, the number of years the system is expected to operate, the base year for analysis and the system load factor. A list of the basic EES model inputs and summary outputs is shown in Table 1.

Table 1. Inputs and Outputs of the EES Model

INPUTS	OUTPUTS
. Energy System Configuration	. Levelized Lifecycle Cost of Power
. Operating Life of System	. Resource Requirements
. Maximum System Capacity	. Manpower Requirements
. Average System Load Factor	. Land and Water Use
. Base Year of Analysis	. Net Energy and Coal Conversion Efficiencies
. Length of System	. Environmental Releases
. Types of Reports Desired	

The EES model uses a comprehensive cost analysis methodology that is based on cost assessment methods recommended by the Electric Power Research Institute [3] and Phung and Rohm [10]. Base capital costs are calculated based on direct and indirect expenses, spare parts allowance, state sales tax, and owners' cost. A standard 15% contingency is included in base capital costs to account for unexpected construction delays, miscalculation of cost estimates and other unpredictable phenomena.

Interest and escalation charges incurred during construction must be factored in when determining total capital requirements. Due to inflation and real escalation of equipment and labor costs over the construction period, as well as interest charges on borrowed capital, total capital requirements exceed standard engineering cost estimates. In order to account for interest and escalation during construction, the EES model employs a methodology developed by Phung [9] that is based on analytical solutions to a variety of construction payout curves. The model uses a modified version of Phung's methodology and currently employs a symmetric S-shaped construction payout curve to determine interest and escalation during construction. These costs, as well as working capital and startup costs, are added to base capital costs to provide the total capital requirements.

Operating, maintenance and fuel costs are calculated annually based on the operating characteristics and financial criteria specified in the data file and the operating file specified by the user. All costs are converted into annual cash flows and discounted to a base year using standard net present value calculations. Costs are then levelized using a minimum revenue requirement approach that determines the annual minimum revenue that is required to offset the total lifecycle cost of the system. The levelized cost of power, reported on a mills per kilowatt-hour basis, allows many different energy systems to be evaluated on a standard basis. This approach is a standard method of evaluating alternative investment decisions and is used widely in electric utility planning.

Some of the features of the EES cost assessment methodology are:

- adjustments for regional cost differences,
- adjustments for economies-of-scale,
- adjustments for alternate cooling and emission control equipment,
- adjustments for alternate construction and payout schedules,
- choice of depreciation schedules,
- choice of inflation and escalation values,
- consideration of investment tax credits and other taxes,
- analysis available for a variety of base years,
- choice of debt and equity structure.

The financial and cost report can be revised and tailored to the requirements of the user.

2.4 Model Limitations

The current application of the EES model is to examine promising alternatives for using the vast coal reserves of Wyoming and Montana to provide bulk electric power to Midwest population centers. However, with this current application, the model is limited in a number of ways.

First, the model is currently designed to examine only coal-based technologies. These include coal extraction, coal-fired power generation, coal gasification, and coal transportation. In addition, a number of electric transmission technologies are included that could be applied to many different fuel-based systems. However, with additional development the model could be adapted to other fuel-based technologies (e.g., nuclear).

Second, the model is currently applicable to only very large-scale energy systems between about 3,000 MW and 10,000 MW. Applications of the model to moderate-scale energy systems (1,000 MW to 3,000 MW) require changes in certain cost relationships and technical assumptions.

Third, in order to measure the relative economics of alternative energy systems, the model evaluates only new plants and equipment. The exception to this requirement is that existing railroad tracks would be used for long-distance rail transportation of coal. Construction of new long-distance rail lines would require a major capital investment and would significantly alter the relative economics of candidate systems. We do, however, account for upgrading of existing track to handle heavy coal traffic as well as construction of some new track to access coal fields and to bypass some population centers along the major route. All technologies examined are considered to be state-of-the-art and commercially feasible by 1990.

Fourth, due to the primary function of the EES model as a general-purpose planning tool, it is not site-specific in nature. That is, cost information and technical assumptions are generic and would require relatively easy adjustments in order to examine specific energy systems for specific sites. However, regional geography and labor rates, which affect costs, are currently taken into consideration. In addition, the model does not now address environmental constraints imposed on proposed systems that result from environmental legislation and regulations with the exception of New Source Performance Standards for new electric generating facilities. The model, however, does provide information on the principle environmental emissions and effluents that result from construction and operation of candidate energy systems.

Finally, the model does not currently assess the likely behavioral responses of competing firms. For example, the model does not take into account the potential for railroads to subsidize specific coal haul routes, due to varying spatial price elasticities of demand, to block development of competing delivery systems (e.g., coal slurry pipelines).

3. MODEL APPLICATION

We will use a hypothetical energy delivery system to illustrate how energy planners could use the model to determine a least-cost system and to examine the sensitivity of this selction to changes in selected key parameters. Our hypothetical example consists of a coal resource base located in the Powder River Basin in Wyoming to be used for electric power needs in Chicago, approximately 1000 miles east. The power requirements are for 3000 megawatts (MW) of base-load power; enough to meet the power needs of a large city.

There are seven generic coal-based delivery systems that could be considered for our analysis. Including coal extraction they are:

1) Unit Train Transport - Conventional Coal-Fired Plant (Load Center)

2) Slurry Pipeline Transport - Conventional Coal-Fired Plant (Load Center)

3) Unit Train Transport - IGCC Plant* (Load Center)

4) Slurry Pipeline Transport - IGCC Plant* (Load Center)

5) SNG Production - Gas Pipeline - Gas-Fired Combined-Cycle Plant (Load Center)

6) Conventional Coal-Fired Plant (Minemouth) - AC Transmission

7) Conventional Coal-Fired Plant (Minemouth) - DC Transmission

For our example we will examine systems 1 through 5.

A number of common key assumptions underlie all systems being examined in our analysis. Our base year for analysis is 1983 and all costs are expressed in 1983 dollars. All systems are planned to be operational in 1990 and have a service life of 30 years. Annual inflation is assumed to be 8.5% as recommended by EPRI [3]. All systems provide 3000 MW of base-load electric power at a 90% load factor (capacity factors for individual plants vary, but average 67% over the 30-year operating period). Total transport distance is 1000 miles from the

---

*Integrated coal gasification/combined-cycle power plant.

minemouth to the load center.

The results of the model runs based on the above scenario are shown in Figure 2. The two systems consisting of solid coal transportation and a conventional coal-fired power generation clearly dominate the selection of a low-cost system. The two systems consisting of solid coal transportation and intergrated coal gasification/combined-cycle power generation are about 25% more costly. The system consisting of coal gasification, gas pipeline transport, and gas-fired, combined-cycle power generation is the most expensive -- almost 50% above the two low-cost systems.

The cost contribution of each component in the delivery systems is provided in Figure 2. Although the combined cost of fuel and transportation is lower for systems containing the integrated gasifier/combined-cycle plant, generation costs are about 40% higher than with a conventional coal-fired plant. The costs of fuel, transportation and generation of the SNG system is very competitive with the two low-cost systems, although the cost of high-Btu gasification is high and increases system costs by about 50%.

The costs of the two systems using conventional coal-fired power generation are very close--within 1% of each other. While the transportation cost of the coal slurry pipeline is lower than the unit train system, coal cost is higher. This is mainly due to the additional coal requirements with coal slurry pipelines due to reduced coal quality resulting from the greater moisture content of the coal [8]. Generation costs for these systems are essentially equal.

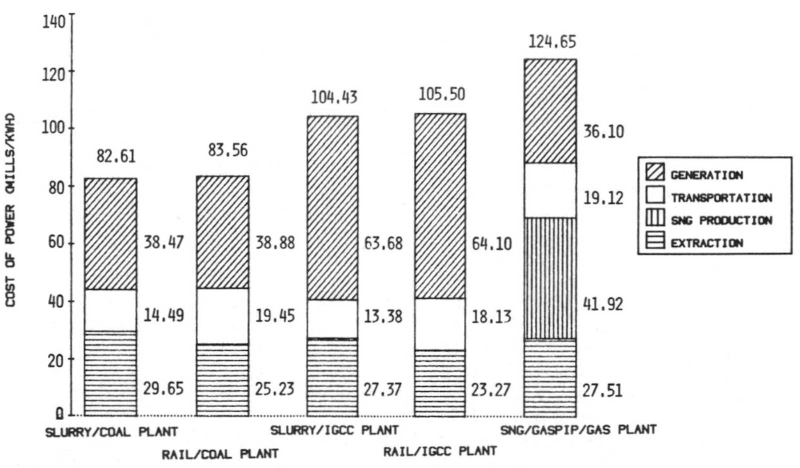

Figure 2. Delivered Cost of Power -- Five Scenarios (mills/kWh)

Because the total costs of the two low-cost systems are very close, we examined the effect of changes in key assumptions on the total cost of power. Several candidate variables were considered:

1. Inflation Rate

2. Transport Distance

3. Coal Cost

4. Depreciation Schedule

5. Size of Generating Complex

6. Cost of Debt and Debt Structure

Sensitivity analyses were performed on the inflation rate, transport distance, and coal cost as these variables were expected to have the greatest impact on relative costs.

For our base case analysis, we used an 8.5% annual inflation rate as recommended by EPRI [3] for energy cost assessments. We then examined total power costs assuming inflation rates ranging from 5.0 to 8.5 percent. Figure 3 shows the effect of changes in the annual inflation rate on the delivered cost of power. For inflation rates under about 7.5%, a unit train delivery system is less costly while above 7.5% a coal slurry system is less costly. This is because annual costs (operating, maintenance and fuel) account for 75% of total transport costs for unit trains but only 40% for coal slurry pipelines. As a result, coal slurry transport costs are less sensitive to inflation than unit train transport costs. However, between 5.5 and 8.5 percent inflation, the cost differences between the two systems are only +1 mill. Because of the error inherent in cost estimation and data sources, this difference is not perceived to be significant in selecting a least-cost system.

In our base case, we assumed the distance between the mine and the load center was 1000 miles. We subsequently examined distances between 700 and 1000 miles to determine the effect on delivered power costs (Figure 4). We found that for distances under about 850 miles, unit train delivery was less costly while above 850 miles coal slurry delivery was less costly. This appears to be due to the greater coal requirements of coal slurry systems compared to unit train systems. In this case, as the transport distance decreases, fuel costs become a greater portion of total power cost, thereby favoring a unit train delivery system. Again, the differences in cost over the 700 to 1000 mile range are +1 mill and are not significant enough to determine the selection of a least-cost system.

Another parameter we examined was real coal price escalation above the general rate of inflation. The coal escalation profile used in the model provides real coal escalation rates developed by EPRI [3] and adopted for the model. We examined the effect of an additional 1, 2 and 3 percent escalation above the base case profile. Figure 5 shows the effect of these different escalation scenarios on delivered power costs. For scenarios employing less than an additional 0.5% above base case escalation, unit train systems are less costly while escalation at more than 0.5% above base case results in coal slurry systems being less costly. Due to the greater coal requirements for coal slurry systems, the impact of higher fuel cost escalation on total power costs is more severe than for unit train systems. As with the other parameters we varied, the relative difference in delivered power costs over the range we examined was not viewed to be significant.

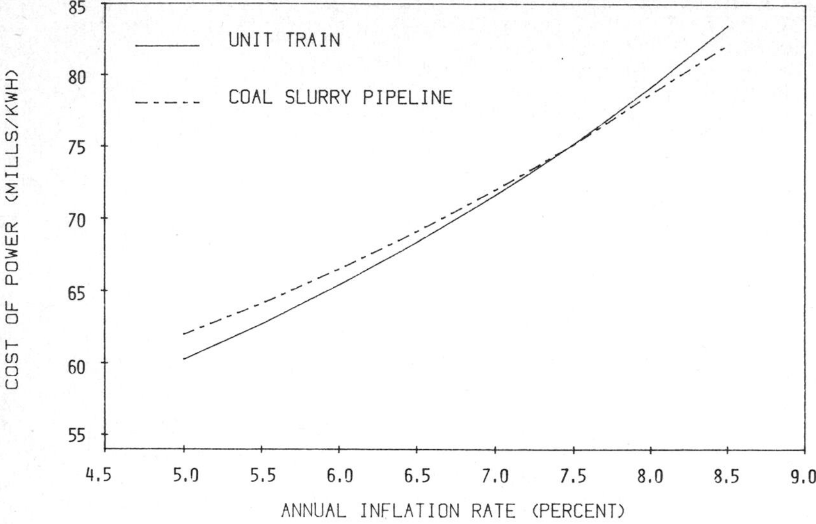

Figure 3. Effect of Inflation Rate on Cost of Power

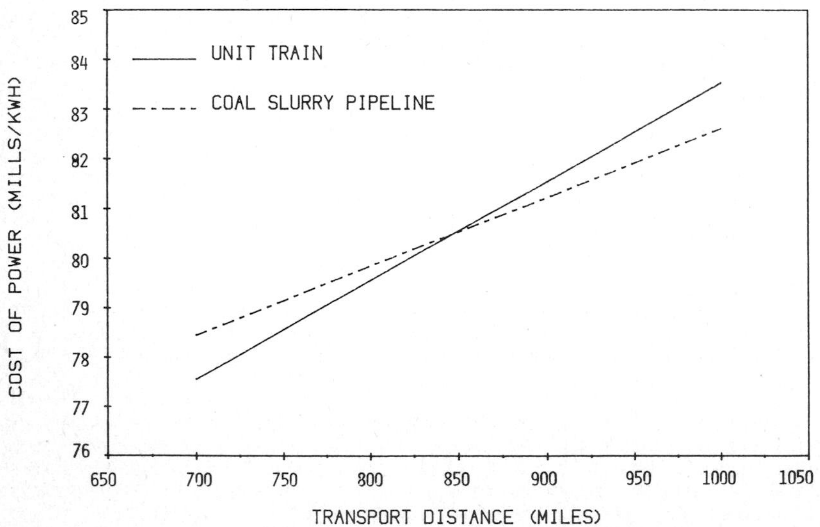

Figure 4. Effect of Distance on Cost of Power

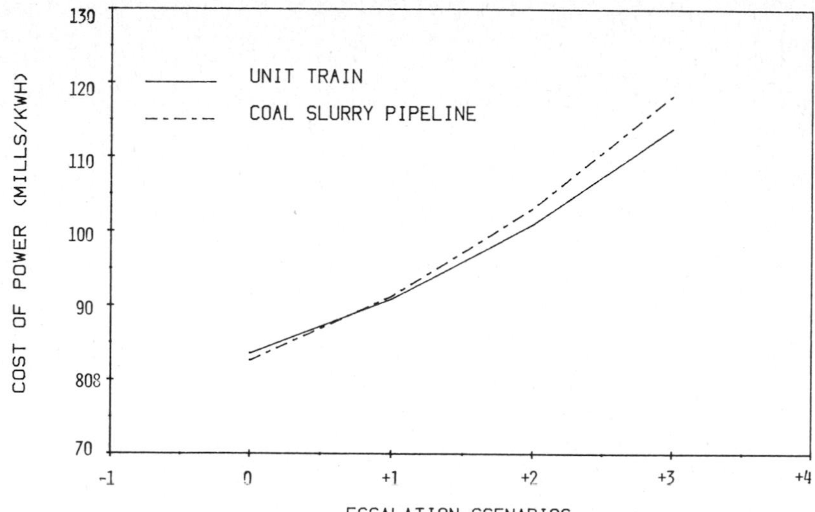

Figure 5. Effect of Coal Escalation Rate on Cost of Power

While our analysis indicates the relative cost advantage of each delivery system under a variety of conditions, it does not suggest a definitive selection of a least-cost delivery system. This is because the differences in cost between the two systems are within unavoidable data inaccuracies. However, the model does provide a screening method to rule out delivery systems that are not cost competitive.

The next stage of analysis to determine a least-cost system would involve gathering and incorporating site-specific information that would be entered in the data files. Alternatively, evaluation of environmental impacts, resource requirements (e.g., water, land, steel), and energy conversion efficiencies could be included in the assessment of a preferred system. Both types of analysis can be easily handled by the model. If these analyses are inconclusive, a detailed engineering cost estimate would be recommended.

4. CONCLUSIONS

The determination of a least-cost electric energy delivery system requires consideration of many technical and economic parameters. An integrated system assessment accounts for the interrelationship of energy system components and aids in the analysis of complex systems. Using such an assessment, we evaluated five generic coal-based electric energy delivery systems and identified the two low-cost systems. Both systems consist of coal extraction and conventional coal-fired power generation; the one supplied by coal slurry pipelines and the one supplied by unit trains. Levelized lifecycle costs for both systems were about 83 mills/kWh.

Sensitivity analysis was performed on three key parameters -- inflation rate, transport distance and coal price escalation -- to determine their effect on delivered power costs. We found that the selection of a least-cost system was affected by changes in each of these parameters but the cost differences between the two systems were not judged to be significant.

The Electric Energy Systems model we used to perform our assessment was useful in screening out delivery systems that were not cost competitive with alternative systems. The model is useful as a generic cost assessment tool that enables easy testing of cost sensitivity to a number of parameters. The model, with its extensive data base, is very flexible and can be used to analyze case-specific problems.

Suggested extensions to our assessment include:

- Consideration of alternating and direct current transmission technologies as a substitute for coal transportation,
- Examination of behavioral responses of competitive firms to transportation pricing,
- Consideration of social costs in determination of a preferred system,
- Evaluation of site-specific factors,
- Evaluation of noneconomic factors such as environmental impacts, resource requirements and energy conversion efficiencies.

The model can be adjusted to handle each of these extensions.

REFERENCES

[1] Eisenhauer, J.L. et al. Electric Energy Supply Systems Comparisons and Choices, Volume I: Technology Description Report (Draft). PNL-3277, Pacific Northwest Laboratory, Richland, WA., 1983.

[2] Eisenhauer, J.L. et al. Electric Energy Supply Systems Comparisons and Choices, Volume II: Assessment Methodology and Model Description Report (Draft). PNL-3754, Pacific Northwest Laboratory, Richland, WA., 1983.

[3] EPRI. Technical Assessment Guide. EPRI-P-2410-SR, Electric Power Research Institute, Palo Alto, CA., 1982.

[4] Harza. "Coal-By-Wire" in The National Power Grid Survey V. 2: Technical Study Reports, DOE/ERA-0056/2. Prepared by Harza Engineering for the U.S. Department of Energy, Economic Regulatory Administration, Office of Utility Systems, Washington, D.C., 1979.

[5] OTA. A Technology Assessment of Coal Slurry Pipelines. Office of Technology Assessment, U.S. Government Printing Office, Washington, D.C., 1978.

[6] Hyde, T.E., An Economic Comparison Between the Coal Slurry Pipeline Proposed by Houston Natural Gas Corporation and Two Comparable Unit Train Models. University of Texas, Austin, Texas., 1979.

[7] Peabody & Associates et. al. Critique and Response to "Coal Transportation." National Science Foundation, Washington, D.C., 1976.

[8] PEDCO Environmental, Inc. Environmental Assessment of Coal Transportation. PB-285-936, Prepared for the U.S. EPA by Industrial Environmental Research Laboratory, Cincinnati, Ohio., 1978.

[9] Phung, D.L. A Method for Estimating Escalation and Interest During Construction (EDC and IDC). ORAU IEA-78-7(M), Prepared by the Institute for Energy Analysis, Oak Ridge Associated Universities, Oal Ridge, Tennessee., 1978.

[10] Phung, D.L. and Rohm, H.H. A Unified Methodology for Cost Analysis of Energy Production. Institute for Energy Analysis, Oak Ridge Associated Universities, Oak Ridge, Tennessee., 1977.

[11] Rieber, M., and S.L. Soo. Comparative Coal Transportation Costs: An Economic and Engineering Analysis of Truck, Belt, Barge and Coal Slurry and Pneumatic Pipelines, Vol 2. Unit Trains. PB 274-380, Urbana-Champaign, Urbana, Illinois., 1977.

[12] Sargent, A. Western Coal Transportation Unit Trains or Slurry Pipelines. Prepared for the U.S. Department of Transportation by Massachusetts Institute of Technology, Cambridge, Massachusetts., 1976.

Analytic Techniques for Energy Planning
B. Lev, F.H. Murphy, J.A. Bloom & A.S. Gleit (Editors)

IDENTIFYING CHANGES IN PATTERNS OF PRODUCTION TO SUPPORT PETROLEUM PRICE CONTROL LITIGATION

Douglas A. Samuelson
3443 Skyview Terrace
Falls Church, Virginia

Petroleum price regulations, in effect during the oil supply squeezes of the 1970's, raised a number of interesting analytical questions, such as: To what extent did price increases result from cost increases? When did significant changes in patterns of production take place for large unitized oil fields? If oil companies were found to have misclassified large amounts of "old" oil as "new" oil what method of repayment would most benefit the customers? Such questions as these, raised originally as part of the Federal enforcement effort, also help us to understanding the workings of international petroleum markets.

1. INTRODUCTION

The Department of Energy's Office of Special Counsel was created in 1978 to expedite the audits of the 35 largest refiners. In assessing whether the refiners had violated Federal price regulations between 1973 and 1980, the Office's staff had to consider not only pricing but also the whole range of exploration, production and distribution, since the maximum allowable price was a function of the costs the refiners incurred.

Some of the questions involved considerable technical detail and sophistication. Therefore, although most of the Office's staff were lawyers and auditors, there were also a few analysts with operations research and related backgrounds to help utilize the oil companies' large, computer-based data files and other quantitative information. These quantitative analysts, of whom I was one from December 1978 through December 1980, were involved in a number of issues and cases, with varying results. Our experience contains an important lesson for the operations research profession: in general, simpler approaches were most effective, as they were easier to explain, to defend in court, and to modify in the course of settlement negotiations.

To illustrate this point, I would like to concentrate on a set of cases based on an especially interesting issue, the treatment of unitization. I regret that I cannot discuss these cases more specifically, because of cases and appeals still pending, but the general description should suffice.

2. UTITIZATION AND PATTERNS OF PRODUCTION

"Unitization" means that an oil company enters into an agreement with a number of owners of mineral leases to enable the oil company to operate the combined holdings as a unit, in order to take best advantage of the geological properties of the oil reservoir. In the largest case, this process involved several hundred owners. The way such an agreement usually works is that each lease's production is calculated as a percentage of the total production for the combined unit, and each owner is to receive the same percentage of the income from the total production from the unit from the date of unitization until the entire operation is shut down. This arrangement enables the operator to shut down some wells and convert some production wells into rejection wells, in order to enhance production from the remaining active production wells.

The enforcement question has to do with "old" and "new" oil. Under the price regulations, the amount of oil already being produced from a given holding as of May 15, 1973 was "old" oil, controlled at a considerably lower price than "new" oil. The difference for most of the price-controlled period was about $10 a barrel. When a field was unitized, the regulations required that "old" oil be calculated on the whole unit, rather than lease by lease.

As a simple example of this rule, suppose two adjoining leases each produced 1000 barrels per month from a common reservoir. An operator could shut down one lease and produce 2000 barrels per month from the other. No additional production would be taking place overall, but if the operator reported on a lease-by-lease basis, he would show 1000 barrels of "new" oil. In addition, the regulations provided that an operator could claim one barrel of "old" oil as "released" oil, which could be sold at the higher price, for each barrel of "new" oil. Thus, in this example, the operator could have converted the entire 2000 barrels per month to the higher price, if he ignored the rule.

The issue in these cases was whether the companies had begun reporting on a unit basis as soon as unitization had, in fact, occurred. Under the regulations, unitization was considered to have taken place upon the earlier of two events: when it was reported in a legal document, such as the unitization agreement or the operator's production reports, or when "a significant change in the pattern of production" occurred. In the largest of these cases, a significant change in the pattern of production appeared to have taken place more than a year before the company acknowledged unitization. Since this was a very large field, the amount of money in dispute was in the hundreds of millions of dollars.

3. ANALYTICAL APPROACHES

How then, could we prove that a significant change in the pattern of production had occurred? Several approaches were considered:

- Using a linear modeling (regression or analysis of variance) approach, attempt to "forecast" production, lease by lease, based on past production; identify those months when production showed statistically significant changes from "predicted" or "accustomed" levels.

- Use the same idea, "predicting" monthly production and identifying changes which appeared significant, but use a time series (ARIMA) model to take into account the time ordering of the data.

- Apply contingency-table techniques, again hoping to identify the significant changes using statistical tests.

- Incorporate into a model based on one or more of the above techniques some independent variables reflecting prices, regulatory changes, and various hypothetical strategies the oil company might have employed.

The time-series approach was quickly discarded because, with several hundred leases, several potential independent variables, and only about 36 months in the period of interest, ARIMA and intervention analysis models would almost certainly be intractable. Contingency table analysis also appeared likely to be intractable, especially if several independent variables turned out to be important.

The linear modeling approach was at least computationally feasible, but interpreting the results was another matter. Even when a model gave what appeared to be statistically significant results - ignoring, for the moment, questions about how well the distributional assumptions were met - it was not clear that a court would be logically compelled to accept statistically significant results as legally significant. Any citation of a standard published statistical technique was likely to result in the oil company's calling the author of the technique, or the leading expert on its use, as an expert witness, with potentially embarrassing results for the Department. Using nonstandard, innovative techniques would only increase the potential for embarrassment, as the stature and reputations of the expert witnesses on both sides would then be even more influential on the court's decision. Therefore, as long as any questions of interpretation remained about our findings, neither the lawyers nor the analysts were eager to present and defend them in court.

After this situation had persisted for some time, we tried a new approach: using a standard statistical package, we generated line printer plots of the production from each lease. Visual examination of the plots confirmed that some leases had apparently had sharp increases in production, and others had sharply decreased, in about a two-month span. We obtained a large map of the oil field and placed a red dot on the map for each lease that appeared to have decreased and a yellow dot for each lease that had increased. When we were finished, we found we had a ring of yellow dots surrounded by a concentric ring of red dots.

When the plots and the map were introduced as evidence, the oil company did not even contest the Department's assertions of fact, let alone call expert witnesses. The judge decided the major case in the Department's favor on a motion for summary judgment, which - as I mentioned earlier - is still under appeal. Regardless of the eventual outcome of these cases, however, it certainly seems evident that the simple approach was easier to present and defend, and almost certainly more convincing.

4. CONCLUSIONS

Analysts who are experienced with litigation support have recognized for some time that simpler approaches often work best, since judges generally refuse to believe what they cannot readily understand. Clearly, analysts who must convince managers rather than judges often face the same problem, perhaps in less obvious form. Certainly, good analysts have learned to resist the temptation to impress rather than convince. What is more difficult, it seems, is to keep reminding ourselves how well simple, seemingly prosaic techniques often work, and how much easier our job can be when the simple techniques suffice.

In particular, in the area of recognizing patterns and changes in patterns, increased sophistication of technique is not necessarily an improvement, especially when the results must be interpreted to skeptical third parties. What was "obvious" to the human eye, when properly summarized and presented, was not clearly identified by any of the statistical tests and techniques we tried. Clearly our model-based techniques still have some way to go before they approach the pattern recognition capabilities of the human mind.

ELECTRIC POWER

Analytic Techniques for Energy Planning
B. Lev, F.H. Murphy, J.A. Bloom & A.S. Gleit (Editors)

REGIONAL ENERGY FACILITY LOCATION MODELS FOR POWER SYSTEM PLANNING AND POLICY ANALYSIS

Benjamin F. Hobbs*

Department of Systems Engineering
Case Western Reserve University
Cleveland, Ohio 44106

Location models can be used to choose locations for sets of power plants and other energy facilities within single or multistate regions. Because such models can simultaneously consider generation, transmission, fuel supply, and environmental constraints and costs, they can assist in electric system planning. They can also facilitate realistic environmental analysis of energy policies by bridging the gap between national energy models, which project regional energy demands, and pollution dispersion models, which require specific facility locations and pollutant discharge rates. Energy facility location models can also be tools of policy analysis in their own right. They have been applied to environmental questions such as the impact of alternative air pollution regulations, and economic issues such as the effect of electric utility deregulation upon electricity prices.

1. INTRODUCTION

Most generation expansion planning models ignore how space influences generation costs: they assume, in effect, that all power plants are at the same point. Yet the location of a new plant relative to fuel and water supplies, other plants, load centers, and areas with stringent environmental standards affects its cost. For example, cost differences among possible sites for a 1600 MW coal plant in southern Minnesota are as large as $50,000,000 per year in the case of make-up water, an equal amount for fuel delivery, and $12,000,000 per year for transmission [22]. The expense of pollution abatement measures can be equally variable. Regional energy facility location models permit inclusion of these location-dependent costs in generation expansion planning.

Location should also be considered in analyses of energy and environmental policy. For example, to estimate the health effects of increased combustion of coal, locations of emission sources relative to population centers must be specified and transport and transformation models applied. Yet national energy models go no further than to sum up residuals (e.g., SO_2) by region [24]. Energy

* Formerly at Oak Ridge National Laboratory, Oak Ridge, Tennessee, operated by the Union Carbide Corporation under contract W-7405-eng-26 for the U.S. Department of Energy.

facility location models can make realistic environmental analyses of energy policy possible by translating regional totals of generating capacity or power demands into estimates of capacity and pollutant emission rates by, say, county [24]. It is possible for such models to explicitly represent pollution standards, land use controls, water laws, population density restrictions, and other regulations that affect the siting of energy facilities and their effluents and resource consumption. Hence, location models can also be used to estimate how changes in environmental regulations would influence power costs and environmental impacts. In addition, evaluations can be made of economic policies, such as power export restrictions or the deregulation of electricity generation.

The purpose of this paper is to summarize formulations and applications of regional energy facility location models. Such models allocate energy facilities or capacity among geographic units of approximately county size, in most cases within a single or multistate region. The intent of such models is to determine a general pattern of facilities, not to propose particular sites. Screening methods for choosing a specific site for a planned facility ([12], [32]) are therefore excluded, as are national models which allocate capacity and output among regions, states, or multicounty areas (e.g., [1], [11]). This paper emphasizes electric power generation and transmission, although location models have also been applied to the coal and natural gas sectors (e.g., [30], [38]). In the next section, how facility location models treat power generation, transmission, and fuel supply is discussed. Subsequent sections survey applications in power system planning and the analysis of environmental and economic policies. Recommendations for methodological improvements conclude the paper.

2. MODEL FORMULATIONS

Power facility location models have been formulated in several ways. Those used for planning are usually more complex than those designed for policy analysis. Most are posed as static optimization problems where the objective is to minimize the cost of generation and transmission subject to demand, environmental, and economic constraints. In such models, loads and generation are located at nodes interconnected by a stylized transmission network. Objectives and solution procedures of energy facility location models are discussed below, as are formulations of the generation, transmission, and fuel supply problems. Environmental, water supply, and other regulatory constraints are presented later in the section on policy applications.

2.1 Objectives

Most energy facility location models adopt cost minimization as their objective ([6], [7], [19], [23], [24], [31], [33], [36]) or cost surrogates such as transmission length or coal hauling distance ([3], [5]). Costs can include, for example, the expense of fuel, water supply, transmission and generation capacity, pollution abatement measures, and taxes on power exports. If electricity demands depend upon price and are to be solved for endogenously, then the objective function can instead be defined as profit or social welfare (the sum of consumer surplus and profit) [13].

Environmental objectives can also be considered. Emanuel et al. [8] chose power plant locations that minimize population exposure to SO_2. Cohon et al. [5] used population within a certain distance of nuclear plants as one of four objectives in a multiobjective model. Honea, Hillsman, and Mader [16] assigned ratings to counties for air quality, population density, and seismic activity which, together with cost criteria, were used in a heuristic power plant location model. Gros [10] defined several objectives, each representing the multiattribute utility function of one interest group.

2.2 Power Generation

The simplist models determine locations of generation capacity whose fuel mix is prespecified (e.g., [5], [8], [16], [24]). Plant output is not explicitly modeled and is assumed to be a constant proportion of capacity. Such models are most useful for policy analysis; they are less suited for planning because they fail to differentiate between peak, intermediate, and base load facilities. Because peak and base demands are distributed throughout a region, the best locations for peaking units will probably differ from those chosen by a model which assumes that peaking units can serve the same demands as base load plants.

More sophisticated models separate the capacity expansion and operating decisions ([13], [19], [29], [33]). Fuel mix can then be optimized rather than prespecified. Most of these models use the deterministic load duration curve method described by Anderson [2]. There, the load duration curve at each node in the network is divided into two or more periods, and the output of each plant during each period is constrained to be less than its expected available capacity. Total generation over the year for each plant can also be constrained to allow for maintenance. The resulting estimate of total generation costs for the system is biased downwards [13]. This is because plants are deterministically "stacked" under the load curve, resulting in an underestimate of generation from the most expensive plants. Such plants would actually be expected to operate at times when, because of random outages, several cheaper plants are forced down simultaneously; but since deterministic models ignore this possibility, the calculated output of these plants will be zero. System marginal costs estimated by the deterministic load curve method, however, are not necessarily biased upwards or downwards.

Lall and Mays [19] use a second approach for calculating operating costs described by Anderson [2]. It requires that the plant merit order be prespecified; that is, plants are ranked in order of increasing operating cost. The available capacity of the mth plant in the merit order is defined as decision variable U_m. The operating cost of the mth plan then equals:

$$C_m \left[G\left(\sum_{1}^{m} U_j\right) - G\left(\sum_{1}^{m-1} U_j\right)\right]$$

where C_m is the operating cost in \$/MWh and G(X) is the integral, in MWh, of the load duration curve from 0 to X MW. The advantage of this method is that no operation variables or constraints are needed, yet operating costs are optimized. But if a model solves for fuel and water sources endogenously, then it may be impossible to determine the merit order *a priori*. Further, the merit order concept loses its meaning in the spatial context, as transmission costs can make it optimal for two or more spatially separated plants to be the marginal sources of power at any given moment. For these reasons, the deterministic load duration curve method is in general to be preferred for location models.

Most location models use continuous decision variables to represent generation capacity. This is unrealistic, since economies of scale dictate that generating units should be of a certain minimum size. Fortunately, computational experience shows that capacity tends to be sited in large lumps because environmental constraints and locational advantages will make a few places significantly more attractive than the others ([5], [25]). Some models, nonetheless, do adopt integer variables for capacity ([4], [16], [33]). Because of the computational burden such variables add, the resulting models are limited in either the size of the region that can be considered or the sophistication with which operating decisions, fuel and water supply, and environmental regulations can be modeled. Policy analysis requires a flexible tool that permits extensive sensitivity analysis; therefore, integer variables are generally omitted from models used for that purpose.

Location models, with few exceptions ([23], [31]), consider the generation system for only a single scenario year. Multiperiod formulations, which are the rule in traditional generation expansion models ([2], [35]), would make many location models impractically large. Thus, one can treat either the time or spatial dimension rigorously, but it is difficult to capture both simultaneously.

System reliability in energy facility location models is handled by imposing a chance constraint: total generating capacity must exceed the peak demand plus a predetermined reserve margin.

2.3 Power Transmission

Sophisticated models for calculating load flows, analyzing system stability, and planning transmission line additions are widely used (e.g., [35]). But the complexity of such models has prevented them from being integrated with generation expansion models. In order to simultaneously consider transmission and generation costs, location models must make more stylized representations of the transmission system. In the simplist models, transmission costs are considered by defining a transmission objective equal to the distance between plants and load centers ([3], [5]). Related to this approach is the transportation formulation that is the basis of several other models ([6], [7], [19], [35]). Transportation cost per kwh in these cases is assumed to be proportional to distance.

More realistic models are formulated as transshipment models which attempt to represent the actual grid ([13], [24], [33]). They can accurately determine power flows in DC networks if line loss is represented as a quadratic function of flow (as in [33]). But if capacitance and inductance are significant, AC flows and losses can only be coarsely approximated. Another cause of distortion is the dependence of flows upon stochastic demands and plant outages. The long transmission flows that can result from several plants within an area being out simultaneously are ignored by deterministic location models, implying that expected transmission distances will be underestimated.

Transshipment formulations allow power flows over a link to be constrained by its capacity. A line's capacity can be set to the minimum of: 1) its thermal capability, a function of voltage and conductor size, and 2) its loadability, as calculated using standard surge impedence loading curves [27]. Capacities calculated in this manner may be too large, however, as the possibility of one or more lines being out of service is ignored. More realistic line capacities can be based on utility contingency planning studies by forcing each link to have spare capacity sufficient to cover line outages elsewhere [13]. Transshipment models allow additions to line capacity to be made at a cost; with few exceptions ([4], [33]), continuous rather than integer capacity variables are used. Determination of the voltage levels of such lines is difficult; they can be based upon utility plans [13], or models can be solved repeatedly with voltages of new lines being adjusted between iterations to accomodate observed flows [29]. Alternatively, integer variables can be used to represent lines of different voltages [33].

2.4 Fuel Supply

In many models, the fuel cost for each generation technology at each node is calculated prior to solving the model and is inserted in the objective function. But where fuel transport costs are significant or there are several alternative fuel sources, it may be desirable to solve endogenously for fuel supplies and costs. For example, Meier et al. [27] constructed transshipment networks reflecting barge and rail costs for each of eight types of coal. The coal types varied in terms of price, percentage sulfur, and heat content. Their model also permitted coal cleaning. Cohon et al. [5] used a simpler transportation formulation for the coal network. Several other models ([19], [23], [36]) have included not only coal networks but also coal gasification plants and gas pipelines.

2.5 Solution Procedures

Most energy facility location models are formulated as LPs. This is because LPs with large, complicated constraint sets can be solved cheaply and sensitivity analyses are easily performed. But to assume linearity is too restrictive for some applications. Mixed integer programming, which permits representation of scale economies, has also been used ([6], [33]). So has nonlinear programming. For example, Lall and Mays [19] apply a generalized reduced gradient method to solve a nonlinear model. But because many of their costs were expressed as power terms with exponents smaller than one, global optimality could not be assured. Velioglu and Brill [36] also had a nonlinear problem; they used variable transformations and separable programming to handle multiplicative terms in their constraint set.

Specialized algorithms have been used by others to solve linear programming location models. For particularly large problems, Matsumoto and Mays [23] proposed use of Benders decomposition together with specialized network algorithms for the subproblems. Application of a network algorithm was also suggested by Church and Bell [3] for a simple energy facility assignment model. Cohon et al. [5] and Gros [10] used multiobjective LPs to generate curves that show tradeoffs among objectives. But the model of Cohon et al. was later changed to a single objective, cost minimization LP because dollar costs were more easily understood by decision makers [7].

A few models, termed baseline screening models, are solved using heuristics instead of mathematical programming ([3], [16], [37]). The intent there is to imitate how utilities actually choose sites using site screening methods. The Oak Ridge Siting Analysis Method (ORSAM) [16] does this by calculating a suitability rating for each county and then allocating capacity first to highly suitable counties close to load centers, and then to ones farther away.

3. USE OF LOCATION MODELS FOR SYSTEM PLANNING

Energy facility location models represent a compromise: in exchange for 1) an integration of transmission and generation and 2) sophisticated treatment of environmental, fuel, water supply, and land use considerations, simplified representations must be made of the generation and transmission systems. Such models can be used by themselves as system planning tools for generation mix optimization and for choosing the most attractive subregions for new plants, or they can be interfaced with more complex AC load flow and generation expansion models. In the latter case, the location model would supply fuel, transmission, and environmental protection costs to the expansion model and plant locations to the load flow model. The expansion model would then return generation mix and reserve margin information to the location model, and the load flow model would provide better transmission loss and cost estimates [29].

Regional energy facility location models have yet to be used in actual planning problems. Examples of hypothetical applications include:

1. Selection of locations for new coal plants and transmission lines in west India [28]. That model used is now being transferred to that country's Central Electricity Authority.

2. Siting of power plants and coal gasification facilities in east Texas [19] and Illinois [36].

3. Site selection for nuclear plants in the Pacific Northwest [6].

These models were static; multiperiod planning models for coal-gas-water-power systems have also been applied to hypothetical problems ([23], [31]).

4. USE OF LOCATION MODELS FOR POLICY ANALYSIS

4.1 General Approach

Planning models are prescriptive: they describe what should be done. In contrast, policy analysis models are predictive; they simulate how the utility industry would react to policy changes under a consistent set of behavioral assumptions. It is desirable for policy analysis models to yield plausible results, to be consistent with theory, and to explicitly include policy "handles" of interest to decision makers [11].

Location models for policy analysis can be of use to regional offices of federal agencies who wish to assess the long run impact of proposed regulations, regional planning bodies such as river basin commissions, and state agencies. For example, the Massachusetts Energy Facility Siting Council, which grants permits for new power plants and transmission lines in that state, has recommended that location models be used to evaluate plant proposals [21]. They argued that such models make clear the long run nature of siting problems and their cumulative implications and would help the staff formulate questions to ask utilities. An example of such an application is given by Meier [25]. A model was used to help the State of New Jersey evaluate a proposal to build power plants in an offshore industrial complex. Issues examined included site cost-effectiveness and the effects of pollution regulations and rail/sea coal terminal congestion upon choice of coal source.

There are two methodological approaches to simulating utility location decisions. The most common one, mathematical programming, was first formulated with an eye to policy analysis rather than planning by Church and Cohon [4]. This approach optimizes the region's power system configuration, in most cases under a cost minimization objective. Environmental regulations and resource costs are explicitly represented. Such models implicitly assume that utilities in the region cooperate to determine the most efficient sites of facilities and allocation of resources. A criticism of this approach is that utilities are not always cost minimizers [11]. For example, environmental and social factors figure prominently in utility power plant siting studies [32], which generally take place after generation mix is optimized. Further, distorted incentives can rise from rate regulation and from lack of coordination among utilities. Finally, utilities are concerned with risk and may therefore, for example, choose to build at nonoptimal locations they already own rather than purchase new sites that a model indicates would minimize expected cost. Nevertheless, there is empirical evidence that utilities do choose cost minimizing sites for new plants

[34]. Furthermore, cost factors are heavily weighted in regional site screenings by utilities (e.g., [22]). Such studies, the first step in the power plant siting process, determine where in a region suitable sites are likely to be found ([12], [32]).

The second approach, baseline screening, attempts to imitate how utilities actually choose sites. ORSAM [16], for example, rates the suitability of counties using a weighted sum of cost and environmental factors. Similar weighting based techniques are used by many utilities to choose sites ([12], [32]). However, there is no evidence that baseline screening methods predict utility decisions better than mathematical programs. For example, a disproportionate number of planned power plants are located in counties that ORSAM has rated as having low suitability [11]. Further, different baseline screening methods can yield startlingly different results [3]. One reason is that different utilities use different screening methods, attributes, and weights, which can by themselves lead to different site choices ([12], [32]). Another reason is that not all utilities apply systematic screening techniques and others may use them simply to rationalize judgmental siting decisions [32]. A second criticism of baseline screening methods is their failure, because of their heuristic nature, to consider cumulative impacts and interrelationships of plants [3]. For example, each county in a river basin may be favorably rated for water supply, but the sum of plants sited there might nonetheless exceed the total water available [11]. Such models also lack the policy handles, such as air quality standards and power export taxes, that mathematical programming location models can include. Finally, marginal costs, which can be obtained from dual solutions of mathematical programs, are not provided by baseline screening methods.

Neither approach is completely satisfactory. Mathematical programming location models seem the best tool for policy analysis because: 1) mathematical programs can explicitly represent environmental and economic policies; and 2) the siting patterns they produce are not obviously less plausible than those yielded by baseline screening models. The only exception to this conclusion is when a single national siting scenario is desired; baseline screening may then be the only practical approach. Applications of location models in environmental and economic policy analysis are surveyed below.

4.2 Disaggregation of National Energy Scenarios

Location models can serve as a bridge between: 1) projections provided by national energy models of generation capacity or demand by region; and 2) environmental impact models that require facility locations and pollutant emission rates. The first such use was in the 1978 National Coal Utilization Assessment of the U.S. Department of Energy (DOE). The Brookhaven Regional Energy Facility Siting model [27] was developed to disaggregate capacity projections for the Northeast for that study, although the assessment's siting scenarios were ultimately obtained using ORSAM [16]. Once facility sites and emission rates were specified, the DOE national laboratories projected the associated socioeconomic water quality, air quality, and water supply impacts. For example, regional transport models were used to estimate ambient levels of SO_2 and SO_4 using projected plant locations and SO_2 release rates. A baseline screening method similar to ORSAM was also used in a later DOE study, the Regional Issue Identification and Assessment [37].

There are tradeoffs between realism and computational feasibility. Region size models can include many details. For national policy analysis, models which allow interregional flows and obtain consistent siting patterns for the entire nation are desired. It was for this reason that ORSAM [16], although simplistic in many ways, was used in the coal utilization assessment. Linear programming location models are being developed for the entire nation [11]; network flow formulations [3], which can be solved very efficiently, hold particular promise.

4.3 Analysis of Environmental Issues

Soon after the DOE coal utilization assessment, energy facility location models became tools of policy analysis in their own right. Solutions of such models would be obtained for several sets of policy assumptions and then compared in terms of power costs, population exposure to pollutants, water consumption, and other relevant measures of performance. Applications to air quality, water quality, and land use issues are surveyed below. Analyses of economic policy are discussed in the next section.

Air pollution regulations in the U.S. take many forms: ambient quality standards, effluent limitations, control technology requirements, and restrictions on fuel sulfur content. Other possible regulatory tools include emission taxes and marketable pollution rights. Any of these can be incorporated in energy facility location models ([18], [27]). Several are included, for example, in the model of Meier [24]. In this model, variables are defined for eight types of coal, coal plants with and without sulfur scrubbers, and coal cleaning, permitting the model to solve for the effluent rate of each plant. Several models incorporate transfer matrices which define ambient concentration of an air pollutant at each node to be a weighted linear function of the effluents at every node ([5], [8], [27]). The linear representation is valid if pollutant dispersion and transformation can be represented by linear differential equations.

Meier ([24], [26]) gives an example of an analysis of air pollution policy. He obtained year 2000 power plant siting scenarios for New York State for two different values of the Federal New Source Performance Standard for SO_2 emissions; 0.6 and 1.2 lb $SO_2/10^6$ BTU. The state imposes a more stringent standard, 0.4 lb/10^6 BTU, in New York City. Although the scenario with the more stringent SO_2 standard yields fewer emissions, it reveals that population exposure to SO_2 could nevertheless increase. The reason is that the stricter standard is so close to the New York City requirement that it becomes more economic to site plants in urban areas and pay more for low sulfur coal than to incur the transmission costs associated with locating plants where standards are less rigorous. Kolstad [18] also uses a location model to analyze air pollution regulation, in this case in the Four Corners region. He examines the economic efficiency of alternative control instruments, including effluent and ambient standards, marketable pollution rights, pollution taxes, and technology requirements, under a range of possible SO_2 damage functions. No one instrument turns out best under all functions.

Measures to prevent thermal pollution can also be modeled. Eagles, Cohon, and ReVelle [7] present a formulation which constrains how much temperature can be increased in a receiving river. They assume that temperature rise is a linear function of rejected heat from once-through cooled power plants. Hobbs and Meier [15] consider the effect upon power costs and water consumption of requiring evaporative cooling towers for all new thermal power plants in the mid-Atlantic states.

In many river basins, low flows are inadequate to support all water uses, while at the same time, political opposition to dams and interbasin diversions makes supply augmentation difficult. Water consumption by utilities is controversial because new plants are large and are often the latest arrivals in such basins. Energy facility location models provide a means of estimating the effect of physical, legal, and institutional water supply restrictions upon power costs and utility water use.

In particular, mathematical programming location models permit detailed treatment of a range of water supply and conservation measures. To be realistic, water supplies in a model must reflect political constraints which, in general, allow less water development than is hydrologically possible. Changes in water laws and policies would be reflected in the assumed cost and availability of water, as in Hobbs and Meier [15]. One source of water included in several models is instream flow, where utilities are allowed to divert up to a certain amount at no cost ([5], [13], [15], [35]). Some models also define variables that represent the firm yield of reservoirs whose costs can be included in the objective function ([5], [13], [15], [19]). More sophisticated formulations, which optimize the size and operation of storage reservoirs, have been proposed ([2], [4], [29]). They would be based on deterministic water system optimization models that find frequent use in river basin planning [20]. Because of surface water shortages, utilities in the West increasingly rely on other sources instead, such as ground water, sewage effluent, and rights transfers from irrigators. Ground water has been considered in a few location models ([19], [31], [36]); procedures for estimating the cost and availability of ground water and other nontraditional supplies are described by Abbey and Loose [1] and Hobbs [14]. Yet another source considered by some models is the interbasin transfer of water ([4], [27], [36]). Finally, if all else fails, utilities can resort to expensive dry or mixed wet/dry cooling. Water demand curves reflecting costs of these water conservation measures can be included in facility location models ([1], [14], [36]).

The effect of land use policies upon power system costs and environmental impacts can also be examined with facility siting models. The simplest means is to delete generation capacity variables for locations that are unsuitable because of population density, seismicity, or conflicting land uses. For example, Hobbs and Meier [15] examined the effect of allowing off-shore floating nuclear plants along the mid-Atlantic states. Strip mining regulations, another land use issue, can be simulated by altering the types, amounts, and prices of coal.

4.4 Analysis of Economic Issues

The primal and dual solutions of mathematical programming models provide information that can be used to analyze economic policies. Applications to be described below include rate setting, geographic equity, fuel choice, and deregulation.

Scherer [33] used a mixed integer program to calculate marginal costs of the New York State Electric and Gas Corporation system. He found that on-peak marginal costs can be ten times off-peak values, which makes a strong case for time-of-day pricing. Because he used integer variables to represent capacity additions, the dual variables, which he interprets as marginal costs, can only represent short run marginal generation costs. Long run marginal costs, which include capacity costs, cannot be estimated this way, nor can short run rationing costs incurred when demand exceeds capacity.

The issue of geographic equity is an important one in siting: a common complaint by residents near proposed facilities is that they will bear the negative impacts of plants which will benefit consumers elsewhere. Some states respond to this concern by taxing power exports or by requiring that a majority interest in plants sited within its borders be owned by instate utilities. Energy facility location models can be formulated so that exports are taxed or restricted [27], or so that each region supplies at least a given fraction of its demand [4].

Export restrictions in New England have been analyzed by Meier and Hobbs [26]. Gros [10] approached the problem differently; he described how each of four interest groups, including local interests, would evaluate siting patterns.

Government actions affecting fuel choice have important siting and power cost consequences. Facility location models can be used to examine the effects of, for example, a nuclear moratorium by imposing a generation mix constraint, as Eagles, Cohon, and ReVelle [7] have done. The cost and air quality consequences of conversion of existing natural gas and oil fired plants to coal can also be assessed by proper definitions of model variables and constraints.

Energy facility location models have been used to estimate how the deregulation of electricity generation might affect bulk power prices [13]. Several proposals for deregulation would separate the industry into its three components: generation, transmission, and distribution. Unregulated generating firms would compete to sell power, which would be transmitted by a publicly owned or regulated transmission grid to large customers and local distribution companies. Because transmission is costly and there are significant scale economies in generation, unregulated generators would be oligopolists, competing with only a few neighbors. In oligopolistic spatial markets, equilibrium prices, in general, exceed marginal cost and profits are nonzero. Economists have proposed models for calculating spatial price equilibria in such markets ([9], [17]), but they usually assume that customer density and production costs are uniform over space and that firms are identically sized. Because this is manifestly untrue in the case of power markets, mathematical programs were developed which can more accurately represent the actual landscape [13].

Equilibrium deregulated prices depend upon spatial price structure and the beliefs each firm has concerning the reactions of rivals to price changes. The price structure assumed in [13] was spatial price discrimination, where differences between prices at different points are not necessarily related to transport cost differentials. Since the beliefs unregulated firms would have concerning rivals' reactions cannot be predicted, two models were developed [13]. One model, based upon the Nash/Bertrand equilibrium described by Hoover [17], represents the most intense level of competition to be expected. In it, each firm naively believes that its neighbors hold their prices fixed; as a result, the equilibrium price at each point equals the second lowest marginal cost among firms. The model defines a separate transshipment network for each firm, which provides dual variables for each firm at each node. After each solution, quantities demanded are adjusted in response to the calculated prices, and a revised solution is obtained. This process is repeated until an equilibrium is reached. The second model developed represents a strategy of limit pricing where prices are set to dissuade entry by new firms. This was assumed to represent an upper bound to deregulated power prices. Limit pricing solutions were calculated in three steps:

1. Post entry prices, under which entrants at nodes where entry is possible expect zero profit, were obtained. Entrants were assumed to build coal fired units;

2. The implied pre-entry prices were then solved for; and

3. A facility location model was used to determine the cost of serving the quantities demanded under the pre-entry prices.

It is also possible to calculate a Cournot/Nash equilibrium, where firms believe that neighbors hold sales at each point fixed, for the spatial price discrimination case [9]. A location model for calculating such an equilibrium would consist of submodels representing the profit maximizing problem for each firm. Each subproblem's objective function would include the firm's revenue as a function of sales at each point. The master problem linking the subproblems would include water supplies, transmission capacities, and other shared resources.

The Nash/Bertrand and limit pricing models were used to define a likely range for deregulated bulk power prices in upstate New York for the years 1980 and 2000 [13]. To focus on the issue of allocative (pricing) efficiency, productive efficiency was assumed to be unaffected by deregulation. The resulting Nash/Bertrand prices were 2 percent above marginal cost, on average, while limit prices were up to 20 percent higher. These prices were significantly above average cost because the marginal source of power at most times is oil. Thus, because estimated unregulated prices were closer to marginal cost than average cost based regulated rates, deregulation was projected to increase allocative efficiency, as measured by the sum of consumer and producer surplus.

5. CONCLUSIONS

Energy facility location models integrate generation, transmission, environmental considerations, and fuel and water supply. Such models can be used for planning power systems and for evaluating environmental and economic policies related to energy.

Several methodological improvements would enhance the usefulness of these models. For example, the models' simple representation of generation and transmission, which makes their comprehensiveness possible, may also be a barrier to their acceptance as planning tools. Integer solutions would be more realistic; it may be possible to extend the network methods discussed by Church and Bell [3] or the decomposition approach of Matsumoto and Mays [23] to obtain them more cheaply. Alternatively, interfacing of location models with traditional generation expansion tools could improve the solutions of both [29]. Improved representations of transmission costs are also desirable. Comparisons of transshipment model solutions with the results of AC load flow analyses and line outage contingency studies would result in better estimates of required reserve margins for transmission lines. Finally, facility location models need to be applied to real planning problems in order to better understand their strengths and weaknesses.

Improvements in the ability of location models to simulate noncost minimizing behavior would make them more useful for policy analysis. Risk aversion, social and environmental objectives, regulation induced biases for or against certain factors of production, lack of coordination among utilities, sequential decision making, public ownership, and the amount of competition all affect productive efficiency and site choices -- but in what direction and to what degree? Generalizations are difficult. Several methodologies might be useful here. An example is multiobjective analysis, the purpose of which is to reveal what tradeoffs there are between cost and noncost objectives ([3], [4], [5]). That approach, however, tends to overload decision makers with information. Risk aversion might be analyzed using portfolio or utility theory. Models which treat each utility separately ([11], [13]) represent a first step toward including the effects of competition and imperfect coordination in location models. These and other approaches need to be developed further.

ACKNOWLEDGEMENT

The author thanks D.R. Alvic, W.R. Emanuel, and J. Matsumoto for their helpful criticisms and Oak Ridge National Laboratory for its support of this work.

REFERENCES

[1] D. Abbey and V. Loose, "Water Supply and Demand in an Energy Supply Model," DOE/EV/10180-2, U.S. Department of Energy, Washington, DC, Dec. 1980.

[2] D. Anderson, "Models for Determining Least Cost Investments in Electricity Supply," Bell J. Econ. Man. Sci., 3(1), Spring 1972, pp. 267-299.

[3] R.L. Church and T.L. Bell, "A Comparison of Two Baseline Screening Approaches to Regional Energy Facility Siting," GeoJournal, Supplementary Issue 3, 1981, pp. 17-36.

[4] R.L. Church and J.L. Cohon, "Multiobjective Location Analysis of Regional Energy Facility Siting Problems," BNL 50567, Brookhaven Natl. Lab., Upton, NY, Oct. 1976.

[5] J.L. Cohon, C.S. ReVelle, J. Current, T. Eagles, R. Eberhart, and R. Church, "Application of a Multiobjective Facility Location Model to Power Plant Siting in a Six-State Region of the U.S.," Comput. and Oper. Res., 7, 1980, pp. 107-123.

[6] R. Dutton, G. Hinman, and C.B. Millham, "The Optimal Location of Nuclear-Power Facilities in the Pacific Northwest," Oper. Res., 22(3), May-June 1974, pp. 478-487.

[7] T.W. Eagles, J.L. Cohon, and C. ReVelle, "Modeling Plant Location Patterns: Applications," EPRI EA-1375, Electric Power Research Institute, Palo Alto, CA, Feb. 1980.

[8] W.R. Emanuel, B.D. Murphy, D.D. Huff, C.L. Begovich, and J.F. Hunt, "An Optimization Model for Air Quality Analysis in Energy Facility Siting," ORNL/TM-6007, Oak Ridge Natl. Lab., Oak Ridge, TN, Sept. 1977.

[9] J.G. Greenhut and M.L. Greenhut, "Spatial Price Discrimination, Competition, and Locational Effects," Economica, 42, Nov. 1975, pp. 401-419.

[10] J. Gros, "Power Plant Siting, A Paretian Environmental Approach," Nucl. Eng. and Design, 34, 1975, pp. 281-292.

[11] E.L. Hillsman, D.R. Alvic, and R.L. Church, "BUILD: A Model of the Future Spatial Distribution of Electric Power Production," ORNL-5969, Oak Ridge Natl. Lab., Oak Ridge, TN, 1983.

[12] B.F. Hobbs, "Multiobjective Power Plant Siting Methods," J. Energy Div., Proc. ASCE, 106 (EY2), Oct. 1980, pp. 187-200.

[13] B.F. Hobbs, "A Location Theoretic Analysis of Competition in Electrical Generation," Ph.D. Dissertation, Cornell Univ., Ithaca, NY, Jan. 1983.

[14] B.F. Hobbs, "Water Supply for Power in the Texas - Gulf Region," J. Water Res. Plan. and Manag., Proc. ASCE (forthcoming, 1984).

[15] B.F. Hobbs and P.M. Meier, "An Analysis of Water Resources Constraints on Power Plant Siting in the Mid-Atlantic States," Water Res. Bull., 15(6), Dec. 1979, pp. 1666-1676.

[16] R.B. Honea, E.L. Hillsman, and R.F. Mader, "Oak Ridge Siting Analysis: A Baseline Assessment Focusing on the National Energy Plan," ORNL/TM-6816, Oak Ridge Natl. Lab., Oak Ridge, TN, Oct. 1979.

[17] E.M. Hoover, "Spatial Price Discrimination," Rev. of Econ. Stud., 4, June 1937, pp. 182-191.

[18] C.D. Kolstad, "An Empirical Analysis of Regulatory Efficiency in Air Pollution Control," LA-UR-81-1727, Los Alamos Natl. Lab., Los Alamos, NM, Nov. 1982.

[19] V. Lall and L. W. Mays, "Model for Planning Water-Energy Systems," Water Res. Research, 17(4), Aug. 1981, pp. 853-865.

[20] D.P. Loucks, J.R. Stedinger, and D.A. Haith, Water Resource Systems Planning and Analysis, Prentice-Hall, Englewood Cliffs, NJ, 1981.

[21] Massachusetts Energy Facility Siting Council, "An Integrated Regional Approach to Regulating Energy Facility Siting," NUREG/CR-0241, Boston, MA, June 1978.

[22] D.L. Matchett and R.P. Kitchell, "Power Plant Siting: Economic Screening Techniques," J. Energy Div., Proc. ASCE, 105 (EY2), Aug. 1979, pp. 277-289.

[23] J. Matsumoto and L.W. Mays, "Capacity Expansion Model for Large-Scale Water-Energy Systems," Water Res. Research, 19 (3), June 1983, pp. 593-607.

[24] P.M. Meier, "Long-Range Regional Power Plant Siting Model," J. Energy Div., Proc. ASCE, 105 (EY1), Jan. 1979, pp. 117-135.

[25] P.M. Meier, "Energy Modelling in Practice: An Application of Spatial Programming," OMEGA, 10(5), 1982, pp. 483-491.

[26] P.M. Meier and B.F. Hobbs, "The Locational Response to Regulatory Policy: A Regional Analysis of Energy Facility Location," Northeast Reg. Sci. Rev., 8(2), 1978, pp. 1-17.

[27] P. Meier, B. Hobbs, G. Ketcham, M. McCoy, and R. Stern, "The Brookhaven Regional Energy Facility Siting Model: Model Development and Application," BNL 51006, Brookhaven Natl. Lab., Upton, NY, June 1976.

[28] P.M. Meier and V. Mubayi, "Application of an Integrated System Planning Model to the Western India Grid: Some Preliminary Results," Brookhaven Natl. Lab., Upton, NY, n.d.

[29] P. Meier, V. Mubayi, and S. Lahiri, "LDC-REFS: A Model for Regional Electric Sector Planning in the Developing Countries," Brookhaven Natl. Lab., Upton, NY, Aug. 1979.

[30] J.P. Osleeb and S.J. Ratick, "A Mixed Integer and Multiple Objective Programming Model to Analyze Coal Handling in New England," Eur. J. of Oper. Res., 12, 1983, pp. 302-313.

[31] G. Provenzano, "A Linear Programming Model for Assessing the Regional Impacts of Energy Development on Water Resources," Res. Rep. 77-0126, Water Resour. Cent., Univ. of Ill., Urbana-Champaign, July 1977.

[32] M.D. Rowe, B.F. Hobbs, B.L. Pierce, and P.M. Meier, "An Assessment of Nuclear Power Plant Siting Methods," BNL-NUREG-51206, Brookhaven Natl. Lab., Upton, NY, Nov. 1979.

[33] C.R. Scherer, "Estimating Peak and Off-Peak Marginal Costs for an Electric Power System: An Ex Ante Approach," Bell J. of Econ., 7(2), Aut. 1976, pp. 575-601.

[34] B.W. Smith, "Analysis of the Location of Coal-Fired Power Plants in the Eastern United States," Econ. Geog., 49, 1973, pp. 243-250.

[35] U.S. Department of Energy, "Regional Power Systems Planning; A State of the Art Assessment," DOE/RA/29144-01, Washington, D.C., Oct. 1980.

[36] S.G. Velioglu and E.D. Brill, Jr., "Planning Models with Alternative Cooling Systems," J. Power Div., Proc. ASCE, 104 (PO2), Apr. 1978, pp. 141-156.

[37] A.H. Weiss, M. Placet, and S.V. McBrien, "Documentation of Electric Utility Models in SEAS for Second Regional Issue Identification and Assessment - Working Paper," MITRE Corp., McLean, VA, 1980.

[38] E.E. Whitlatch, Jr., "Coal Gasification and Water Resources Development," J. Water Res. Plan. and Man. Div., Proc. ASCE, 103 (WR2), Nov. 1977, pp. 299-314.

Analytic Techniques for Energy Planning
B. Lev, F.H. Murphy, J.A. Bloom & A.S. Gleit (Editors)

PLANNING MODELS ARE FOR INSIGHT NOT NUMBERS: A COMPLEMENTARY MODELLING APPROACH*

J.S. Rogers

Dept. of Industrial Engineering
University of Toronto
Toronto, Canada

This paper describes a complementary modelling approach to the design of a system of models for planning new energy policies. It focuses on the distinction between complementary and auxiliary models and shows that much of the current literature can be interpreted in this way. The strengths and limitations of this approach are illustrated by a specific model built to complement a large 4-region 6-time period model of inter-regional electric energy supply in Canada.

1. INTRODUCTION

In this paper we describe an approach to modelling energy policy which we call "complementary" modelling. The idea is to design a system of models whose results taken together aid the decision maker rather than trying to design a single model of the energy system. This approach is an extension of the evolution of models in the energy and electric power planning fields in which multiple computational models have been used. We emphasize the use of analytic models both as auxiliary models and as complementary models. Specifically we suggest the need for a tight link between the results of large computational models and the design of analytic models. A sample application shows how useful insights into the results from computational models can be derived from the use of a complementary analytic model.

This paper consists of the following sections. Section 2 is a brief review of the literature on the use of multiple models to study a particular set of policy alternatives. Section 3 distinguishes between complementary and auxiliary models and describes the basic concept of complementary models. Sections 4, 5, and 6 describe an application of the complementary modelling approach to the analysis of the output of a large scale LP model of the Canadian electric power system, the Canadian Inter-Regional Electricity Model (CIREM). Section 4 describes the computational model and Section 5 describes a complementary analytic approach. In it, the computational and analytic models are used in a complementary way to gain insight into the conditions under which inter-regional transmission of electric energy makes a significant difference in the amount of nuclear generation capacity built.

2. REVIEW OF PREVIOUS WORK

Earlier work has focused primarily on using one or more large scale models

---

*This paper was sponsored by the Natural Sciences and Engineering Research Council of Canada under grant No. A8587. We thank J.A. Bloom for helpful comments on an earlier version.

to study a particular energy system planning issue. A good example of the use of multiple computational models is the work of A.S. Manne and associates on energy planning for Mexico [10]. Only in the last few years has the need for analytic models been perceived among operations research and system planning analysts.

The idea of using analytic models to explain the results of experiments has, of course, been normal practice in scientific and engineering disciplines (e.g. "The purpose of computing is insight not numbers" (Hamming [11])). Similarly, many of the analytic models in the literature (e.g. Hogan and Manne [12], Levin et al. [16] and Saraf et al. [26]) come indirectly from attempts to understand phenomena seen in practice or as output from computational models. However, the need for the tight link between large scale computer models and a group of explanatory analytic models has not been noticed until recently (e.g. Geoffrion [9] and Richels [21]). As discussed in Section 3, there are two alternative approaches: the auxiliary model approach and the complementary model approach.

2.1 The Use of Computational Models

For the last 25 years, the electric utility industry has used large scale computer models (Anderson [2]). Moreover, the use of a set of computational models in planning electric power system expansion is a widespread practice. Thus the evolution of this practice in this sector of the energy system yields useful insights into the effective use of multiple models to study the broader energy planning issues.

Perhaps the best expositions of this approach are Anderson [2], Knight [15] and Albouy et al. [1]. Figure 1 summarizes the central idea of these authors. This idea is that each type of model works well when focused on a certain set of issues but does not work well when used to analyze other issues. The upper line in Figure 1 represents a level of reasonable computational resources and the lower line represents the minimum level of detail that is sensible for the given type of planning problem.

The basic issues of the long term mix of generation capacity by fuel type are typically expressed as a linear programming model. However, this requires information on appropriate levels of reserve margins. This can only come from a more detailed intermediate term model which considers the sequencing and timing of generating units entering service and contains an explicit reliability model. This type of planning model is typically a dynamic programming (Rogers [22], Booth [6]), or integer programming (Noonan [19]) model. In turn, these intermediate term models take the mixture of generation capacity by fuel type from the long term model. Moreover, their estimates of fuel costs only approximate the results of the short term models. The short term models take the sequence of capacities and fuel types of generating units as fixed, and compute fuel costs based on very detailed models of system operating procedures. These models often have optimizing submodels, but are usually a complex combination of stochastic and other models, and so in essence become simulations. Figure 2 is a schematic diagram of the iterative process that utility planners often undertake.

Efforts to reproduce the heuristic iterative approach of the working planner in an explicit modelling framework are reported by Beglari and Laughton [3] and Schweppe et al. [27]. However, later papers by these groups (Cote and Laughton [8] and Bloom [5]) indicate that the problems caused by iterating among standard models were great enough that it is preferable to simplify the models somewhat and then use an explicit decomposition framework such as Benders' Decomposition (Benders [4]). Cote and Laughton [8] consider integer variables for generation and use an equal load carrying capability approach for reliability. In contrast, Bloom [5] uses continuous variables for the former and expected energy unserved

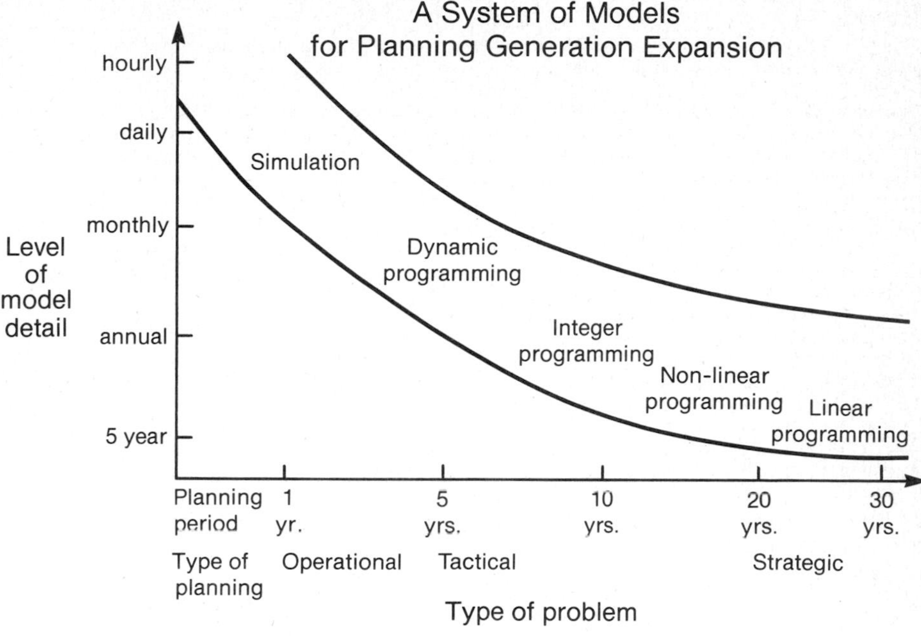

Figure 1. An Appropriate Model for Each Problem

for the latter.

2.2 The Use of Analytic Models

The use of a mixed set of analytic and computational models is described by Manne [18]. In this book, the results from simple analytic models are used to supply a rationale for the structure of the larger scale computational models. Similarly, the results of an integer programming model are used to motivate the structure of a heuristic procedure designed to work on the largest and most general model considered in the book.

Recently, there have been some papers which have focused on the development of simple analytic models to explain the results of parametric analysis done with a large scale computational model. Geoffrion [9] uses the term "auxiliary" models to describe models which are simplifications of a computational model. Ignall et al. [13] derive basic functional relationships from the output of simulations. Janischewskyj and Rogers [14] describe an approach in which this was done by regression.

The use of analytic models to enhance and extend the domain of applicability of the results of large scale computational models is the focus of the next section.

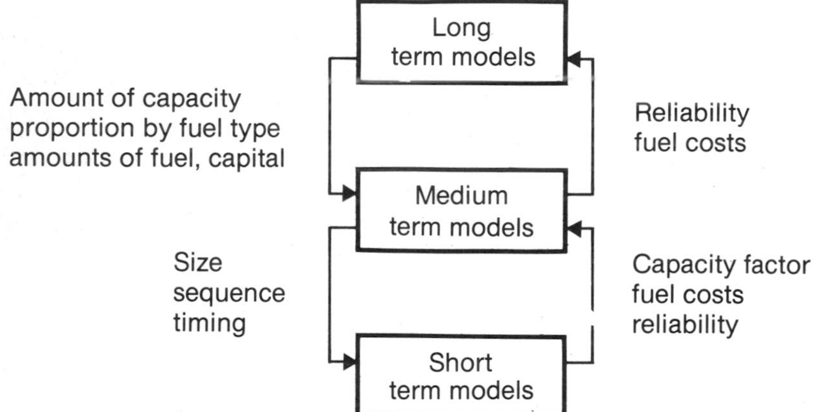

Figure 2. The Iterative Procedure of the Planning Process

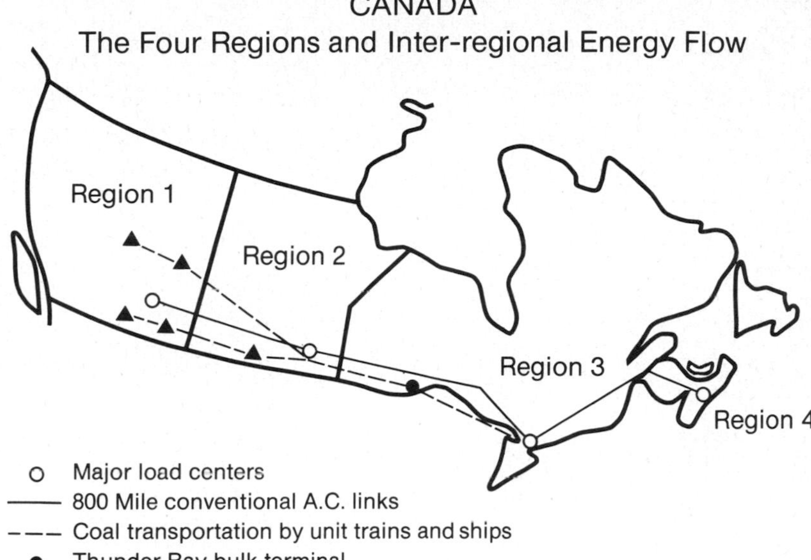

Figure 3. The Regions of the CIREM Model

3. ANALYTIC MODELS: COMPLEMENTARY VS AUXILIARY

In this section we distinguish between the use of complementary models and auxiliary models. Complementary is defined as "mutually supplying each other's lack" (Woolf [28]). In a set of complementary models, no one model is correct and the results come from integration by the analyst or, in some less complicated cases, another integrating model. On the other hand auxiliary is defined as "functioning in a subsidiary capacity" (Woolf [28]). In this case there is a correct model: it is the large computational model. "Auxiliary" analytic models are special cases of the computational model.

The structure of each auxiliary model is a subset of the structure of the large computational model. Many of the parameters of the large model are aggregated into a single parameter in the auxiliary model. Phillips, D. et al. [20] use an analytic model of the static generating mix problem to motivate their multi-period non-linear programming model. Thus, in use, an auxiliary model focuses on one aspect of the results generated by the computational model, and shows that these results can be explained in terms of a highly aggregated view of the problem.

On the other hand, complementary models are ones which are significantly different in their portrayal of at least one aspect of the system. For example, the computational model described in Section 4 contains a stepwise approximation to the load duration curve and a very detailed characterization of the changing relative prices and availability of different types of generating units, fuels, etc. over the planning horizon. In contrast, the complementary analytic model of Section 5 contains an exact portrayal of the annual load duration curve of each region in the target year, but assumes that all variation in prices and availability over the planning horizon can be aggregated into equivalent one period values. In at least one dimension, each of these models is "more accurate" than the other. Thus the modelling problem is not to build "a model for system planning", but rather "a system of models for planning" (Rogers [23]).

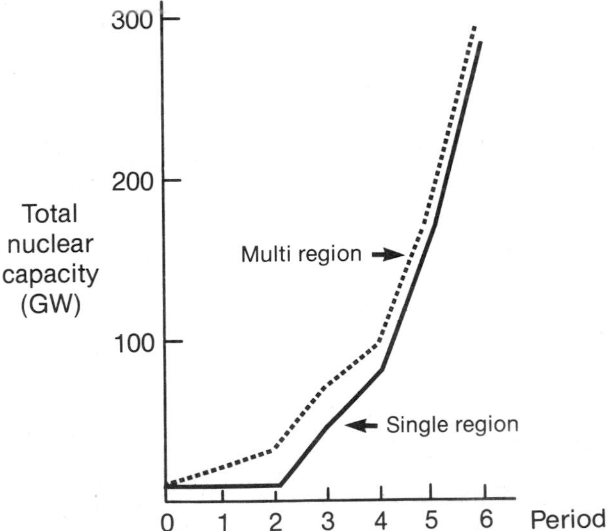

Figure 4. Single and Multi Region Results from CIREM

From this perspective, the practice in the electric utility industry of using multiple computational models to study a particular planning problem (as described in Section 2) is a complementary modelling approach. Thus we propose that it and similar approaches to the broader issues of energy planning be extended explicitly to include analytic models. Then the new complementary modelling procedure would be like the example described in Section 6.

4. THE COMPUTATIONAL MODEL

4.1 Basic Structure

The Canadian Inter-Regional Electricity Model (CIREM) used to generate the empirical results was described in detail by Rogers and Choudhury [24]. It consists of a 30 year, six period, four region linear programming model which allows expansion and operation of three types of thermal generating capacity within each region and inter-regional transmission of electricity. Figure 3 shows the transportation options superimposed on a map of southern Canada which displays the four regions. CIREM minimizes the present value of capital and operating costs of generation and transmission and has regional reliability standards. It also contains supply functions for each of three types of coal. The sequence of planned hydro-electric generating facilities is assumed fixed, and so in each period the available hydraulic base load and peaking capability is removed from the system load duration curve to create a load duration curve for the thermal units. This "thermal" load duration curve is used as input to the model.

4.2 Numerical Results

Figure 4 shows the total amount of nuclear capacity in the system. The upper line shows the results for the multi region (or base) case. By setting the capital and operating costs of transmission to zero, we create a "single region" case in which all generation and load is at one point. This model then is a small degenerate version of CIREM. The difference in the amount of nuclear capacity built in the multi and single region cases is an estimate of the size of the regional effects (or the error caused by neglecting the regional effects).

Since the focus of this paper is on the simplest model which will represent the effect of transmission on the amount of nuclear capacity, we are interested in this value at the end of the planning period and not the temporary differences which occur in the early periods. The numerical values show that in the last period the difference in the amount of nuclear capacity is about 11 GW out of a total thermal capacity in all regions of 346 GW or about 3%.

5. A COMPLEMENTARY ANALYTIC MODEL

5.1 Structure of the Model

The design of the structure of the analytic model is based on choosing the simplest model which will yield understanding of the principal determinants of the variation in the long term amount of nuclear capacity shown by the CIREM model for the two cases studied. To approach this problem we designed a simple analytic model of thermal generation and inter regional transmission expansion for two regions. This analytic model is based on an extension of the work described by Phillips, D. et al. [20]. Region 1 in Figure 5 represents Region 3 in Figure 3. Similarly, Region 2 in Figure 5 represents Region 1 in Figure 3. The general characteristics of the CIREM optimal solution are incorporated into the structure of the analytic model. These characteristics are the following:

1. Nuclear units can be built in both regions at the same capital and operating cost.

2. Coal-fired units can be built in both regions at the same capital cost.

3. The coal-fired units in each region use the same type of coal and so the cost of fuel in region one equals the cost in region two plus the transportation cost.

4. The capital cost of a nuclear unit is higher than that of a coal-fired unit but its operating cost is lower than the coal cost in the cheapest region (i.e., two).

5. The usefulness of electric power transmission is both in transmitting electric energy from region two to region one instead of transporting coal, and in transmitting nuclear generated electricity from region one to region two to reduce the amount of coal burned in region two.

6. During the planning period both types of capacity will be built in both regions so that the amount of transmission capacity allowed affects only the amount of each type of capacity built, not whether or not it would be built. A somewhat different and more complex model is explored by Choudhury [7].

7. The efficiency of transmission is 100%.

The effects of these considerations are illustrated by the two region electric energy exchange in Figure 5. Rogers and Choudhury [25] describe the equations and the details of the analysis. Following this structure, we can formulate the total annual cost of supplying the two thermal load duration curves as the following expression:

$$
\begin{aligned}
TC(x_1,x_2,T) &= c_1(x_1,x_2) + c_t T + c_2(P_1-x_1-T+P_2+T-x_2) \\
&+ \int_0^{s_1}[\gamma_N x_1+(\gamma_C+t)(P_1(s)-T-x_1)]ds + \int_0^{s_1}[\gamma_N x_2+\gamma_C(P_2(s)+T-x_2)]ds \\
&+ \int_{s_1}^{s_2}[\gamma_N x_1+ \gamma_N x_2)ds + \gamma_C \int_{s_1}^{s_2}[P_1(s)-x_1+P_2(s)-x_2]ds \\
&+ \gamma_N \int_{s_2}^{s_3}[(P_1(s) + T) + x_2]ds + \gamma_C \int_{s_2}^{s_3}[P_2(s)-T-x_2]ds \\
&+ \gamma_N \int_{s_3}^{1}[P_1(s) + P_2(s)]ds \qquad (1)
\end{aligned}
$$

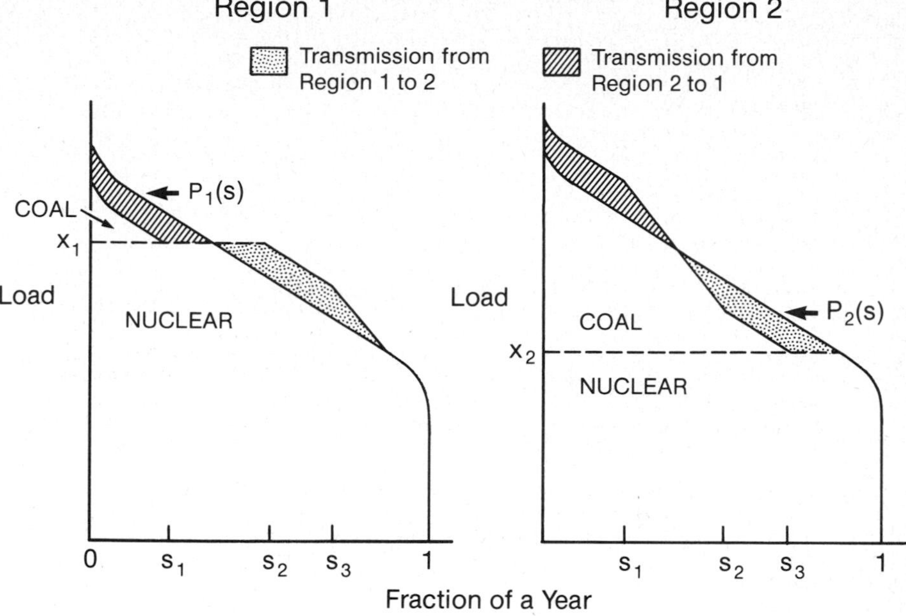

Figure 5. Generation and Transmission Between Two Regions

Before defining the symbols we will describe the rationale for each integral in equation (1).

1. In the range of 0 to s_1, both coal and nuclear generating units operate in both regions and the amount of power transmitted is limited by the capacity of the transmission line. The first integral computes the operating costs for Region 1 and the second for Region 2. We note that the coal-fired units in Region 1 incur transportation cost, t, per unit of energy produced in addition to the operating costs of the units in Region 2.

2. Over the range of s_1 to s_3, coal-fired units operate only in Region 2 but nuclear units operate in both regions. For the range of s_1 to s_2 the third integral computes the nuclear operating costs for both regions while the fourth integral computes the coal operating cost in Region 2. Similarly in the range s_2 to s_3, the fifth integral computes the nuclear operating costs for both regions while integral six computes the coal operating costs only. We note that in the range of s_1 to s_2 the amount of power transmitted is limited by the demand or supply. However, in the range of s_2 to s_3 the amount transmitted is limited by the capacity of the transmission line.

3. In the range of s_3 to 1 only nuclear generation is operating and so integral seven computes its operating costs. We note that in this range the power transmitted is limited by the demand.

The fact that the transmission link is used at capacity in the ranges of 0 to s_1 and s_2 to s_3 means that the duration of maximum utilization is a very nonlinear function of the amount of capacity. It is this fact that makes the value and proper sizing of inter regional transmission much more difficult to estimate than the corresponding quantities for generating units.

The symbols have the following meaning:

For nuclear generating capacity,

x_i = capacity in region i

c_1 = capital cost per unit of capacity

γ_N = variable operating cost per unit of energy produced.

For coal-fired generating capacity,

c_2 = capital cost per unit of capacity

γ_C = fuel production cost per unit of energy produced

t = fuel transportation cost per unit of energy produced in region one.

For transmission capacity,

T = capacity of the inter-regional transmission link

c_t = capital cost per unit of capacity

For the load,

P_i = the required thermal capacity in region i

$P_i(s)$ = the thermal load duration curve in region i.

The variable s represents a fraction of a year. We note from Figure 5 that we can define

$$s_1 \text{ by } P_1(s_1) = x_1 + T, \tag{2}$$

$$s_2 \text{ by } P_1(s_2) = x_1 - T \tag{3}$$

$$\text{and } s_3 \text{ by } P_2(s_3) = x_2 + T. \tag{4}$$

5.2. Analytic Results

Taking the partial derivatives of equation (1) with respect to x_1, x_2 and T we get the following expressions:

$$(\partial TC/ \partial x_1) = \Delta c - ts_1 - \Delta\gamma s_2 \tag{5}$$

$$(\partial TC/ \partial x_2) = \Delta c - \Delta\gamma s_3 \tag{6}$$

$$(\partial TC/ \partial T) = c_t - ts_1 + \Delta\gamma s_2 - \Delta\gamma s_3 \tag{7}$$

where

(Δc) equals $(c_1 - c_2)$

and

$(\Delta\gamma)$ equals $(\gamma_C - \gamma_N)$.

Since $TC(x_1,x_2,T)$ is convex (Rogers and Choudhury [25]), a sufficient condition for the global optimum is that the three partial derivatives be zero (Luenberger [17]). Then equation (5) can be interpreted as requiring that the unit capital cost difference between coal and nuclear units be balanced by the sum of the coal transportation cost over duration s_1 and the fuel cost difference over duration s_2. Similarly, equation (6) requires that the capital cost difference balance the fuel cost difference over duration s_3. In the same fashion, equation (7) requires that the unit capital cost of transmission be balanced by the sum of the coal transportation cost over duration s_1 and the fuel cost difference over duration $(s_3 - s_2)$. Hence from (6) we have $s_3 = \Delta c/\Delta\gamma$, and from (5) and (7) we have $s_1 = c_t/2t$ and $s_2 = (\Delta c/\Delta\gamma) - (c_t/(2\Delta\gamma))$.

6. SINGLE VS MULTI-REGION RESULTS: AN APPLICATION OF COMPLEMENTARY MODELLING

There are several analyses that can be undertaken using this analytic model and the computational model as complementary models. As a sample study to illustrate the usefulness of the concept of complementary models, we show, in this section, how the main causes of the numerical results from the CIREM model reported in Section 4 can be derived from the results of the analytic model of Section 5. The specific issue we focus on is the difference between the amount of nuclear capacity in the system in period six as computed by the multi-region version of CIREM and that computed by the single-region version. We show that the analytic model not only gives a good (perhaps unreasonably so) numerical estimate of this difference but also yields insight into which parameters of the model most influence the value of this difference.

6.1 Analytic

Now, for the two region analytic model of Section 5, by adding equations (3) and (4) the total amount of nuclear capacity in the system is

$$X_{NM} = x_1 + x_2 = P_1(s_2) + P_2(s_3).$$

The alternative case is created by assuming all generation and load is at a single point (i.e. free transmission). We call this the single region model and note that it can be derived from the multi-region case by setting $c_t=0$. Then we have essentially a generation mix like that of region two to supply the total load. Thus in the single region case, $s_1 = 0$ but $s_2 = s_3$ above and s_3 is unchanged. Hence for this case, the total amount of nuclear capacity in the system, called X_{NS}, is found by evaluating the combined load duration curves of both regions at duration s_3. Thus,

$$X_{NS} = P_1(s_3) + P_2(s_3)$$

We now have

$$X_{NM} = X_{NS} + P_1(s_2)-P_1(s_3) \tag{8}$$

where the values of s_2 and s_3 are computed from the two region results.

If $c_t > 0$, we have $s_2 < s_3$ and so $X_{NM} > X_{NS}$. We note that equation (8) shows that $(X_{NM}-X_{NS})$, the difference in nuclear capacity between the multi-region and single region solutions, is dependent upon the shape of the thermal load duration curve only in region one, and the relative size of $c_t/2$ to Δc. The difference is zero if $c_t/2$ is negligibly small but it becomes substantial as $c_t/2$ approaches Δc in magnitude.

A particularly interesting case occurs when the thermal load duration curve is approximately linear in the range $[((\Delta c/\Delta\gamma) - (c_t/2\Delta\gamma)), (\Delta c/\Delta\gamma)]$ (ie: between s_2 and s_3 in the two region model). Then

$$P_1((\Delta c/\Delta\gamma) - (c_t/2\Delta\gamma)) - P_1(\Delta c/\Delta\gamma) \simeq mc_t/2\Delta\gamma$$

where $m=-(dP_1(s)/ds)$.
We then have

$$X_{NM}-X_{NS}=mc_t/2\Delta\gamma. \tag{9}$$

From this we see two types of results:

1. quantitative explanations

   a. The difference between the estimates of nuclear capacity produced by the single and multi-region versions of the CIREM model can be computed from equation (9).

2. qualitative insights

   a. The load duration curve in the region with the less expensive coal has no effect.

   b. The transportation cost of coal has no effect.

   c. The capital costs of generation have no effect if the load duration curve in the region with the high cost coal is approximately linear near its center.

Since much of the structure of the analytic model was taken from the optimal solution to the multi-region CIREM model, these general conclusions are valid in the neighborhood of the optimum CIREM solution and as long as the solution to the analytic model is an interior one.

6.2 Numerical

The matrix generator for the multi-region CIREM model produces a "thermal" load duration curve for region one in period six. In that period the corresponding CIREM solution adds transmission capacity to only half of the region one-to-three link, so for the latter half we use the "value in the system" (i.e., cost-reduced cost) from the CIREM solution. The values of all of the other parameters are taken from the corresponding inputs to the CIREM model in period 6. We note that this is not normally a useful procedure if many of the reduced costs on the corresponding variables are "greatly" different from zero.

We compute $\Delta\gamma$, the difference in fuel cost between nuclear and coal fired plants in region one of the CIREM model, as 17.7($$10^3$/MW Yr). Hence, we have $X_{NM}-X_{NS}$ = ((0.32X5.5)/(2X17.7))230GW = 11.4 GW. The actual CIREM solution was 11GW (see Section 4.2). The value in the system of half the transmission link from region one to two was the only number used that was not available without running the CIREM multi-region case. If we had used the actual capital cost of that link, the estimate of $X_{NM}-X_{NS}$ would be 14.8 GW, still a useful estimate.

7. CONCLUSION

In this paper, we introduced the idea of comlementary modelling with particular emphasis on the close relationship between analytic and computational models in the analysis of energy policies. We found it useful to distinguish between two types of models: auxiliary and complementary. The former has been discussed previously. We illustrated the usefulness of the latter concept in a sample application to the Canadian Inter-Regional Electricity Model. The insights obtained from this procedure are, in our view, well worth the effort required to formulate and solve the analytic model.

REFERENCES

[1] Albouy, Y., G. Joly, M. Launay, P. Martin, R. Cristerna, E. Salinas, F. Sosapavon, C. Urdaibay. "An Integrated Planning Method for Power Systems--Parts 1,2 & 3", Power Industry Computer Applications Conference, 1975.

[2] Anderson, D. "Models for Determining Least Cost Investments in Electricity Supply," Bell Journal of Economics and Management Science, Spr. 1972, 3 (1), pp. 267-299.

[3] Beglari, F. and M.A. Laughton. "The Combined Cost Method for Optimal Economic Planning of an Electric Power System", IEEE Transactions on Power Apparatus and Systems, Nov. -Dec. 1975. 94(6), pp. 1,935-1,942.

[4] Benders, J.F. "Partitioning Procedures for Solving Mixed Variables Programming Problems", Numerische Mathematik, 1962, 4, pp. 238-252.

[5] Bloom, J.A. Decomposition and Probabilistic Simulation in Electric Utility Planning Models, PhD thesis, Operations Research Center, Massachusetts Institute of Technology, 1978.

[6] Booth, R.R. "Optimal Generation Planning Considering Uncertainty", IEEE Transactions on Power Apparatus and Systems, Jan. -Feb. 1972. pas-91, pp. 70-77.

[7] Choudhury, S.K. "A Regional Model for Planning the Expansion of the Electric Generation and Long Distance Transmission System in Canada (1980-2010): A Linear Programming Approach", Master's thesis, Dept. of Industrial Engineering, Univ. of Toronto, 1977.

[8] Cote, G. and M.A. Laughton, "Decomposition Techniques in Power System Planning: The Benders' Partitioning Method", Electric Power and Energy Systems, 1979, 1(1), pp. 57-64.

[9] Geoffrion, A.M. "The Purpose of Mathematical Programming is Insight, Not Numbers", Interfaces, 1976, 7(1), pp. 81-92.

[10] Goreux, L.M. and A.S. Manne, Editors. Multi-Level Planning: Case Studies in Mexico. Amsterdam: North-Holland 1973.

[11] Hamming, R.W. Numerical Methods for Scientists and Engineers. New York: McGraw-Hill 1962.

[12] Hogan, W.W. and A.S. Manne, "Energy-Economy Interactions: The Fable of the Elephant and the Rabbit", In Advances in the Economics of Energy and Resources,: JAI Press Inc., 1979.

[13] Ignall, E.J., P. Kolesar and W.E. Walker. "Using Simulation to Develop and Validate Analytic Models: Some Case Studies", Operations Research, 1978, 26(2), pp. 237-253.

[14] Janischewskyj, W. and J.S. Rogers. Economic Design and Governing Criteria-Well-Head Generation and Long Distance Transmission, pages 1-16 of paper 1.1/5. Fifth Power Systems Computation Conference, Cambridge U.K., 1975.

[15] Knight, U.G. Power System Engineering and Mathematics. Oxford: Pergamon Press 1972.

[16] Levin, N., A. Tishler and J. Zahavi. "Time Step vs Dynamic Optimization of Generation Capacity Expansion Programs of Power Systems", 1982, forthcoming in Operations Research.

[17] Luenberger, D.G. Introduction to Linear and Nonlinear Programming. Reading, Mass.: Addison-Wesley 1973.

[18] Manne, A.S. Investments for Capacity Expansion: Size, Location and Time-Phasing. Cambridge, Mass.: MIT Press 1967.

[19] Noonan, F. Optimal Investment Planning for Electric Power Generation. PhD thesis, Dept. of Industrial Engineering and Operations Research, Univ. of Massachusetts, 1973.

[20] Phillips, D., F. Jenkin, J.A.T. Pritchard and K. Rybicki. A Mathematical Model for Determining Generating Plant Mix. Third Power Systems Computation Conference, Rome, Italy, 1969.

[21] Richels, R. "Building Good Models is Not Enough", Interfaces, 1981, 11(4), pp. 48-54.

[22] Rogers, J.S. A Dynamic Model for Planning Capacity Expansion: An Application to Plant Reliability in Electric Power Systems. PhD thesis, Dept. of Operations Research, Stanford University, 1970.

[23] Rogers, J.S. "An Approach to Modelling Energy Systems," Presented to Symposium on Canada's Energy Resource Development sponsored by Deans of Engineering, Toronto, June 1975.

[24] Rogers, J.S. and S.K. Choudhury. Planning Inter-regional Electric Energy Supply in Canada (1980-2010): A Linear Programming Approach, pages 22-29 vol. 1. Sixth Power Systems Computation Conference, Darmstadt, West Germany, 1978.

[25] Rogers, J.S. and S.K. Choudhury. "An Analytic Model for Determining the Long Term Amount of Nuclear Generating Capacity in Canada: An Explanation of the Multi Region and Single Region Model Results," Working Paper #81-004, Dept. of Industrial Engineering, Univ. of Toronto, Feb. 1981.

[26] Saraf, S., F.H. Murphy and A.L. Soyster. "On the Effect of Fuel Prices in Electric Utility Capacity Expansion Planning," 1983.

[27] Schweppe, F.C., D. H. Marks, D.L. Farrar, J. Gruhl, M.F. Ruane. P.F. Shiers, and F. Woodruff. Economic Environmental System Planning. IEEE Power Engineering Society Summer Meeting, 1974.

[28] Woolf, H.B. et al. Webster's New Collegiate Dictionary. Toronto: Thomas Allen and Son Ltd. 1981.

Analytic Techniques for Energy Planning
B. Lev, F.H. Murphy, J.A. Bloom & A.S. Gleit (Editors)

AN ANALYTIC STUDY OF CRITICAL TERMINAL CONDITIONS IN LONG RANGE GENERATION EXPANSION PLANNING FOR ELECTRIC UTILITIES*

Jane Chumley Ammons

School of Industrial and Systems Engineering
Georgia Institute of Technology
Atlanta, Georgia 30332

Long range planning of generation capacity is a complex and expensive task for electric utilities. Planning decisions are based on results from intricate models which incorporate key aspects of the generating environment, including uncertainties describing the final portion of the planning horizon. The critical nature of some of these terminal conditions have been examined analytically using the computer implementation of a nonlinear mixed integer programming generation expansion model.

1. INTRODUCTION

Generation expansion planning (GEP) for electric utilities is a large scale and complex problem composed of many complicated and interacting issues. In overview, GEP can be stated as the selection of types and sizes of electric generating units to construct over a specified long range planning horizon while respecting limitations imposed by construction budgets, demand requirements, and reliability guarantees in order to minimize total discounted system cost. Models developed for the planning of investments in electric generating capacity are reviewed in the survey articles by Anderson [2], Sassoon and Merrill [39], and Knight, et. al. [24].

Modeling approaches include linear programming (Anderson, [2], Masse' and Gibrat [27], and Bessiere and Masse' [5]), mixed integer programming (Ammons [1], Iwayemi [18], Noonan and Giglio [30], Rowse [37], and Sawey and Zinn [40]), nonlinear programming (Philips, et. al. [36], Bloom [7], Jenkins [19], Bessiere [4], and Paramantier [33]), heuristics incorporating simulation (Booth [8], Lansdowne, et. al. [25], Marsh, et. al. [26], and Jenkins and Joy [20]), dynamic

*This research was supported in part by National Science Foundation Grant No. ECS-8206612 and in part by the New Faculty Research Development Program of the Georgia Institute of Technology. Reproduction in whole or in part is permitted for any purpose of the U.S. Government.

programming (Garver [14], Henault, et. al. [16], Irisari [17], Morin and Jenkins [28], Oatman and Hamant [31], Peschon and Jamoulle [34], and Peterson [35]), and combinations of these (Beglari and Laughton [3], and Farrar and Woodruff [11]). Solutions of GEP problems are expensive: development of a viable model may cost up to 1.5 million dollars, and one subsequent extensive study may cost upwards of $300,000.

The specification of a forecasted scenario is required for each GEP study, with resulting impact on the model's solution. The scenario is prescribed by data requirements which include (1) fixed and operating costs characteristics for existing and proposed generation units; (2) time windows for commissioning, construction time and cost schedule for proposed units; (3) financial considerations including capital expansion budget, inflation rates, long and short term rates of return; (4) reliability characteristics of current and proposed units and corresponding system reliability requirements for each time period; and finally, (5) electricity demand forecasts including expected peak load per time period in the planning horizon.

Because the planning horizon may be of twenty to thirty years length, many of the forecasted quantities have uncertainty associated with them which greatly increases over the more distant future periods. Furthermore, different optimal solutions to GEP may be obtained for studies which differ only in the length of the planning horizon. In order to obtain the desired validity for solution results associated with the near future, studies of adequate length with appropriate terminal conditions must be run. However, the length of a study is a crucial determinant of its cost: as years are added to the planning horizon, data costs escalate linearly and computational requirements exponentially. Thus, terminal conditions have a critical impact on both the solution outcome and cost of GEP.

This paper presents the preliminary results for the analysis of terminal conditions in GEP. The next section develops inherent assumptions in GEP, followed by a discussion of uncertainty and complexity issues. Finally, their impact on "optimal" expansion schedules is presented.

2. INHERENT ASSUMPTIONS IN LONG RANGE GEP

In both the modeling and data construction phases of long range GEP, explicit as well as hidden assumptions are required. Typically assumptions are generated for such reasons as model feasibility, computational tractibility, convenience in data assimilation, etc. However, inherent in the GEP planning process are certain assumptions which are not necessarily explicit nor apparent. These assumptions are related to trends which continue past the end of the planning horizon: trends in such areas as costs, demands, technologies, and the potential environment.

2.1 Trends In Costs And Financial Factors

Implicit in the modeling of long range GEP are critical assumptions concerning trends in costs and financial factors. As for costs, assumptions are required as to the behavior over time of the fixed costs associated with generating units. Also, the magnitude and functional characteristics of the unit operating costs must be specified for the planning horizon. Trends and relationships in both fixed and variable costs then implicitly extend past the end of the planning horizon.

Similarly, certain critical assumptions are required concerning the behavior of key GEP financial factors. Included in this category are trends in annual inflation rates, short and long term rates of return, magnitude of capital expansion budget and cash flow considerations, and construction costs and schedules. Again, trends in these assumptions extend past the given planning horizon.

Studies have tried to assess the impact of these assumptions on the outcome of GEP solutions. Galloway, et. al. [13] investigated the resulting plant mix structure when the cost of fossil and peaking steam plants were varied while the nuclear and gas turbine costs were held fixed. Similarly, Felak, et. al. [12] varied unit characteristics (fixed and operating costs) in a simulation study to assess resulting financial impact. Garver [14] shows the relationship of GEP plant mix added over a 20 year horizon as a function of the inflation rate. Effect of the discount rate upon expansion schedules has been studied by Rowse [38]. These studies demonstrate the critical nature of cost and financial assumptions in GEP.

2.2 Trends In Demand

Similar to the inherent assumptions associated with trends in costs and financial factors are those related to demand for electricity. Implicit in GEP models are trends in peak load growth, load duration curve shape, load management, etc. -- trends which are assumed to extend past the end of the planning horizon. These trends are critical assumptions because demand is the driver of GEP problems, forcing expansions to be incurred.

2.3 Trends In Technology

Related to the trends in costs, financial factors, and demand are trends in the technical environment of electric power generation. These issues include such items as future hydro availability, the licensing/operating/political environment for nuclear production, emergence of "new" sources such as solar, wind, tidal, etc., development of transmission modes with higher efficiencies, and coal/gas availabilities in the future. By inclusion or omission in the modeling or data determination steps of GEP, trends in technologies are inherent assumptions. Impact studies on just the reliability sector of GEP have been performed for solar (Jordan, et. al. [22]) and nuclear (Panichelli, et. al. [32]) technologies, for load management (Billinton and Alam [6]), and for load shape dynamics (Jordan, et al. [21]).

2.4 Length Of Planning Horizon

In addition to inherent assumptions associated with trends in costs and financial factors, demand, and technologies, the selection of a planning horizon for GEP imposes other assumptions. Smaller planning horizons discriminate against units with large expansion costs because the benefits of their reduced operating costs may not be completely recovered within the planning horizon. A common assumption to overcome this problem uses the unit "extended costs" technique which assigns costs to each unit as though identical unit replications occur into an infinite extension period by assuming system status at the last year of the planning horizon will prevail forever (see Bloom [7]). Often this assumption is required to assure computational tractability of the GEP model; however, the assumption has inevitable consequences upon unit selection, assumed trends, etc. Desired is the determination of "near planning horizons" as proposed for other simple planning problems (e.g., see Shapiro and Wagner [43]).

2.5 Uncertainty and Complexity Issues

Interacting with the aforementioned trends and assumptions associated with planning horizon length are issues imposed by uncertainty and complexity with GEP. Planning for the future induces uncertainty into GEP; this uncertainty combined with intricate relationships between various aspects of GEP enforces it. Certainly one of the most challenging and possibly the most studied issues in GEP is the dynamic nature of the electricity generating environment. For a planning horizon of twenty to thirty years, who can predict with any certainty the correct scenario for the last portion of the planning horizon? Certain studies have focused on uncertainty in demand (Mount and Chapman [29], Borison, et. al. [10]), which is a critical segment because demand growth forces expansion in GEP. However, also important is the uncertainty associated with every other factor (cost, capacity, reliability, etc.) pertinent to GEP. And the interaction of the uncertainty associated with these factors is critical.

2.6 Factor Interrelationships

Currently there is a shift in GEP approaches to recognize "the phenomena of interest today are the complex interactions" of various aspects of the planning problem (p. 7, Taylor [42], p. 89, Graves [15]). For example, an upward shift in the inflation rate will have a definite impact on the outcome of the solution to GEP because of its interrelationship with other factors. Typically inflation rates in GEP are applied in a discounting fashion with an upward shift in inflation rate. The capital expansion budget should inflate accordingly - but not necessarily uniformly as is commonly modeled. Similarly, construction costs, fixed costs, and production costs should increase; but, in reality, all units may not inflate identically. An upward shift in inflation has uncertain responses in the corresponding behavior of short and long term rates of return, peak load demand, load duration curve shape, trends in peak management, etc. Therefore, because of the interaction of various aspects of GEP, parametric changes in one factor induce nonobvious yet critical changes in others. This significant interaction is magnified when the effects of inherent uncertainty are considered.

3. ANALYSIS

Assessing the impact of terminal conditions in long range GEP for electric utilities involves recognition of the inherent assumptions and factors mentioned above in both the modeling and computational planning stages. The modeling step requires capturing explicitly the factor(s) of interest - as in the modeling of demand uncertainty by Borison, et al. [9]. However, realistically modeling all critical factors and their intricate interactions is such a challenge that traditionally empirical studies employing parametric variation have been substituted. Also, modeling effort in this area is dependent upon the GEP approach employed.

Some preliminary studies have been performed using data representative of a large Southeastern utility. The implementation is based upon the GEP mixed integer programming approach developed previously by the author (see Ammons [1]). As a brief overview, the model is given as follows:

$$\text{(P)} \quad \text{Minimize} \quad \sum_j f_j y_j + \sum_{ti} \Big[\sum_j (V_{1jt} x^2_{jit} + V_{2jt} x_{jit} + V_{3jt}) h_{it} \Big] \tag{1}$$

$$\text{subject to} \quad \sum_j x_{jit} \geq P_{it} \quad \text{for every } i,t \tag{2}$$

$$L_{jt} y_j \leq x_{jit} \leq U_{jt} y_j \quad \text{for every } i,j,t \tag{3}$$

$$\sum_j a_{jt} U_{jt} y_j \geq (1+m) P_t \qquad \text{for every } t \qquad (4)$$

$$S_t - (1+r_t)\, S_{t-1} + \sum_j c_{jt} y_j = B_t \qquad \text{for every } t \qquad (5)$$

$$LOLP_t\,(\{y\}) \leq LOLP_{t\text{-}max} \qquad \text{for every } t \qquad (6)$$

$$\sum_{\{Jk\}} y_j = 1 \qquad \text{for every } k \qquad (7)$$

$$y_j \in \{0,1\} \qquad \text{for every } j \qquad (8)$$

$$S_t \geq 0 \qquad \text{for every } t \qquad (9)$$

where

y_j = zero-one valued integer variable indicating whether unit j is to be constructed

x_{jit} = operation level of unit j in interval i of period t

f_j = sum of discounted fixed costs (taxes, maintenance, etc.) associated with unit j over the planning horizon

$V_{.jt}$ = discounted coefficients of quadratic production cost function for unit j in period t

h_{it} = number of hours in interval i of period t

P_{it} = power demand level in interval i of period t

L_{jt} = lower bound on production level on unit j in period t

U_{jt} = upper bound on production level on unit j in period t

a_{jt} = availability factor for unit j in period t, $0 \leq a_{jt} \leq 1$

m = portion of capacity reserve margin required when peak demand occurs

P_t = peak demand during period t

S_t = construction budget funds unused in period t, $S_0 = 0$

r_t = short term rate of return for period t

c_{jt} = construction funds required for unit j in period t

B_t = additional construction budget funds available in period t

$LOLP_t(\{y\})$ = the loss of load probability of system $\{y\}$ during period t

$LOLP_{t\text{-}max}$ = the maximum allowable loss of load probability during period t

$\{Jk\}$ = set of indices belonging to mutually exclusive projects, e.g., generalized upper bounds, system structural constraints.

(P) is a mixed integer nonlinear programming problem with a quadratic objective function and linear and nonlinear constraints. In the objective function (1), to be minimized is the discounted sum of fixed and operating costs associated with the expansion projects that are constructed. Operating costs are quadratic as experienced in industry (see Kirchmayer [23]). Constraint (2) assures demand satisfaction for every interval of the load duration curve. The load duration curve is a familiar representation for system demand during a time period, where demand level is shown as a function of amount of time the load is incurred during the period, a set of (h_{it}, P_{it}) points. For more detail, see Anderson [2]. Constraint (3) insures that unit operation meets capacity bounds. Reserve margin, or the assurance that enough capacity exists on the system to exceed peak demand when it occurs, is expressed in constraint (4). Construction budget limitations are explicit in (5). Constraint (6) represents the requirement that the system reliability, as measured by the loss of load probability, is guaranteed through the expansion schedule. Finally, constraint (7) prohibits a prospective unit from being initiated in more than one year.

Using a Benders' Decomposition approach, the model was implemented on a CDC 70/74-6400 as reported in Ammons [1]. A base problem was constructed of 123 existing generating units and 25 potential expansion projects with 10 generalized upper bounds. Studies were performed over a planning horizon of 20 years. The base problem used twenty points to approximate the load duration curve points of (h_{it}, P_{it}). Criteria of 0.10 was used each year for loss of load probability, (0.05) * (peak load) for expected deficit, and 0.25 for reserve margin. For the base problem, the inflation rate for every time period was set at 0.10, with short term rate of return on surplus construction funds being 0.09 for each time period. The long term rate of return used to discount all costs to the present was set at 0.12. For all test problems the size of the base problem, the core requirements were approximately 82k decimal words.

Because demand is the forcing function in GEP, issues regarding its representation, associated uncertainty, etc. must be acknowledged. Aggregation of demand representation is a significant issue, especially when one considers the tradeoff between computational requirements and accuracy of forecasts at the end of the planning horizon. Sawey and Zoraster [41] have reported the impact of demand aggregation on unit mix solution. For this base problem, it was expected that as the number of points decreased, the total costs would be overestimated but that solution time would decrease. As Table 1 shows, the first anticipation was confirmed but the second was not. Upon examination of the results, the increase in solution time as the number of points decreased might be explained by convergence properties of the procedure.

However, no change in optimal expansion schedule was obtained when the short rate of return in the base problem was varied from 0.00 to 0.09. Similar results were obtained for parametric variation of the discount rate. For levels of inflation higher than 10%, no feasible solution could be found to the original problem.

As anticipated, varying the length of the planning horizon yielded different optimal solutions. Table 2 shows the effect of varying the number of years in the planning cycle on execution time and solution value. As may be seen in Figure 1, the same construction schedule was obtained for planning horizon lengths of 9 and 10 years, while different schedules were obtained for runs of 14 and 20 years, respectively. Choice of additions seemed to follow logical tradeoffs between fixed and variable costs while respecting construction budgets.

4. SUMMARY

GEP is an expensive and complex task for electric utilities. Planning decisions are based on results from intricate analytical models which attempt to capture key components of the generating environment. Included in these models are the inherent assumptions and crucial interrelationships described above, which impact critically on the "optimal" expansion schedule. Some of these factors may be explicitly included in the GEP model, but a more common approach is to perform parametric sensitivity analysis at a computational price. For illustration, preliminary empirical results were presented for some simple one- factor variation studies.

ACKNOWLEDGEMENTS

Dr. Leon F. McGinnis participated in initial discussions of the subject. Chris Berry performed some of the computational runs.

REFERENCES

[1] Ammons, J.A. "A Generation Expansion Planning Model for Electric Utilities," Ph.D. Dissertation, Georgia Institute of Technology, 1982.

[2] Anderson, D. "Models for Determining Least-cost Investments in Electricity Supply," Bell Journal of Economics and Management Science, 3, pp. 267-285, 1972.

[3] Beglari, F. and M. A. Laughton. "The Combined Costs Method for Optimal Economic Planning of an Electrical Power System," IEEE Transactions of Power Apparatus and Systems, 94-6, pp. 1935-1942, 1975.

[4] Bessiere, F. "The 'Investment 85' Model of Electricite in France," Management Science, 17-4, pp. 192-211, 1970.

[5] Bessiere, F. and P. Masse'. "Long Term Programming of Electrical Investments," in J. R. Nelson, Marginal Cost Pricing in Practice, Englewood Cliffs, N.J., Prentice-Hall, Inc., pp. 235-252, 1964.

[6] Billinton, R., and M. Alam. "Outage Postponability Effects in Operating Capacity Reliability Studies," presented at the IEEE PES Winter Meeting, New York, NY, 1978.

[7] Bloom, J. A. "Decomposition and Probabilistic Simulation in Electric Utility Planning Models, " Ph.D. Thesis, Department of Mathematics, Massachusetts Institute of Technology, 1978.

[8] Booth, R. R. "Optimum Generation Planning Considering Uncertainty," IEEE Transactions on Power Apparatus and Systems, PAS-91, pp. 70-77, 1971.

[9] Borison, A. B., P. A. Morris, and S. S. Oren. "A State-of-the-World Decomposition Approach to Dynamics and Uncertainty in Electric Utility Generation Expansion Planning," submitted to Operations Research, 1982.

[10] Borison, A. B., P. A. Morris, S. S. Oren, and M. N. Thapa. "Optimal Electric Utility Capacity Expansion Under Demand Uncertainty," presented at the Joint National ORSA/TIMS Meeting, Chicago, IL, April, 1983, 1983.

[11] Farrar, D. L. and F. Woodruff, Jr. "A Model for the Determination of Optimal Electrical Generating System Expansion Patterns," MIT Energy Lab Report, PB-223-995, 1973.

[12] Felak, R. P., W. D. Marsh, R. W. Moisan, and R. M. Sigley. "Adding Financial Simulation to Long Range Generation Planning," presented at the American Power Conference, Chicago, IL, April 1977.

[13] Galloway, C. D., W. D. Marsh, and K. F. Miller. "An Investigation of Long Range Trends in Systems Generation Composition," presented at the Joint ASME-IEEE Power Generation Conference, Charlotte, NC, September, 1969.

[14] Garver, L. L. "Electric Utility Planning Models," ORSA/TIMS Joint National Meeting, Chicago, 1975.

[15] Graves, J. S. "Developing Generation Construction Plans for the Potomac Electric Power Company: Management Science in Utility Regulation," Interfaces, 12, pp. 83-104, 1982.

[16] Henault, P. H., R. B. Eastveldt, J. Peschon, and L. P. Hajdu. "Power System Long-term Planning in the Presence of Uncertainty," 6th Power Industry Computer Application Conference Proceedings, pp. 635-645, 1969.

[17] Irisari, G. "Power System Expansion Planning," Ph.D. Dissertation, Purdue University, 1975.

[18] Iwayemi, A. "Investment Resource Allocation in the Electric Power Supply Industry in Nigeria," Ph.D. Dissertation, The Johns Hopkins University, 1975.

[19] Jenkin, F. P. "Power System Planning in England and Wales," presented at the IEEE PES Winter Meeting, Jan. 29-Feb. 3, 1978.

[20] Jenkins, R. T. and D. S. Joy. "Wien Automatic System Planning Package (WASP) - An Electric Utility Optimal Generation Expansion Planning Code," ORNL-4945, Oak Ridge National Laboratory, Oak Ridge, TN., 1974.

[21] Jordan, G. A., W. D. Marsh, R. W. Moisan, and J. L. Oplinger. "The Impact of Load Factor on Economic Generation Patterns," presented at the 1976 American Power Conference, Chicago, IL, 1976.

[22] Jordan, G. A., R. W. Moisan, and G. P. O'Brien. "Impact of Solar Energy on Electric Utility Generation System Reliability and Operations," presented at the American Power Conference, Chicago, IL, April, 1977.

[23] Kirchmayer, L. K. Economic Operation of Power Systems, Wiley, New York, 1958.

[24] Knight, U. G., R. R. Booth, S. A. Mallard, and D. M. Lewis. "Computers in Power Systems Planning," Proceeding of the IEEE, 62-7, pp. 872-883, 1974.

[25] Lansdowne, Z. F., C. L. Rudasill, and O. S. Yu. "Power System Expansion Model for Energy R&D Planning," presented at the Spring TIMS/ORSA Joint National Meeting, San Francisco, 1977.

[26] Marsh, W. D., R. W. Moisan, and H. G. Stoll. "Solving Today's Capital and Fuel Supply Problems in the Selection of New Generation," 1975 American Power Conference, Chicago, 1975.

[27] Masse, P. and R. Gibrat. "Application of Linear Programming to Investments in the Electric Power Industry," Management Science, 3, pp. 149-166, 1975.

[28] Morin, T. L. and R. T. Jenkins. "OPTIMIZER: An Enhanced Dynamic Program for Generation Planning," Proceedings of the Conference on Electric System Expansion Analysis, March, 1981.

[29] Mount, T. C. and L. D. Chapman. "Capacity Planning for Electric Utilities," in Aronofsky, J. S., A. G. Rao, and M. E. Shakun, eds., Energy Policy, TIMS Studies in the Management Sciences, 10, North-Holland Publishing Company, 1978.

[30] Noonan, F. and R. J. Giglio. "Planning Electric Power Generation: A Nonlinear Mixed Integer Model Employing Benders Decomposition," Management Science, 23, pp. 946-956, 1977.

[31] Oatman, E. N. and L. J. Hamant. A Dynamic Approach to Generation Expansion Planning," IEEE Transactions on Power Apparatus and Systems, PAS-92, pp. 1888-1897, 1973.

[32] Panichelli, S., L. Salvaderi, and M. Valtorta. "Impact of Bulk Nuclear Capacity on Generating System Reliability," presented at the IEEE PES Winter Meeting, New York, NY, February, 1979.

[33] Paramantier, J. "Optimal Heat and Power System Planning," presented at the Spring TIMS/ORSA Joint National Meeting, New Orleans, LA, 1979.

[34] Peschon, J. and E. Jamoulle. "An Integrated Set of Power System Planning Models," presented at the Spring Joint National ORSA/Tims Meeting, Chicago, IL, 1975.

[35] Petersen, E. R. "A Dynamic Programming Model for the Expansion of Electric Power Systems," Management Science, 20-4, pp. 656-664, 1973.

[36] Philips, D., F. P. Jenkins, J. A. Pritchard, and K. Rykicki. " A Mathematical Model for Determining Generating Plant Mix," presented at the Third PSCC, Rome, Italy, 1969.

[37] Rowse, J. "Toward Optimal Capacity Expansion for an Electric Utility: A Mixed Integer Programming Approach to Generation Planning," Ph.D. Dissertation, University of Minnesota, 1974.

[38] Rowse, J. "Optimal Power Supply Expansion and the Discount Rate: Evidence for Saskatehewan Power," submitted to Engineering Economist, 1979.

[39] Sassoon, A. and H. D. Merrill. "Some Applications of Optimization Techniques to Power Systems Problems," Proceedings of the IEEE, 62, pp. 959-972, 1974.

[40] Sawey, R. M. and C. D. Zinn. "Mathematical Model for Long Range Expansion Planning of Generation and Transmission in Electric Utility Systems," IEEE Transactions on Power Apparatus and Systems, PAS-96, pp. 657-665, 1977.

[41] Sawey, R. M. and S. Zoraster. "Sensitivity of Electric Utility Capacity Expansion Models to Approximations for the Load Duration Curve," presented at the Third International Conference on Mathematical Modelling," University of Southern California, Los Angeles, CA. July 29-31, 1981.

[42] Taylor, L. L. "Adapting Planning Models to The Changing Nature of Utility Planning," presented at the Fall ORSA/TIMS Joint National Meeting, San Diego, CA, 1982.

[43] Shapiro, J. F. and H. M. Wagner. "A Finite Renewal Algorithm for the Knapsack and Turnpike Models," Operations Research, 15, pp. 318-341, 1967.

Table 1. Effect of Varying the Number of Points Used to Represent the Load Duration Curve

NUMBER OF POINTS	5	10	BASE PROBLEM 20
Total executive time (cpu secs)	89.744	84.041	79.159
Optimal solution value(V_i) 10^6	48.76	48.06	47.75
$(V_i - V_{20})/V_{20}$ * 100%	2.1%	0.6%	0.0%
Number of iterations run	3	3	3
Execution time requirements (cpu secs)			
Problem initialization	2.540	2.648	2.599
Initial feasible solution	37.638	38.369	35.460
Master problem solution	50.156	43.132	40.783
Subproblem solution	1.579	2.075	2.342

Table 2. Effect of Varying the Number of Years in the Planning Horizon

NUMBER OF YEARS	9	10	14	BASE PROBLEM 20
Total execution time (cpu secs)	76.63	94.207	108.18	87.77
Optimal solution value (V_i)	$.223x(10)^8$	$.246x(10)^8$	$.341x(10)^8$	$.477x(10)^8$
Number of iterations run	1	1	3	3
Execution time requirements (cpu secs)				
Problem initialization	2.40	2.24	2.56	2.42
Initial feasible solution	6.13	8.13	17.64	39.79
Master problem solution	69.0	82.76	81.51	42.39
Subproblem solution	0.28	0.32	1.52	2.63

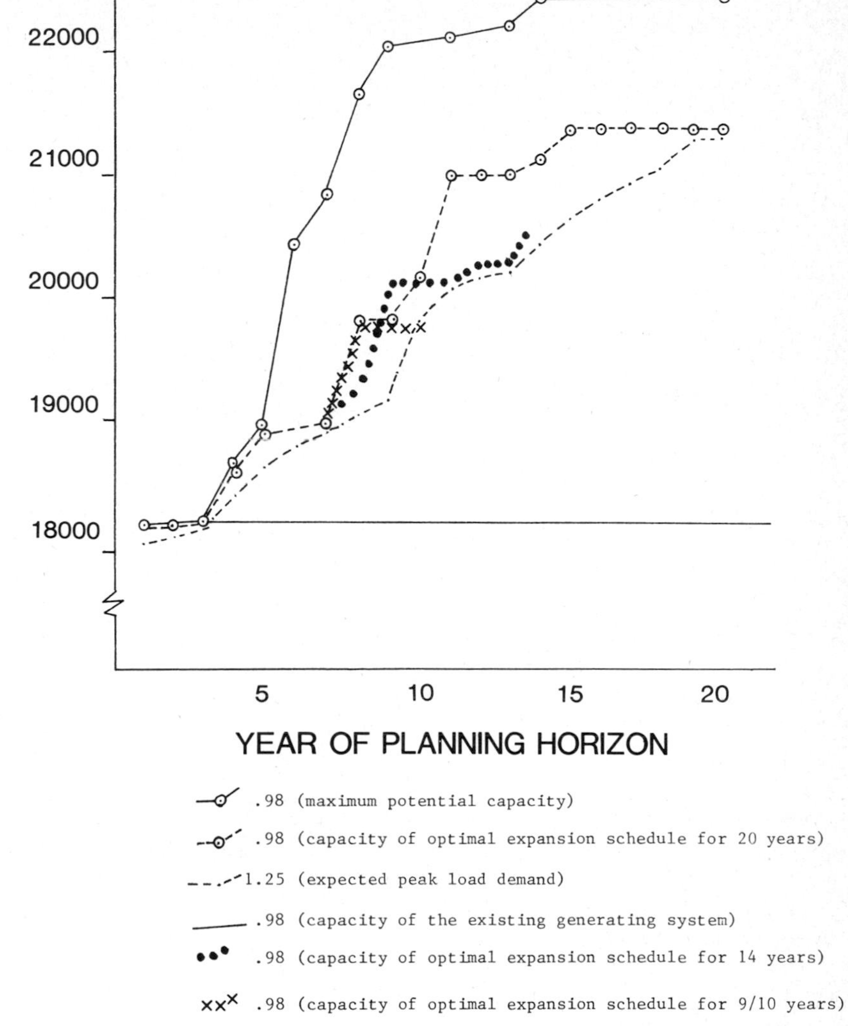

Figure 1. Capacity of Optimal Expansion Schedule for Alternate Planning Horizon Lengths

Analytic Techniques for Energy Planning
B. Lev, F.H. Murphy, J.A. Bloom & A.S. Gleit (Editors)

ASSESSMENT OF ELECTRIC POWER CONSERVATION AND SUPPLY RESOURCES IN THE PACIFIC NORTHWEST: AN OVERVIEW

J.C. King

Battelle, Pacific Northwest Laboratories
Richland, Washington 99352

The Pacific Northwest Electric Power Planning and Conservation Act of 1980 mandated the preparation of a Regional Plan to meet the power needs of the region for the next twenty years. This paper explores the selection of the conservation and generation resources incorporated into the Plan. The initial selection of resources was facilitated by development of resource supply functions, each depicting the cost of a given resource vs. its availability at a specific point in time. Given anticipated electrical demand, it was possible to identify preferred conservation and generation resources.

1. INTRODUCTION

The Pacific Northwest, comprising the states of Washington, Oregon, Idaho, and the portion of Montana west of the continental divide, is served by eight investor-owned electric utility companies and over 100 public-owned electric utilities. The investor-owned utilities typically own and operate generating plants, transmission, and distribution systems, similar to private utilities elsewhere in the United States. In contrast, most of the public utilities provide distribution and retail sales services only. These utilities purchase wholesale electric power from the Bonneville Power Administration.

The Bonneville Power Administration (BPA), a federal agency, was chartered to transmit and market electric power from federally-owned and operated hydroelectric projects (The Federal Columbia River Power System). BPA today markets electricity from thirty federally-owned and operated hydroelectric projects and two nuclear generating plants to public and private utility customers throughout the Pacific Northwest and adjacent areas. Surplus electricity is also marketed to the Southwest. Generating projects from which BPA markets power total approximately 22,100 MW of installed capacity and provide approximately 11,300 average MW[1] of annual energy. These resources represent over 60% of the installed electric generating capacity available to the region and over 65% of the electric energy available to the region.

Unlike the Tennessee Valley Authority, the Bonneville Power Administration was not empowered to develop or operate generating resources. BPA could merely transmit and market power generated by other federal agencies and "wheel" power generated and used by others over its transmission system. The Pacific Northwest thus had no integrated mechanism for electric power planning and development since the agency on which the majority of utilities within the region relied for their electric power supply was unable to develop generating facilities to meet new demands.[2] The problem became acute in the mid-to late 1960's when rapid load growth made it evident that the existing federal hydroelectric system upon which BPA relied for its electric power supply would be insufficient to meet future demands of BPA customers.

For years the region's private utilities, through development of their own hydro projects and through purchases from BPA, as well as the region's public utilities, through their purchases from BPA, had relied upon inexpensive electric power generated by the abundant hydroelectric resources of the region. Nearly all economically and environmentally acceptable hydroelectric sites had been developed by the mid-1960s and it became evident that alternative sources of electric energy would be required to meet forecasted load growth. The region consequently embarked upon an ambitious thermal power plant construction program, including a number of coal and nuclear power plants.

As construction on the thermal plants proceeded, the region learned what most of the nation had grown accustomed to long before - that the cost of power generated by thermal plants was expansive - an order of magnitude more expansive than power generated by hydroelectirc plants. This came as a shock to a region heavily dependent on abundant cheap electric power for uses such as water heating, space heating, and industrial process applications.

The high cost of electricity from thermal sources increased the value of the very low cost power marketed by BPA from the Federal Columbia River Power System. Not all Northwest consumers, however, had equal access to this power. Under the Bonneville Power Act and subsequent legislation, preference rights to Federal power were granted to the public utilities of the region. Private utilities could purchases Federal power only after the needs of the public customers had been satisfied. Because of continuing growth in electrical needs of the public utilities, BPA, in 1973, was forced to deny further contracts for firm power to investor-owned utilities (although these utilities continued to purchase "non-firm" surplus Federal power when available). Private utilities were thus forced to rely to a greater extent than the public customers of BPA upon more expensive thermal power. Forced to pay higher prices for power than customers of neighboring public utilities, customers of private utilities maintained that they were being unfairly denied access to inexpensive Federal power.

The Pacific Northwest Electirc Power Planning and Conservation Act of 1980 (PL 96-501) as designed to alleviate these and other issues. Key provisions of the Act include the following:

- The Act establishes a mechanism for long-term regional power planning
- The Act provides authority for the Bonneville Power Administration to acquire electric power and conservation resources
- The Act establishes a mechanism providing access by residential and agricultural customers of private utilities to low-cost power from the Federal Columbia River Power System.
- The Act requires the development and implementation of a plan for mitigating the impact of the Federal Columbia River Power System on the fish and wildlife resources of the region.

2. THE REGIONAL CONSERVATION AND ELECTRIC POWER PLAN

The Regional Act establishes a Northwest Power Planning Council comprised of eight members, two from each of the four Northwest states, appointed by the governors of the states. The Act mandates the Council to "...prepare, adopt and promptly transmit to the Administrator (of the Bonneville Power Administration) a regional conservation and electric power plan" (Public Law 96-501 Section 4(d)(1)). The plan is to contain the following elements:

- an energy conservation program including model conservation standards

- a forecast of power resources required to meet the obligations of BPA
- a methodology for determining environmental costs and benefits of electric power development
- a demand forecast of at least twenty years
- an analysis of reserve and reliability requirements
- a program to protect, mitigate and enhance fish and wildlife
- a methodology for calculating surcharges as required to encourage implementation of electrical conservation measures.
- recommendations for research and development

The Bonneville Power Administration is empowered by the Act to acquire conservation and generation resources consistent with the plan as required to meet the obligations of BPA.

3. THE PLANNING PROCESS

A five-step process was devised for development of the Regional Plan (Figure 1).

- Resource Assessment: The cost and availability, environmental impacts and constraints to development of existing and potential Pacific Northwest electric power conservation and generating resources were assessed. The products of this work include a set of resource supply functions depicting the cost and availability of new electric power resources and a resource data base containing cost, performance and environmental characteristics of new and existing resources.
- Demand Forecast: A demand forecasting model, consisting of several end-use submodels, was used to forecast Pacific Northwest electric power demand over the next twenty years. The product of this work is a set of four demand forecasts for high, medium-high, medium-low, and low regional growth scenarios. An estimated probability was attached to each. Because electricity demand is sensitive to price, the demand forecasting model includes a submodel to balance loads and resources. Resource cost and performance characteristics are drawn from the resource data base. Iterative runs of the demand model may be performed as the resource schedule is refined through operation of the Strategic Resource Planning Model and the System Analysis Model.
- Resource Selection: Preliminary resource schedules, identifying the type, timing and amount of new resources, were assembled, based upon the supply functions developed in the resource assessment. The Strategic Resource Planning Model, a large-scale linear programming model, was used to identify a preliminary schedule of conservation and generation resource additions that would minimize cost of building and operating the future Northwest electric power system.
- Testing of the Resource Schedule: The preliminary resource schedule was tested using the System Analysis Model. The System Analysis Model simulates the operation or the Northwest Power System. Resource additions are evaluated on the basis of systemwide present value cost to the region. The product was a final schedule of resource types, timing and amounts.

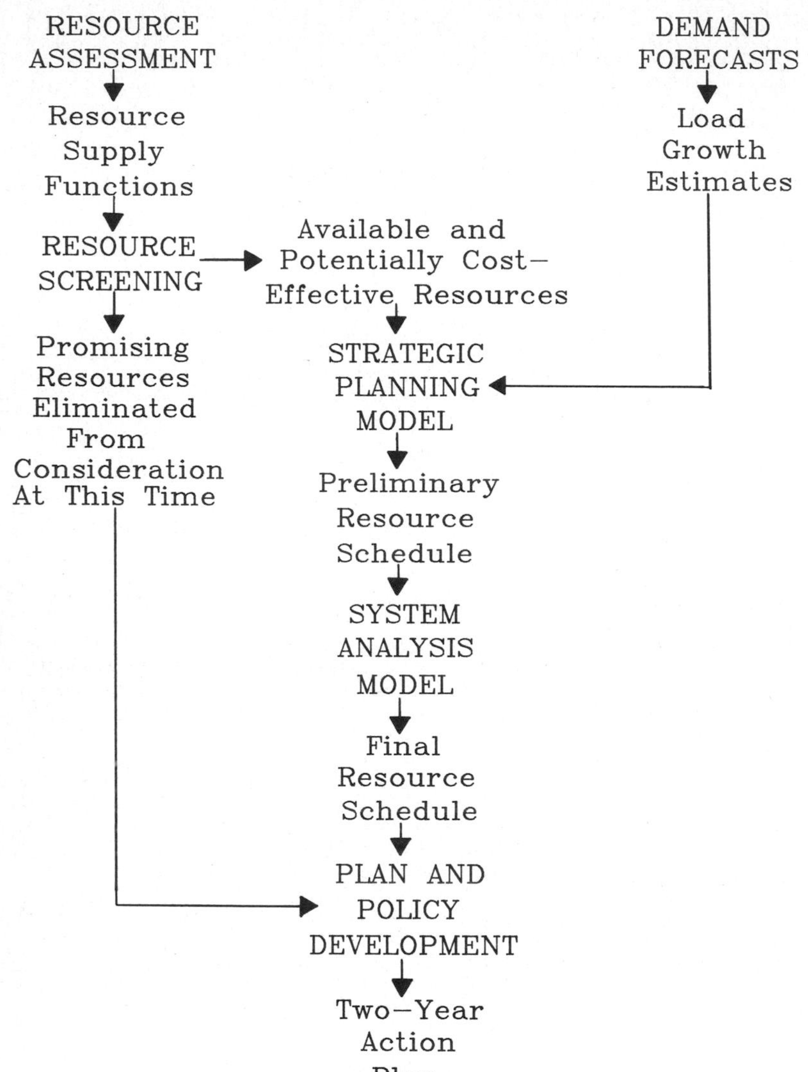

Figure 1. Regional Planning Process

- Plan and Policy Development: The product of the planning effort was a schedule of resource additions identifying the type, timing and amount of resource additions required over the 20-year planning period. The resource schedule is sufficiently flexible to accomodate the range of likely load growth over the period. Based on the resource schedule, a two-year action plan was developed, containing recommendations for resource acquisitions and purchase of resource options. Recommendations for research and development of promising resources not included in the present resource schedule are also provided.

4. THE RESOURCE ASSESSMENT

The Regional Act requires a variety of resources to be considered in the development of the regional plan. These include electric power conservation, generating resources based on renewable energy sources, generating resources utilizing waste heat (cogeneration), generating resources of "high fuel conversion efficiency" and "all other" resources (Table 1). Four basic criteria are provided, upon which the selection of resources is to be based:

- Reliability
- Availability
- Cost-effectiveness
- Resource type

With respect to reliability and availability, the Act simply states that the resources are to be "reliable" and "available within the time it is needed". This implies that consideration must be given to issues such as performance characteristics, technology development and construction lead times.

Resources are to be selected on the basis of cost-effectiveness. Cost-effectiveness is to be evaluated based on total system cost including all direct costs of system development and operation and "such quantifiable environmental costs and benefits ... directly attributable to such measure or resource" (hence the requirement for a methodology for determining environmental costs and benefits of electric power development as a component of the plan).

Under the Act not all resource types are created equal. Conservation, defined "as increases in the efficiency of energy use, production or distribution" is given a 10% cost-effectiveness credit. Thus a conservation measure costing up to 110 percent of a competing resource (and equally available and reliable) is to be given preference. In addition a priority ranking of resources is established as follows:

1) Conservation
2) Renewable resources
3) Generating resources utilizing waste heat or of high fuel conversion efficiency
4) All other resources

Given resources of equal reliability, availability and cost-effectiveness (and considering the 10% conservation credit) resources are to be given preference as established by the priority ranking.

The cost-effectiveness of all resources was estimated using a consistent set of financial assumptions. The "most likely" sponsor was identified for each option, and debt and equity financing consistent with that sponsor was used to assess the resulting cost of energy. Conservation measures were treated as a power-producing resource and costs per kilowatt-hour saved were calculated to facilitate comparison with generating options. All costs were calculated as levelized lifetime revenue requirements of project development, operation and retirement. All calculations were done in "real" terms, exclusive of general inflation, but including forecasted rates of real escalation in capital, operation and fuel costs.

Methods used to assess the availability and cost of the different resource types were as follows:

4.1 Conservation

- Building Conservation: Representative building designs were developed for three generic residential structures and seven generic commercial structures found in the Pacific Northwest. Conservation measures were identified for each. The cost of installing and operating each conservation measure was estimated by architects, engineers and building contractors. For each generic building type, energy consumption was calculated for sequential application of conservation measures in order of estimated cost-effectiveness using the SUNCODE and DOE-2.1. A building energy simulation models for residential and for commercial structures, respectively. The levelized lifetime cost per kilowatt conserved was then calculated for each conservation measure.

  Estimates of existing and future building populations were obtained from BPA. Estimates were prepared to the total potential availability of conservation savings by conservation measure, building type and climate zone. Potential availability was constrained by estimates of existing conservation measure penetration and structural restrictions on conservation measure installation.

- Industrial Conservation: This assessment was limited to lighting and motor drive end uses, estimated to account for approximately 43% of electricity consumed by the industrial sector in the Pacific Northwest. (Resistance heating and electrolytic uses account for most of the balance of consumption.) Energy conservation measures applicable to industrial lighting and motor drives were identified. Estimates of cost and unit (per horsepower or lumen) energy savings were assembled for each conservation measure, allowing costs per kilowatt saved to be estimated. Estimates of the current population of candidate motors and lights for retrofit of energy conservation measures were developed for eight industrial sectors from previous estimates of industrial electrical end use in the Northwest and estimates of the distribution of various motor and light fixture types. Future motor and light populations were estimated based on forecasted industrial growth rates. Potential availability of conservation savings were calculated, considering the estimated percentage of existing retrofits.

- Agricultural Conservation: The principal use of electric energy in Pacific Northwest agriculture is for irrigation. Three basic energy conservation measures were identified including application system improvements, pumping system improvements and irrigation scheduling. Estimates of the cost and unit (per acre) energy savings were prepared for each measure. The energy savings resulting from these conservation

Table 1. Resources and Associated Technologies Considered in the Resource Assessment

Resource	Technologies
Residential Building End Uses	Measures to reduce heat loss and gain Solar hot water and space heating Efficient equipment and appliances
Commercial Building End Uses	Measures to reduce heat loss and gain Solar hot water, space heating and lighting Efficient equipment Building cogeneration
Industrial End Uses	Efficient motors and lighting Industrial cogeneration
Agricultural End Uses	Efficient irrigation equipment Irrigation scheduling
Biomass	Wood-fired steam electric plants MSW-fired steam electric plants
Geothermal	Flashed-steam electric plants Binary cycle electric plants Direct space heating applications
Hydroelectric	Large, intermediate small-scale and micro-hydro plants
Solar	Central photovoltaic stations Central thermal receivers
Wind	Central wind energy systems
Coal	Direct-fired steam-electric plants Fluidized bed combustion plants Gasification-combined cycle plants Gasification-fuel cell-combined cycle plants
Natural Gas	Direct-fired steam-electric plants Combustion turbines Combined cycle plants Fuel cell stations
Fuel Oil	Combustion turbines Combined cycle plants Fuel cell stations Diesel generators
Nuclear	Light water reactor plants
Imports	--

measures are a function of the pumping lift, volume of water applied annually, and type of irrigation systems in current use. Estimates of existing and prospective irrigated acreage, acres irrigated by type of irrigation system, average annual water use and average pumping lift were compiled for each of fourteen agricultural subregions in the Pacific Northwest. Conservation measures were then ranked in order of estimated cost-effectiveness for each subregion and estimates prepared of potential energy savings vs. cost.

4.2 Renewable Resources

- Biomass: Estimates of the current and future availability, price and distribution of wood residue (mill and forest residue) and municipal solid waste were compiled. Cost and technical performance information was developed for steam-electric plants using wood residue and municipal solid waste as fuel. From this information, were developed estimates of the potential availability and cost of electricity generated from wood residue and from municipal solid waste.

- Geothermal: The subsurface temperatures, depth and estimated energy content of the high-temperature hydrothermal convection systems of the Pacific Northwest were compiled. Promising sites were screened for environmental acceptability. An appropriate geothermal electric generation system (binary cycle or flashed steam) was chosen for each. Using the GEOCOST model, which simulates the design, development and operation of geothermal well fields and power plants, the cost and availability of electric power for ten promising geothermal resource areas were calculated.

  An estimate was also prepared of the availability and cost of space heating using geothermal district heating systems. The subsurface temperature and energy content of intermediate-temperature hydrothermal resources were compiled. Communities of 10,000 population or larger within economically feasible transmission distance of these resources were identified. Using the GEOCITY model, which simulates the design, development and operation of geothermal district heating systems, estimates of the cost of serving customers in these communities were prepared.

- Hydroelectric: Numerous surveys of the undeveloped hydroelectric resources of the Pacific Northwest are available. These studies lack consistency of treatment, especially with respect to estimates of cost. The technical characteristics and available cost information were assembled for 154 potential hydroelectric projects ranging from micro-scale to large-scale in size. Cost information was adjusted to common year dollars and to a common scope of development activities. Levelized lifetime costs were calculated for each project.

- Solar: Information on solar isolation was compiled for the Pacific Northwest. Cost and design information was compiled on central photovoltaic stations and central thermal receivers using current technology. The performance of a prototype central photovoltaic station and a prototype central receiver was estimated under the most favorable Pacific Northwest conditions. Cost of power estimates were then prepared for the two prototypes. The quantity of power potentially available from the solar resource would be essentially unlimited due to the large amount of undeveloped land in the more favorable areas of the Northwest.

- Wind: Seven promising Pacific Northwest wind resource areas were identified. Cost information was compiled on three generic wind turbines suitable for central wind farm applications. The performance of each type of machine was estimated under the conditions presented by each of the seven wind resource areas. A development scenario was postulated for each promising wind resource area. Based on the postulated development scenarios, the cost of power was estimated for each wind resource area.

4.3 Non-Renewable Resources

- Coal: Large quantities of inexpensive low-sulfur sub-bituminous coal are available from the Northern Great Plains of eastern Montana and Wyoming. The future cost of this coal, both at minemouth and delivered within the Pacific Northwest region, was estimated. The cost and performance characteristics and construction lead times of current and advanced coal conversion technologies were assembled. From this information, estimates of the cost of power from current and advanced coal-fired generating plants, located both within the region and at minemouth, were developed.

- Natural Gas: Natural gas is available to the region by pipeline from Canadian and domestic sources. Estimates of future gas prices to the region were compiled. Information on the technical performance, cost, and availability of current and advanced electric power generating technologies fueled by natural gas was compiled. From this information, estimates of the cost of power from current and advanced power plants using natural gas were developed.

- Oil: Oil is imported to the region from Alaskan and contiguous domestic sources. Historically, the use of oil for generation of electricity has been limited to peaking plants. Little future use of oil is anticipated due to price and availability considerations and constraints established by the Powerplant and Industrial Fuel Use Act. The cost of oil-fired generation was, however, estimated for completeness. Estimates of the future prices of distillate and residual fuel oils were compiled. Current and advanced oil-fired electric generation technologies were identified, and cost, performance characteristics, and availability information assembled for each. From this information were developed estimates of the future cost of electricity using oil-fired power plants.

- Nuclear: Of the nine nuclear plants in various stages of development in the Pacific Northwest at the beginning of this study, four units were terminated and one additional unit deferred in the period during which the Regional Plan was in development.[3] Thus the focus of the nuclear resource assessment was on the costs-to-complete and anticipated performance of planned and partially completed nuclear plants. From the resulting information were developed estimates of the potential availability and cost of electricity generated from nuclear sources.

- Imports: Electric power could be imported to the Pacific Northwest from Western Canada (coal and hydro sources), the Northern Great Plains (coal), or the Arizona-New Mexico Region (coal). In addition, due to differing load profiles, seasonal exchanges with California are possible. The cost and availability of electric power from these sources were each estimated.

5. FINDINGS

The findings of the resource assessment are summarized in the resource supply function of Figure 2.

The supply function depicts the cost and availability of new resources at a given point in time. The supply function of Figure 2 is for the year 1995 - about the time major new generation resources (in addition to those currently under construction) would be required under the high load growth case. Similar supply

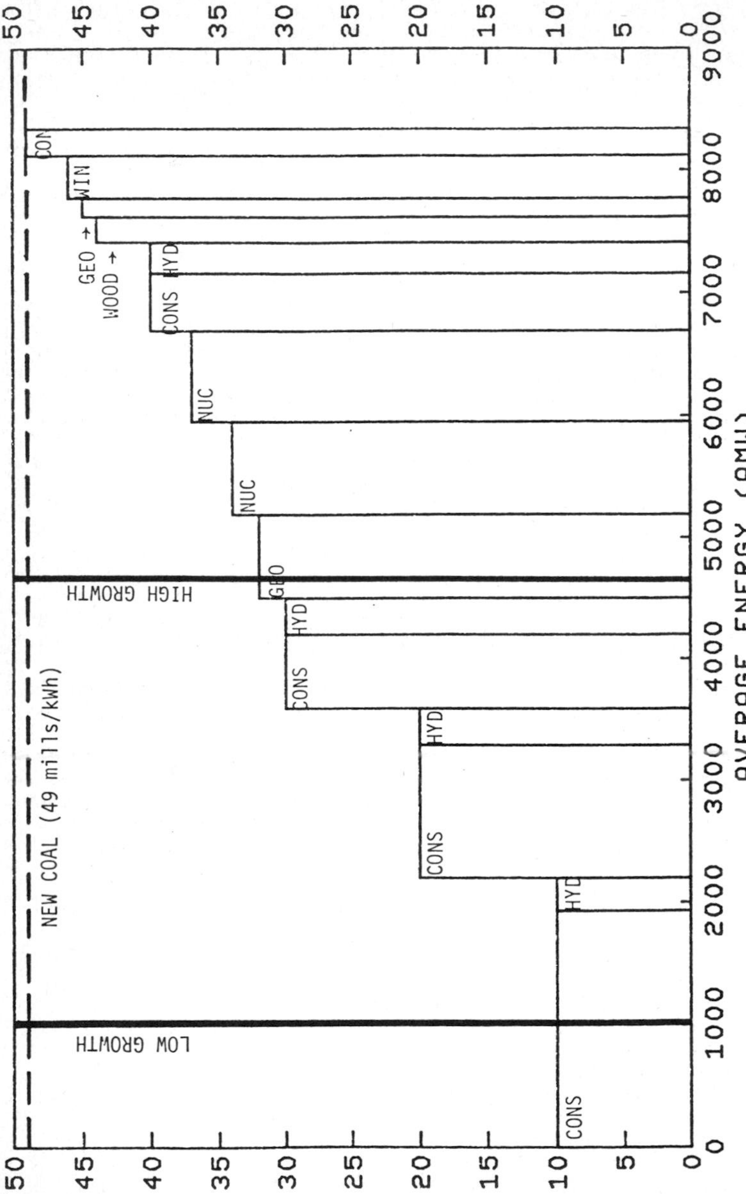

FIGURE 2. Conservation and Supply Resoucres: Pacific Northwest - 1995

functions could be prepared for other points in time. Estimated costs would change due to price escalation effects. Resource availability would be affected by development lead times, construction of new building stock, retirement of old building stock, acreage brought under irrigation and industrial growth rates.

The horizontal axis of Figure 2 shows the availability of electric energy[4] from various resources. Energy availability is measured in terms of average megawatts (AMW).

The cost of energy from the various options is shown on the vertical axis. All costs are estimated in 1980 dollars using real (inflation free) costs of capital.

The resource options are depicted as blocks, dimensioned by cost and energy availability, arranged in order of cost-effectiveness. Given a forecasted need for additional energy, a preliminary schedule of resources likely to meet the forecasted demand in a cost-effective manner can be readily compiled. (Because of the effects of resource cost on electrical demand and because of the effects of power system operation on the cost-effectiveness of certain resources, it is necessary to further assess the preliminary schedule of resources, as discussed in the preceding section.)

The set of potentially cost-effective resources is bounded by the cost of the most cost-effective resource whose availability is essentially "unlimited" with respect to the potential needs of the region. Three resources are candidates: coal, nuclear, and solar. Levelized lifetime revenue requirements were estimated to be 110-190 mills/kwh for solar (central receivers), 49 mills/kwh for coal (steam-electric plants) and 42 mills/kwh for nuclear (light water reactor plants), suggesting that new light water reactors would bound the set of potentially cost-effective resources.

Comparative analysis of the performance of coal and nuclear plants in the context of the Northwest power system using The System Analysis Model, suggests, however, that new coal plants are as cost-effective as new nuclear plants. This seemingly anomalous result is primarily due to the opportunity to shut down the region's thermal plants during good water years. Coal plants are characterized by a much higher ratio of variable-to-fixed costs than nuclear units and shutdown of these plants during good water years results in cost savings to the region that offset the lower cost of nuclear units observed under constant capacity factor operation.

Because new coal plants appear to be as economical as new nuclear units for Pacific Northwest conditions, the levelized lifetime cost of new coal units is taken as the boundary of potentially cost-effective resources (Figure 2).

Over 8000 AMW of potentially cost-effective resources are available to the region, greatly exceeding forecasted needs by 1995 (Figure 2, vertical lines). These resources include building conservation, agricultural conservation, industrial conservation, hydro, geothermal, wood, wind and two partially completed nuclear units.

5.1 Building Conservation

Through implementation of building conservation measures over 3450 AMW of annual energy savings are estimated to be obtainable at costs of less than 49 mills per kilowatt-hour saved. Of this amount, 1650 AMW are estimated to be available at costs of less than 10 mills per kilowatt-hour saved. These estimated savings would result from improvements in building equipment and appliance efficiencies and improvements in building shell thermal performance. Additional savings are available through implementation of building equipment and designs using renewable resources such as daylighting and solar-assisted space and hot water heating.

5.2 Agricultural Conservation

In the agricultural sector over 400 AMW of annual energy savings are estimated to be available at costs of less than 49 mills per kilowatt hour. Of this amount, over 180 AMW are estimated to be available at costs less than 10 mills per kilowatt-hour. The majority of these potential savings would be obtained through implementation of irrigation scheduling programs. Lesser amounts would be saved through pump and application system efficiency improvements.

5.3 Industrial Conservation

In the industrial sector, approximately 440 AMW of annual energy savings are estimated to be available at costs of less than 49 mills per kilowatt-hour saved. These savings would result from implementation of efficient motors, variable speed controllers and more efficient lighting. Additional savings, not assessed in this work,[5] may be available in resistance heating and electrolytic end uses. Industrial cogeneration projects, potentially producing in excess of 550 AMW, were also identified (not shown on Figure 2).

5.4 Hydroelectric

One hundred twenty-nine hydroelectric projects, providing approximately 1140 AMW of energy annually[6] were identified as having energy production costs of 49 mills per kilowatt-hour or less. These projects range from micro-scale (less than 1MW) to large scale (more than 25 MW) and include additions to existing hydroelectric projects, additions to existing non-power water resource projects (irrigation, water supply and flood control), and new hydroelectric projects. Many of the additions to existing power and non-power projects can be developed without substantial environmental impacts.

5.5 Geothermal

Based on current understanding of their characteristics, two geothermal resource areas, Newberry Caldera and Mickey Hot Springs, both in Oregon, could be developed for power production at estimated costs of 32 mills per kilowatt-hour for Newberry Caldera and 45 mills per kilowatt-hour for Mickey Hot Springs. Estimated annual power output of these areas is 150 AMW for Mickey Hot Springs and 690 AMW for Newberry Caldera. The flashed steam technology that would likely be used for power production is well developed; however, the characteristics of these two resource areas are not well enough understood to guarantee the availability of this power. Further exploration of these resource areas appears to be warranted.

5.6 Nuclear

WNP #4 and WNP #5 are two partially completed nuclear plants on which construction has been terminated due to lack of funding and demonstrated need for power in the near-term. The plants could, however, be preserved for later completion. At estimated levelized lifetime revenue requirements of 34 and 37 mills per kilowatt-hour for WNP #4 and WNP #5, respectively (based on capital costs-to-complete), completion of these plants appears to be potentially cost-effective should rapid growth in electrical demand materialize. However, the long lead time required to complete these plants (8 1/2 years), coupled with the low probability of high load growth, poses a high risk of excess capacity development.

5.7 Wood

One wood-fired power plant is nearing completion in the Pacific Northwest and sufficient mill and forest residue is thought to be available in the region to support an additional 300 MW of wood-fired capacity, producing approximately 215 AMW of energy annually. Levelized lifetime revenue requirements of the typical plant, a 25 MW capacity steam-electric unit, are estimated to be 44 mills per kilowatt-hour.

5.8 Wind

Of the seven wind resource areas investigated, five show potential for producing power at costs ranging from 45 to 47 mills per kilowatt-hour in 1995. The aggregate capacity of these sites would be about 1020 MW. The machines would produce approximately 340 AMW annually. Additional development would be possible at each site. These costs assume certain economies of scale from site development; thus, costs early in the site development process would be substantially greater (70 to 80 mills per kilowatt-hour) than the costs of fully developed sites. Additionally, the wind machine costs used for these estimates were based on levels of wind turbine production which would be achieved only if substantial demand for wind turbines materializes.

Finally, because wind is a non-firm resource, these costs should be compared to the cost of power potentially displaced by the wind-generated power. In the Northwest, the displaced power would likely be that of coal steam-electric plants. The cost savings (value of displacement power) would be the variable costs of coal steam - electric plant operation.

5.9 Coal

Essentially unlimited amounts of energy with respect to anticipated Northwest needs are potentially available from coal. Average production costs for a four-unit 2000 MW project were estimated to be 49 mills/kwh (costs for the first unit would be greater). The principal uncertainties relative to the future use of coal relate to environmental concerns and the susceptibility of fuel and operating costs to inflation and escalation.

6. CONCLUSION

The most promising electric power resources for near term and mid-term development in the Pacific Northwest are conservation and hydro. Together, these resources are sufficient to meet the needs of the region for all but the highest rates of electrical load growth through 1995. Should rapid growth in electrical demand occur, additional resources may be required beginning about 1995.

Coal and nuclear are two demonstrated resources that could be used to meet post-1995 needs under conditions of high load growth. Although the levelized production costs of coal units appear to exceed those of nuclear units, the high proportion of variable-to-fixed costs of coal-fired power plants result in long-term production costs comparable to nuclear units in the context of the hydro-dominated Pacific Northwest electric power system. Because the shorter construction lead times of coal plants reduce the risk of overbuilding, coal is presently favored over nuclear should the need for new thermal capacity arise.

More advanced resources may be cost-effective by the mid- to late 1990's, offsetting the need for additional conventional thermal capacity. Advanced coal combustion concepts such as fluidized bed combustion and plants using fuel derived by gasification of coal offer the promise of lower production costs and less environmental impact than conventional coal plants.

Certain geothermal and wind resource areas also show promise of cost-effective and environmentally acceptable electricity generation by the mid to late 1990's.

FOOTNOTES

[1]"Average Megawatts" is commonly used as the measure of electric energy in the Pacific Northwest. One average megawatt (AMW) is the amount of electric energy generated by one megawatt of capacity operating continously for a period of one year. One average megawatt is equivalent to 8.76 gigawatt-hours.

[2]During the first phase of the Hydro-Thermal Power Program, BPA agreed to acquire the output of thermal plants sponsored by publically-owned utilities by purchasing an amount of power from a sponsoring utility equal to that utility's share in the plant (all new thermal plants in the Northwest are jointly owned). BPA would remunerate the utility through "net-billing" whereby the charges for the utility's power purchase from BPA would be reduced by cost of the thermal power. BPA thus guaranteed purchase of the output of the thermal plants at cost. This arrangement ceased to be used for newer thermal plants primarily because the escalating cost of the net-billed thermal plants exhausted the capacity of utility power purchases from BPA to support net-billing.

[3]Since this writing two additional units have been terminated and one additional unit deferred.

[4]Because of the large fraction of hydroelectric capacity, the Northwest electric power system is energy-constrained rather than capacity-constrained. Therefore the potential supply of energy is of interest.

[5]Separate estimates of potential savings in the major industrial sectors were submitted to the Council by industrial representatives.

[6]The estimated availability of hydroelectric resources was subsequently extended through an assessment conducted by the Pacific Northwest Utilities Conference Committee.

REFERENCES

[1] Battelle, Pacific Northwest Laboratories. 1982/1983. Assessment of Electric Power Conservation and Supply Resources in the Pacific Northwest, Volumes I through XVI. Prepared for the Northwest Power Planning Council, Portland, OR.

[2] Northwest Power Planning Council. 1983. Regional Conservation and Electric Power Plan: 1983. Portland, OR.

Analytic Techniques for Energy Planning
B. Lev, F.H. Murphy, J.A. Bloom & A.S. Gleit (Editors)

OPTIMIZATION OF HYDROELECTRIC POWER SYSTEM OPERATION*

H. Habibollahzadeh
J.A. Bubenko
Royal Institute of Technology
Stockholm, Sweden

D. Sjelvgren
Swedish State Power Board
Stockholm, Sweden

G. Larsson
N. Andersson
Krangede AB
Stockholm, Sweden

The operation planning problem in hydro electric power systems exhibits certain complex features and requires special solution methods. This paper presents the development of a solution method which reforms the problem into a network formulation and employs a fast Network Flow Algorithm. Extensions to the network flow theory are introduced to consider:

1) additional linear constraints

2) piecewise linear nature of hydro power production and

3) head dependence of power production

1. INTRODUCTION

The operation planning problem in hydro electric power systems is characterized by external security constraints, head dependence and piecewise linear nature of objective function, and the large number of variables involved, e.g. 839 variables per hydro plant in the weekly operation planning considered in this paper. It is clear that such a problem is beyond the scope of general algorithms and special solution methods are required.

In this paper a solution method is presented that exploits the special characteristic of the large number of constraints involved in the problem.

2. HYDRO RESERVOIR DYNAMICS

The dynamics of the hydro reservoir can be represented by the following difference equation:

$$x_i(k+1) - x_i(k) + u_i(k) - u_{i-1}(k) + s_i(k) - s_{i-1}(k) = r_i(k) \quad (1)$$

$$\underline{x}_i \leq x_i(k) \leq \bar{x}_i \quad (2)$$

$$\underline{u}_i \leq u_i(k) \leq \bar{u}_i \quad (3)$$

*This research was supported by Krangede AB, Stockholm, Sweden.

$s_i(k)$ = the spillage from the ith reservoir during hour k

$u_{i-1}(k)$ and $s_{i-1}(k)$ represent the discharge and spillage from the upstream reservoir and are equal to zero if no such reservoir exists. Equations (2) and (3) represent the maximum and minimum limits on the reservoir contents and discharges. These limits are defined according to the environmental requirements and the hydro plant's actual limits. For example, there could be a non-zero minimum discharge requirement or a maximum discharge requirement less than the maximum limit of plant discharge (referred to as u_{max} in this paper). There are two assumptions implicit in this formulation:

- the travelling time for the water from one reservoir to the next is much less than the one hour time step of the model;
- no reservoir has more than one reservoir directly up- or down-stream from it.

These two assumptions are for the specific problem considered here. The general case can be handled with slight modification of the procedure.

3. HYDRO PRODUCTION CURVES AND MARGINAL COSTS

The hydropower benefit is dependent on hydropower production and marginal costs. The power production of a hydro plant is a function of water flow and reservoir head. Figure 1 illustrates the power production curve of a hydro plant versus discharge at a given head. This curve is concave (typical for the power plants in Sweden) and consists of K line segments. The η's are the slopes of the different segments and depend on the reservoir head. The best operating points (or the best efficiency points) for 1, 2 and 3 generators in operation are also shown as u_{b1}, u_{b2}, u_{b3} respectively.

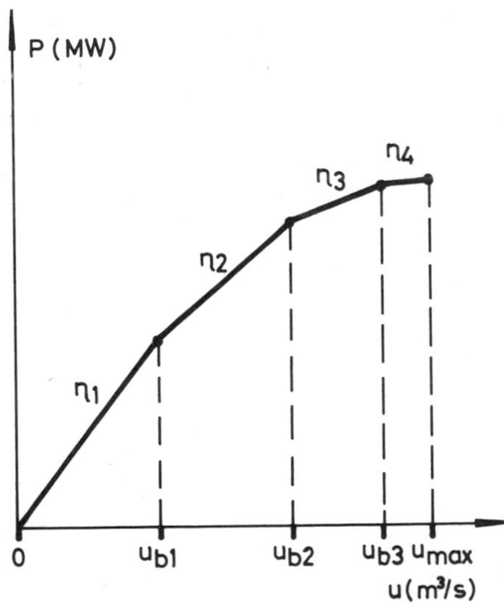

Figure 1. Piecewise linear representation of power production curve for a given head (K = 4)

The power output for a hydro station, station i, at a given head during hour k is:

$$P_i(k) = \sum_{j=1}^{K} \eta_{ij}\, u_{ij}(k) \tag{4}$$

η_{ij}'s are the slopes of different line segments of the power production curve at plant i and $u_{ij}(k)$'s are components of $u_i(k)$, each corresponding to one of these line segments. Thus,

$$u_i(k) = \sum_{j=1}^{K} u_{ij}(k) \tag{5}$$

The head (h) variations for the problem considered here are small. These variations are linearly dependent on the reservoir content within its boundaries:

$$h_i = \alpha_i x_i + \beta_i$$

α_i and β_i are constants.
The energy production for hydro station i during hour k is then,

$$e_i(k) = T\, P_i(k) \tag{6}$$

T in this model is one hour. The total energy production at hour k, e(k), is the sum of energy production at each plant,

$$e(k) = \sum_{i=1}^{M} e_i(k) \tag{7}$$

where M is the total number of hydro plants in the system. The hydro plants benefit function can now be written as,

$$f = \sum_{k=1}^{N} e(k)\, b(k) \tag{8}$$

where N is the number of time intervals in the optimization period (N = 168 in the weekly problem) and b(k) is the marginal benefit at hour k.

The hydro system considered in this paper is a part of a large hydrothermal power system consisting of several utilities. So the marginal benefits used in this paper correspond to the total system and are obtained from optimization of this system [18]. Due to the negligible marginal cost of hydroelectric generation, this optimization is a problem of how to use, in a given time, the water availability for hydroelectric generation to reduce the thermal production. This optimization is done by iteratively solving the thermal subsystem and hydro subsystem and results in the marginal benefits for hydro energy production.

4. SYSTEM REQUIREMENTS

There are usually other constraints that must be considered. One example of these constraints is the reserve requirement, as follows:

$$\sum_{i=1}^{M} (P_{maxi}(k) - P_i(k)) \geq R_{req} \tag{9}$$

where

$P_{maxi}(k)$ = maximum possible power generation at plant i during hour k

R_{req} = system reserve requirement

The maximum possible power generation at plant i during hour k can be written as a function of discharge:

$$P_{maxi}(k) = \sum_{j=1}^{K} \eta_{ij}\, \bar{u}_{ij} \tag{10}$$

where η_{ij}, j=1,...,K, are the slopes of line segments in the hydro production curve, Figure 1, and $\bar{u}_{ij}$'s are the components of $\bar{u}_i$ along these line segments. Substituting equations (4) and (10) in equation (9), the following equation for reserve requirement as a function of water discharges is obtained:

$$\sum_{j=1}^{K} \eta_{ij}(\bar{u}_{ij}-u_{ij}(k)) \geq R_{req} \tag{11}$$

5. OPTIMIZATION MODEL

As described previously, the hydro system considered in this study is a part of a large system and does not affect the marginal costs. So the problem of weekly planning for this hydro system can be described as maximization of total benefit versus hourly marginal benefits. This can be written from equation (1) through (11) as follows:

maximize

$$f = \sum_{k=1}^{N} b(k) \sum_{i=1}^{M} T \sum_{j=1}^{K} \eta_{ij}\, u_{ij}(k) \tag{12}$$

subject to

$$x_i(k+1) - x_i(k) + \sum_{j=1}^{K} u_{ij}(k) - \sum_{j=1}^{K} u_{i-1j}(k)$$

$$+ s_i(k) - s_{i-1}(k) = r_i(k) \tag{13}$$

$$\sum_{i=1}^{M} \sum_{j=1}^{K} \eta_{ij}(\bar{u}_{ij}(k) - u_{ij}(k)) \geq R_{req} \tag{14}$$

$$\underline{x}_i \leq x_i(k) \leq \bar{x}_i \tag{15}$$

$$\underline{u}_{ij} \leq u_{ij}(k) \leq \bar{u}_{ij} \tag{16}$$

$$i=1,\ldots,M,\ k=1,\ldots,N,\ j=1,\ldots,K$$

Letting [x] be the set of all state variables, x_i's, control variables, u_{ij}'s, and spillage, s_i's, such as below:

$$[x] = \begin{cases} [x_i(k)] - [\underline{x}_i] \\ [u_{ij}(k)] - [\underline{u}_{ij}] \\ [s_i(k)] \end{cases}$$

and [c] be the set of all unit costs, c_m, where each coefficient corresponds to an element of [x] such as below:

$$c_m = \begin{cases} 0 & \text{if m corresponds to a state variable or spillage} \\ -b(k)\ \eta_{ij}T & \text{if m corresponds to a control variable} \end{cases}$$

Vector [c] is head dependent because (as explained before) η_{ij}'s are head dependent. Equations (12) through (16) can now be written respectively as follows:

minimize

$$[c]^t[x] \tag{17}$$

subject to

$$[A_1][x] = [r_1] \tag{18}$$

$$[A_2][x] \geq [r_2] \tag{19}$$

$$0 \leq [x] \leq [\bar{x}] \tag{20}$$

6. OPTIMIZATION METHOD

The weekly operation planning as described in the previous section is a large linear programming problem with two groups of constraints. The first group, equation (18), consists of hydro reservoir dynamics and has a network structure. There are 168 constraints per reservoir in this group and they constitute a major part of the total constraints. The second group, equation (19), contains the reserve requirement and has a non-network structure. There are only 168 constraints in this group, which is considerably lower than the first group.

Fast network flow algorithms [13] can be applied to solve this problem when only the first group of constraints are involved. These algorithms are about one hundred times faster than standard methods, but to solve the problem with both groups of constraints involved, the Dantzig-Wolfe decomposition method [5] must be used to exploit the network structure of the large number of constraints involved. This is due to the fact that the subproblem of this method will have a purely network structure and network flow algorithms can be applied to solve it. The CPU time requirement of the decomposition method depends on the size of its master problem and consequently on the number of constraints in the second group. The CPU time requirements are demonstrated later in the conclusions.

The general procedure for solving the weekly operation planning problem using the Dantzig-Wolfe decomposition method is to start solving the problem with only the first set of constraints and add the violated constraints in the second group as they are detected. The head variations are updated in each iteration. Since the constraints of this problem, equations (18) and (20), are not head dependent, they are the same in all iterations. So the solution from one iteration is feasible for the next iteration, and only the dual variables must be modified in accordance with the new cost coefficient vector. The head variations in this problem are very small and they add only few iterations to the solution of the problem with fixed head. In general, if the iterations for head updating did not converge, the head dependence equations could be added to the second group of constraints and considered in the decomposition method.

In practice, the general procedure is reduced to a more simplified procedure as shown in Figure 2. In this procedure a fast network flow algorithm is employed to solve the problem with the second group of constraints ignored. A major part of the constraints in the second group are met by this primary solution. To comply with the few constraints that are not met, the Dantzig-Wolfe decomposition method is used. This procedure reduces the size of the master problem for the decomposition and consequently the CPU time requirement. The head variations are updated in each iteration. The head updating procedure adds only 2-4 extra iterations and a very small amount of CPU time to the problem solution with fixed head. This is due to the fact that in all iterations, except the first iteration, there is a feasible solution from the previous iteration. About 90% of the CPU time is used in the first iteration because we have to start with an all artificial solution.

7. EXAMPLE

The topological structure of a six reservoir example is shown in Figure 3. The final destination of the water is a sea which is also included, because it is used as the reference node in the application of network flow algorithms. For illustrative convenience, the sea is omitted in the next figures but, in fact, it is assumed to be the destination of any arc that is drawn one-ended in the figures of this paper. The expansion of topological structure of the

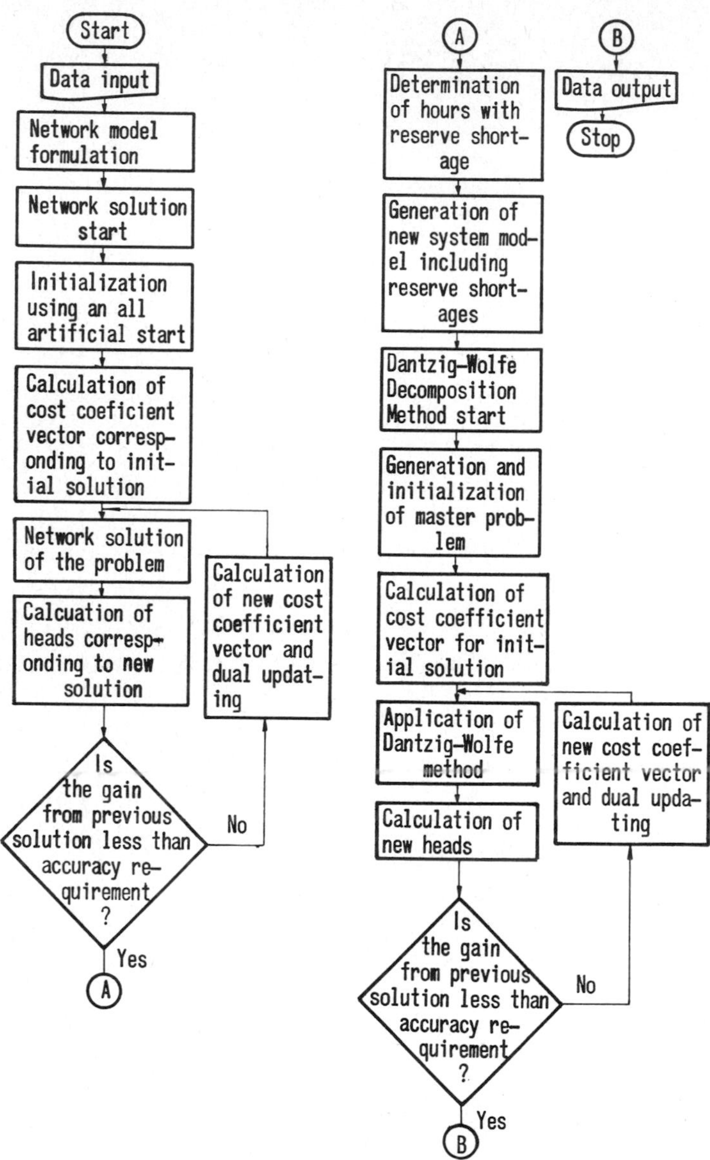

Figure 2. The flow chart for optimization

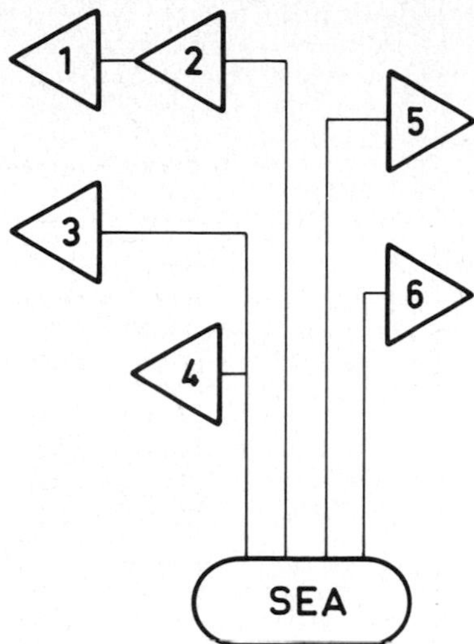

Figure 3. A six reservoir system

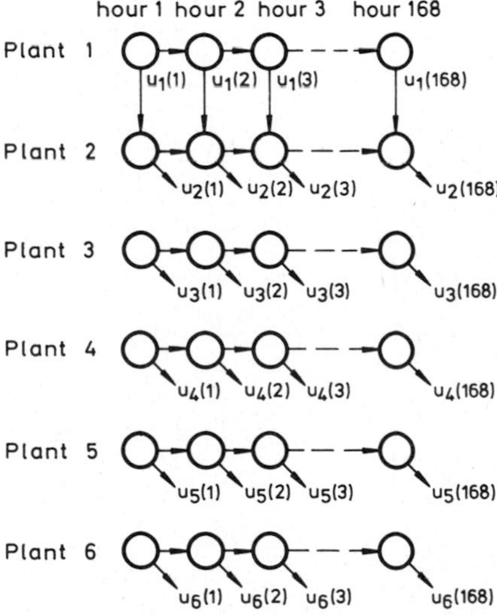

Figure 4. The expanded topopological diagram of the six reservoir system over a period of 168 hours

system over a period of 168 hours is drawn in Figure 4. The matrix $[A_1]$ in the system equations (17)-(20) is the node arc incidence matrix of expanded topological diagram over the optimization period. So, matrix $[A_1]$ does not have a full rank; this is a specific character of network programs.

An all artificial initial solution is used to start the procedure. This initial solution consists of artificial arcs connecting every node to the root node. The flow of each arc is set according to the requirement of the corresponding node. The unit cost along these arcs and their upper-bounds are set to infinity.

In the pricing step of the network solution, since the size of the candidate set is very large at the early iterations, a maximum size is appointed to this set. Once a candidate set is generated, its elements are entered into the basis. A new candidate set is generated when there are no more elements with negative reduced cost in the existing candidate set.

An interesting feature of the optimal tree in this case is that a major part of non-basic arcs represents the discharges at the different hours. This means that the discharges are usually at lower-bound, upper-bound or one of their best operating points.

The discharges at the hours with high marginal costs reach their upper limit so they violate the reserve requirements. To comply with the reserve requirements at these hours, the Dantzig-Wolfe decomposition method is employed. Sparsity methods are used in the application of the Dantzig-Wolfe method since very sparse martrices are involved.

Sample results for a reservoir from application of the procedure discussed are shown in Figures 5 and 6. Figure 5 illustrates the marginal cost, reservoir head and discharge variations for a week when there is no reserve requirement. Figure 6 illustrates the same problem when there is some requirement. The plants have three generators so the discharges corresponding to the best operating point, when one, two or three generators are in operation, are also given.

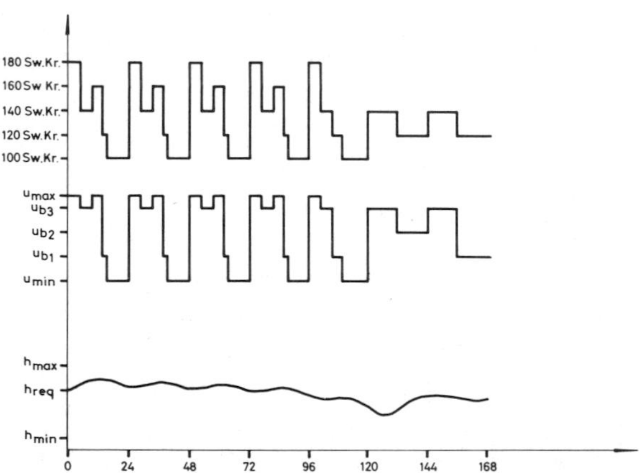

Figure 5. Sample output data for a reservoir when there is no reserve requirement

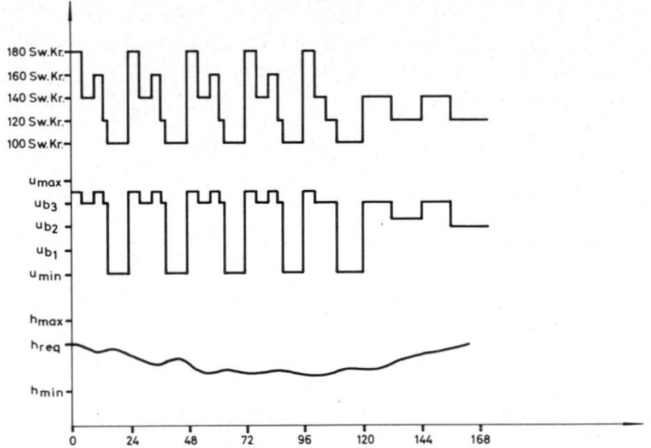

Figure 6. Sample output data for a reservoir when there is a reserve requirement

8. CONCLUSIONS

A computer program has been developed for the application of this method to hydro system short-term scheduling. An efficient basis tree labeling system, suitable for the physical context of the problem, and sparsity techniques are employed in the program. The procedure has been efficient since it:

- exploits the network structure of the large number of constraints involved and employs network flow algorithms;
- reduces the number of constraints with non-network structure to a very low number.

Table 1. The CPU times when there is no reserve requirement

TYPE	No. VARIABLES	CPU TIME (s)
DAILY	238	2.5
WEEKLY	1678	20

Table 2. The CPU times when there is a reserve requirement

TYPE	No. VARIABLES	No. SECUR. CONST.	CPU TIME (s)
DAILY	238	3	8
		5	15
WEEKLY	1678	10	130
		20	360

The program is intended for maximization of benefits in six hydro plants (Figure 3) but due to lack of data it has only been tested on the two cascade plants in the system, plants number 1 and 2. The efficiency of the program in the daily and weekly planning is shown in Tables 1 and 2. The computation time in these tables are on a Vax-11-780 computer.

The alternative to the decomposition method is the partitioning method (compact inverse method), [9]. The only draw back of this method is that after reducing the number of security constraints, the new unsatisfied constraints cannot be added before a full solution of the problem; where in the decomposition method they can be picked up in the intermediate states.

REFERENCES

[1] Bazarra, M.S. and Jarvis, J.J., Linear Programming and Network Flows, John Wiley & Sons, New York, 1977.

[2] Bubenko, J.A. and Waern, B.M., "Short-Range Hydro Scheduling", IEEE Conference 1972, paper C 72456-2.

[3] Chen, S. and Saigel, R., "A Primal Algorithm for Solving a Capacitated Network Flow Problem with Additional Linear Constraints", Network, Vol. 7, 1977.

[4] Cunningham, W.H., "A Network Simplex Method", Mathematical Programming, 11-2, 1976.

[5] Dantzig, G.B. and Wolfe, P., "The Decomposition Algorithm for Linear Programs", Econometrica, Vol. 29, No. 4, 1961.

[6] El-Hawary, M.E., "Optimal Economic Operation of Electric Power Systems", Academic Press, N.Y., 1979.

[7] Engles, L., Larson, R.E., Peschon, J. and Stanton, N., "Dynamic Programming Applied to Hydro-Thermal Generation Scheduling", A report from Systems Control Inc., 1976.

[8] Gagnon, C.R. and Bolton, J.F., "Optimal Hydro Scheduling at the Bonneville Power Administration", IEEE Summer Meeting, Mexico City, Mex., 1977.

[9] Glover, F. and Klingman, D., "The Simplex Son Algorithm for LP/Embedded Network Problems", Research report CCS 317, University of Texas, Austin, Texas, 1977.

[10] Glover, F., Klingman, D. and Stutz, J., "Augmented Threaded Index Method for Network Optimization", Infor., Vol. 12, No. 3, 1974.

[11] Habibollahzadeh, H., "Optimal Short-Term Operation Planning of Hydroelectric Power Systems", Research report, Royal Institute of Technology, Stockholm, 1983.

[12] Heidari, M., Chow, V.T., Kokotovic, P.V. and Meredith, D., "Discrete Differential Dynamic Programming Approach to Water Resource System Optimization", Water Resource Research, Vol. 7, No. 2, 1970.

[13] Kennington, J.L. and Helgason, R.V., Algorithms for Network Programming, John Wiley & Sons, New York, 1981.

[14] Lasdon, L.S., Optimization Theory for Large Systems, Macmillan, London, 1970.

[15] Rosenthal, R.E., "A Nonlinear Network Flow Algorithm for Maximization of Benefits in a Hydroelectric Power System", Operation Research, Vol. 29, 1981.

[16] Sjelvgren, D. and Dillon, T.S., "Modeling and Organization of Production Planning System for Hydro-Thermal Regulation in the Swedish State Power Board", PSCC VII, Lausanne, 1981.

[17] Sjelvgren, D. and Dillon, T.S., "Seasonal Planning of a Hydro-Thermal System Based on the Network Flow Concept", PSCC VII, Lausanne, 1981.

[18] Soares, S., Lyra, C. and Tavares, H., "Optimal Generation Scheduling of Hydrothermal Power Systems", IEEE Trans., PAS-99, No. 3, pp.1107-114, 1980.

[19] Turgeon, A., "Optimal Short-Term Hydro Scheduling from the Principal of Progressive Optimality", Hydro-Quebec, Canada, 1981.

[20] Turgeon, A., "Optimal Short-Term Scheduling of Hydro Plants in Series - A Review", Hydro-Quebec, Canada, 1981.

Analytic Techniques for Energy Planning
B. Lev, F.H. Murphy, J.A. Bloom & A.S. Gleit (Editors)

THE EMISSIONS STRATEGY INTEGRATION MODEL: A PROPOSED CONCEPTUAL APPROACH*

Edward H. Pechan
Kristin Graves

E.H. Pechan & Associates, Inc.
5537 Hempstead Way
Springfield, VA 22151

The acid precipitation problem has the potential to play a significant role in energy use decisions made in the next several years. For example, some proposed acid deposition control measures being considered by Congress would require significant reductions in emissions of sulfur oxides from fossil fuel combustion. This would either require shifts in sources of coal used in the Midwest and/or installation of a substantial amount of new pollution control hardware.

This paper discusses a proposed approach for development of an Emissions Strategy Integration Model (ESIM) discussed in more detail in [14]. The ESIM is being developed under joint sponsorship of the Assessments and Policy Analysis Task Group and the Man-Made Sources Task Group, two components of the National Acid Precipitation Assessment Program (NAPAP). The Assessments Task Group is responsible for development and use of analytic methods to evaluate the effects of possible acid deposition control and/or mitigation measures.

A prototype version of the model to be implemented in 1983 based on the design presented here will enable the development of cost-effective regional control strategies covering all significant emitting sectors. The model will also allow consideration of the effects of sources located in different regions on deposition of acidic substances on user-designated "sensitive areas."

1. INTRODUCTION

The Acid Precipitation Act of 1980 established an Interagency Task Force on Acid Precipitation and called for a comprehensive ten-year research program to identify causes of acid precipitation, evaluate its effects, and identify potential mitigation measures to reduce its adverse effects.

The National Acid Precipitation Assessment Program (NAPAP) operates through a set of ten Task Groups each with specific research responsibilities. The Emissions

*Although the information described in this paper has been funded by the United States Environmental Protection Agency under Assistance Agreement No. CR-80946101 to the University of Illinois and Subcontract No. 81-132 to E.H. Pechan & Associates, Inc., it has not been subjected to the Agency's peer and administrative review and therefore does not necessarily reflect the views of the Agency and no official endorsement should be inferred.

Strategy Integration Model (ESIM), discussed in this paper, is designed to provide support to the Assessments and Policy Analysis and the Man-Made Sources task groups relative to the integration of emissions data, control scenarios and costs, and atmospheric relationships.

The ESIM, described more fully in [14] , will be designed to allow expansion at a later date to include information from other assessment components, such as effects and economic damages, as appropriate quantitative data become available.

The ESIM will be a computerized system designed to permit policy analysts to examine issues related to pollutant species, emission sectors, geographic regions, control scenarios, and control costs. The major inputs to the ESIM will be information on emissions, cost and emission effects of possible alternative control policies, and information relating region and species-specific emissions in specified source regions to the deposition of target pollutants in specified receptor regions. The model will use a non-linear optimization technique to derive cost-effective solutions which meet user specified emissions and/or deposition targets. The model is designed to consider possible control alternatives on all major emitting sectors.

2. SYSTEM REQUIREMENTS

The requirements of the ESIM have been separated into two groups. The first group of requirements represents the minimum capabilities for the prototype model which are to be implemented and tested this year; the second group represents possible future extensions which may be required in later versions of the model, depending upon the outcomes of current and planned research activities.

The following characteristics are included within the scope of the prototype model to be implemented initially:

- Emissions and costs for source regions are to be included at the state level of geographic detail for specified years of data.
- Receptor regions are to include source regions as well as optional "sensitive areas." These will be specified by the system user.
- Sulfur dioxide, nitrogen oxides, primary sulfates, and volatile organic compounds are to be the emitted pollutant species included.
- Regional emission and/or deposition constraints will be accommodated for the four species above, plus other user defined intermediate and final transformation products, e.g., total wet sulfur.
- Sectors to be included in any given analysis will be user-specified. At a minimum, the prototype system will include information on electric utilities, industrial activities, residential and commercial space heating and transportation.
- Individual source-receptor relationship coefficients for each pollutant, source region, and receptor region will be accommodated. The model will be designed to accommodate simple "weighting" relationships as well as more sophisticated types of "transfer matrix" inputs such as the use of different linear coefficients for different relative levels of emission reduction.

In addition to these prototype capabilities, the model will be designed to permit possible future extensions in the following areas:

- Seasonal detail may be included as appropriate.
- Emissions and costs for sub-state regions may be accommodated for one or more economic sectors.
- Source-receptor relationships may be given a more sophisticated treatment; quantitative non-linear relationships are to be a part of this treatment.
- Uncertainty may be treated analytically within the model.
- Quantitative data may be included which relate deposition estimates to effects and damages if appropriate. If this path of model development is taken, the model will also be enhanced to include effects and/or damage measures within its objective functions and constraints.

3. ENERGY/ECONOMIC/EMISSIONS COMPONENTS

The magnitude of the analytic problem posed by the acid deposition issue is too great to allow the development of an entirely new modeling system with the limited time and resources available. As a result, the proposed treatment of energy, economic, and emissions components is designed to utilize as many analytic tools which are already available as possible.

Figure 1 identifies the various ESIM components along with the hierarchical approach used to analyze linkage concerns. These linkage questions are being addressed in detail in a separate report [15]. For the purposes of the ESIM design, however, it is important to note that analytic and data linkages are designed to move both down and within the levels of Figure 1. For example, this implies the assumption that the types of cost-effective strategies selected by ESIM (Level III) will not be so significant as to affect overall macro-economic variables (Level I). It is obvious that a major relaxation of this assumption would require that the entire problem at all three levels be solved within a general equilibrium framework -- a task which might be impossible to achieve.

4. SYSTEMS DESIGN

The overall conceptual operation of the model is illustrated in Figure 2. The major external inputs to the model are the regional emissions and costs data and the source-receptor relationship data. Also included, although not shown on this figure, are the user-specified inputs; these consist of deposition and/or other constraints.

The system is designed to be modular so that different sectoral models can be utilized as desired by the user. As such, it will operate in three stages:

- stage 1 - setup of emissions and cost files
- stage 2 - setup of source-receptor information
- stage 3 - operation of the ESIM itself.

The general structure of the system will include the following: (1) translators designed to convert results from other models into the required ESIM formats, (2) the set of summary files from the various scenarios examined with the individual contributing models, and (3) the integration model itself.

Each sector model will be run once for each of the policies to be included in the ESIM analysis; additional sector model runs would also be required for

FIGURE 1.

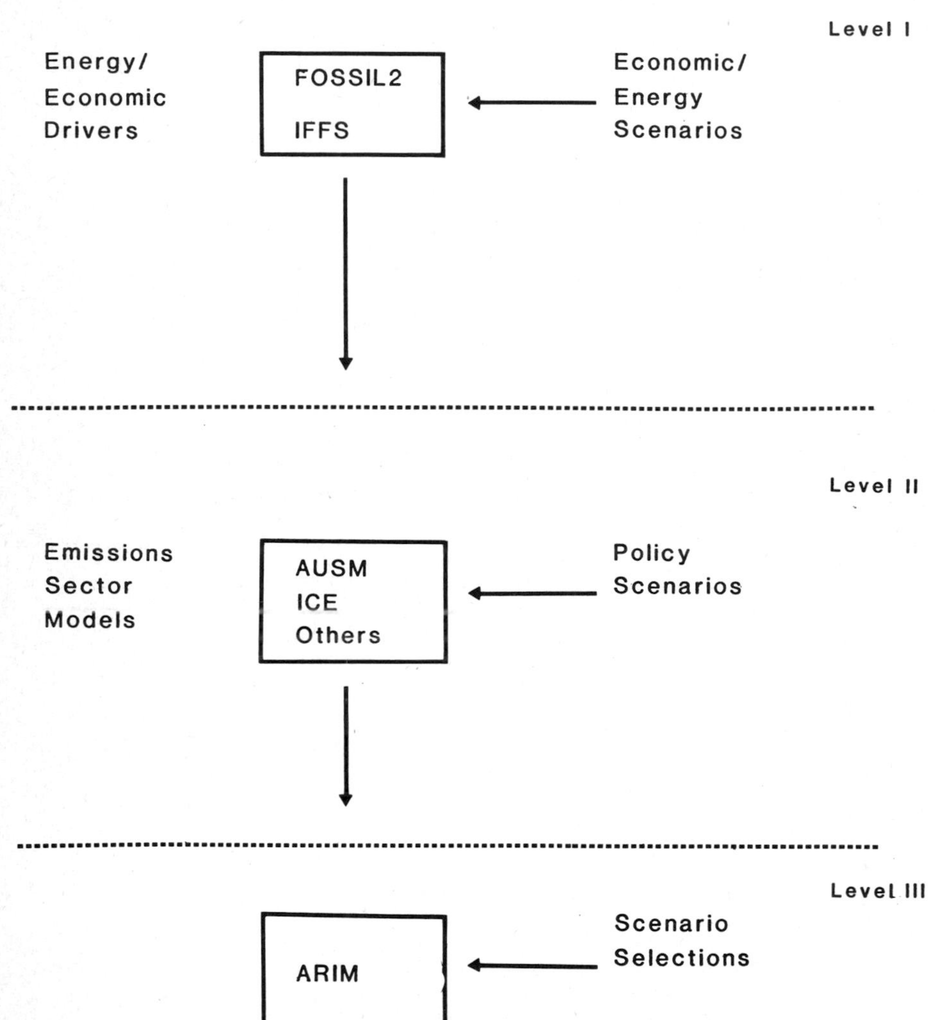
Energy/Economic/Emissions Components
Level I
Energy/
Economic
Drivers
FOSSIL2
IFFS
Economic/
Energy
Scenarios
Level II
Emissions
Sector
Models
AUSM
ICE
Others
Policy
Scenarios
Level III
ARIM
Scenario
Selections

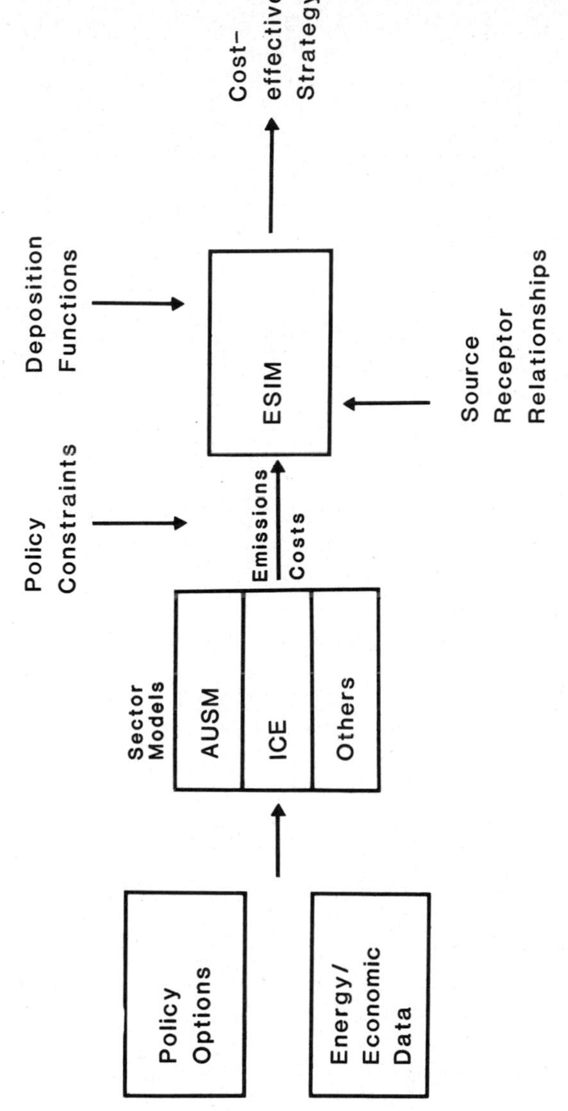
Control Strategies Assessment Structure Overview
Policy Options
Energy/ Economic Data
Sector Models
AUSM
ICE
Others
Emissions
Costs
Policy Constraints
Deposition Functions
ESIM
Source Receptor Relationships
Cost-effective Strategy

FIGURE 2.

alternative economic/energy assumptions. The outputs from each of these runs would then be saved. As the outputs would be relatively small, there should be no problem in saving the results from a large number of alternative scenario runs.

Several alternative models are being considered for inclusion in the ESIM. So far, these alternatives have only been examined with regard to those aspects associated with the mechanical integration of the model outputs within the ESIM framework. The inclusion of specific models does not represent an endorsement of their methodologies and/or results.

The models considered under each sector are listed along with literature references to current documentation:

- Electric Utilities

  The Advanced Utility Simulation Model ([1], [19])

  The National Coal Model/Coal and Electric Utilities Model ([2], [3], [8])

  The AIRCOST/FORECAST Models ([11], [12], [13])

- Industrial Sources

  The Industrial Combustion Emissions Model ([9], [17])

  Scoping models (discussed below)

- Other Emitting Sectors

  The Environmental Trends Analysis Model [5]

  The Strategic Environmental Assessment System ([10], [20])

  The Residuals Accounting Model [4]

  MOBILE2 and MOBILE 2.5 ([16], [18])

Information on source-receptor relationships are needed to permit the assessment of the relative significance of emissions from each source region on ultimate deposition values. "Transfer matrices" containing information from several long range transport models have been developed for earlier studies. These matrices could be easily adapted for use within the ESIM analysis framework. It is important to note, however, that most of the modeling work reflected in these transfer matrices has considered only sulfur emissions and deposition. Calibration and verification of the models has generally been limited to estimates of wet sulfur deposition and ambient sulfate at selected receptor sites.

An alternative to transfer matrices is the use of simple weighting schemes to consider some aspects of source receptor relationships. An example of the use of a simple weighting scheme might be to apply a single numerical weight to all sources of a particular pollutant species. Another approach would be to use source-receptor weightings associated with species and distance from source to receptor. In the prototype model, the importance of these assumptions to the model results can be determined by sensitivity analyses.

5. ANALYTIC APPROACH

The solution methodology to be applied in the prototype model is a modification of a solution technique designed to solve a variety of integer programming problems with many dichotomous variables. To reduce the computer time required to solve the model, a heuristic algorithm is employed.

The optimization problem is specified as:

$$\min \sum_{c,s} K_{c,s}(i)$$

subject to:

(1) Deposition constraints

$$\sum_{c,s} E_{c,s,p}(i) * t_{s,r,p} \leq D_{r,p} \quad \text{for all } r,p$$

(2) Emissions Constraints

$$\sum_{c} E_{c,s,p}(i) \leq L_{s,p} \quad \text{for all } s,p$$

with the following variables:

$K_{c,s}(i)$ = annualized cost of ith control alternative of source category c in region s

$E_{c,s,p}(i)$ = emissions at ith control alternative of pollutant p from source category c in region s

$t_{s,r,p}$ = transfer coefficient for pollutant p from source region s to receptor region r

$D_{r,p}$ = maximum deposition permitted of pollutant p in receptor region r

$L_{s,p}$ = maximum emissions permitted of pollutant p from source region s

where:

c = category of source

s = source region

r = receptor region

p = pollutant

A large number of control alternatives is permitted for each source category/source region combination.

The terminology used above is somewhat simplified in that it does not show the actual dichotomous variables. For example, consider the case of a source category "c" in source region "s" with five possible control alternatives. At any given time, only one of the five control scenario alternatives can be included in the current solution vector; therefore, the values for four of the dichotomous variables used to identify control alternatives "i" will be 0 and the value for one of the variables will be 1.

Another factor not shown above is the need to permit more than one emitted pollutant to simultaneously affect one or more of the deposition indicator variables. To simplify the presentation and discussion, it is assumed below that each emitted pollutant is also a deposition indicator; the actual model implementation will permit simultaneous effects.

A list of potential control alternatives is needed for each source modeled. A measure of both cost and emissions, specific to each source category/source region combination is associated with each control alternative.

The decision variables for this problem are the individual control alternatives selected for each source category/source region combination. The objective function to be minimized expresses the sum of the costs incurred by each source category in each source region. The explicit constraints of the model are these: (1) deposition targets for each receptor region/pollutant combination, and/or (2) emission constraints for each source region/pollutant combination. For a solution to satisfy the deposition constraint imposed in receptor region "r" for pollutant "p", the transfer coefficient for pollutant "p" from source region "s" into receptor region "r" is first summed over all source categories and regions. Next, the sum is multiplied by the amount of emissions that remain uncontrolled at each source category/source receptor combination. The resultant product must fall below the deposition target, D, to satisfy the deposition constraint imposed in receptor region "r" for pollutant "p".

In the prototype model, the assumption is made that any reduction in the emissions of an individual source category/source receptor combination causes a linear reduction in the deposition realized in each receptor region, although it is clear that this assumption can easily be relaxed.

5.1 Analytic Basis for the Solution Technique

The solution algorithm is derived from that of Senju and Toyoda [7] and is here referred to as the S-T method. Our technique takes advantage of the fact that only one control alternative is permitted at any given time for each source category/source region combination.

This modified S-T solution technique employs the use of an effective gradient, calculated for each source category/source region combination having the ability to employ a more stringent emissions control alternative. The technique measures the relative efficiency of implementing a more stringent control alternative in terms of the required deposition and/or emissions constraints.

The modified S-T method was selected for initial implementation in the ESIM for a number of reasons. The method is widely known and has been independently determined to be an effective and efficient technique [21]. In addition, the method has been successfully applied to a number of problems in the past, including similar environmental problems. The AIRMOD model, developed to estimate regional cost-effective solutions to ambient air quality problems [6] also used the S-T method and has been used by a number of researchers. Finally, the S-T method was used successfully in an earlier unpublished scoping study which attempted to compute cost-effective solutions for a single pollutant acidic deposition problem.

Although the modified S-T method is being implemented in the prototype ESIM model, additional literature reviews are being conducted to identify alternative solution methods which might have advantages over the S-T method.

5.2 Beginning the Solution

The calculation begins with an infeasible solution (i.e., that of no controls) and moves iteratively to bring the tentative solution into feasibility in terms of the deposition and emissions constraints.

Before beginning the solution technique, the problem is "initialized" by deleting any control alternatives which are clearly inferior. Control alternative "j" is considered to be clearly inferior to alternative "i" (and is deleted from the problem) if all of the following conditions hold: (1) the annualized cost for alternative "j" is at least equal to that for alternative "i", (2) corresponding emission figures from emissions vector $E_{c,s,p}$ from alternative "j" are never less than those from alternative "i", and (3) for at least one pollutant, the corresponding emissions from alternative "j" are numerically greater than those from alternative "i". In other words, alternatives are discarded that both result in additional emissions of at least one pollutant and do not represent any cost savings.

For the initial control alternative selected (i.e., the base case), the control alternative indicator "i" is set equal to the first level.

5.3 Selecting the Next Control Level

Once initialization is complete, the analysis proceeds step by step. At each step, one source category in one source region is moved to a more stringent control alternative and the solution moves closer to meeting deposition and/or emissions constraints. At any given step in the analysis, then, each source category in each source region is at a specified level of control "i".

The modified S-T method computes a benefit value "B" for each possible control alternative "j" in which (1) no member of the emissions vector $E_{c,s,p}$ has a value greater than its value at its current level "i", and (2) at least one member of $E_{c,s,p}$ has a value lower than its value at level "i". By virtue of the initialization procedure, each control alternative which meets criteria (1) and (2) above must have a higher cost value $K_{c,s}$ than control alternative "i".

The benefits value "B" is a "figure of merit," which represents the reduction in the infeasibility of each successive control alternative. As it will generally be more costly to achieve extra emissions reductions as the emissions level is reduced, the benefit "B", at any step, is weighted by the remaining amount of deposition or emissions reduction which must be achieved.

Deposition benefits are computed for each receptor region and pollutant, and emissions reduction benefits are computed for each source region and pollutant. The total benefit "B" of an alternative is the sum of all of the non-zero terms. A weighting factor is computed and applied to each term in the sum. This weighting factor is computed as the difference between the deposition at the current stage "m" of the problem (defined as $C_{r,p}(m)$), and the maximum deposition permitted, i.e., $D_{r,p}$. If the difference

$$C_{r,p}(m) - D_{r,p}$$

is less than or equal to zero (i.e., the deposition limit for a particular pollutant at a particular receptor region is already being achieved), this receptor region/pollutant combination does not contribute to the benefit term, and its weight is set equal to zero. If the difference is positive, it is multiplied by the incremental reduction that would be achieved by moving from control alternative "i" to control alternative "j", i.e.,

$$(E_{c,s,p}(i) - E_{c,s,p}(j)) \quad * \quad t_{s,r,p}$$

The product of these terms is added into the total benefit for the alternative being considered. A similar procedure is followed for each emissions constraint.

For those receptor region/pollutant and/or source region/pollutant combinations that are unconstrained, the deposition and/or emissions targets are set to an extremely high value so that these combinations do not figure into the problem solution.

Once the total value of B is computed, the benefit to cost ratio B/K is computed. After a ratio is calculated for each control alternative, the alternative with the highest B/K value is selected for inclusion in the problem solution.

5.4 Termination

Each time a control alternative is selected using the above procedure, the current deposition and emission values are recalculated and checked against the constraints. If all values are within the permitted levels, the problem is solved and the calculation procedure terminates. If one or more additional constraints are still unmet, the program attempts to reduce deposition and/or emissions by repeating the procedure discussed above. If at any stage no incrementally more stringent control alternatives exist or no alternative has a nonzero benefit value, the problem is considered to be infeasible and the program stops.

REFERENCES

[1] AUSM, "AUSM - Analytical Documentation," Vols. I, II, III, Assembled by the EPA Industrial and Environmental Research Laboratory, Prepared by members of the Universities Research Group on Energy, March 1983.

[2] Federal Energy Administration, ICF, Inc., "The National Coal Model: Description and Documentation," Contract CO-05-50198-00, October 1976.

[3] ICF, Inc., "Coal and Electric Utilities Model Documentation," May 1980.

[4] McBrien, S.V. and Jones, L.R., "Scenario Reference Manual for the Residuals Accounting Model," MTR-81W180, EPA Contract 68-02-3680, Project 1074A, Department W-51, September 1981.

[5] Pechan, E. and Graves, K., "The Environmental Trends Analysis Model: Technical Documentation," Prepared for Belinda Briggs, Office of Policy, Planning and Analysis, U.S. Department of Energy, April 1983.

[6] Pechan, E. and Strathmeyer, S., "A Computer-Assisted System for Developing Regional Cost-Effective Air Pollution Control Strategies (AIRMOD)," Prepared for the Office of Planning and Evaluation, U.S. Environmental Protection Agency, July 1980.

[7] Senju, S. and Toyoda, Y., "An Approach to Linear Programming with 0-1 Variables," Management Science, Vol. 15, No. 4, December 1968.

[8] U.S. Department of Energy, Energy Information Administration, "National Coal Model: Executive Summary," Prepared by the Office of Coal, Nuclear, Electric and Alternate Fuels, April 1982.

[9] U.S. Department of Energy, Energy and Environmental Analysis, Inc., "Industrial Fuel Choice Analysis Model Primary Model Documentation," Prepared for Office of Policy and Evaluation, January 1980.

[10] U.S. Department of Energy, The Mitre Corporation, "SEAS: Introduction to the Strategic Environmental Assessment System," MTR-80W115, Prepared for the Assistant Secretary for Environment, Office of Environmental Assessment, Regulatory Analysis Division, Contract DE-AC02-79EVI0092, October 1980.

[11] U.S. Environmental Protection Agency, E.H. Pechan & Associates, Inc., "AIRCOST Model: Preliminary User Documentation," Draft, Prepared for Paul Schwengels, Acid Deposition Research Staff, December 1982.

[12] U.S. Environmental Protection Agency, E.H. Pechan & Associates, Inc., "FORECAST Model: Technical Documentation," Prepared for Paul Schwengels, Acid Deposition Assessment Staff, March 1983.

[13] U.S. Environmental Protection Agency, E.H. Pechan & Associates, Inc., "AIRCOST Model: Technical Documentation," Prepared for Paul Schwengels, Acid Deposition Assessment Staff, April 1983.

[14] U.S. Environmental Protection Agency, E.H. Pechan & Associates, Inc., "Emissions Strategy Integration Model (ESIM): Conceptual and Preliminary Design Document," Prepared for Paul Schwengels, Acid Deposition Assessment Staff, May 1983.

[15] U.S. Environmental Protection Agency, E.H. Pechan & Associates, Inc., "Emissions Strategy Model Linkages: Preliminary Design Document," Under preparation for Paul Schwengels, Acid Deposition Assessment Staff, July 1983.

[16] U.S. Environmental Protection Agency Emission Control Technology Division, "Modifications to MOBILE2 Which Were Used by EPA to Respond to Congressional Inquiries on the Clean Air Act," May 1982.

[17] U.S. Environmental Protection Agency, Energy and Environmental Analysis, Inc., "Development of an Industrial Combustion Emissions (ICE) Model for Acid Rain Analysis: Draft Task I Report," EPA Contract 68-02-3930, February 1983.

[18] U.S. Environmental Protection Agency Motor Vehicle Emission Lab, "User's Guide to Mobile2 (Mobil Source Emissions Model)," February 1981.

[19] U.S. Environmental Protection Agency, Universities Research Group on Energy (URGE) Project Office, "The Advanced Utility Simulation Model: System Design," April 1983.

[20] Wilson, M.L. and Jones, L.R., "The Status of the Strategic Environmental Assessment System," MTR-80W206, EPA 68-01-5064, September 1980.

[21] Zanakis, S.H., "Heuristic 0-1 Linear Programming: An Experimental Comparison of Three Methods," <u>Management Science</u>, Vol. 24, No. 1, September 1977.

ENERGY USE

Analytic Techniques for Energy Planning
B. Lev, F.H. Murphy, J.A. Bloom & A.S. Gleit (Editors)

RESIDENTIAL ENERGY USE AND IMPROVED BUILDING THERMAL EFFICIENCY: AN ECONOMETRIC ANALYSIS*

R.J. Moe
R.C. Adams

Pacific Northwest Laboratory
P.O. Box 999
Richland, Washington 99352

This paper presents an econometric analysis of residential space conditioning energy consumption. Seasonal demand functions for space conditioning energy were estimated using a sample of single-family residences. Explanatory variables included average and marginal prices, income and other economic and demographic variables, and the shell thermal efficiency. The shell thermal efficiency of each residence was calculated using a two-step procedure. In the first, the shell efficiency for selected homes was computed using DOE II, a thermal simulation program. An equation summarizing DOE II was statistically estimated using these results. In the second step, the shell thermal efficiency was calculated for all residences in the sample using the estimated summary equation.

1. INTRODUCTION

In recent years, a large number of subsidized residential energy conservation programs have been instituted in the United States. Such programs are typically sponsored by public or private utilities or federal power marketing agencies, such as the Bonneville Power Administration, and focus on reducing the energy consumed for home heating by increasing the thermal efficiency of the residential building shell. These programs typically take the form of free energy audits of residences; free or subsidized installation of storm windows, insulation, hot water blankets, and other conservation measures; and low-interest loans for consumers who install such measures on their own.

The savings in energy used for space conditioning (heating, cooling) that result from such programs are uncertain, as are the increases in consumer welfare of those who participate. To date, only engineering methods have been used to assess these issues. In such an assessment, a thermal analysis program such as DOE 2.1 is used to simulate annual energy consumption for a residence, both with and without a particular conservation measure (e.g., storm windows). The difference in annual energy consumption between the two cases is attributed to the conservation measure, since all other

* Work supported by Bonneville Power Administration under a Related Services Agreement with the U.S. Department of Energy under Contract DE-AC06-76-RLO 1830

characteristics of both the residence and the residents, including consumer behavior, are held constant in the analysis. Multiplication of these per-household savings by the number of residences which will have the corresponding conservation measure installed under the program's sponsorship provides an estimate of the aggregate annual energy savings generated by the program. The benefits to an individual consumer of having the measure installed are then calculated by multiplying the estimated energy savings per household by the price of energy.

As Khazzoom [5] has shown in a study of household applicance efficiency standards, such an engineering analysis is by no means complete because it explicitly holds consumer use patterns constant. In fact, increases in the energy efficiency or productivity of an energy-using device have an economic effect which serves to increase energy use; therefore, an efficiency increase of a given percentage (defined in engineering terms) will not necessarily result in an equal percentage reduction in energy consumption by the device. Similar results were found by Burright and Enns [1] in a study of automobile gasoline usage and by Warren-Boulton [13] in an analysis of factor productivity.

Put in terms of household space-conditioning energy consumption, each of these researchers found that an increase in a building's thermal efficiency (i.e., its ability to prevent heat generated within the building from escaping outside) lowers the price the consumer must pay to maintain a particular internal comfort level (temperature). The reduction in the price of comfort induces the consumer to increase his consumption of comfort; i.e., in the winter, the resident sets the thermostat at a higher level. The higher thermostat setting causes energy consumption to be greater than that predicted by the engineering analysis, which held the thermostat setting fixed after the increase in the building's thermal efficiency.

These findings have several important implications. First, engineering estimates of the per-household or aggregate energy savings associated with any particular conservation measure are biased upwards, since they do not account for the price-induced energy consumption increase. Second, related to this, the corresponding estimates of consumer benefits are biased downwards, since they do not account for the increases in consumer welfare that result when a resident moves down his demand curve to a lower-price, higher-quantity position. Finally, econometric studies of residential energy demand which do not include variables representing a residence's thermal shell efficiency will produce biased estimates of own- and cross-price demand elasticities because of a left-out variable; in such a case, the price elasticities incorrectly contain the estimated effect on consumption of the thermal shell efficiency.

In this paper, the analytical framework of Khazzoom, Burright and Enns, and Warren-Boulton is applied to the case of increases in residential building thermal efficiency. Econometric estimates of the effects of increases in thermal efficiency on winter space heating electricity consumption in the Pacific Northwest are provided, as are estimates of the benefits to consumers of such increases.

2. THEORETICAL FRAMEWORK

The theoretical framework for analysis of thermal shell efficiency increases begins with household production theory, which has a rich history in the economics literature (Lancaster [6], Muth [10], Muellbauer [9]). Consumers are assumed to derive utility (satisfaction) from three goods: space conditioning (H), other residential services (L), and a composite commodity (Z) that represents all other goods and services. The utility function is assumed to be homothetic and separable between the two residential services and the composite commodity. Households produce space conditioning by combining energy (Q), the building's thermal efficiency (T), and a set of environmental variables (N). Other residential services are produced by the household, using energy (E), the stock of appliances and the efficiency of this stock (A), and a second set of environmental variables (V). Summarizing,

$$U = U(H,L,Z) \quad (1)$$
$$H = H(Q,T,N) \quad (2)$$
$$L = L(E,A,V) \quad (3)$$

In the long run, the consumer maximizes utility subject to the prices of Q, T, N, E, A, V and his income, which together form the budget constraint; from this maximization, the long-run demand functions for Q, T, E, and A are derived[1]:

$$Q = Q^*(P_Q,P_T,P_E,P_A,P_Z,N,V,Y) \quad (4)$$
$$T = T^*(P_Q,P_T,P_E,P_A,P_Z,N,V,Y) \quad (5)$$
$$E = E^*(P_Q,P_T,P_E,P_A,P_Z,N,V,Y) \quad (6)$$
$$A = A^*(P_Q,P_T,P_E,P_A,P_Z,N,V,Y) \quad (7)$$

where "*" denotes the long-run demand function, P_i denotes the price of commodity i, and Y is income. Note that in the long run the thermal efficiency (T) does not determine energy consumption for space conditioning (Q); instead, both are choice variables, jointly determined by prices, environmental variables, and income.

In the short run, however, both the thermal efficiency of a residence (T) and the appliance stock (A) are considered fixed; the consumer faces a utility maximization problem similar to that in the long run, with the exception of these two additional constraints. From this modified utility-maximization process, the short-run demand functions for Q and E are derived:

$$Q = Q^{**}(P_Q,P_E,P_Z,\overline{T},\overline{A},N,V,Y) \quad (8)$$

$$E = E^{**}(P_Q,P_E,P_Z,\overline{T},\overline{A},N,V,Y) \quad (9)$$

where "**" denotes short-run demand functions, and $\overline{T}$, $\overline{A}$ are the fixed, parametric values of the thermal efficiency and appliance stock variables. In the short run, energy consumption for space conditioning is a function of the thermal shell efficiency of the residence, which is under the influence of policymakers.[2]

Using equation (8) one could estimate the relationship between household energy use for space conditioning and the price of energy, the efficiency of the residence's shell, and other factors. However, equation (8) does not contain any information about the nature of this relationship; e.g., that the effects of price and thermal efficiency are somehow linked as suggested in the introduction. Information of this sort can be discovered, however, by investigating the production relationship between residential space conditioning services (H), and energy use for space conditioning (Q), thermal efficiency (T), and the environment (N).

What can be said about the relationship among the variables given in equation (2)? First, one could reasonably assume that the relationship is multiplicative:

$$H = G(Q,T) \cdot M(N) \tag{10}$$

where "•" denotes multiplication; G( ) defines energy measured in efficiency units; and M( ), the energy required to obtain a particular comfort level imposed by the environment. The appropriate form of G( ) would also seem to be multiplicative between energy use in physical units and thermal efficiency: 1) if thermal efficiency increased one percent, one would expect a one-percent increase in energy measured in efficiency units, when energy in physical units is held constant; 2) holding thermal efficiency constant, one would expect a one-percent increase in energy measured in physical units to be associated with a one-percent increase in energy measured in efficiency units. Thus, defining F as energy measured in efficiency units,

$$F = G(Q,T) = Q \cdot T \tag{11}$$

In defining P_F, the price of energy in efficiency units, an obvious constraint is that the expenditure on energy for space conditioning be identical whether it is calculated in physical or efficiency units; i.e.,

$$P_F F = P_Q Q \tag{12}$$

which gives

$$P_F = \frac{P_Q Q}{F} = \frac{P_Q}{T} \tag{13}$$

When the short-run utility-maximization process described above is performed in terms of space-conditioning energy use measured in efficiency units, the thermal efficiency of the residence no longer determines energy use; energy use in efficiency units is instead determined by the space-conditioning energy price measured in efficiency units (P_F), the appliance energy price measured in efficiency units (P_V), and P_Z, N, V, A, and Y:

$$F = F^{**}(P_F, P_V, P_Z, N, V, A, Y) \tag{14}$$

F** is the short-run demand function for space-conditioning energy measured in efficiency units. Equation (14) can be collapsed into:

$$F = F^{**}(P_F, X) \tag{15}$$

where X represents P_V, P_Z, N, V, A, and Y.

Constraints on the estimated elasticities of space-conditioning energy demand can be derived using equation (15) in the following manner. First, converting to physical units,

$$Q^{**}(P_F, X, T) = \frac{F^{**}(P_F, X)}{T} \tag{16}$$

is the short-run demand for space-conditioning energy in physical units associated with equation (15). Taking derivatives with respect to T,

$$\frac{\partial Q^{**}}{\partial T} = \frac{-F^{**}(P_F, X)}{T^2} + \frac{1}{T}\frac{\partial F^{**}}{\partial P_F}\frac{\partial P_F}{\partial T} \tag{17}$$

But $\frac{\partial P_F}{\partial T} = \frac{-P_Q}{T^2}$ by equation (13),

$$\text{so} \quad \frac{\partial Q^{**}}{\partial T} = \frac{-F^{**}}{T^2} - \frac{1}{T^2}\frac{\partial F^{**}}{\partial P_F}\frac{P_Q}{T} \tag{18}$$

which, after using equations (11) and (13), yields:

$$\frac{\partial Q^{**}}{\partial T} = -\frac{Q}{T}\left\{1 + \frac{\partial F^{**}}{\partial P_F}\frac{P_F}{F^{**}}\right\} \tag{19}$$

$$\text{or} \quad \varepsilon_{QT} = -1 - \varepsilon_{FP} \tag{20}$$

where ε_{ij} denotes the elasticity of i with respect to j. Equation (20) states that the elasticity of space-conditioning energy demand measured in physical units with respect to thermal efficiency is equal to the sum of negative unity and the efficiency-unit demand price elasticity. But this price elasticity is independent of units; i.e., the price elasticity measured in physical units is identical to the price elasticity measured in efficiency units.[3] Thus, we have:

$$\varepsilon_{QT} = -1 - \varepsilon_{QP} \tag{21}$$

$$\text{or} \quad \varepsilon_{QT} + \varepsilon_{QP} = -1 \tag{22}$$

Measured in physical units, the sum of the space-conditioning energy demand price elasticity and the space-conditioning energy thermal efficiency elasticity must equal negative unity.

This result is appealing, given the intuitive argument presented in the first section. When the thermal efficiency of a home increases B percent, B percent fewer Btu's are required to heat the home to maintain a constant comfort level. Holding internal comfort constant, energy use for space conditioning falls B percent. Thus, B percent fewer dollars are required to heat the home with a constant level of internal comfort (or energy measured in efficiency units). The price of internal comfort has dropped B percent, as has the price of energy measured in efficiency units (the two are synonomous given constant environmental factors).

This B percent reduction in the price of internal comfort causes a $B \cdot |\varepsilon_{FP}|$ percent increase in consumption of internal comfort, where $|\varepsilon_{FP}|$ is the (absolute value) price elasticity of internal comfort demand (or price elasticity of efficiency-unit energy for space-conditioning demand). This causes energy consumption to increase $B \cdot \varepsilon_{FP}$ percent. Adding together the two change (which have different signs) in energy consumption, one obtains the net percentage change in energy use for space conditioning given a B percent change in thermal efficiency:

$$\varepsilon_{QT} \cdot B = -B - B \cdot \varepsilon_{FP} \quad (23)$$

or $$\varepsilon_{QT} = -1 - \varepsilon_{FP} \quad (24)$$

Thus, a B percent increase in the thermal efficiency of a shell leads to a reduction in energy use for space conditioning of less than B percent.

The benefits to consumers of this B percent thermal improvement can be analyzed in a similar framework using the concept of consumer surplus. Consumer surplus for an individual unit of a purchased commodity is defined as the difference between what a consumer was willing to pay to obtain that unit and what he in fact did play. Summed across all of the units consumed of a specific commodity, consumer surplus represents the gains to a consumer of being permitted to purchase the commodity in question at the prevailing price. When the price falls exogenously, consumer surplus increases; the difference in consumer surplus calculated at the two prices measures the gain accruing to the consumer due to the price change.

It was shown above that the B percent thermal-efficiency increase could be treated as a B percent reduction in the price of internal comfort (energy measured in efficiency units). In Figure 1, the price of internal comfort falls from P_0 to P_1, causing an increase in consumption from Q_0 to Q_1. The increase in consumer surplus is equal to the sum of areas A and B. An engineering analysis of consumer benefits associated with thermal improvements would count only area A, since internal comfort would be held constant at Q_0.

Using standard formulas for computing changes in consumer surplus (see Halvorsen and Ruby [4]), the increase in consumer surplus measured in terms of internal comfort is given by:

$$\Delta CS = BP_0Q_0 \ (1 - 0.5\varepsilon B) \quad (25)$$

where ΔCS represents the change in consumer surplus, B is in decimal units (one percent is 0.01), P_0 and Q_0 are in units of internal comfort (or efficiency-unit energy) and ε is the internal-comfort price elasticity of demand (equal to the efficiency-unit energy price elasticity of demand as well as the physical-unit energy price elasticity of demand). Converting to physical units of energy,

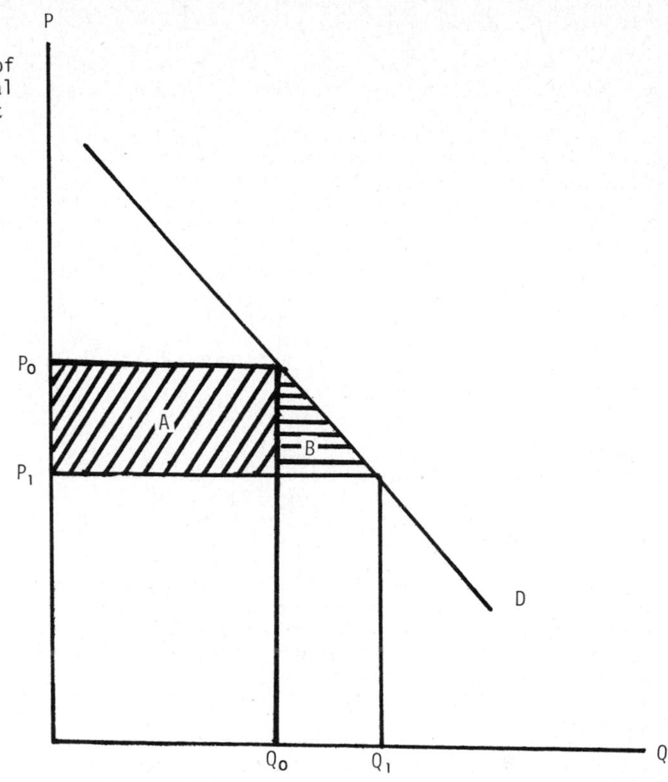

FIGURE 1. Consumer Surplus

equation (25) can be rewritten:

$$\Delta CS = Q_0 P_0 B \ (1 - 0.5 \ \varepsilon_{QP} B) \qquad (26)$$

where Q_0 and P_0 are the initial quantity and price of space-conditioning energy measured in physical units, and ε_{QP} is again the price elasticity of space-conditioning energy demand measured in physical units. Since ε_{QP} is negative, the engineering estimate of consumer benefits ($Q_0 P_0 B$) underestimates true consumer benefits by $Q_0 P_0 B \cdot 0.5 \, |\varepsilon_{QP}| \, B$, or by $100 \cdot 0.5 \, |\varepsilon_{QP}| \, B$ percent. Also, the larger ε_{QP} is, in absolute value (i.e., the closer it is to negative unity), the greater are the benefits of a given thermal improvement. In such a case, given equation (22), the energy savings are smaller than if ε_{QP} were smaller in absolute value.

3. IMPLEMENTATION OF THEORY

A winter space-conditioning electricity demand function was estimated for Pacific Northwest single-family residences using the theory presented in Section 2. Implementation of the theory is discussed in the present section.

The data used in the analysis was taken from the 1979 Pacific Northwest Residential Survey, prepared by Elrick and Lavidge, Inc. [2]. Among other information, the Survey contained data for 1437 electrically heated single-family residences in the Northwest. Information on monthly energy consumption and expenditure by fuel type, building characteristics, appliances and climate was collected from each resident.

The thermal efficiency of each building in the survey was not available (in fact, this is an unobservable variable). To fill this void, 150 homes from the sample were randomly selected. The physical space-conditioning energy requirements of each of these residences were simulated using the thermal analysis program DOE 2.1. The simulated energy requirements varied from one residence to the next because of variations in: square footage of living area; climate; wall, ceiling, and floor insulation; number of windows, storm windows, doors, and storm doors; and the amount of caulking, weatherstripping, and plastic covering. The DOE 2.1-predicted energy requirements of the 150 residences were then regressed on the physical characteristics of the homes to obtain the DOE 2.1 summary thermal equation presented in Table 1, which was used in place of DOE 2.1 to calculate the predicted DOE 2.1 energy requirements of all 1437 residences in the sample. The thermal efficiency of each residence, T, was then defined as square footage of living area divided by the predicted DOE 2.1 energy requirements.

Electricity use for heating is likewise not included in the sample; only total monthly electricity consumption data is available. To account for electricity use by appliances, an appliance electricity-use index was constructed using information on the appliances present in each residence. Weights for the index were taken from a study performed using the same data base (Scanlon and Hofferd [11]).

Because of declining block rate structures, the marginal price of electricity is not typically equal to the average price. In the Northwest survey, only average prices were available. However, as Taylor [12], Halvorsen [3], and others have shown, the appropriate price to include in estimation of an electricity demand equation is the marginal price.[4]

This study employed a unique technique to overcome this problem. An average price equation of the form

$$\log P_a = a + b \log Q + c\, 1/Q + d(\log Q \cdot STATE1) + e(\log Q \cdot STATE2) + f(\log Q \cdot PUBLIC) + gX + U \quad (27)$$

was estimated using two-stage least squares, where a, b, c, d, e, and f are estimated coefficients; g is a vector of coefficients; "log" denotes natural logarithm; P_a, average winter electricity price; Q, winter electricity consumption; STATE1 and STATE2 are dummy variables for the state of residence; PUBLIC, a dummy variable for type of utility; X, a set of other explanatory variables; and U, the error term. Assuming a continuous price schedule,

$$P_a Q = \int_{q=0}^{q=Q} P_m dq \quad (28)$$

where P_m is the marginal price. Substituting (27) into (28) and differentiating both sides with respect to Q yields:

$$P_m = P_a \{1 + b - c/Q + d\ STATE1 + e\ STATE2 + f\ PUBLIC\} \quad (29)$$

Equation (29) was used to calculate the marginal price for each observation in the sample for inclusion in the electricity demand equation.

A number of functional forms were analyzed in this study; the final equations were estimated using a form first presented by Mount, Chapman, and Tyrell [8], in which the log of the dependent variable is regressed on the logs and reciprocals of the independent variables. In demand analysis, this form produces variable elasticity estimates; i.e., estimates of price, income and other elasticities that vary according to the value of the corresponding variable (price, income, etc.). In the equation

$$\log Q = a + b \log P_m + c\, 1/P_m + + + \quad (30)$$

where + + + represents the other independent variables in the equation, the price elasticity using the MCT functional form is equal to $b - c/P_m$.

In the equation

$$\log Q = a + b \log P_m + c\, 1/P_m + d \log T + e\, 1/T + + \quad (31)$$

the price elasticity (ε_{QP}) is equal to b - c/P_m, while the thermal efficiency elasticity (ε_{QT}) is equal to d - e/T. We know from equation (22) that

$$b - c/P_m + d - e/T = -1 \tag{32}$$

$$\text{or} \quad d = -1 - b + c/P_m + e/T \tag{33}$$

This constraint was imposed in the estimation by substitution; i.e., d was replaced in equation (31) by the right-hand side of (33), yielding the estimating equation

$$(\log Q + \log T) = a + b\ (\log P_m - \log T) + c\ (1 + \log T)/P_m$$
$$+ e\ (1 + \log T)/T + + + \tag{34}$$

and elasticities

$$\varepsilon_{QP} = b - c/P_m \tag{35}$$

$$\varepsilon_{QT} = -1 - b + c/P_m \tag{36}$$

Notice that the expression for ε_{QT} does not involve the coefficient e or the value of T, but varies only according to price.

Finally, to account for the simultaneity among price and quantity which appears because of the use of rate schedules instead of a single price, two-stage least squares was employed in order to obtain consistent estimates of the coefficients in equation (34). Since the thermal efficiency of a residence is also simultaneously determined in the long run with both price and quantity, a third equation explaining T was added to the price-quantity system.

4. STATISTICAL RESULTS

The estimated winter space-heating electricity demand equation is presented in Table 2. The auxiliary price and thermal efficiency equations are available from the author. Only one coefficient in the equation, on the reciprocal of income, is not statistically significant from zero at the five-percent level; signs are as expected; and the overall fit of the equation is reasonable for a cross-section sample.

In Table 3, estimates of the thermal efficiency elasticity are presented for the minimum, mean, and maximum sample prices within 95 percent confidence intervals. For the mean price, the point estimate of the elasticity is -0.546: a one-percent increase in thermal efficiency causes a 0.546 percent reduction in winter space-conditioning electricity consumption. At the mean and all prices at least as great as the mean, all estimates of the elasticity are negative but significantly different from negative one. Thus, this equation supports the hypothesis that the percentage reduction in space-conditioning energy use is less than the associated percentage

Table 1. Estimated DOE 2.1 Summary Thermal Equation

```
LDOEII = -4.95542 + 0.00051 GAREA
         (-3.3669)  (2.4906)

         +0.00045 SPACH + 1.70335 LHDD
         (9.5088)         (9.7867)


         -0.00122 PSDAREA - 0.00109 PSGAREA
         (-2.1663)          (-2.0246)

         -0.0000026 RINACTIC - 0.000106 RINACT2W
         (-2.3269)             (-11.4299)

         -0.21451 FOUNDBAS - 0.10767 CAKSOM
         (-4.3109)           (-1.7911)

         -0.08036 WSTALL
         (-1.7548)
```

t - statistics in ( )

R^2 = 0.7287 $\bar{R}^2$ = 0.7092 R^2 (physical units) = 0.7230

$\bar{R}^2$ (physical units) = 0.7031 DF = 139

Key to Regression Equation

LDOEII	=	LOG of output from DOE 2.1 simulations (kwh/year)
GAREA	=	Square feet of glass area
SPACH	=	Square feet of heated living space
LHDD	=	LOG of heating degree days, 65° base
PSDAREA	=	Percentage of doors with storm doors
PSGAREA	=	Percentage of glass area with storm windows
RINACT3W	=	RWALLALL * CALHDD
RWALLALL	=	dummy = 1 if all walls insulated
CAKSOM	=	dummy = 1 if caulking on some walls
FOUNDBAS	=	1 if foundation is basement
RINACT1C	=	RCEIL * SPACH
WSTALL	=	dummy = 1 if weatherstripping on all windows/doors
RCEIL	=	Ceiling R-value
CALHDD	=	Heating degree days, 65° base

TABLE 2. Pacific Northwest Winter Space Heating Electricity Demand Equation

$$\mathrm{Log(KWH)} + \mathrm{Log(T)} = \underset{(8.533)}{-8.199} - \underset{(0.041)}{0.439}\ \mathrm{Log}(P_m)$$

$$+\underset{(0.00011)}{0.00028}\ (\mathrm{Log(T)} + 1)/P_m$$

$$+\underset{(0.056)}{0.111}\ \mathrm{Log(Y)} + \underset{(518.05)}{328.23}\ 1/\mathrm{Y}$$

$$-\underset{(0.963)}{2.762}\ \mathrm{Log(HDD)} - \underset{(865.14)}{2718.06}\ 1/\mathrm{HDD}$$

$$+\underset{(0.292)}{2.383}\ \mathrm{Log(APP)} + \underset{(1402.55)}{4474.94}\ 1/\mathrm{APP}$$

$$-\underset{(0.350)}{0.820}\ \mathrm{Log(AGE)} - \underset{(14.339)}{29.086}\ 1/\mathrm{AGE}$$

$$+\underset{(0.037)}{0.325}\ \mathrm{Log(NUMBER)} + \underset{(0.00007)}{0.00031}\ 1/\mathrm{NUMBER}$$

$\bar{R}^2 = 0.3913$ D.F. = 1424

Asymptotic Standard Errors in ( ).

Key

KWH = winter (October-April) electricity consumption

T = thermal efficiency index

P_m = marginal price of electricity, \$/kwh

Y = annual gross income, \$

HDD = heating degree days, 65° base

APP = appliance electricity use index

AGE = age in years of head of household

NUMBER = rumber of residents

increase in thermal shell efficiency.

For the mean sample marginal price and mean sample quantity of winter electricity consumption, the increase in consumer surplus resulting from a ten-percent increase in thermal efficiency was calculated using equation (25).

Table 3. Estimates of Winter Space Heating Electricity Demand Thermal Efficiency Elasticity[a]

	Lower Bound[b]	Point Estimate	Upper Bound[c]
Evaluated at Minimum Sample Price	0.482	0.400	0.318
Evaluated at Mean Sample Price	-0.464	-0.546	-0.628
Evaluated at Maximum Sample Price	-0.471	-0.553	-0.635

(a) Defined as $\hat{\varepsilon}_{QT} = -1 + 0.439 + 0.00028/P_m = -0.561 + 0.00028/P_m$

(b) Bounds of 95 percent confidence interval, defined as $\hat{\varepsilon}_{QT} \pm 1.96\ \hat{s}$, where $\hat{\varepsilon}_{QT}$ is the point estimate for a given P_m, and $\hat{s}$ is the corresponding standard error of $\hat{\varepsilon}_{QT}$.

Here, B is equal to 0.1. The estimated increase in consumer surplus per household was $21.23 per winter. If the second half of equation (25) had been ignored, as would occur in an engineering calculation of per-household benefits, this estimate would fall 2.3 percent to $20.74 per winter.

5. SUMMARY

This paper considered the following energy policy question: if the thermal efficiency of a home is increased by a given percentage because of installation of a conservation measure, by what percentage will energy use for space conditioning decrease? It was found that the thermal efficiency increase creates economic incentives for consumers to increase their consumption of internal comfort or space conditioning. Thus, space-conditioning energy use falls by a smaller percentage than the thermal efficiency increase.

This theoretical framework was applied to a sample of some 1437 Pacific Northwest single-family residences to estimate a winter space-heating electricity demand equation. Several unique features of the implementation were: 1) inclusion of a variable representing the thermal shell efficiency of each residence as an explanatory variable in the equation; 2) calculation of the marginal price econometrically; and 3) imposition of a constraint on the estimated coefficients of the equation, forcing the sum of the demand own-price and demand thermal efficiency elasticities to equal negative unity.

In the estimation process it was found that a one-percent increase in the thermal efficiency of a residence led to a 0.546 percent reduction in winter space-heating electricity use (evaluated at the mean sample price). This is considerably less than the one-percent reduction implied by engineering analyses of the problem. It was also discovered that a ten-percent increase in the thermal shell efficiency of a residence would, at the mean sample price and quantity, create benefits to the residents of the home equal to $21.23 per winter, which is 2.3 percent higher than the benefits calculated using an engineering approach.

FOOTNOTES

[1]For details, see Moe, Owzarski, and Streit [7].

[2]Even in the long run, Q is under the influence of policymakers, who can change P_T; however, estimation of the impacts of thermal efficiency increases on household energy consumption is enhanced by use of this short-run model.

[3]Just as the price elasticity of demand measured in dollars is identical to the price elasticity measured in cents.

[4]Use of average price leads to elasticity estimates which in absolute value are biased upwards because of the inclusion of an income effect.

REFERENCES

[1] Burright, B.K. and J.H. Enns, "Econometric Models of the Demand For Motor Fuel", (R-1561-NSF/FEA), Rand Corporation, Santa Monica, California, 1975.

[2] Elrick and Lavidge, Inc., "The Pacific Northwest Residential Survey, Volume 1, Executive Summary", Prepared for the Bonneville Power Administration and the Pacific Northwest Utilities Conference Committee, 1980.

[3] Halvorsen, R., Econometric Models of U.S. Energy Demand, Lexington Books, Lexington, Massachusetts, 1978.

[4] Halvorsen, R. and M.G. Ruby, Benefit-Cost Analysis of Air Pollution Control, Lexington Books, Lexington, Massachusetts, 1981.

[5] Khazzoom, J.D. "Economic Implications of Mandated Efficiency in Standards for Household Appliances," The Energy Journal, 1 (1980), pp. 21-40.

[6] Lancaster, K., "A New Approach to Consumer Theory", Journal of Political Economy, 74 (1966), pp. 132-157.

[7] Moe, R.J., S.K. Owzarski, and L.P. Streit, "Impact of Conservation Measures on Pacific Northwest Residential Energy Consumption", PNL-4717, Pacific Northwest Laboratory, Richland, Washington, 1983.

[8] Mount, T.D., L.D. Chapman, and J.J. Tyrell, "Electricity Demand in the United States: An Econometric Analysis," ORNL-NSF-3P-49, Oak Ridge National Laboratory, Oak Ridge, Tennessee, 1973.

[9] Muellbauer, J. "Household Production Theory, Quality, and the 'Hedonic Technique,'" American Economic Review, 64 (1974), pp. 977-994.

[10] Muth, R.F., "Household Production and Consumer Demand Functions," Econometrica, 34 (1966), pp. 699-708.

[11] Scanlon, T. and D. Hofferd, "A Conditional Demand Approach to Appliance Usage Estimates for Single-Family Homes in the Pacific Northwest," unpublished working paper, Bonneville Power Administration, 1981.

[12] Taylor, L.D., "The Demand for Electricity: A Survey," Bell Journal of Economics, 6 (1975), pp. 74-110.

[13] Warren-Boulton, F.R., "The Effect of Factor-Augmenting Technical Change on Factor Demand, and the Response by Factor Supplies," Paper presented to the Western Economics Association, June 1978, Honolulu, Hawaii.

Analytic Techniques for Energy Planning
B. Lev, F.H. Murphy, J.A. Bloom & A.S. Gleit (Editors)

FORECASTING ELECTRICITY DEMAND WITH AN END-USE/ECONOMETRIC MODEL*

Michael J. King
Michael J. Scott

Battelle
Pacific Northwest Laboratories
Richland, Washington 99352

A key variable in power system planning is the forecast of electricity demand. Recently, more sophisticated models have been developed to predict electricity demand, taking into account equipment efficiency, fuel prices, and economic conditions. This paper will examine one of the forecasting techniques that has recently come into vogue--end-use/econometric models. An example of one of these models will be discussed, including its treatment of conservation, fuel prices, and energy efficiency. The discussion includes results from the Railbelt Electricity Demand (RED) model developed for the State of Alaska.

1. INTRODUCTION

Electricity sector demand models have been among the more popular modelling exercises of the past few years. While most economists believe they understand the concepts underlying electricity demand, in practice a variety of problems with limited data, measurement of theoretical variables and differences in purpose have led to a wide variety of approaches. For example, there is the "all fuels" approach, which estimates total energy demand and then allocates demand to single fuels based primarily on relative prices. Examples of this approach include Baughman-Joskow [2] and Mathematical Sciences Northwest [8]. In this approach, electricity demand for a sector is derived from the demand for energy in that sector. A second approach that has proved popular is the electricity-only econometric approach, typified by models such as ORNL-SLED [4], CAPCO econometric model [1], and Mount, Chapman, and Tyrell [9]. A third variation is the end-use engineering model, which builds up an estimate of total electricity demand from estimates of the stock of appliances and engineering estimates of electricity use per appliance. Few pure end-use models exist, since engineering and econometric approaches can easily be combined, but examples include WISE [6] and Northeast Utilities Service Company model [10]. These models are more commonly used for policy simulation than forecasting. Most sophisticated models incorporate the first and third or second and third approaches to take advantage of economists' insights into electrical customer behavior, research estimating the market penetration of appliances, and engineering data on the limits of and improvements in electrical consumption by certain types of appliances. Examples of these types of models include the ORNL Residential Model [7], the PNUCC model [11], and the California Energy Commission models [3]. The model Railbelt Electricity Demand (RED) reported in this paper fits into the category of

*Parts of this research were sponsored by the Energy Information Administration, U.S. Department of Energy, and the Office of the Governor, State of Alaska. We gratefully acknowledge the assistance of Sarah L. Owzarski.

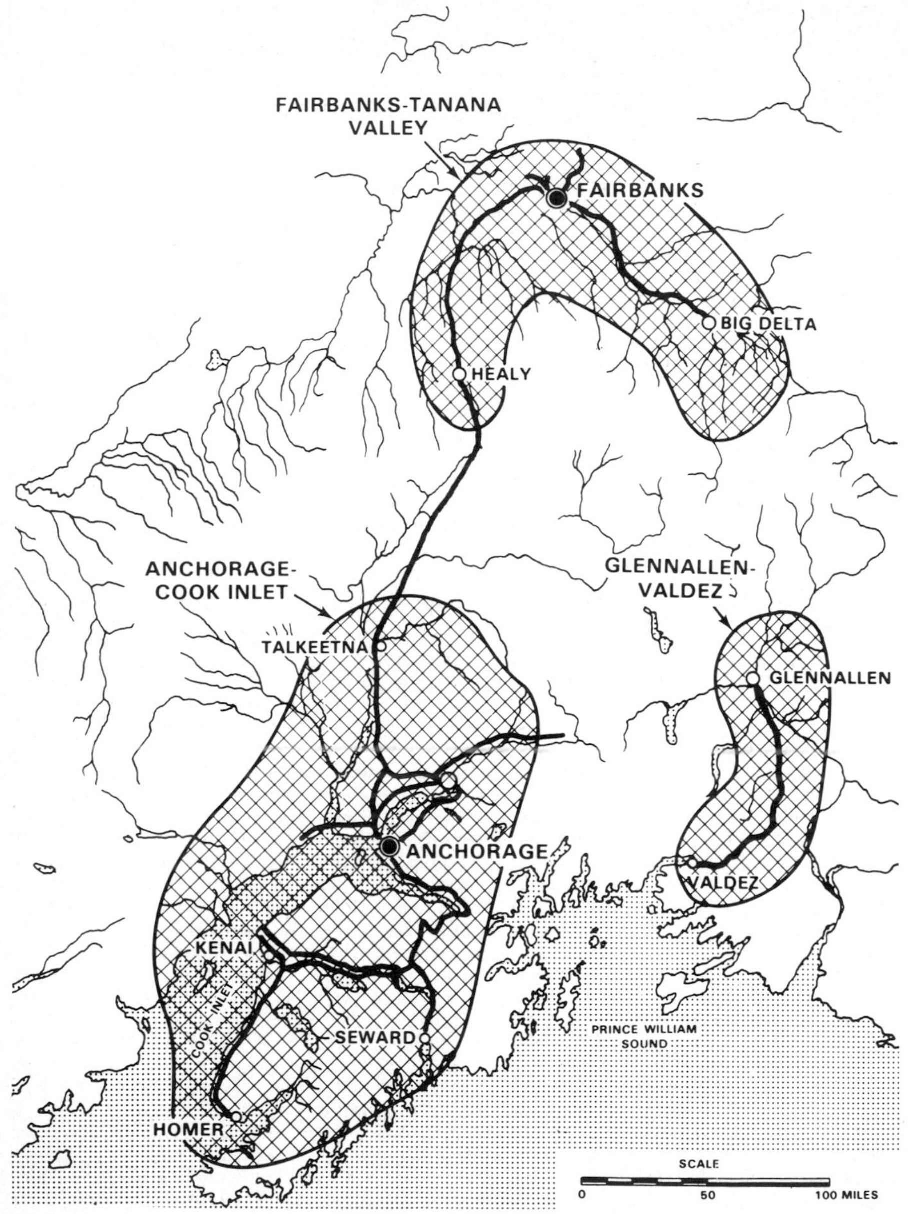

Figure 1. Railbelt Area of Alaska Showing Electrical Load Centers

combined engineering end-use/econometric approaches and is an electricity-only model custom designed to allow for Alaska's unique data problems.
The RED model was developed and utilized in response to requirements of the State of Alaska's Railbelt Electric Power Alternatives Study and Department of Energy/Energy Information Administration's Regional Analysis Program. The Alaska Railbelt Electric Power Alternatives Study was an electric power planning study for the State of Alaska, Office of the Governor and the Governor's Policy Review Committee. Begun in October 1980 and extending into April 1982, the study's objectives were to forecast the demand for electric power through the year 2010 for the Railbelt region of Alaska and to estimate the monetary, socioeconomic, and environmental costs of all options (including conservation) that could be used to supply this power. The Regional Analysis Program was a program at the various national laboratories to provide coordinated regional analysis capabilities, to review and analyze midterm and long term factors which affect long term energy development. Alaska's future demand and supply of energy was an issue of particular interest in the Pacific Northwest region. The RED Model was used to provide forecasts for both programs.

2. THE MODEL

The Railbelt Electricity Demand (RED) Model is a simulation model designed to forecast annual electricity consumption for the residential, commercial-industrial-government and miscellaneous end-use sectors of Alaska's Railbelt region (see Figure 1). The model also takes into account government intervention in the energy markets via conservation programs in Alaska and produces forecasts of system annual peak demand. The forecasts of consumption by sector and system peak demand are produced in five-year steps for three Railbelt load centers:

- Anchorage and vicinity (including Anchorage, Matanuska-Susitna Borough and Kenai Peninsula)
- Fairbanks and vicinity (including the Fairbanks-North Star Borough)
- Glennallen/Valdez (including settlements along the Richardson Highway).

When run in Monte Carlo mode, the model produces a sample probability distribution of forecasts of electricity consumption by end-use sector and peak demand for each load center for each forecast year: 1985, 1990, 1995, 2000, 2005, 2010. This distribution of forecasts can be used for planning electric power generating capacity. The RED model is accordingly designed to be run in tandem with a separate electric capacity planning and dispatching model which produces forecasts of retail electricity rates.

Figure 2 shows the basic relationships among the seven modules that comprise the RED model. The model begins a simulation with the Uncertainty Module, selecting a trial set of model parameters, which are sent to the other modules. These parameters include price elasticities, appliance saturations, and regional load factors. Exogenous forecasts of population, economic activity, and retail prices for fuel oil, gas, and electricity are used with the trial parameters to produce forecasts of electricity consumption in the Residential Consumption and Business Consumption Modules. These forecasts, along with additional trial parameters, are used in the Conservation Module to model the effects of subsidized conservation and dispersed generating options such as windmills or microhydro installations on electricity sales. The revised consumption forecasts of residential and business (commercial, small industrial, and government) consumption are used to estimate future miscellaneous consumption and total sales of electricity. Finally, the consumption forecasts are used along with a trial system load factor forecast to estimate peak demand. The model then returns to

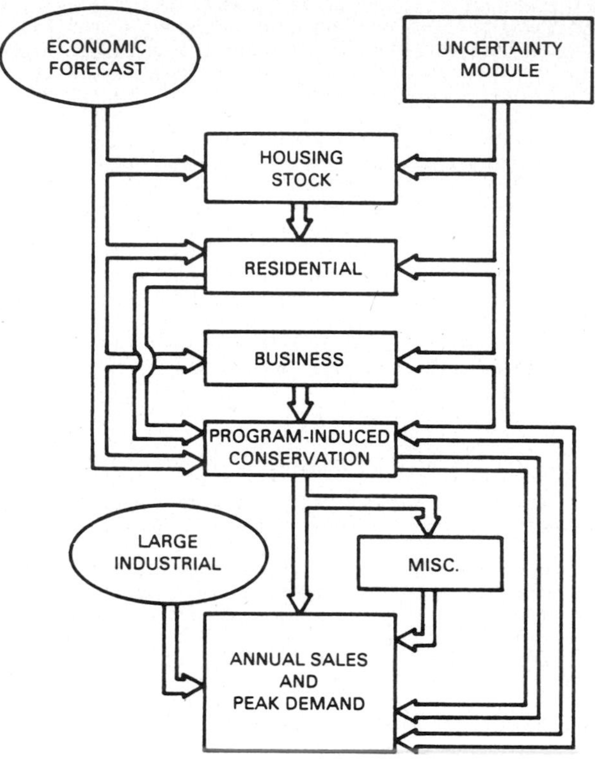

Figure 2. Information Flows in the RED Model

start the next Monte Carlo trial. When the model is run in certainty-equivalent mode, a "default" set of parameters is used and only one trial is run. The remainder of this section presents brief descriptions of each module.

2.1 Uncertainty Module

The purpose of the Uncertainty Module is to randomly select values for individual model parameters that are considered subject to forecasting uncertainty. These parameters include the market saturations for major appliances in the residential sector; the own-price and cross-price elasticities of demand for electricity in the residential and business sector; the market penetration of conservation and dispersed generating technologies; the intensity of electricity use per square foot of floor space in the business sector; and the electric system load factors for each load center.

These parameters are generated by a Monte Carlo routine, which uses information on the distribution of each parameter (such as its expected value and range) and the computer's random number generator to produce sets of parameter values. Each set of generated parameters represents a "trial." By running each successive trial set of generated parameters through the rest of the modules, the model builds distributions of annual electricity consumption and peak demand. The end points of the distributions reflect the probable range of annual electric consumption and peak demand, given the level of uncertainty.

The Uncertainty Module need not be run every time RED is run. The parameter file contains "default" values of the parameters that may be used to conserve computation time.

2.2 The Housing Module

The Housing Module calculates the number of households and the stock of housing by dwelling type in each load center for each forecast year in which the model is run. Using exogenous regional forecasts of the number of households and regional forecasts of total population, the housing stock module first derives a forecast of the size of households in each load center. Next, using a statewide forecast of the age distribution of Alaska's population and headship rates, it estimates the distribution of households by age of head and size of household for each load center. Finally, it forecasts the demand for four types of housing stock: single family, mobile homes, duplexes, and multifamily units.

The supply of housing is calculated in two steps. First, the supply of each type of housing from the previous period is adjusted for demolition and compared to the current period's demand. If demand exceeds supply, construction of additional housing begins immediately. If excess supply of a given type of housing exists, the model examines the vacancy rate in all types of housing. Each type is assumed to have a maximum vacancy rate. If this rate is exceeded, demand is first reallocated from the closest substitute housing type, if needed, then from other types. The end result is a forecast of occupied housing stock for each load center for each housing type in each forecast year. This forecast is passed to the Residential Consumption Module.

2.3 Residential Consumption Module

The Residential Consumption Module forecasts the annual consumption of electricity in the residential sector for each load center in each forecast year including the effects of price-induced conservation and fuel switching. Explicit government intervention to promote residential electric energy conservation or self-sufficiency is covered in the Conservation Module. The Residential Consumption Module employs an end-use approach that recognizes nine major end uses of electricity, and a "small appliances" category that encompasses a large group of other end uses and extra water heating for clothes washers and dish washers.

A number of other end-use models have sophisticated methods for determining appliance and fuel mode choices. (See, for example, Hirst and Carney [7]). In Alaska, however, the data base necessary to support these models is non-existent. We instead chose to use a simple, straightforward approach where we could use what information was available. We needed an estimate of the stock and fuel mode of the existing end uses in the Railbelt Region. A simple one page questionnaire was mailed to 4,000 randomly chosen customers of the electric utilities in the region. Due to the simplicity of the survey instrument and a postage free return envelope, the response rate was forty four percent.

The survey yielded estimates of the number of appliances or stock of electric end-uses. The estimates of the future saturation of the end-uses in the Railbelt, however, had to be based on professional judgment, which considered the increases in real income, conditions in the 48 contiguous states, etc. Similarly, the net impact of increased appliance efficiency (due solely to technical change) and increasing capacities on average energy use per new unit had to be judgmentally derived.

Again, these parameter forecasts had to be independent of the effects of real energy price changes because the impacts of energy prices on electricity demand are explicitly modeled. The specific form of the price adjustment mechanism is described later in this paper.

An end-use model is basically an accounting model: a stock of appliances or end-uses is built up, additions and retirements are tracked, and the average energy use characteristics of each vintage are melded into an average consumption rate for the stock. By multiplying together the average consumption rate and the number of installed appliances, a preliminary forecast of energy use can easily be derived.

Finally, the Residential Consumption Module receives exogenous forecasts from the Uncer- tainty Module of residential fuel oil, natural gas, and electricity prices, along with "trial" values of parameters used to derive price elasticities and cross-price elasticities of demand for electricity. It adjusts the preliminary consumption forecast for both short- and long-run price effects on appliance use and fuel switching. The adjusted forecast is passed to the Conservation and Peak Demand Modules.

2.4 Business Consumption Module

The Business Consumption Module forecasts the consumption of electricity by load center in commercial, small industrial, and government uses for each forecast year (1980, 1985, 1990, 2000, 2010). Because the end uses of electricity in the commercial, small industrial and government sectors are more diverse and virtually unknown (no end use survey or load research has been conducted on this sector) the Business Consumption Module forecasts electrical use on an aggregate basis rather than by end use.

RED uses a proxy variable (the stock of commercial floor space) for the stock of capital equipment to forecast the derived demand for electricity in the commercial, light industrial, and government sectors. Using exogenous forecasts of employment, the module forecasts the regional stock of floor space. Next, econometric equations are used to predict the intensity of electricity use for a given level of floor space in the absence of any relative price changes. Finally, a price adjustment similar to that in the Residential Consumption Module is applied to derive a forecast of business electricity consumption (excluding large industrial demand, which must be exogenously determined). The Business Consumption Module forecasts are passed to the Conservation and Peak Demand Modules.

2.5 Price Adjustment Mechanism

RED employs estimates of the own-price and cross-price elasticities of demand to estimate the impacts of energy price changes on electricity demand. Three alternative fuels are considered in the model--natural gas, liquified petroleum gas (propane), and fuel oil.

Elasticities are a measure of responsiveness of consumers to a change in the price of a good, a substitute good, or a complement good. The elasticity, specifically, measures the percentage change in quantity consumed of a good in response to a one percent change in either the price of the good, or its substitutes/complements.

Elasticities are usually derived with econometric regression techniques. The optimum situation, for the demand modeller, is to have a data base capable of supporting estimates of elasticities for the area modelled. Unfortunately, the data base for the Railbelt is extremely sparse; therefore, we were forced to rely on estimates from the lower 48 states.

After an extensive literature review, we settled on the estimates derived by Mount, Chapman, and Tyrell [9]. These estimates were derived from pooled time series cross-sectional data for the 48 contiguous states from 1946-1970. The two most attractive features are the explicit adjustment mechanism from the short run to the long run and the variable elasticity formulation.

The variable elasticity formulation implies that the response to a change in price is dependent not only on the magnitude of the change, but also the level of price. One would certainly expect individuals who are currently paying three cents a kWh to respond differently to a ten percent increase in price than consumers facing thirteen cent power.

The long run adjustment is desirable because it does not force the modeller to make arbitrary definitions of the long- and short-run. It also allows smooth adjustments from the short run to the long run.

Exogenous forecasts of fuel prices, therefore, are translated into price index factors in RED with the "trial" parameter estimates from Mount, Chapman, and Tyrell [9] (the parameters are allowed to vary within their 95 percent confidence intervals when RED is run in Monte Carlo mode). These indices are then applied to the residential and business estimates of consumption in the absence of price changes to derive forecast of electricity consumption for the two sectors.

2.6 Conservation Module

Because of the potential importance of government intervention in the market place to encourage conservation of energy and substitution of other forms of energy for electricity, the RED model includes a module that permits explicit treatment of technologies and programs that are designed to reduce the demand for utility-generated electricity. The module structure is designed to incorporate assumptions on the technical performance, costs, and market penetration of electricity-saving innovations in each end use, load center, and forecast year. The module forecasts the aggregate electricity savings by end use, the costs associated with these savings, and adjusted consumption in the residential and business sectors.

The Conservation Module requires a set of off-line calculations by a nested computer program called CONSER. These calculations are more complex in the residential than the commercial sector, since more data are available on residential sector conservation options. In the residential sector, the model user supplies information to CONSER on the technical efficiency (electricity savings), electricity price, and costs of installation. Government market intervention in the form of capital subsidies or low-interest loans is incorporated in lowered installed cost to the consumer. CONSER then calculates the incremental internal rate-of-return on the option to the consumer. That rate of return must exceed the passbook savings interest rate if the option is to gain assumed market acceptance. The Conservation Module then calculates the option's payback period for technologies considered "acceptable" by the user, and a payback decision rule links the payback period to a range of market saturations for the technologies. The savings per installation and market saturation of each option are used to calculate residential sector electricity savings and costs for the incremental investment above what would be adopted without the program. In the business sector, the model user must specify the technical potential for new and retrofit energy-saving technologies. The user must also specify the range of conservation saturation as a percent of total potential conservation. The Conservation Module then calculates total electricity savings due to market intervention in new and retrofit applications and adjusts residential and business consumption for each load center and forecast year.

2.7 Miscellaneous Consumption Module

The Miscellaneous Consumption Module forecasts total miscellaneous consumption for second (recreation) homes, vacant houses, and other miscellaneous uses, such as street lighting. The module uses the forecast of residential consumption (adjusted for conservation impacts) to predict electricity demand in second homes and vacant housing units. The sum of residential and business consumption is used to forecast street lighting requirements. Finally, all three are summed together to estimate miscellaneous demand.

2.8 Peak Demand Module

The Peak Demand Module forecasts the annual peak hour demand for electricity. A two-stage approach using load factors is used. The unadjusted residential and business consumption, miscellaneous consumption, and load center load factors generated by the Uncertainty Module are first used to forecast preliminary peak demand. Next, displaced consumption (electricity savings) calculated by the Conservation Module is multiplied by a peak correction factor supplied by the Uncertainty Module to allocate a portion of electricity savings from conservation to peak demand periods. The allocated consumption savings are then multiplied by the load factor to forecast peak demand savings, and the savings are subtracted from peak demand to forecast revised peak demand.

3. THE FORECAST

Figure 3 presents a sample forecast with three sensitivity tests. The base forecast has oil prices escalating at 1.7 percent annually, gas at 3.3 percent, and electricity at 1.6 percent (all real). The major impact is from the own price response, which reduces demand by 1,000 GWh from the level which would have occurred in 2010 if electricity prices had remained constant. The cross price response accounted for a 150 GWh reduction due to oil prices and a 400 GWh reduction due to gas price increases. With constant electricity prices demand increases at about 3.5 percent per year or about 1.4 percent per year per capita. Real electricity price increases of 1.6 percent per year reduce year 2010 demand by about 15 percent or take 0.5 percent per year off the growth rate. Holding the other prices constant cuts year 2010 demand another six percentage points. Two policy implications can be derived from this sample forecast: 1) if the economic forecasts driving RED are correct, major additions to Railbelt generating capacity would be required, even with conservation, and 2) the forecast is quite sensitive to prices of fuels. Thus, major cost increases or capital-intensive generating projects could significantly affect demand for the projects.

REFERENCES

[1] Arthur D. Little, Inc., "Independent Demand Forecast Assessment for CAPCO Power Pool. Complete Final Report to Ohio Power Siting Commission," (Arthur D. Little, Inc., Cambridge, Massachusetts, 1976).

[2] Baughman, M.L. and Joskow, P.L., "The Future Outlook for U.S. Electricity Supply and Demand", Proceedings of the IEEE 65(4). (1977).

[3] California Energy Commission, "California Energy Demand 1982 to 2002. Forecast for Consideration in the Proceedings on the Fourth Biennial Report, Volume I, Technical Report, Staff Report," Demand Assessment Office, Assessment Division, California Energy Commission, Sacramento, California. (1982).

[4] Chern, W.S. et al., "Regional Econometric Model for Forecasting Electricity Demand by Sector and by State", ORNL/NUREG/49, Oak Ridge National Laboratory, Oak Ridge, Tennessee. (1978).

[5] Energy Modelling Forum, "Electric Load Forecasting. Probing the Issues with Models", EMF Report 3, Stanford University, Stanford, California. (1980).

[6] Foell, W.K., "The Wisconsin Energy Model - A Tool for Regional Energy Policy Analysis", Institute for Environmental Studies, University of Wisconsin, Madison, Wisconsin. (1974).

[7] Hirst, E. and Carney, J., "The ORNL Engineering-Economic Model of Residential Energy Use", ORNL/CON-24, Oak Ridge National Laboratory, Oak Ridge, Tennessee. (1978).

[8] Mathematical Sciences Northwest. Northwest Energy Policy Project Energy Demand Modeling and Forecasting. Final Report., (1977).

[9] Mount, T.D., Chapman, L.D. and Tyrell, T.J., "Electricity Demand in the United States: An Econometric Analysis", ORNL-NSF-49, Oak Ridge National Laboratory, Oak Ridge, Tennessee. (1973).

[10] Northeast Utilities Services Company, "Electric Energy Demand 1978-1987",

Research Section of Northeast Utilities Company, in: Energy Modelling Forum, Electric Load Forecasting, Probing the Issues with Models, EMF Report 3, Energy Modelling Forum, Stanford University, Stanford, California. (1980).

[11] Pacific Northwest Utilities Conference Committee, Econometric Model -Electricity Sales Forecast Technical Appendix. (1980).

[12] Taylor, L.D., "The Demand for Electricity: A Survey", The Bell Journal of Economics, 6(1):(1975) pp. 74-110.

SYMBOLS

Y = income per household or per capita
HS = avg. family size
SHU = single detached housing units (fraction of total)
NU = nonurban housing units (fraction of total)
W = mean December temperature
S = mean July temperature
Yi = income per capita (67 dollars)
N = population density
Pi = energy price index relative to CPI (dollars per Btu)
MT = avg. temperature of warmest three months of year (^{o}F)
LT = avg. temperature of coldest three months of year (^{o}F)
mpe = marginal price of electricity
fce = fixed charge for electricity
x = total personal income
ddh = heating degree days
ddc = cooling degree days
C_r = number of residential customers
P_{rm} = marginal price of electricity
Y^* = per capita personal income
J = average July temperature
D = heating degree days
Z = population per square mile
R = percent rural population
H = percent of housing units in single-unit structures
E = number of housing units per capita
P_R = average real price of residential electricity, in cents per KWH
Y_H = average real income per capita, in thousands of dollars
A = index of real wholesale prices of selected electric appliances
U = percentage of population living in rural areas
M = percentage of housing units in multiunit structures
H_A = average size of households
T = time
HT = stock of occupied housing units
HS_A = average size of housing units
C = the fraction of households with a particular type of equipment
T1 = thermal performance of housing units
EU = average annual energy use for the type of equipment
U = usage factor

g_{t-1} = lagged personal consumption expenditure for electricity per capita in 1958 dollars.

X_t = total personal consumption expenditure per capita in 1958 dollars

p = implicit deflator for electricity/implicit deflator for PCE (1958=100)

Y_j = value of retail sales

PE_j = average deflated price per KWH of electricity

$Q_{it}\text{-}1_j$ = lagged per capita fuel consumption

P = population

PE = price of electricity (mills per KWH)

Q_{t-1} = lagged demand in millions of KWH.

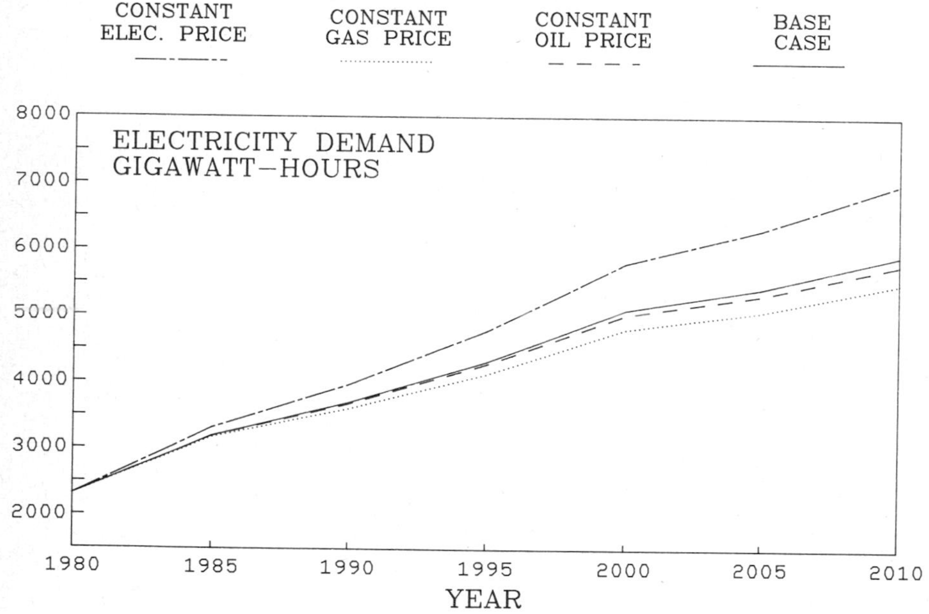

Figure 3. Sample R E D Forecast

Table 1. Residential Electricity Demand Survey

Author	Type of Elasticity	Time Frame	Type of Data	Substitute Prices	Other Demand Determinants[(a)]
Anderson, K.P. (1972) Residential Demand for Electricity: Econometric Estimates For California and the United States. The Rand Corporation, Santa Monica, CA	Constant	Long run	Cross-section 1969, states	Average price of Natural Gas	
Anderson, K.P. (1973) Residential Energy Use: An Econometric Analysis R-1297-NSF. The Rand Corp., Santa Monica, CA	Constant	Short run long run	Cross-section 1969, states	Fuel oil, bottled gas, coal	Y, HS, SHU, NU, W, S
Baughman, M.L., Joskow, P.L., Dilip, K.P. 1979 Electric Power in the United States: Models and Policy Analysis. MIT Press, Cambridge, MA	Constant	Short run long run	Time series 1968-1972 48 states	Energy price index	Yi, N, MT, LT, P_i
Blattenberger, G.R., Taylor, L.D., Rennhack, R.K. 1983, "Natural Gas Availability and the Residential Demand for Energy". The Energy Journal. 4(1):23-45	Constant	Short run long run	Time series 1960-1975 states	Marginal price natural gas, fixed charge natural gas, price of fuel oil	mpe, fce, x, ddh, ddc
Halvorsen, Robert. 1976 "Demand For Electric Energy in the United States". Southern Econ Journal. 42(4):610-625.	Constant	Long run	Cross-section 1969 states	Average price per therm for all types of gas purchased by sector	c_r, P_{rm}, Y*, J, D, Z, R, H, E
Halvorsen, Robert. 1978 Econometric Models of U.S. Energy Demand. D.C. Heath and Co., Lexington, MA	Constant	Long run	Pooled 1961-1969 48 states	Average real gas price for all types of gas in cents	P_R, Y_H, A, D, J, U, M, H_A, T per therm
Hirst, Eric, and Carney, Janet. 1979. "The ORNL Residential Energy-Use Model: Structure and Results". Land Economics. 55(3):319-333	Constant	Short run long run	Cross-section 1970		HT, HS_A, C, T1, EU, U
Houthakker, H.S. and Taylor, L.D. 1970. Consumer Demand in the United States. Harvard Univ. Press, Cambridge, MA	Constant	Short run	Time series		g_{t-1}, X_t, P
Mount, T. D., Chapman, L. D., and Tyrrell, T. J. 1973. Electricity Demand in the United States: An Econometric Analysis.	Variable	Short run long run	Cross-section 1947-1970 States	Price of gas-includes natural, liquid petroleum, manufactured and mixed gas.	Population, per capita income, avg. electricity price, price index for appliances, mean January temperature

(a) For symbols, see glossary at end of section.

Table 2. Commercial Electricity Demand Survey

Author	Type of Elasticity	Time Frame	Type of Data	Substitute Prices	Other Demand Determinants[a]
Beierlein, James G., Dunn, James W., McConnon, James C. 1981. "The Demand for Electricity and Natural Gas in the Northeastern United States". The Review of Economics and Statistics. August 1981, pp. 403-408.	Constant	Short-run long-run	Cross-section time series 1967-1977 regional NE	Natural gas, fuel oil	Y_j, PE_j, Q_{it-1j}
Mount, T. D., Chapman, L. D., and Tyrell, T. J. 1973. Electricity Demand in the United States; An Econometric Analysis. Contract No. W-7405-eng-26. ORNL, Oak Ridge, Tennessee	Variable	Short-run long-run	Cross-section 1947-1970 States	Gas	Y, P, PE, Q_{t-1}

(a) For symbols, see glossary at end of section.

Analytic Techniques for Energy Planning
B. Lev, F.H. Murphy, J.A. Bloom & A.S. Gleit (Editors)

MASTER: A FORECAST MODEL OF REGIONAL ECONOMIC ACTIVITY*

R.J. Moe
R.C. Adams
M.J. Scott

Pacific Northwest Laboratory
P.O. Box 999
Richland, Washington 99352

Forecast models of local economic activity are frequently employed in energy-related uses by both public and private decision-makers. The Metropolitan and State Economic Regions (MASTER) model was designed to provide such local forecasts and impact analyses. MASTER forecasts economic activity in all 268 Standard Metropolitan Statistical Areas (SMSA's) and 48 Rest-of-State Areas (ROSA's) in the continential United States. Employment and wages in 12 industrial sectors are determined within the model, as are construction in 25 categories, total personal income and its components, and population. Exogenous variables which affect local economic activity include local energy and construction prices, and national interest rates and national industrial output. MASTER was statistically estimated using historical cross-section/time-series data for the individual SMSA/ROSA's.

1. INTRODUCTION

During the 1970s and early 1980s, an acute need developed in energy-related fields for models of economic activity in substate areas (counties, Standard Metropolitan Statistical Areas, BEA Economic Regions). The need has arisen from a number of sources, all related to the fact that energy market conditions and hence the severity of the "energy problem" vary substantially between areas, even those within the same state.

First, planners in public and private utilities require forecasts of electricity demand in one or more utility service districts to determine electricity generation and transmission capacity requirements. The models which provide such demand forecasts are typically driven by forecasts of population, residential units, commercial floorspace, industrial employment by sector and other measures

*Work sponsored by the U.S. Department of Energy under Contract DE-AC06-76-RLO 1830

of economic activity in each of the corresponding service areas.

Second, planners in federal, state, and local government frequently require forecasts of population, personal income, and other general measures of economic activity for many metropolitan areas and other substate regions to determine the local demand for schools, hospitals, highways, and other public facilities. Since local energy prices in part determine these variables, the forecasts of the variables should vary as energy prices vary.

Third, in a similar manner, planners in private business require forecasts of demand and production costs in many locations to determine a firm's desired quantity and location of future additions to productive capacity. Since both local demand and production costs may be determined in part by local personal income, population, etc., which in turn may be determined by local energy prices, the forecast values of demand should vary as energy prices vary.

Fourth, to assess the impacts on local economic activity of proposed energy-related policies, such as those that would cause direct changes in energy prices, construction prices, or construction employment, energy policymakers require models in which these and other variables appear as policy instruments.

Thus, planners and policymakers in energy-related fields needed and continue to need, both for forecasting and policy analysis, models of economic activity and substate regions that 1) can forecast activity in all of the corresponding geographic units in the United States; 2) forecast the specific variables required as input into energy demand models; 3) include energy prices as determinants of local activity; and 4) include as determinants of local activity other variables under the influence of energy policymakers, such as construction prices and construction employment. Despite the clear need for a national multiregional model of economic activity in substate areas with these qualities, no presently operational model has these capabilities. In fact, only two currently operational models which have been presented in the literature forecast economic activity in both substate areas and in every geographic unit in the nation. The Multiregion Multi-Industry Model developed by Harris [9] forecasts industrial output and employment in 98 sectors as well as construction in 28 categories for every county in the United States. The MULTIREGION model (Olsen, et al. [13]) forecasts economic activity in all 173 BEA Economic Regions in the country. Neither, however, is appropriate for energy uses; neither includes energy prices as a determinant of local economic activity and only one of them contains enough disaggregation in the industrial and construction sectors to drive typical energy demand models. A large number of economic models of single substate areas or multiple areas in a small region have also been presented in the literature (Ballard and Glickman [2], Crow [3], Duobinis [4], Engle, et al. [5], Glickman [7], Hall and Licari [8], Loxley [11], Rubin and Erickson [14], Taylor [15]). Despite variations in model structure and the types of variables considered, the basic geographic unit considered and the number of such units, all have one common feature: they are inappropriate for application to energy-related problems, since neither energy prices nor typical energy policy instruments are included in the models.

In this paper the Metropolitan and State Economic Regions (MASTER) model is presented. This model is unique in that it was constructed specifically in response to the need for a national multiregional model of economic activity in substate areas which can be used for forecasting, planning, and policymaking in energy-related fields. Unlike any other currently operational model, MASTER 1 forecasts economic activity in all 268 Standard Metropolitan Statistical Areas (SMSAs) and 48 non-SMSA Rest-of-State Areas (ROSAs) in the continental United States; 2) accounts for the role of local electricity and natural gas prices in determining economic activity in each SMSA and ROSA; 3) includes such energy policy instruments as local construction prices and local energy prices as determinants of local economic activity, permitting analysis of energy policies on local activity; and 4) forecasts the specific variables, primarily disaggregated employment and construction, required to "drive" most energy demand models, such as those constructed at Oak Ridge National Laboratory.

2. MODEL DESCRIPTION

MASTER consists of four submodels, one for each U.S. Census Region (Northeast, North Central, West, South). Each submodel can be used to forecast annual economic activity in any SMSA or ROSA in the corresponding Census Region. Each submodel contains 53 stochastic[1] equations linked together by over 100 identities. MASTER is an econometric model; the stochastic equations of each submodel were statistically estimated using a time-series/cross-section sample of data for the years 1967-1976 for each SMSA/ROSA in the corresponding Census Region.

2.1 Model Specification

Specification of an econometric model refers to selection of 1) the endogenous or dependent variables of the model, 2) the exogenous or explanatory variables of the model, 3) the forms of the functions through which the exogenous variables determine the endogenous variables, and 4) the interactions between the endogenous and exogenous variables.

The variables which MASTER forecasts for every SMSA and ROSA in the United States are listed in Table 1. These variables were selected to provide energy policymakers and planners with a tool applicable to forecasting and policy analysis problems. The set of variables includes the primary measures of local economic activity (total employment, personal income, and population), so the impacts of various policies can be summarized by the changes in these general activity variables; the set of forecast variables also includes sufficient disaggregation in the employment and construction blocks to drive many energy demand models, including the Oak Ridge Industrial, Commercial, and Residential models.

The exogenous variables employed by MASTER are listed in Table 2. Exogenous variables were selected according to two criteria. First, variables that are under the influence of energy policymakers were included in the model where possible, in order to provide a tool for policy analysis. Second, those variables which economic theory suggests would determine local economic activity were included where possible.

The functional forms used in each block of the model were selected primarily according to consistency with economic theory and how well each equation could be applied to a wide range of local conditions. For example, the dependent variable in each stochastic employment equation is the annual percentage change in employment, because this functional form could most easily be applied to both small and large SMSAs.

The interactions between the endogenous and exogenous variables are displayed in Figure 1. In the figure, the arrows are representative of causation, ovals represent sets of exogenous variables, and rectangles sets of endogenous variables. The following paragraphs provide a brief guide to how each of MASTER's endogenous variables is determined in the model. Further information is available in Adams, et al. [1].

Table 1. MASTER Forecast Outputs

Employment and Annual Wages by Sector

Agriculture
Agricultural Services, Forestry, and Fishing
Mining
Construction
Non-Durable Manufacturing
Durable Manufacturing
Public Utilities, Transportation, and Communications
Wholesale Trade
Retail Trade
Finance, Insurance, and Real Estate
Services
Government

Income, by Source

Wage Bill
Rent, Interest, and Dividends
Transfer Payments
Social Insurance Payments
Residence Adjustment
Total Personal Income
Per Capita Income

Population, by Category

Births
Deaths
Net Migration
Population

Construction of New Commercial Buildings, by Building Category

Retail - Wholesale
Office Building
Auto Repair
Warehouse
Education
Health
Public
Religious
Hotel - Motel
Miscellaneous

Commercial Construction, Additions and Alterations, by Building Category

Same as New Commercial Building Construction Categories

Residential Construction, by Building Category

Apartments, Five or More Units, One-Three Stories
Apartments, Five or More Units, Four or More Stories
Apartments, Three to Four Units
Single-Family, Detached
Duplexes

Table 2. MASTER Exogenous Variables

National Annual Wage Rates, by Sector

Same as Employment Sectors

National Annual Industrial Output, by Sector

Same as Employment Sectors

Local Energy Prices

Electricity
Natural Gas

Local Construction Prices, by Building Category

Same as Commercial and Residential Building Categories

Miscellaneous

National Unemployment Rate
National Consumer Price Index
National Interest Rates (90-day Treasury Bill, AAA Bond Rate)

2.1.1 Employment

The annual percentage change in employment in each sector is determined by the logarithms and percentage changes of 1) the sector real wage, 2) real electricity and/or natural gas prices, 3) real personal income; and by 4) the change in real national output in the sector and 5) the interest rate. Employment in each sector is computed in an identity using the previous year's sector employment and the predicted change in sector employment. Local employment in a specific sector is thus, in part, determined by national activity in the sector as measured by output; however, local employment is not simply determined as a "share" of national employment, as is done in many regional models.

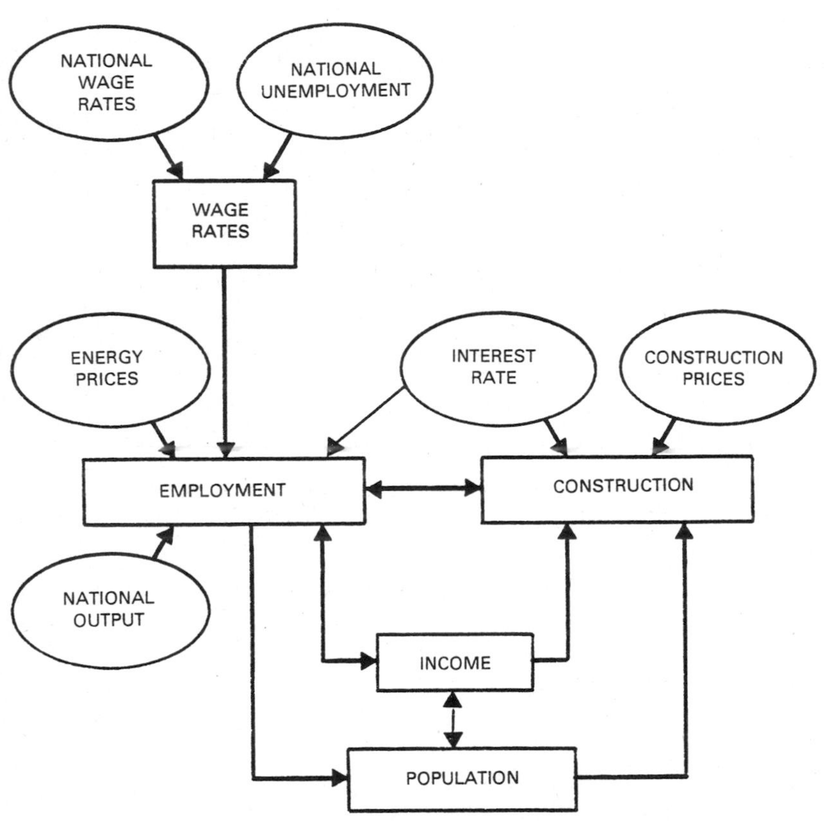

FIGURE 1. MASTER Model: Simple model schematic.

2.1.2 Annual Wage

The nominal annual wage in each sector is determined through an identity by the previous period's nominal wage and the predicted year-to-year change in the sector nominal annual wage. This predicted annual change is determined by 1) the change in the sector national real annual wage, 2) the change in the national consumer price index, 3) the change in the national unemployment rate, and 4) the previous period's ratio of nominal local wage rate to nominal national wage rate. Wages in the model are not currently determined by local factors such as employment.

2.1.3 Construction

The predicted commercial construction variable in each category is square feet of construction. The construction equation specification follows the stock adjustment formulation commonly employed in modeling construction activity (Follain [6], Muth [12]). In each equation, square feet of construction is determined by 1) the previous period's construction in the corresponding category; and by the second lags and lagged differences of 2) the AAA bond rate, 3) the real price per square foot of construction in the category, and 4) a category-specific "driver" variable. The "driver" is analogous to a scale variable in a building-stock demand equation; for example, in the Retail-Wholesale category, the driver is combined retail-wholesale employment. The residential construction equations are similar to the commercial equation; the stock adjustment formulation is again employed, and in each category the predicted variable is square feet of construction. Residential construction by building category is determined by 1) the previous period's construction in the category; and lagged and differenced values of 2) the real price per square foot of construction in the category, 3) population, and 4) a variable representing liquidity available for residential mortgages.

2.1.4 Income

Total personal income is equal to the sum of its four non-wage and one wage components. The four non-wage components are 1) transfer payments, which are payments by the government to SMSA/ROSA residents; 2) rent, interest, and dividend (property) income received by residents; 3) social insurance payments, which are taxes paid to the government by residents; and 4) residence adjustment, which accounts for income earned in one SMSA/ROSA by residents of another SMSA/ROSA. The wage bill is equal to the sum of the wage bills for the twelve sectors; each sector's wage bill is equal to the product of employment in the sector and the sector's annual wage. Nominal per capita transfer payments are determined by the previous period's value and the predicted percentage change; nominal property income is determined in the same manner. The nominal residence adjustment equals the previous period's adjustment plus the predicted year-to-year change; residence adjustment can be either positive or negative. The predicted variable in the social insurance payments is the logarithm of nominal payments. Each of these predicted variables is determined by levels, logarithms, year-to-year changes, and/or percentage changes in 1) population, 2) total employment, 3) nominal wage bill, 4) the consumer price index, and/or 5) the national unemployment rate.

2.1.5 Population

Population in each SMSA and ROSA is calculated using the previous period's population and the current period's predicted births, deaths, and net migration. The logarithms of births and deaths are determined by 1) the logarithm of popultion and 2) the logarithm and percentage change of real per capita income. Predicted net migration is determined by the lagged change in total employment.

2.2 Data Sources

County- and state-level data for the period 1967-1976 was collected from a number of sources for estimation and simulation of each MASTER submodel. County-level employment and income information for each county in the United States was collected from the Bureau of Economic Analysis and aggregated to the SMSA/ROSA level. County-level construction data for each U.S. county was obtained from F.W. Dodge and aggregated in a similar manner, as was the population data collected from the Census Bureau. State-level energy price information was taken from the Department of Energy/Energy Information Administration's State Energy Price System. No SMSA/ROSA-level data was synthesized from state-level data through sharing techniques, as is done in a number of other substate models.

2.3 Model Estimation

Each stochastic equation in each submodel was estimated using a pooled time-series/cross-section data base covering 1) the years 1967-1976 and 2) every SMSA and ROSA in the corresponding Census Region. Each equation was estimated individually using a time-series/cross-section regression procedure suggested by Kmenta [10]. Despite considerable simultaneity in the structure of the model, a simultaneous-equations estimation procedure was not employed due to computational burdens. The estimation procedure used adjusts coefficient estimates for 1) systematic heteroscedasticity of the disturbance terms for each SMSA/ROSA, 2) contemporaneous correlation of disturbance terms between two distinct SMSA/ROSAs, and 3) autocorrelation of the disturbances of each SMSA/ROSA over time. Besides coefficient estimates for each equation, the procedure produces an estimate of the autoregressive parameter for each SMSA/ROSA in the sample.

The estimation results are too voluminous to present here but are presented in Adams, et al. [1]. Generally, the results were quite good, with expected signs and levels of statistical significance exceeding those found in typical time-series/cross-section estimates. The 100 construction equations estimated (25 for each region) were by far the best fitting, while the weakest equations were those whose dependent variable was the percentage change in local sectoral employment. Despite this, the model forecasts employment (not its percentage change) quite accurately. Employment equations for the West Census Region Model are displayed in the Appendix as an example of the estimation results.

2.4 Model Simulation

In the process of forecasting for an individual SMSA or ROSA, two adjustments are made to the estimated equations. First, because a time-series/cross-section data base was used in estimating the equations, the sum of the residuals for a given stochastic equation computed for a single cross-section does not equal zero, as it would if each equation was estimated individually for each SMSA/ROSA using ordinary least squares. Thus, it is possible that the estimated equation "misses" the entire historical experience of a particular SMSA/ROSA by consistently over-predicting (or under-predicting) the values of the dependent variable. To overcome this problem, dummy variables are frequently used in econometric analysis of pooled samples; their presence causes the sum of residuals for each cross-section to equal zero. As part of the simulation process, dummy variables, or intercept adjustments, are calculated for each stochastic equation and each SMSA/ROSA in the Region. These adjustments ensure that the mean 1967-1976 predicted value of the dependent variable is equal to the mean actual value for each dependent variable for each SMSA/ROSA in the Region.

The second adjustment concerns the autoregressive parameters. A "false start" forecast is made to generate predicted 1976 values for each stochastic variable for each SMSA/ROSA. These predicted values are subtracted from the actual values to obtain the 1976 residual for each stochastic-equation dependent variable in each SMSA/ROSA. When the true forecast is generated, the 1976 residuals are combined with estimates of the autoregressive parameters to generate forecast values in 1977, 1978, and beyond.

For the actual forecast simulation, the 1) intercept adjustments, 2) calculated 1976 residuals, and 3) autoregressive parameters corresponding to each stochastic dependent variable in the model for each SMSA/ROSA in the Region are entered into a data set with 4) actual values of the exogenous and endogenous variables for 1974-1976, which "prime" the forecast simulation, and 5) forecast values of the exogenous variables. Alternative forecasts of economic activity in any SMSA or ROSA can be made by changing the values of these exogenous variables.

3. POTENTIAL APPLICATIONS OF THE MASTER MODEL

The MASTER model was designed for application to a number of energy-related issues. Several of these have been mentioned above in the context of requirements of a model of regional economic activity which can be used to analyze energy-related issues. In this section, potential applications are discussed in greater detail. The model applications naturally fall into two categories, 1) forecasting and 2) policy-impact analysis, which depend not on how the model is used but on the information that the user requires from the model.

3.1 Forecasting

In this category are applications in which MASTER is used to forecast SMSA, state, or national economic activity under one or more scenarios, but in which the user is not explicitly interested in comparing the forecasts associated with different scenarios. In this setting, "scenario" refers to a set of values of the exogenous variables. Perhaps the most straightforward application of the model is simply in providing forecasts of general local economic activity to planners in business and all levels of government. These forecasts can be used to plan construction of additional public facilities or private productive capacity. In situations where the user has reason to believe that energy or construction prices may change dramatically from their historical values, in turn dramatically changing economic activity, the MASTER model is clearly an appropriate forecasting tool because the effects of such changes are contained in the model's stochastic equations.

A second application of the MASTER model deals with construction. Because of its highly disaggregated commercial and residential construction blocks and its explicit consideration of additions and alterations to the existing commercial stock, MASTER has been used at PNL and other national laboratories to generate national construction forecasts. These forecasts have typically been used with current stock estimates to forecast building stocks. These stock estimates are in turn used in determining the potential effect of various policies. For example, national residential forecasts provided by MASTER have been used by researchers at Lawrence Berkeley Laboratory to forecast the number of homes with refrigerators, which in part determines the potential energy savings from mandated increases in refrigerator energy efficiency.

A third application in the forecasting category is in local energy demand forecasting. The MASTER model's industrial and construction disaggregation enables it to drive economic/end-use energy demand models, such as those constructed at Oak Ridge National Laboratory for the industrial, commercial, and residential sectors. These models could not previously be easily applied at the SMSA level because estimates of industrial activity by sector, commercial floorspace by building category, and residential floorspace by building category were not typically available. MASTER permits use of these and other types of energy demand models requiring forecasts of local economic activity, and thus allows local energy planners to better forecast generation and transmission capacity requirements.

3.2 Policy Analysis

The MASTER model was also designed to assess a number of energy-related policy impacts. Measuring policy impacts requires using MASTER to generate two forecasts: one for a base case and one for the alternative scenario. In this alternative scenario, one or more of MASTER's exogenous variables are changed from the base case, which causes changes in MASTER's forecast of economic activity. The policy impact is calculated by comparing the forecast values of key variables (e.g., total employment, personal income) in the two cases. For example, many energy conservation programs considered by the U.S. Department of Energy, such as the Building Energy Performance Standards, would increase construction costs (and therefore construction prices) by requiring higher levels of insulation and other conservation measures in new homes and commercial buildings. The impacts of such policies can be expected to vary from one region to another due to variation in regional energy market conditions (e.g., energy prices) and construction market conditions (e.g., construction prices, existing building stocks, economic growth). The effects of such policies on local construction activity and economic activity can be measured using MASTER, since local construction prices are explicitly included in the model as determinants of construction which in turn is a determinant of employment, personal income, etc.

Other federal, state, and local policies affect energy prices. Such policies (e.g., natural gas decontrol) can be expected to have impacts which vary from one region to another because of varying local energy market conditions. Evaluation of these differential local impacts is required by the Federal Energy Administration Act of 1974. Because the MASTER model considers energy prices in determining employment and economic activity, it can be used to assess the differential local impacts of such policies.

Another potential application of the MASTER model is in assessing the impacts of exogenous changes in one or more of the model's endogenous variables. For example, construction of an energy-generation facility or a waste-storage facility in a particular SMSA or ROSA would directly affect employment in construction and some of the sectors (e.g., durable manufacturing) which supply the construction industry. Local economic activity is increased because of the facility, as these new employees purchase goods and services from the wholesale, retail service, construction, finance, insurance, and real estate sectors. Further increases in employment (on top of those required for the construction project) in these sectors result. In combination with regional input-output tables, MASTER can be used to assess these "induced" effects caused by construction of such a facility or by any other event or policy which directly changes employment in one of the MASTER industrial sectors.

4. EXAMPLE APPLICATIONS OF THE MASTER MODEL

In the previous section, potential applications of the MASTER multiregional economic model were discussed. In the present section, these capabilities are displayed. Four separate forecasts were prepared for each of nine U.S. SMSAs (one from each Census Division). The cities are Hartford, Connecticut; Pittsburgh, Pennsylvania; Minneapolis-St. Paul, Minnesota; Kansas City, Kansas-Missouri; Albuquerque, New Mexico; San Diego, California; Abilene, Texas; Jackson, Mississippi; and Atlanta, Georgia. At first, a base case forecast was developed. In this base case, local real energy prices and local real construction prices are held at their 1976 values through 2000. In the second case, real energy prices in each of the nine SMSAs were allowed to increase five percent per year from 1980 to 2000. In the third case, real construction prices increase five percent per year from 1980 to 2000. In the fourth case, the impact of constructing an energy-waste facility within each of the SMSAs is simulated.

Average annual rates of forecast growth in total employment, personal income, and population between 1980 and 2000 are displayed in Table 3 for each of the nine SMSAs under 1) the base case and 2) the energy price increase case. The nine-city average of average annual employment growth falls from 1.77 in the base case to 1.04 in the scenario, a reduction of 0.73 percent per year, while the corresponding average rates fall 0.58 percent per year for personal income and 0.57 percent per year for population. Local economic activity is thus seen to be relatively sensitive to energy price increases.

The percentage reductions (increases) in year 2000 employment, commercial construction, and residential construction between the base case and the construction price increase case are shown in Table 4. Employment in 2000 in the nine SMSAs is, on average, 0.24 percent lower in the scenario than in the base case. Commercial construction in the year 2000 falls, on average, 0.32 percent due to the price increases, while residential construction increases 10.17 percent on average. In six of the nine SMSAs, residential construction increases; in each of these cases, apartment construction rises dramatically while single family and duplex construction falls only slightly. In the three cities with year 2000 residential construction decreases, the non-apartment reductions are greater than elsewhere. The variance of employment and construction changes, caused by the construction price increases, lends weight to the hypothesis that energy policy impacts vary substantially among regions and thus must be assessed with a substate economic model; a more geographically aggregated model could not discern these variations. In the construction project impact forecast, a hypothetical nuclear waste storage facility was constructed in each SMSA. The results are applicable to any construction project with similar requirements.

TABLE A.1

DEPENDENT VARIABLE = PERCENT CHANGE EMPLOYMENT AGRICULTURE

INDEPENDENT VARIABLE	B VALUES	T STATISTICS
INTERCEPT	0.0226658	2.7314
% CHANGE, REAL WAGE	-0.0584061	-11.270
% CHANGE REAL PERSONAL INCOME	0.281780	6.3435
REGION FIVE DUMMY	-0.0443636	-3.2971
DEGREES OF FREEDOM =	455	
TRANSFORMED MEAN SQUARE ERROR =	0.16723198	

TABLE A2.

DEPENDENT VARIABLE = PERCENT CHANGE EMPLOYMENT AGRICULTURE SERVICES, FORESTRY, AND FISHING

INDEPENDENT VARIABLE	B VALUES	T STATISTICS
INTERCEPT	0.0613228	5.3851
% CHANGE, REAL WAGE	-0.694115	-21.268
CHANGE US AG SVC OUTPUT/POPULATION	36.8624	4.7537
LOG REAL PERSONAL INCOME	0.403032	3.4280
% CHANGE REAL PERSONAL INCOME	0.208995	8.4509
90 DAY TREASURY BILL RATE	-0.00634467	-10.095
REGION FIVE DUMMY	0.00743968	3.5613
DEGREES OF FREEDOM =	452	
TRANSFORMED MEAN SQUARE ERROR =	0.16891986	

TABLE A.3

DEPENDENT VARIABLE = PERCENT CHANGE EMPLOYMENT MINING

INDEPENDENT VARIABLE	B VALUES	T STATISTICS
INTERCEPT	-0.179574	-5.3600
LOG REAL PERSONAL INCOME	0.0123368	5.9169
REGION FIVE DUMMY	0.0409553	3.5166
% CHANGE, REAL WAGE	-0.108993	-14.968
%CHANGE REAL NATURAL GAS PRICE	0.236958	9.2056
DEGREES OF FREEDOM =	454	
TRANSFORMED MEAN SQUARE ERROR =	0.16167814	

TABLE A.4

DEPENDENT VARIABLE = PERCENT CHANGE EMPLOYMENT CONSTRUCTION

INDEPENDENT VARIABLE	B VALUES	T STATISTICS
INTERCEPT	-0.0326891	-7.6978
%CHANGE, TOTAL CONSTRUCTION (SQ FT)	0.0528998	8.6768
% CHANGE REAL PERSONAL INCOME	1.53033	26.812
DEGREES OF FREEDOM =	456	
TRANSFORMED MEAN SQUARE ERROR =	0.16479117	

TABLE A.5

DEPENDENT VARIABLE = PERCENT CHANGE EMPLOYMENT NON-DURABLE MANUFACTURING

INDEPENDENT VARIABLE	B VALUES	T STATISTICS
INTERCEPT	0.0131508	0.12336
% CHANGE, REAL WAGE	-0.658904	-12.890
% CHANGE REAL PERSONAL INCOME	0.476182	14.731
LOG REAL WAGE	-0.0717228	-1.9891
LOG REAL PERSONAL INCOME	0.0100386	2.3304
REGION FIVE DUMMY	0.00811243	1.3110
DEGREES OF FREEDOM =	453	
TRANSFORMED MEAN SQUARE ERROR =	0.16068745	

TABLE A.6

DEPENDENT VARIABLE = PERCENT CHANGE EMPLOYMENT DURABLE MANUFACURING

INDEPENDENT VARIABLE	B VALUES	T STATISTICS
INTERCEPT	0.00131830	0.12127
REGION FIVE DUMMY	0.0337253	7.9873
% CHANGE REAL PERSONAL INCOME	1.25710	59.861
LOG REAL ELECTRICITY PRICE	-0.0292272	-5.7549
% CHANGE, REAL ELECTRICITY PRICE	0.201149	12.130
DEGREES OF FREEDOM =	454	
TRANSFORMED MEAN SQUARE ERROR =	0.16978812	

TABLE A.7

DEPENDENT VARIABLE = PERCENT CHANGE EMPLOYMENT WHOLESALE TRADE

INDEPENDENT VARIABLE	B VALUES	T STATISTICS
INTERCEPT	0.185529	4.4298
% CHANGE, REAL WAGE	-1.21464	-10.539
90 DAY TREASURY BILL RATE	-0.00131737	-0.87762
% CHANGE, REAL ELECTRICITY PRICE	0.135576	2.8813
LOG REAL ELECTRICITY PRICE	-0.0855811	-3.2997
% CHANGE REAL PERSONAL INCOME	0.241367	4.5547
DEGREES OF FREEDOM =	453	
TRANSFORMED MEAN SQUARE ERROR =	0.14693999	

TABLE A.8

DEPENDENT VARIABLE = PERCENT CHANGE EMPLOYMENT RETAIL TRADE

INDEPENDENT VARIABLE	B VALUES	T STATISTICS
INTERCEPT	-0.0373716	-1.3424
CHANGE US RETAIL OUTPUT/POPULATION	0.500803	9.1278
% CHANGE, REAL WAGE	-0.374890	-9.1235
% CHANGE, REAL ELECTRICITY PRICE	-0.0541318	-4.4082
% CHANGE REAL PERSONAL INCOME	0.441880	14.275
LOG REAL PERSONAL INCOME	0.00320614	1.5973
REGION FIVE DUMMY	0.0128246	3.5232
DEGREES OF FREEDOM =	452	
TRANSFORMED MEAN SQUARE ERROR =	0.16556913	

TABLE A.9

DEPENDENT VARIABLE = PERCENT CHANGE EMPLOYMENT FINANCE, INSURANCE, REAL ESTATE

INDEPENDENT VARIABLE	B VALUES	T STATISTICS
INTERCEPT	-0.0302099	-0.56416
CHANGE US FINANCE OUPUT/POPULATION	1.15298	15.242
LOG REAL PERSONAL INCOME	0.00437110	1.2394
% CHANGE REAL PERSONAL INCOME	0.428551	16.418
% CHANGE, REAL ELECTRICITY PRICE	-0.180835	-4.6723
LOG REAL ELECTRICITY PRICE	-0.0212571	-2.0873
% CHANGE, REAL WAGE	-0.0407273	-1.0004
DEGREES OF FREEDOM =	452	
TRANSFORMED MEAN SQUARE ERROR =	0.16224223	

TABLE A.10

DEPENDENT VARIABLE = PERCENT CHANGE EMPLOYMENT SERVICES

INDEPENDENT VARIABLE	B VALUES	T STATISTICS
INTERCEPT	0.0216509	2.7889
% CHANGE, REAL WAGE	-0.601620	-29.793
CHANGE US SERVICES OUTPUT/POPULATION	0.525624	9.4526
LOG REAL PERSONAL INCOME	0.00285331	5.5942
% CHANGE REAL PERSONAL INCOME	0.208995	8.4509
90 DAY TREASURY BILL RATE	-0.00634467	-10.095
REGION FIVE DUMMY	0.00743968	3.5613
DEGREES OF FREEDOM =	452	
TRANSFORMED MEAN SQUARE ERROR =	0.16891986	

Table 3. Summary of Growth Rates in Base Case and Energy Price Increase Case

	Base	Scenario	Base	Scenario	Base	Scenario
Hartford	0.9	0.4	1.1	0.9	0.5	0.1
Pittsburgh	-0.7	-1.3	-0.4	-0.7	-1.2	-1.7
Minneapolis-St. Paul	2.1	1.1	1.9	0.9	1.4	0.6
Kansas City	1.4	0.6	1.2	0.4	1.0	0.3
Albuquerque	2.4	1.9	4.8	4.4	2.0	1.6
San Diego	2.2	1.8	5.0	4.7	2.1	1.8
Abilene	1.9	1.1	3.6	2.9	0.7	0.1
Jackson	1.5	1.0	2.6	2.1	0.8	0.4
Atlanta	4.2	2.8	5.1	3.8	3.3	2.3

Table 4. Percentage Changes in Year 2000 Employment, Commercial Construction, and Residential Construction Between Base Case and Construction Price Increase Case

	% Change Year 2000 Employment	% Change Year 2000 Commercial Construction	% Change Year 2000 Residential Construction
Hartford	-0.10	-0.39	97.00
Pittsburgh	-0.12	-0.36	48.59
Minneapolis-St. Paul	-0.04	-0.02	20.45
Kansas City	-0.08	-0.03	30.59
Albuquerque	-0.52	-0.48	121.77
San Diego	-0.21	-0.16	16.65
Abilene	-0.73	-0.83	-76.04
Jackson	-0.09	-0.14	-81.01
Atlanta	-0.31	-0.48	-86.45

For such a project, employment in each sector increases for two reasons. First, the construction itself directly requires construction employees and indirectly requires employees in manufacturing, trade, and other sectors to supply materials for the facility. The assumed direct and indirect manpower requirements of the hypothetical construction project for each of the five years required to construct the facility are listed in Table 5. Second, these direct and indirect changes in SMSA employment lead to changes in SMSA personal income and population, which, as explained in the previous section, induce further increases in employment in each sector.

The induced changes in economic activity were calculated by 1) forecasting economic activity in the base case; 2) forecasting activity in the presence of the project, with the direct and indirect employment changes exogenously imposed onto the economy; 3) calculating the difference between employment (or income, etc.) in the scenario case and employment in the base case; and 4) subtracting from this difference the direct and indirect employment (or income, etc.) increases. These induced changes are presented in Table 6. Each entry in the employment column is equal to the difference between total 1989 employment in the scenario forecast and total 1989 employment in the base case, less 2205, the direct plus indirect employment change in 1989 employment. Entries in the population column were calculated in a similar manner, using the 1989 forecast population values and again substracting 2205 from the difference. For personal income, the difference between the two 1989 values was calculated; from this was subtracted the wage bill associated with the direct plus indirect employment.

Table 6 shows that the induced effects of such construction activity can be substantial. The nine-city average induced change in forecast 1989 employment was 1870, compared to a direct plus indirect employment change of 2205. This induced impact varied substantially between regions, with a low of 926 persons in Kansas City and a high of 5106 in Atlanta. The induced changes in personal income and population show similar degrees of magnitude compared to the direct and indirect changes, as well as similar degrees of variance between SMSAs.

Table 5. Assumed Direct and Indirect Employment Changes Caused By Construction of Nuclear Waste Facility

	1985	1986	1987	1988	1989
Construction	1100	1500	1800	1600	1500
Mining	33	45	54	48	45
Non-Durable Manufacturing	44	60	72	64	60
Durable Manufacturing	165	225	270	240	225
Public Utilities, Transportation	33	45	54	48	45
Wholesale Trade	110	150	180	160	150
Retail Trade	22	30	36	32	30
Finance, Insurance, Real Estate	11	15	18	16	15
Services	99	135	162	144	135
TOTAL	1617	2205	2646	2352	2205

Table 6. Induced[(a)] Changes in 1989 Economic Activity Caused By Construction of Nuclear Waste Facility

	Net Change In Employment[(b)]	Net Change In Personal Income[(c)]	Net Change In Population[(d)]
Hartford	1325	14495	3801
Pittsburgh	1365	21685	4471
Minneapolis-St. Paul	1007	12246	2969
Kansas City	926	11745	2994
Albuquerque	1098	16215	3564
San Diego	1025	19563	3897
Abilene	2412	33679	5399
Jackson	3468	38358	6736
Atlanta	5106	60304	9109

(a) Total change in variable minus the direct plus indirect change. For personal income, the direct plus indirect change is the change in the wage bill due to the direct plus indirect employment changes. For population, the direct plus indirect change is identical to the direct plus indirect change in employment.
(b) Number of persons.
(c) Thousands of real, 1972 dollars.
(d) Number of persons.

FOOTNOTE

[1]"Stochastic here refers to a variable which has a fixed or structural component as well as a random component; i.e., a variable with a probability distribution. See Theil [16] for details.

REFERENCES

[1] Adams, R.C., et al. The Metropolitan and State Economic Regions (MASTER) Model Documentation. PNL-4698, Pacific Northwest Laboratory, Richland, Washington, 1983.

[2] Ballard, Kenneth and Norman J. Glickman. "A Multiregional Econometric Forecasting System: A Model For the Delaware Valley," Journal of Regional Science, 17 (1977), 161-177.

[3] Crow, Robert T., et al. "An Econometric Model of the Buffalo SMSA: A Progress Report," School of Management, State University of New York at Buffalo, 1973 (mimeo).

[4] Duobinis, Stanley F. "An Econometric Model of the Chicago Standard Metropolitan Statistical Area," Journal of Regional Science, 21 (1981), 293-319.

[5] Engle, Robert F., Franklin M. Fisher, John R. Harris, and Jerome Rothenberg. "An Econometric Simulation Model of Intra-Metropolitan Housing Location: Housing, Business, Transportation, and Local Government," American Economic Review, 62 (1972), 87-97.

[6] Follain, James R., Jr. "The Price Elasticity of the Long-Run Supply of New Housing Construction," Land Economics, 55 (1979), 190-199.

[7] Glickman, Norman J. Econometric Analysis of Regional Systems. Academic Press, New York, 1977.

[8] Hall, Owen P. and Joseph A. Licari. "Building Small Region Econometric Models: Extension of Glickman's Structure to Los Angeles," Journal of Regional Science, 14 (1974), 337-353.

[9] Harris, Curtis, Jr. The Urban Economies, 1985. Lexington Books, D.C. Heath and Company, Lexington, Massachusetts, 1973.

[10] Kmenta, Jan. Elements of Econometrics. MacMillan Publishing Co., Inc., New York, 1971.

[11] Loxley, Colon. "A Quarterly Econometric Model of the Cleveland SMSA," unpublished Ph.D. dissertation, Case Western Reserve University, 1975.

[12] Muth, Richard. "The Demand for Non-Farm Housing," in The Demand for Durable Goods, ed. Arnold C. Harberger, University of Chicago Press, Chicago, 1960.

[13] Olsen, R.J., et al. MULTIREGION: A Simulation-Forecasting Model of BEA Economic Region Population and Employment. ORNL/RUS-25, Oak Ridge, Tennessee, 1977.

[14] Rubin, Barry M. and Rodney A. Erickson. "Specification and Performance Improvements in Regional Econometric Forecasting Models: A Model for the Milwaukee Metropolitan Area," Journal of Regional Science, 20 (1980), 11-35.

[15] Taylor, Carol A. "Econometric Modelling of Urban and Other Substate Areas," Regional Science and Urban Economics, 12 (1982), 425-448.

[16] Theil, Henri. Principles of Econometrics. John Wiley and Sons, Inc., New York, 1971.

Analytic Techniques for Energy Planning
B. Lev, F.H. Murphy, J.A. Bloom & A.S. Gleit (Editors)

ECONOMIC AND ENERGY END-USE ASSESSMENT*

T.J. Secrest

Pacific Northwest Laboratory
Richland, Washington 99352

Battelle, Pacific Northwest Laboratories is assisting DOE in the assessment of R&D funding options for improving the efficiency of energy use in the residential and commercial building sectors. The structure of this effort is to integrate the use of two economic and two end-use energy models to develop detailed forecasts of end-use energy consumption in the residential and commercial sectors. The FORSYS Macro-economic model is used to construct a national economic forecast of economic activity to drive the MASTER regional economic model. This model is simulated to generate forecasts of commercial and residential sector construction activity for input into the two energy end-use models. The ORNL engineering-economic commercial and residential energy end-use models are then used to provide detailed forecasts of energy consumption by major end-use, building type and fuel type.

1. INTRODUCTION

The purpose of this analysis is to lay a rational, analytical foundation for Department of Energy (DOE) program decisions related to energy use in the residential and commercial sectors of the economy. The effort is based on an assessment made by the Office of Building Energy Research and Development (BERD) of the energy, economic, and technological environment that will prevail in these areas for the 1982-2000 time period under two sets of conditions. First is a baseline projection of the energy, economic and technological environment that will exist with no or minimal activity on the part of DOE/BERD. Second, the projected impacts of BERD programs in the residential and commercial sectors and in community systems will be measured against this baseline projection so that program costs, benefits, and impacts can be measured within a consistent methodological framework.

It must be recognized that any projection of energy and economic conditions is critically dependent on the assumptions and methodology used to make the simulation. The projections of energy use in the residential and commercial sectors are based on results from the Residential and Commercial Energy End Use Models originally developed for the Building Energy Research and Development Division by the Oak Ridge National Laboratory (ORNL). The Pacific Northwest Laboratory (PNL) FORSYS and MASTER models are used to provide forecasts of the economic environment. The FORSYS model provides the national level forecasts of economic activity and the MASTER model provides the local level economic forecasts.

The nature of this work is an ongoing assessment of BERD programs and translating these into model inputs, running the models and interpreting the results to help

*Work Supported by the Pacific Northwest Laboratory under Contract DE-AC06-76RLO 1830

evaluate the effectiveness of alternative programs in terms of both energy and economic impacts against the baseline projection. At this point in time the baseline projection has been completed. It should be mentioned that the baseline is itself subject to change given new information such as fuel prices.
This paper is organized to first present a brief description of each of the four models used in the analysis. The FORSYS and MASTER Model descriptions are abbreviated as a more detailed discussion of these two models was presented in this session of the conference. This is followed by a discussion of the integration effort to link the models. The fourth section presents baseline forecasts of the economic environment and end-use energy consumption using the January 1982 EIA fuel price forecasts.

2. MODEL DESCRIPTION

This section contains brief descriptions of the two end-use energy models and the two economic models used to perform the program assessment. These descriptions relate the models' structure, operation and key underlying assumptions.

2.1 ORNL Commercial and Residential Energy End-Use Models

The demand for energy in the residential and commercial sectors is derived from the demand for end-use services that the energy provides, i.e., space heating, air conditioning, water heating, etc. However, to satisfy the demand for end-use services, energy must be used in conjunction with a stock of capital goods that mechanically transforms basic energy to a usable form. The total demand for energy (energy consumption) in the two sectors, can then be seen as a function of three components: the intensity of demand for the particular end-use service (utilization rate); the stock of capital goods that supplies the service; and the efficiency with which the stock transforms raw energy into a usable form of energy for meeting end-use demands. The two end-use energy demand models perform the simulations by interacting these three components.

The approach taken in the two models is to forecast each of the three components of energy demand in the residential and commercial sectors for the period 1982-2000 and then to aggregate them to yield projections of total energy consumption. The analysis relies on two models initially developed at Oak Ridge National Laboratory (ORNL): the ORNL Engineering-Economic Model of Residential Energy Use and the ORNL Commercial Energy Use Model. The residential model has subsequently undergone significant revision at the Lawrence Berkeley Laboratory and the most recent version is used for this analysis. The commercial model has also received continued attention at ORNL and the most recent version of this model was obtained for this exercise.

Both models are highly disaggregated in their end-use energy projections. The residential model calculates annual energy use in the residential sector for four fuel types (electricity, gas, oil, other), eight end uses (central space heating, room space heating, air conditioning, water heating, food refrigeration, food freezing, cooking, and clothes drying); three housing types (single-family, multifamily, mobile home); and two housing states (new, existing). The commercial model calculates annual energy use in the commercial sector for the same four fuel types, five end uses (space heating, air conditioning, water heating, lighting, other); and ten building types (retail-wholesale, offices, auto repair, warehouse, educational, hospitals, public, religious, hotel-motel, miscellaneous).

The structure of the two models is very similar. Both operate on the premise that energy is consumed in conjunction with the operation of capital goods and in the short run (the period of time in which the stock of capital goods is fixed) total energy consumption is estimated by simply estimating the equipment stock and the utilization rate of the stock (the intensity with which the stock is used). Over a longer period of time, changes in the stock of capital goods and in the energy-using characteristics of capital goods must also be considered.

The residential model estimates the stock of capital goods (appliances) by combining estimates of the stock of occupied housing units, adding increases to the stock (new construction), and then estimating the saturation of each type of capital good in the housing stock. Similarly, the commercial model uses estimates of the stock of commercial floor square footage, the yearly additions to that stock, and the percentage of the total stock of floor space that is served by a particular end-use appliance.

The utilization rate of the stock of equipment is estimated from the price of capital equipment and per capita income, among other variables. From this estimation, short- and long-run usage elasticities are derived. The usage elasticities give the percentage change in the utilization rate of capital equipment in response to a percentage change in the fuel price.

In the short run then, the ORNL models operate in accordance with the following logical sequences. An increase in the price of fuel increases the operating cost of supplying any particular end-use service. Since the capital stock is fixed in the short run and, thus, so are the energy-using characteristics of the stock (i.e., the efficiency of the stock), households and commercial establishments can only respond to fuel cost increases by cutting back in their use of capital equipment. The magnitude of the cutback is determined from the short-run usage elasticities.

In the long run, as old capital equipment is retired and as new capital equipment is purchased to meet the demand created by new construction, the energy-use characteristics of capital equipment can change (the energy efficiency of new capital stock improves). Thus, household and commercial establishments may not only change the intensity of use of capital equipment in response to fuel price changes, but may also purchase more energy-efficient equipment and structures (for space heating and air conditioning end uses). Detailed technology curves have been developed that show the relationship between increases in the energy efficiency of equipment and structures due to technological design options and increases in the first cost of the equipment or application that would result from incorporating the design option. Thus, these technology curves show the incremental improvement in energy efficiency brought about by incremental increases in purchase price.

As fuel prices rise in the long run, again increasing the operating costs of supplying any particular end-use service, households and commercial establishments will purchase equipment that is more energy efficient for replacement and new construction needs to offset the increase in operating costs. This more efficient equipment also has a higher capital cost. In determining the level of energy efficiency that will be purchased, the models perform a life-cycle cost analysis within this framework. Consumers are presumed to buy more efficient equipment as long as the sum of the discounted incremental operating cost savings is larger than the incremental increase in purchase price. In other words, the models posit that consumers are attempting to minimize life-cycle cost in their equipment purchases.

In any given year, the models determine the energy consumption of additions to the capital stock from the life-cycle cost analysis and add this amount to the energy consumption of the existing stock to obtain total energy consumption. Note that as equipment becomes more efficient over time, its use may rise; the greater efficiency (reduction in relative energy cost) of the equipment will offset to some extent the energy savings due to the efficiency improvements.

The technology curves referred to earlier are a mathematical description of the tradeoff between capital cost and energy use. These curves are the means that the two ORNL simulation models use to reflect the technological potential for more efficient end-use energy consumption. The technology curves reflect the basic concept that, for any end-use and fuel combination, the available technological alternatives can be represented in terms of their first cost and energy-use efficiency. The most attractive of these combinations can be expected to fall in the neighborhood of a curve such as that shown in Figure 2.1. This curve demonstrates the expected properties, of decreasing energy use with increased first cost, while the marginal increase in efficiency diminish with succeeding increases in first cost.

The curve can be approximated by a variety of algebraic expressions. The commercial model uses the expression:

$$E = a + \exp^{b-d(c-1)} \tag{1}$$

where

E = energy-use requirement for standard operating conditions relative to baseline energy use E^*

c = capital cost of equipment, relative to baseline capital cost c^*

a,b,d = parameters of the function, specific to the end use and fuel type combination represented.

The residential model uses the expression:

$$E = d + (b+1)/(b+c)^a(1-d) \tag{2}$$

where the variables E, c, a, b, and d are defined as above.

The technology curves are estimated by the general process of defining a baseline energy-using system (e.g., a building shell, a furnace, a refrigerator) with a baseline energy use (under standard operating conditions) and a baseline capital cost, then comparing the estimated performance and capital cost of successive modifications to that baseline system. A sophisticated computer simulator model of heat transfer (DOE-2) was used, together with well-documented estimates of material and equipment costs, to define the data points for estimating the technology curves.

In some cases, the process of deriving the curves resulted in technological options that are clearly inefficient. For example, modification A is inefficient if it has a capital cost that is equal to or greater than modification B and also uses more energy than B. In such cases, the technology curve includes modification B and not the economically inefficient modification A.

The technology curves are used in simulating the choice of efficiency level of new structures and equipment in the projection period. This is made possible by assuming that purchases of new equipment are influenced by the general principle of minimizing the life-cycle cost of equipment. That is, they will move toward that combination of efficiency and first cost (i.e., along the technology curve) which results in the lowest sum of first cost and future energy costs (discounted to the present using an appropriate discount rate). This sum can be expressed, for each end use and fuel type combination, as follows:

$$LCC = c \times c^* + \sum_{t=0}^{n-1} (E \times E^* \times p^f \times (1 + e)^t)/(1 + r)^t) \quad (3)$$

where

LCC = life-cycle cost

E, E*, c, c* are defined as in Eq. (1)

p^f = price of fuel in year of evaluation ($\$/10^6$ Btu)

r = real discount rate

e = real rate of expected fuel price increase

t = year of interest

In the case of the commercial model:

$$c = \frac{b - \ln (E-a)}{d} + 1 , \quad (4)$$

Substituting (4) into (3) yields:

$$LCC = Ac^* + B \quad (5)$$

where

A = equation (4)

B = LCC - (c x c*)

The level of E that minimizes LCC is determined by setting $\frac{d}{dE}$ (LCC) = 0 and solving for E. This results in:

$$E = (c^*/ (p^f \times E^* \times d^{\,n-1} ((1+e)^t / (1+r)^t) + a) \quad (6)$$

which is the expression used in the commercial model to simulate the choice of efficiency of new structures and equipment for the heating, cooling, and lighting end uses for each year of the simulation. A similar derivation and expression are used in the residential model.

Equation (6) clarifies how the parameters a, b, and d, which represents the technology curves for each end-use and fuel type combination, influence the simulation of choice of efficiency of equipment and structures. These parameters are input to the models and can be changed from year to year to reflect changes in policy or the state of the world. Such changes might include:

- tax credits for conservation investments (a reduction in capital cost to the consumer of energy-efficient equipment, which translates to a shift to the left of a technology curve such as that in Figure 2.1 and an equivalent shift in the parameters a, b, and d)
- technological change that makes more efficient or cheaper equipment available to consumers (a shift down or to the left of the relevant technology curve, with equivalent shifts in parameters a, b, and d in an earlier year of simulation, for example, 1983 instead of 1986).

Equation (6) also shows that the discount rate r, which is used by the consumer to discount future energy cost savings to their present value, influences the efficiency level E that is simulated. The ORNL models have usually been run with discount rates r intended to reflect the effects of such factors as uncertainty about the performance of energy conservation measures, separation of the costs and benefits of conservation investments (such as between landlords and renters), institutional rigidities in capital markets, and the like. These factors operate to make observed investment decisions less energy-conserving than those that would be simulated by using a value for at or near the real market rate of interest. As a result, the values for used in the ORNL models are higher than the real market rate of interest, and the simulated investment decisions are influenced by these differences.

Finally, two caveats deserve mention. First, the analysis on which the technology curves are based is costly. Consequently, it has been necessary to choose baseline systems and modifications such that the results represent the best estimate for a generally-representative system, rather than a precise analysis valid for every variation of climatic condition, usage patterns, etc. This means that the technology curves used in the two ORNL models are almost certain to be wrong for some specific situations, even though they are believed to be reasonably accurate for the sector as a whole. Additional engineering analyses would help to reduce this problem (e.g., developing region-specific technology curves for building shell), but it is difficult to imagine completely eliminating the problem and the model's structure and operation of the model would become more complicated.

Second, it is likely that the technology curves used in the models slightly underestimate the available choices for the latter part of the simulation period (the 1990s). The curves currently used represent equipment and structural options which are either available in the market now or are sufficiently understood that their entry in the next few years is likely. Other technical breakthroughs will probably also occur in the next 10 to 15 years but, in the absence of the data necessary to evaluate their performance, they are not represented in the model's run.

2.2 FORSYS Macroeconomic Model

The current version of the FORSYS model can be described as an annual, dynamic, macroeconomic model of the U.S. economy with an imbedded 112-sector input-output (I/O) system. Prices and wages are determined by the I/O sector within the model and are used to determine net incomes to business and consumers. Relative prices and incomes are determinants of consumption and investment decisions. For this analysis, interest rates and other monetary variables are exogenous to the model.

A very important feature of the model is that it can be modified to reflect anticipated or hypothetical changes in the economy. The changes can be incorporated into the technical I/O coefficients, the consumption functions, other components of final demand, and the labor and investment functions. This flexibility allows a user to easily model changes in supply conditions, technological improvements, and a variety of government policy actions.

2.3 Master Regional Economic Model

Pacific Northwest Laboratory has recently completed the Metropolitan and State Economic Regions (MASTER) Model. MASTER is a simultaneous equation econometric model designed for application to the 268 standard metropolitan statistical areas (SMSAs), the 48 non-SMSA state areas, and any combination of these areas. MASTER provides forecasts of six major areas of activity: industrial and commercial value of shipments by SIC; employment by SIC; wage rates by SIC; labor market clearing; population; and income. The major exogenous variables used to drive the model are total value of shipments by SIC, U.S. wage rates by SIC, prices for non-labor production inputs, consumer price index/GNP deflator, U.S. interest rates, initial commercial building stock, population age distribution, and climate.

The MASTER model has a number of applications. First, the comprehensive database can be used to investigate historical trends in economic activity by country, SMSA/non-SMSA state area, and state. Second, MASTER can forecast regional economic activity for purposes of business and/or government planning. Third, MASTER can assess the implications of federal, state, and local government and business decisions on SMSA and/or non-SMSA state area economies. For example, MASTER can assess the regional economic changes caused by changes in energy prices, changes in national economic activity, climate variations, or the introduction of a large construction project (e.g., a power producing facility). Finally, the output from MASTER can drive other models, such as regional energy demand models.

3. MODEL INTEGRATION AND OUTPUTS

This section briefly discusses model outputs and how they interface to produce the integrated energy and economic forecasts. Figure 3.1 shows the models used and the linkages between them to produce the integrated energy and economic simulations. All of the models are driven by one or more exogenous inputs. These inputs are forecasted values of the six variables labeled, with the forecasts done outside the model structure. The purpose of the exogenous variables is to key the model simulations to a common base and, in some cases, to override the values of some variables that are internal to the models themselves.

As mentioned previously, the ORNL commercial and residential models produce forecasts of end-use energy consumption for the commercial and residential sectors. Both models are driven by forecasts of fuel prices and personal income. In addition, forecasts of annual housing starts and additions to commercial floorspace are inputs to the respective models. The construction forecasts were obtained from the baseline MASTER simulation of the entire set of SMSA and non-SMSA regions in the U.S. This MASTER simulation was keyed to the FORSYS baseline forecast for this analyis.

The output of the residential model provides detail on annual energy consumption for the forecast period by three housing types, eight end-uses and four fuel types as follows:

Housing type	vs	End Use	vs	Fuel Type
single family		central space heat		electricity
multifamily		room space heat		natural gas
mobile home		central air conditioning		oil
		room air conditioning		other - liquid gases
		water heating		
		refrigerators		
		freezers		
		clothes dryers		

for a total of 96 categories of energy consumption. Other information generated by the model includes:

- annual appliance installations by the 96 categories
- annual average fuel consumption per appliance by the 96 categories
- annual thermal integrity of new construction by housing type vs fuel type
- annual thermal integrity of the housing stock by housing type vs fuel type for central space heat, room space heat and air conditioned residences
- cumulative energy consumption by fuel type vs appliance type
- annual fuel costs by fuel type
- cumulative fuel and equipment costs by fuel type vs appliance type.

The output of the commercial energy end-use model provides detail on annual energy con-sumption on five-year increments over the forecast period by 10 building types, five end- uses and four fuel types as follows:

Building Type	vs	End Use	vs	Fuel Type
retail-wholesale		space heating		electricity
office		space cooling		natural gas
auto repair		water heating		oil
warehouse		lighting		other -
education		other		liquid gases
health				
public				
religions				
hotel				
miscellaneous				

for a total of 200 end-use categories. Other information generated by the model includes:

- annual energy use by end use, by fuel and by fuel vs end use
- annual energy use by the above 200 categories vs building vintage for three vintage categories
- annual energy use per square foot of floor space by the above 200 categories
- annual fuel cost by fuel type and equipment costs.

The policy/program options are effected in the two advance models by making changes in model inputs and/or parameters. One option is to simulate improvements in appliance and building shell efficiencies by redefining the energy use relationships for the specific appliance and building types, as could be brought about by DOE-backed R&D efforts. Another option is to simulate the effect of DOE information programs by changing parameters in the consumer decision-making framework.

To effect the program options in the two economic models, the changed energy demands produced by the two end-use models are applied as inputs to the FORSYS model. Changes in the values of these two demands between the base and policy cases becomes the basis simulating the national level effects of the policy/program option under study. Key national level indicators generated for this analysis are:

- Gross National Product
- total employment
- sectoral shifts in employment
- net energy demand
- net oil consumption and imports

The policy/program cases are effected in the MASTER model primarily through changes in the levels of the driver variables obtained from the national level forecasts produced by the FORSYS model. For the baseline case, the MASTER model produced forecasts for two SMSA's, Albany, New York and Portland, Oregon and the outputs include:

- employment
- income
- construction

4. BASELINE FORECASTS

The baseline energy consumption forecasts for the commercial and residential sectors for the period 1982-2000 are shown in Tables 4.1 and 4.2, respectively. These tables show total projected energy consumption in quads and the share of total by major end use, fuel type and building type.

Total energy consumption in the residential sector is about 45 percent greater than commercial initially and declines to about 35 percent greater at the end of the forecast period. Total projected consumption in the commercial sector increases at an annual compound rate of about 0.9 percent compared to about 0.5 percent for the residential sector.

Commercial sector energy consumption shows a decrease in the share of energy accounted for by space heating. This is almost entirely counted for by the increase in energy consumed for space cooling and to a lessor extent other uses. Electricity consumption increases significantly from about 60 to 74 percent of total at the expense of the other three fuel types. Consumption between building types does not exhibit significant changes in the share of totals except for modest adjustment in warehouse, education and health buildings.

The distribution of residential energy consumption by end use shows only modest adjustments, with most of the adjustment occuring in the first four end-uses. The share of consumption by fuel type again shows a significant increase in electricity. This is again offset by the other three fuel types, with the share of natural gas declining much more than in the commercial sector. Consumption between housing types shows a modest shift between single and multi-family housing.

The macroeconomic baseline forecast is summarized in Table 4.3. Results of simulation of FORSYS/EXPLOR suggest a very modest growth path of real GNP over the coming two decades. From 1980 to 1985, the growth of GNP will average about 2.75 percent per year. In the following five years, the growth rate will accelerate to about 2.9 percent per year. But the decade of the 1990's exhibits somewhat slower growth, about 2.4 and 2.0 percent in the first and second halves of the decade, respectively. The slow growth in the 1990's is explained largely by declining growth rates of the labor force.

But the components of GNP grow at rates that suggest increased competitiveness in the world economy and a shift to a larger proportion of investment to total output. Recovery after 1982 sharply increases the rate of growth in fixed investment, raising it to over 6 percent from 1980-1985. Although it slows somewhat in the next 5 year period (to 3.8 percent), fixed investment grows at a rate of 5.25 percent from 1990 to 1995 and at a 3 percent rate the last five years of this century. In 2000, total fixed investment is projected to account for some 20 percent of GNP, as compared to 16 percent in 1978. At the same time, our trade balance first narrows, bringing imports almost into balance with exports by 1995, but then exports grow more rapidly than imports. By 2000, our exports are growing nearly 1 percent per year faster than imports.

Over the forecast period, nonresidential construction is projected to grow at a rate of 3.1 percent per year, measured on a constant dollar basis. This compares with forecasts of commercial structures that grow at a rate of 4.5 percent per year when measured on a floorspace basis. This difference can be accounted for by the fact that the floorspace forecasts cover neither industrial buildings nor utilities. When these building categories are eliminated from the constant dollar forecasts, the constant dollar forecasts are much closer to the floorspace forecasts.

Residential investment grows at a somewhat faster rate than residential floorspace forecasts reflecting a continuation of trend increases in real costs per square foot of construction. Constant dollar growth of residential investment over the forecast period is at a rate of 5.4 percent per year, while floorspace forecasts grow at an annual rate of about 3 percent. Since these figures include multifamily and single family housing combined, the difference in growth rates could be caused by changes in the size of dwellings, improvements in quality, or a continuation of relative scarcity of residential housing.

The MASTER baseline forecasts of economic activity for Albany, New York and Portland, Oregon for the period 1980-2000 are shown in Table 4.4. The level of economic activity forecasted for Albany is modest at best, with personal income as the only area showing any increase. Commercial construction shows a very slight increase and all other variables decreasing. The forecast for Portland indicates significant growth for all of the economic indicators.

MASTER runs can be produced for any of the 268 SMSA and 48 non-SMSA State areas in addition to the two sample locations presented. More detail is available for all of the above forecasts and this detail would be used as necessary to show the projected effects of anticipated programs to promote the efficient use of energy in buildings. In addition to changes in the energy consumption patterns shown in Tables 4.1 and 4.2, information about the cost of the energy efficient measures and the value of the energy savings to building owners is provided. Changes in the economic indicators are also available in much more detail by specific sectors to help identify likely effects that a particular program may have upon income and employment by sector as well as construction activity.

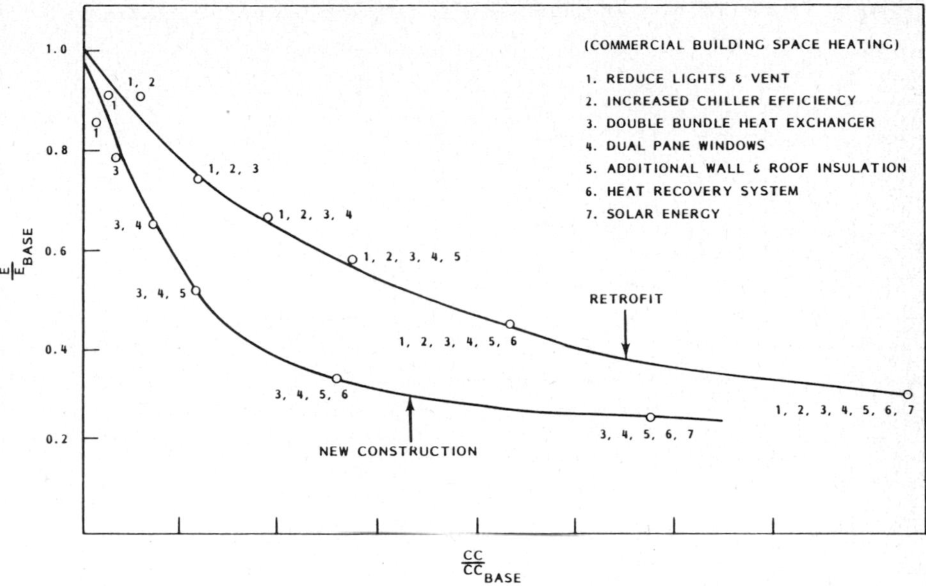

Figure 2.1 Capital-Efficiency Curve for Commercial Building Space Heat

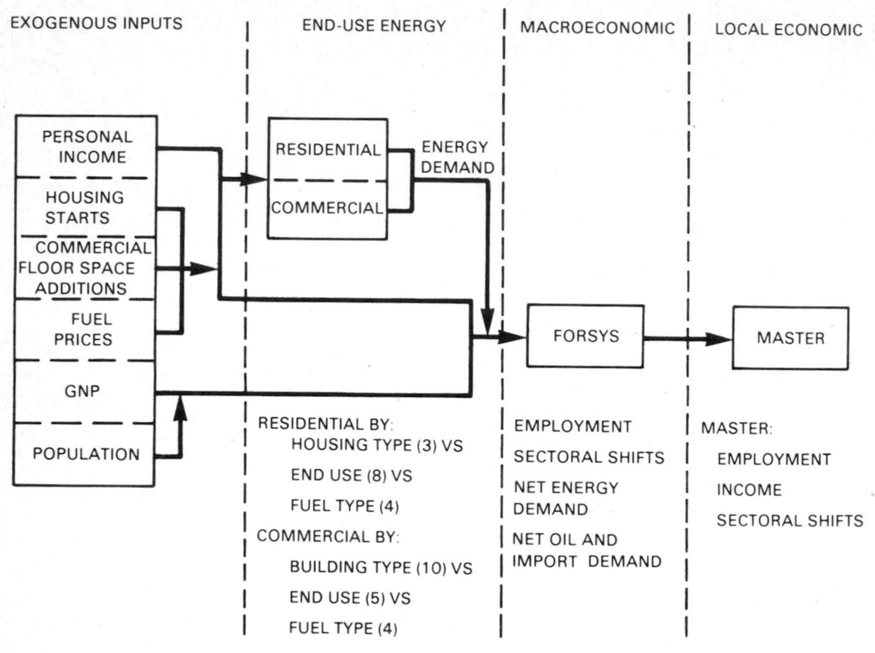

Figure 3.1 Model Integration Diagram

TABLE 4.1. Commercial Energy Consumption by Use Category

	Percent of Total					
By End Use	1982	1985	1990	1995	2000	Cumulative (1982-2000)
Space Heating	44.5%	42.3%	38.9%	35.6%	32.5%	38.8%
Space Cooling	25.1	26.4	29.0	31.6	34.2	29.1
Water Heating	2.6	2.6	2.7	2.7	2.8	2.7
Lighting	19.8	20.3	20.5	20.5	20.3	20.4
Other	7.9	8.3	9.0	9.6	10.2	9.0
	100%	100%	100%	100%	100%	100%
By Fuel Type						
Electricity*	60.5%	64.1%	68.2%	71.2%	74.2%	67.8%
Gas	25.3	23.9	22.5	20.9	19.5	22.4
Oil	13.0	11.2	8.7	7.4	5.9	9.1
Other	0.9	0.8	0.6	0.5	0.4	0.6
	100%	100%	100%	100%	100%	100%
By Building Type						
Retail-Wholesale	24.4%	24.7%	25.2%	25.5%	25.4%	25.1%
Office	17.1	17.2	17.6	18.2	19.1	17.8
Auto Repair	1.2	1.2	1.3	1.3	1.3	1.3
Warehouse	3.8	4.3	5.2	6.2	7.4	5.3
Health	11.4	11.1	10.5	9.9	9.0	10.4
Public	4.4	4.5	4.7	4.7	4.7	4.6
Religious	2.9	2.8	2.7	2.6	2.4	2.7
Hotel	5.8	5.6	5.4	5.3	5.2	5.4
Miscellaneous	11.5	11.5	11.3	11.2	11.2	11.3
	100%	100%	100%	100%	100%	100%
Total Quads	9.64	9.92	10.33	10.79	11.40	196.68

*Electricity consumption is expressed in primary Btu's

TABLE 4.2. Residential Energy Consumption by Use Category

	Percent of Total					
By End Use	1982	1985	1990	1995	2000	Cumulative (1982-2000)
Central Heat	36.6%	35.4%	34.2%	33.3%	32.9%	34.2%
Room Heat	12.2	11.6	11.0	10.7	10.5	11.1
Air Conditioning	13.3	13.8	14.4	15.0	15.2	14.5
Water Heating	17.0	18.1	19.9	21.5	22.5	20.2
Refrigeration	7.7	7.5	6.5	5.7	5.2	6.4
Freezing	3.1	3.2	3.2	2.9	2.6	3.0
Cooking	6.2	6.4	6.5	6.7	6.7	6.5
Dryers	3.8	4.0	4.2	4.3	4.4	4.2
	100%	100%	100%	100%	100%	100%
By Fuel Type						
Electricity*	53.0%	57.4%	64.8%	71.3%	74.8%	65.6%
Gas	29.9	27.5	22.8	18.8	16.7	22.3
Oil	13.0	11.7	9.8	8.1	7.2	9.6
Other	3.9	3.4	2.6	1.8	1.3	2.4
	100%	100%	100%	100%	100%	100%
By Housing Type						
Single Family	74.8%	74.1%	73.3%	72.6%	71.8%	73.3%
Multifamily	20.8	21.4	22.2	23.0	23.8	22.2
Mobile Home	4.5	4.5	4.4	4.3	4.3	4.4
	100%	100%	100%	100%	100%	100%
Total Quads	13.97	13.66	13.94	14.54	15.38	270.59

*Electricity consumption is expressed in primary Btu's

TABLE 4.3. Baseline Macroeconomic Indicators, 1980-2000

Macroeconomic Variables	History 1978	History 1980	Forecasts 1985	Forecasts 1990	Forecasts 1995	Forecasts 2000
Gross National Product (Billions, $1972)	1438.6	1474.0	1692.5	1952.1	2203.5	2432.9
Implicit Deflator (1972=1.0)	1.504	1.786	2.62	3.64	4.68	5.80
Personal Consumption Exenditures (Billions, $1972)	903.4	930.5	1081.9	1241.6	1360.5	1456.2
Fixed Investment (Billions, $1972)	220.7	213.3	286.8	347.5	454.0	525.44
Residential	62.4	47.2	54.7	60.9	72.2	88.6
Non-Residential	153.4	166.1	210.6	253.7	329.8	386.1
Structures		48.5	65.2	84.7	92.3	88.5
Government Purchases (Billions, $1972)	274.6	284.6	301.2	346.9	385.5	429.3
Net Exports (Billions, $1972)	24.0	50.6	25.6	27.1	30.0	43.8
Population (Millions)	222.63	227.65	238.67	249.55	259.02	266.84
Labor Force (Millions)	102.25	106.94	114.58	121.57	128.07	131.93
Unemployment (Percent)	6.9	7.6	7.4	6.1	5.0	4.9
Manufacturing to Total Output (Percent)	24.0	22.1	21.1	21.0	20.9	20.4

TABLE 4.4. Baseline Economic Indicators for Albany, New York and Portland, Oregon, 1980-2000

Economic Variables	1980	1985	1990	1995	2000
Albany, New York					
Employment	317,492	311,337	310,111	306,639	305,646
Commercial Construction (sq.ft.)	2,566,666	2,736,398	2,747,562	2,678,760	2,754,478
Residential Construction (sq.ft.)	2,470,520	2,069,179	2,024,756	2,105,294	2,026,790
Personal Income ($x10^3$ 1972 $)	3,841,129	4,000,739	4,164,953	4,216,251	4,294,771
Population	801,315	789,173	785,985	781,673	779,961
Portland, Oregon					
Employment	551,135	636,451	749,154	873,807	1,044,634
Commercial Construction (sq.ft.)	9,218,534	13,122,631	15,475,164	18,695,412	24,760,355
Residential Construction (sq.ft.)	21,462,411	22,222,247	23,385,605	24,554,927	27,747,911
Personal Income ($x10^3$ 1972 $)	6,922,504	8,617,380	10,925,608	13,730,770	17,921,367
Population	1,218,418	1,362,957	1,543,218	1,739,903	1,999,256

Analytic Techniques for Energy Planning
B. Lev, F.H. Murphy, J.A. Bloom & A.S. Gleit (Editors)

OPPORTUNITIES FOR COGENERATION IN COMMERCIAL BUILDINGS*

David Strom

Office of Technology Assessment
U.S. Congress
Washington DC 20510

Although the opportunities for cogeneration in industry are numerous and diverse, cogeneration in commercial buildings appears to have a much smaller market potential. Commercial enterprises typically require less heating than industrial concerns. As a result, the economics of cogeneration systems for commercial buildings traditionally have been much less favorable than those of industrial systems.

OTA reviewed the literature on commercial cogeneration and found it to be sparse and extremely site-specific. Therefore, we developed and applied a mathematical capacity expansion model to determine the market potential for commercial cogeneration for the rest of the century.

The results show that the opportunities for commercial cogeneration would be very limited, because cogenerators will have difficulty competing with central-station, coal-fired, baseload generation. Even when cogenerators compete with oil-fired electricity generators, the high capital costs of the cogenerators more than offset any savings from more efficient fuel use; and these high costs resulted in little significant penetration of cogeneration. When baseload expansion was constrained, however, cogenerators penetrated the utility system significantly and provided much of the heating demands and peak and intermediate electricity for the system.

Our results were highly dependent on assuming natural gas and distillate oil prices were equal. Lower gas prices would result in greater penetration of natural gas-fired cogeneration, particularly if competing with oil-fired electricity.

1. INTRODUCTION

While there is a large body of literature concerning the opportunities for industrial cogeneration, only a few prior studies have examined the potential for commercial cogeneration. These include a Federal Energy Regulatory Commission (FERC) study that estimated the amount of cogeneration that would be stimulated by the Public Utilities Regulatory Policies Act (PURPA); a study by the American Gas Association (AGA) that compares gas-fired cogeneration with two conventional heating systems in a hospital in

---

* This paper summarizes the analysis reported in Industrial and Commercial Cogeneration, OTA-E-192, February 1983.

area and by the State of California for State-owned buildings such as universities, hospitals, and prisons.

Each study has its drawbacks. The FERC study concentrates on large commercial buildings and ignores incentives other than PURPA such as tax benefits. The AGA study is limited to hospitals, which, unlike other commercial buildings, have a relatively constant energy demand. The conclusions of both the Consolidated Edison and California studies are relevant primarily for their regions and cannot be extended nation-wide.

Because the commercial cogeneration literature is sparse and has limited application for national policy, OTA undertook its own analysis. The goals of the analysis were to identify the parameters that significantly affect the use of cogeneration in commercial buildings and to estimate the future potential for cogeneration for the remainder of this century, based on these parameters. We constructed a computer model[1] -- the Dispersed Electricity Technology Assessment (DELTA) model -- that simulates decisionmaking by electric utilities and commercial building owners in choosing new capacity. While the model cannot be used to forecast future cogeneration capacity, it does give insight into how cogeneration might compete with new central station capacity to supply commercial electricity demand. The model can also be used to estimate the effect of such factors as thermal load profiles on utility decisions to construct either central-station or cogeneration facilities. The remainder of this paper describes the critical assumptions and limits of the DELTA model and the opportunities for commercial cogeneration.

2. CRITICAL ASSUMPTIONS AND LIMITS OF THE DELTA MODEL

The DELTA model uses a linear programming algorithm similar to those in use by utility planners. However, while utility models focus on minimizing costs of electricity production, OTA's model has the objective of minimizing the cost for producing both electricity and thermal power during the 1981-2000 period. The model simulates the addition of grid-connected cogeneration in three kinds of large new commercial buildings, with different types of daily load cycles, to supply electricity, space heating and cooling demands. Several scenarios were constructed to explore the sensitivity of utility investments in cogeneration for these buildings to regional utility and climate characteristics, fuel price changes, and different technological specifications.

2.1 Model Structure

The DELTA model differs from existing utility planning models in that its objective function is the minimization of total annual energy costs for both utilities and their commercial building customers. The model includes both the fixed and operating costs of producing power and providing space cooling and heating. Thus, DELTA goes beyond traditional utility planning, which usually analyzes those costs borne only by the power system. The strategy selected through this hybrid cost minimization may not exactly match either the strategy chosen by the utility or by the customer acting alone, but will tend to produce an average between both parties.

2.2 Demand Assumptions

The DELTA model only analyzes grid-connected cogeneration, because the PURPA provisions on purchases of cogenerated power are intended to benefit only those cogeneration systems that provide energy and capacity diversity to the electric utility system. The model specifies hourly demands for three types of energy: electricity, space heating and space cooling. The analysis begins in 1980 with a specified thermal demand baseline of zero load and zero capacity, and an electrical demand baseline of 1000 MW load. The analysis also assumes the existing capacity mix of three sample regions (which represent actual geographic conditions), each normalized to that 1000 MW electrical load (see Table 2 for a description of the three

Table 1.—Technology Characteristics (all costs are for 1980 in 1980 dollars)

Technology type	Cap cost ($/kW)	Fixed O&M ($/kW-yr)	Variable O&M ($/kWh)	Availability[a] (percent)	Heat rate[b] (Btu/kWh)
Base	1,014	14.0	0.001	88	10,300
Intermediate	200	1.4	0.0015	88	10,500
Peak	200	0.3	0.003	93	14,000
Cogeneration—high	750	0.0	0.008	95	9,751
Cogeneration—low	575	0.0	0.008	95	9,751
Thermal boiler	100	0.0	0.0	95	4,266
Thermal storage	2[c]	0.0	0.0	—	—
Electric air-conditioners	700	0.0	0.0	95	1,138
Absorption air-conditioners	110	0.0	0.0	95	5,251

[a] Availability is the maximum percent of time that capacity can serve demand - thus 88 percent means the baseload equipment is out of service a total of 12 percent of the year.

[b] The cogeneration heat rate shown is the heat rate for electrical service on;y: the net heat rate (including the energy in steam produced by the cogenerator) is 5,333 Btu/kWh. Both of the heat rates shown for air-conditioners are calculated in Btu/kWh of heat removed from commercial buildings.

Sources: Electrical Power Research Institute, The Technical Assessment Guide, Special Report PS 1201 SR, July 1979, specifies capital cost, variable and fixed O & M costs, heat rates, and availabilities for coal steam plants with flue-gas desulfurization, for distillate oil-fired steam plants, and for oil-and gas-fired combustion turbine plants. OTA multiplied the costs for these plants by the Consumer Price Index inflator to bring 1978 costs to 1980 costs, and used the Gross National Product inflator to bring 1978 dollars to 1980 dollars.

Table 2.—Sample Utility Configurations

Region	1980 capacity installed (MW) Base	Intermediate	Peak	Total	Electrical demand growth[a]	Annual peak in	1980 reserve margin
1	500	740	150	1,390	1%	Summer, winter	39%
2	1,020	0	237	1,257	2%	Summer	26%
3	285	1,107	50	1,442	3%	Summer	44%

[a] Annual growth in both electrical peak demand and total energy demand.

Source: Office of Technology Assessment

regions used).
While electric capacity was normalized to facilitate inter-regional comparisons, thermal demands and capacity were set at zero due to lack of data. This is equivalent to only allowing cogeneration in new buildings; in this case, cogeneration competes only with new centralized capacity.[2]

The total yearly energy demand (for heating, cooling and electricity) was separated into eight different "typical days" in order to observe more clearly the range and frequency of utility operating characteristics. Each typical day has a specific load pattern and frequency for each region and year. For example, the load cycle patterns for region 1 during 1990 are shown in Figure 1 for three typical days (the fall/spring weekday which occurs 108 times a year, the summer peak day which occurs eight times a year, and the winter peak day which occurs six times a year).

In addition to specifying the annual energy demand, OTA disaggregated the entire commercial buildings sector space heating and cooling demand into three different building types (called subsectors). The electric demands were not disaggregated in the model because it was our goal to capture the interaction of the cogenerators with the centralized utility system. Therefore, it was necessary to use regional load profiles, rather than those of individual buildings.[3]

The three subsectors -- hospitals/hotels, office buildings and multifamily buildings -- were chosen for their different thermal load patterns. For example, the region 1 space heating demands for hospitals and hotels are the lowest of all three subsectors, with small peaks at 8 a.m. and 9 p.m. Multifamily buildings use somewhat more energy and have similarly occurring peaks, while offices use the most energy of the three subsectors and have the most pronounced peak during the winter days at 6 a.m.

2.3 Supply Assumptions

In the DELTA model, different sets of fuel prices and technological and operating characteristics are specified in order to simulate utility and commercial building characteristics in the three different regions. OTA used two different sets of fuel prices to test the sensitivity of estimated cogeneration to changes in fuel prices. Because the outputs from the two sets of price assumptions differed by less than two percent, we report only the results from the lower price path here.

The major technologies used in the DELTA model include three different types of central electricity generating plants representing capacity used to serve base, intermediate and peaking loads; several space heating and cooling technologies such as conventional steam boilers, absorptive and electric air conditioners, and thermal storage; and the cogenerators. Table 1 summarizes the characteristics of each technology. To simplify the analysis, we assume the new baseload capacity in all three regions uses coal, while the new intermediate and peaking capacity uses either natural gas or oil. Cogenerators use either natural gas or distillate oil, depending on the region.[4] Because the linear programming algorithm is deterministic, the model cannot change the type of fuel used in either electric generating or thermal equipment from their original specifications in Table 1.

Two sets of capital cost for cogenerating capacity were used: \$750/kW and \$575/kW (in 1980 dollars). This is typical of the range of costs for cogeneration technologies presently available in the marketplace. Other operational assumptions included a fixed planning reserve margin for the electric utilities of 20 percent (although 1980 reserve margins were all above this threshold), a fixed electricity to steam ratio of 227 kWh/MMBtu for an overall thermodynamic efficiency of 80 percent, and a fixed efficiency for thermal storage of 90 percent (no electrical storage is considered).

The specification for the three sample utility regions are summarized in Table 2. As mentioned earlier, the electrical demand and initial 1980 capacity for each region was normalized to 1000 MW.

Figure 1.— Comparison of Electric Demand for Three Types of Days
(for region 1 during 1990)

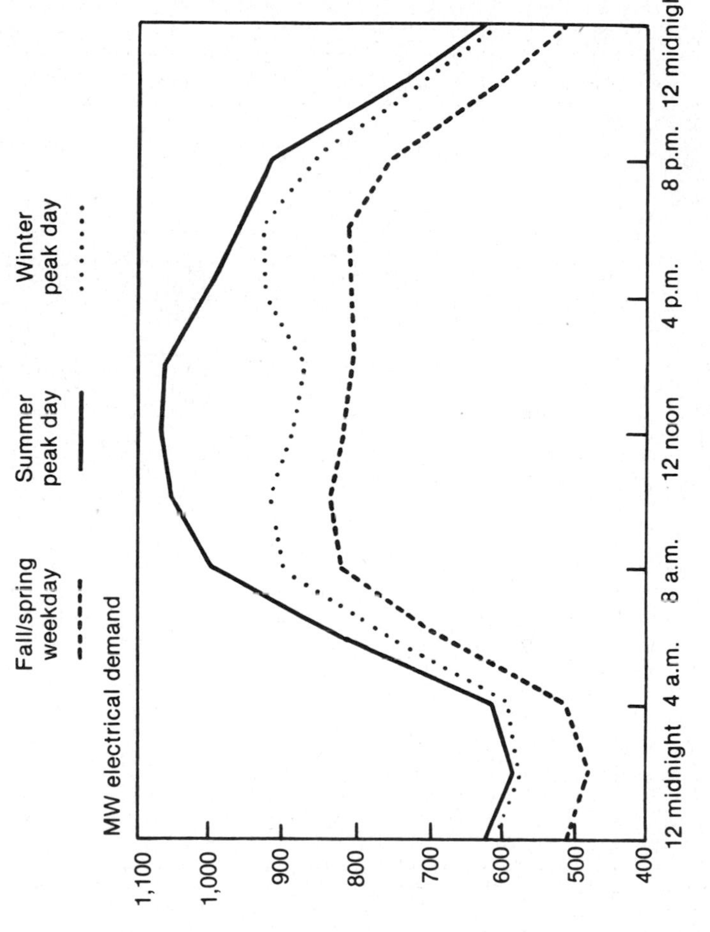

SOURCE: Office of Technology Assessment.

Figure 2.—Electrical Capacity Additions 1990–2000

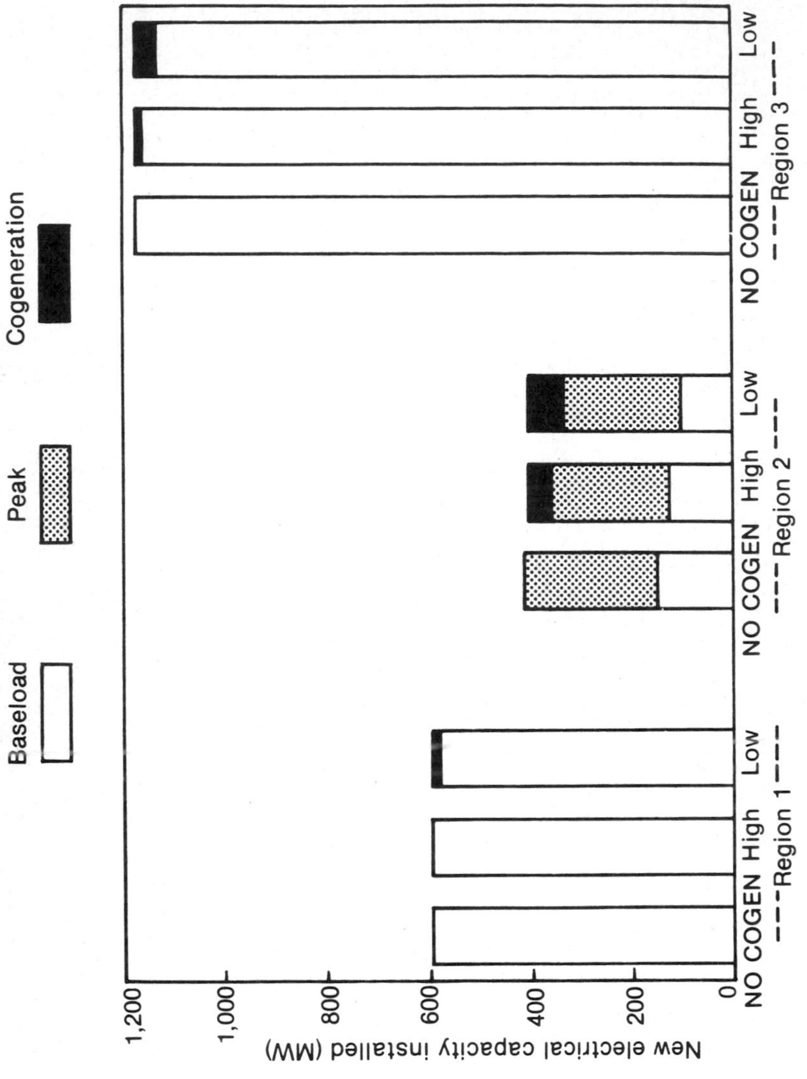

Baseload Peak Cogeneration

New electrical capacity installed (MW)

1,200
1,000
800
600
400
200
0

NO COGEN High Low
Region 1

NO COGEN High Low
Region 2

NO COGEN High Low
Region 3

SOURCE: Office of Technology Assessment.

2.4 Scenario Description

Based on the above demand and supply assumptions, OTA used the model to simulate nine standard and five special scenarios to investigate commercial cogeneration opportunities. The standard scenarios were grouped into three sets of three to represent the three regions: a base case in which no cogeneration is allowed and only utility powerplants are used to supply electricity and two cogeneration cases using higher and lower capital costs of the cogenerators. The special scenarios, formulated to investigate the effects of constraining the addition of baseload capacity and of using a zero capital cost cogenerator, will be described later.

3. COMMERCIAL COGENERATION OPPORTUNITIES

OTA's analysis of cogeneration capacity and its effects on utility system operations was concerned with two issues: first, whether a minimum-cost capacity expansion plan would include significant amounts of cogeneration; and second, how the cogeneration equipment that is added is used to supply electric and thermal energy.

3.1 Cogeneration Capacity

To see if cogeneration capacity would be economically attractive compared to central station generation for our set of assumptions, OTA compared the electric generating capacity additions for the base-case scenarios -- in which no cogeneration is allowed -- with the scenarios in which cogeneration can be added. The results, summarized in Figure 2, show that the greatest opportunity for cogeneration occurs when the match between thermal space heating and electrical demands is the closest. Thus, the largest proportion of cogeneration capacity is added in Region 2, which has the highest thermal demand of the three regions. Region 3, on the other hand, adds more total capacity (both cogeneration and central station) because it has the largest growth in electricity demand. With our assumptions, therefore, commercial cogeneration in new buildings is competitive with central station technologies only when there is a significant need for space heating and at least a moderate growth in electricity demand. Baseload capacity is cheaper than new cogeneration capacity when electricity is needed but very little or no heating is required. The baseload capacity is cheaper because it uses coal, which is less expensive than the oil used to fire cogenerators. This fuel price differential, considered over a 20-year planning period, overwhelms the capital costs of the cogenerators.

One way to test the impact of fuel prices on the attractiveness of cogeneration is to vary the capital cost of the cogenerator. By going to the extreme case of zero capital cost, the limit of cogeneration penetration can be shown under our fuel cost assumptions.[5] We tested this case for Region 2 and found that the cogeneration technology was more competitive with the coal baseload capacity and more cogeneration was installed than in the other cogeneration scenarios for Region 2. However, the amount of electricity produced from cogeneration did not increase significantly. This is because the electricity produced from the zero-cost cogenerators is still more expensive than the existing (i.e., also zero capital cost) coal-fired baseload central-station units.

Another set of special scenarios was formulated restricting the amount of baseload capacity additions in Regions 1 and 3. These scenarios simulate conditions where coal burning may be prohibited for environmental reasons, or where nuclear units have been restricted. For each region, one scenario restricted both baseload and cogeneration capacity, and one only restricted baseload capacity but allowed cogeneration capacity to be added. These restrictions increase the economic attractiveness of cogeneration in both regions. For example, in one special scenario in Region 3, 17 percent of new electrical capacity would be cogeneration, about four times the proportion of cogeneration installed in the standard scenarios.

Figure 3.—Thermal Supply and Demand for Winter Peak Day

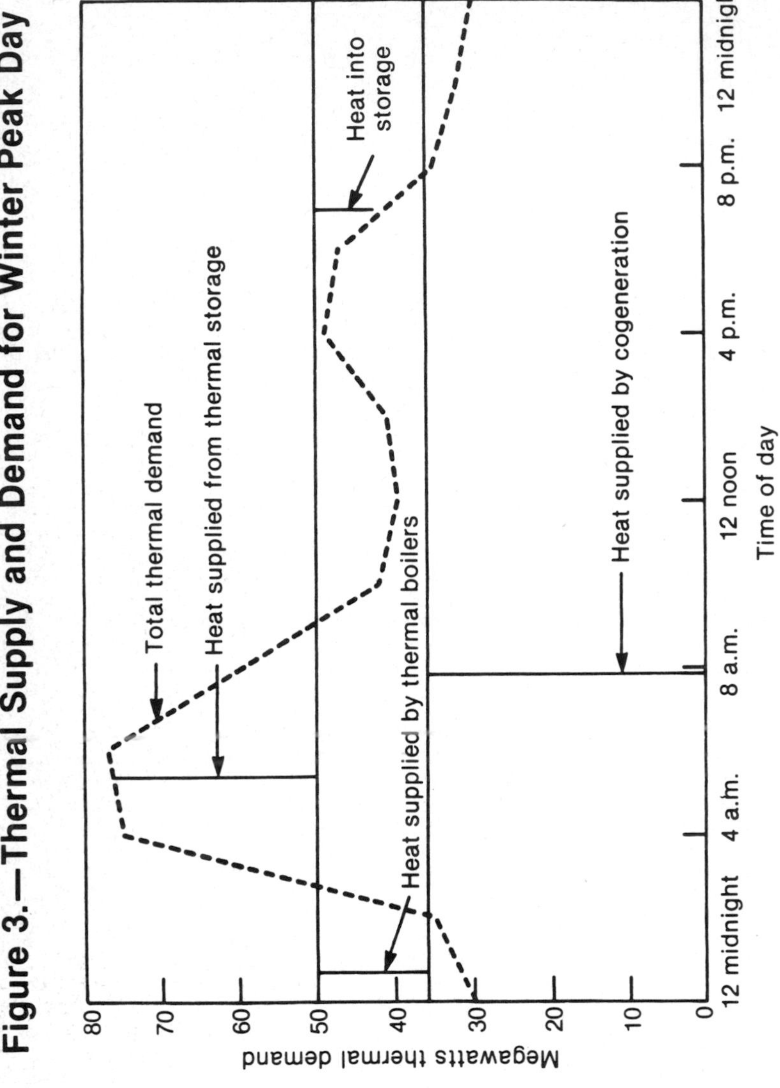

[a]For 1990, scenario 1—LOW-COST COGEN/COAL-LIMITED.

SOURCE: Office of Technology Assessment.

Figure 4.—Electricity Supply for Winter Peak Day

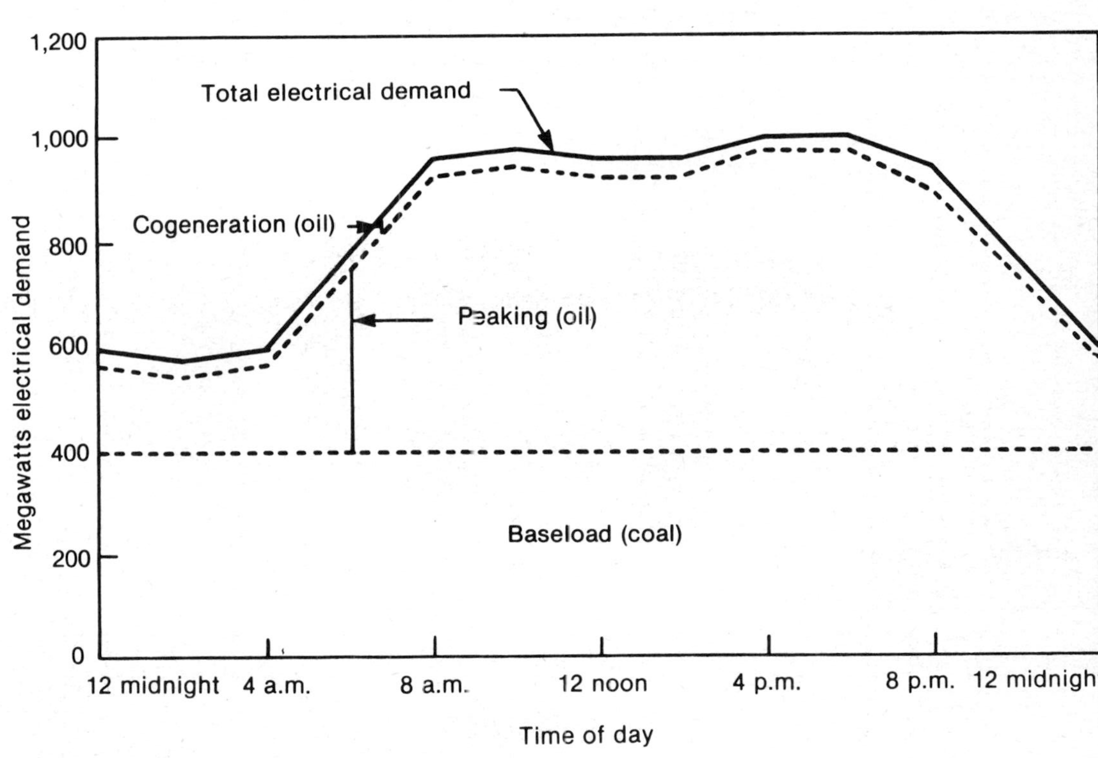

[a]For 1990, scenario 1—LOW-COST COGEN/COAL-LIMITED.

SOURCE: Office of Technology Assessment.

Figure 5.—Fuel Used in 1990 and 2000 for Coal-Limited Scenarios

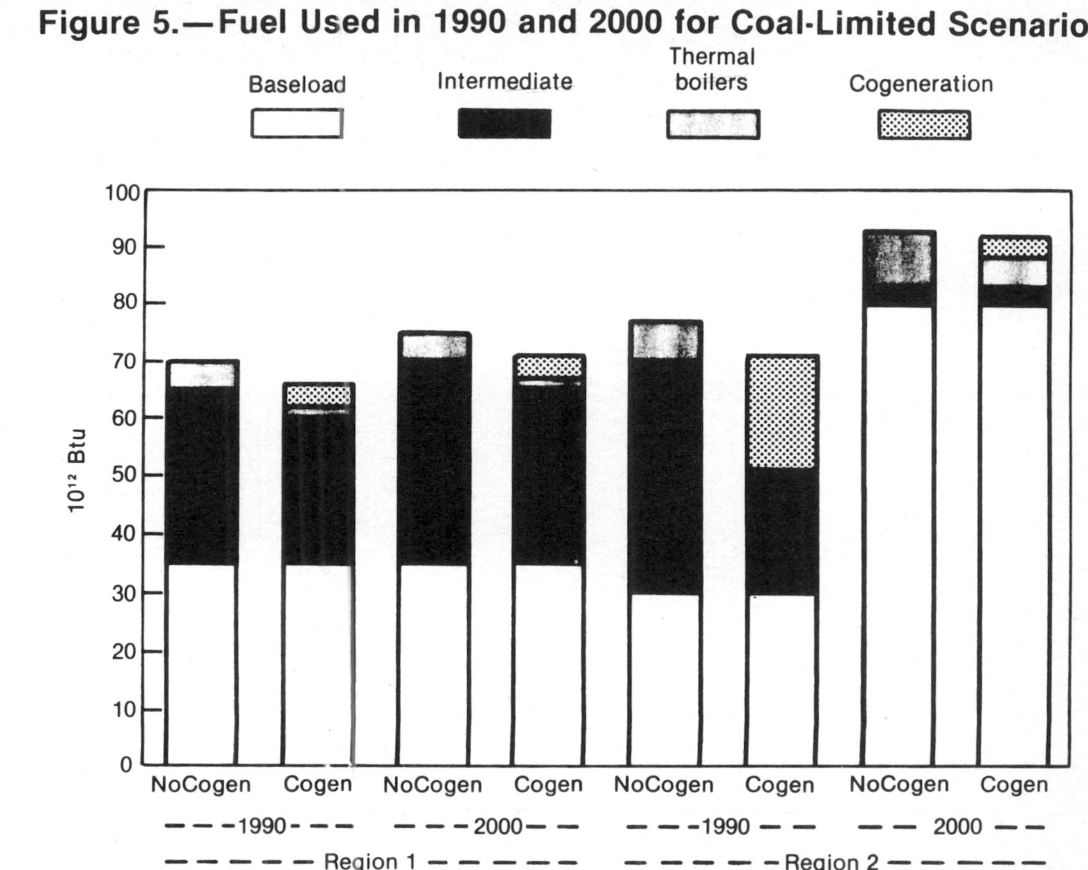

SOURCE: Office of Technology Assessment.

3.2 Cogeneration Operation

The details of how electrical and thermal loads are met in commercial buildings help explain the simulated cogeneration capacity. OTA calculated the capacity factor for both the cogeneration and baseload electric generation capacity in each of the scenarios. Most of the baseload capacity operates 66 to 70 percent of the time, while the cogenerators operate less than 30 percent of the time. This low capacity factor for the cogenerator results from its inability to generate electricity at a price competitive with central station electricity. As discussed previously, the cogenerated electricity is more expensive because of our assumptions about fuel prices.

In the nine standard scenarios, cogenerators are only operated when their electricity output is needed to meet intermediate or peaking demands that otherwise would be supplied by oil-fired utility units. The higher fuel prices of these units, combined with the high overall efficiency of the cogenerator, allows the latter to compete economically in the market for intermediate and peaking power. However, when coal is prohibited in the special scenarios, the cogenerators become more competitive with baseload utility plants. In this case, the cogenerators are operated more frequently, over 50 percent. These capacity factors only describe the general performance of each generator in the special scenarios, averaged over all eight typical days. Figures 3 and 4 provide a more detailed description of the hourly dispatch of all units in region 1 for space heating and electrical demands (respectively) on the winter peak day in 1990 under the special coal-limited cogeneration scenario.

During the 1990 winter peak day in this coal-limited scenario, the cogenerators provide about 37 MW of heat to meet thermal demands that vary between 30 and 78 MW, operating about 95 percent of the time. Thus, seen from the perspective of a commercial building owner, cogenerators operate as a "baseload" heating system during colder days.

The situation is different from the utility's perspective, however. Figure 4 shows that cogenerators only contribute to the peak load during the same winter peak day. The small numerical value of this contribution is partly due to our assumptions of zero thermal demand and 1000 MW of electrical demand for 1980. If a larger thermal demand had been assumed (incorporating the load of existing buildings and allowing for retrofit opportunities), the electricity contribution of the cogenerators would have substantially increased.

3.3 Fuel Use

OTA also analyzed the change in proportion of fuels used by both the utilities and commercial building owners in the sample utility regions to determine if cogeneration would displace any oil or gas. We assumed that cogeneration equipment used distillate fuels in Regions 1 and 2 and natural gas in Region 3. The results showed that cogeneration accounted for less than one percent of the total fuel used in all standard scenarios, so that it had little impact on total regional fuel mix. This is because cogeneration cannot compete with new baseload electricity from coal. Cogenerators operate only a small fraction of the time, therefore they use only a small fraction of the total fuel.

While fuel mix is unaffected by cogeneration in the standard scenarios, some changes in fuel use do occur in the special scenarios which limit baseload additions. Figure 5 shows that the addition of cogeneration to the sample system decreases total fuel use, when the cogeneration scenarios are compared to the base-case (no-cogeneration) scenarios. This is the result of two factors. First, there is considerably more cogeneration that operates higher capacity factors, as shown above. Second, this greater penetration allows the higher overall fuel efficiency of cogeneration to significantly affect total fuel use.

Overall, cogeneration has only a small effect on utility fuel use as long as electricity can be produced more cheaply with other types of technologies. However, in the special coal-limited scenarios, cogeneration causes less total oil to be used.

4. SUMMARY

By using the DELTA model and a set of technical and economic assumptions, OTA was able to determine the interaction of cogeneration with several hypothetical centralized utility systems. Under most circumstances, cogeneration additions in new commercial buildings were very limited because they could not compete economically with central station coal-fired generation. As a result, fuel usage did not change greatly from an all-centralized system. When coal-fired expansion was constrained, however, cogenerators penetrated the utility system significantly, providing much of the heating demands for commercial buildings and peak and intermediate electricity for the commercial buildings in the region.

Two specific conclusions can be drawn from this analysis. First, given our fuel price assumptions, cogenerated electricity cannot compete with new central station coal-fired capacity. Therefore, in commercial buildings, cogeneration will only contribute to peak and intermediate electricity demands. Lower-cost natural gas could change these economics, and in some regions, natural gas-fired cogeneration is preferable to existing central stations that are near retirement.

Second, if oil- and natural gas-fired cogenerators are used, their best opportunity is in three types of regions: (1) those regions with high heating loads (greater than 6,000 heating degree-days) and moderate electrical growth (at least 2 percent annual growth in both peak and total energy), such as the northern Midwest and Northwest; (2) regions where utilities are caught in a capacity shortfall; or (3) regions where the utility has a high percentage of oil-fired capacity and where cogenerators can use a fuel that is significantly less costly than oil. However, even if these conditions are met, cogeneration's competitiveness in the commercial sector will be subject to certain limiting factors such as competing with conservation measures that have a lower capital cost and shorter paybacks, the ability to supply significant amounts of power to the grid, and economic and regulatory uncertainties.

FOOTNOTES

[1]For a complete description of the model, as well as a list of references, see the full OTA report, Industrial and Commericial Cogeneration.

[2]While the exclusion of retrofits tends to understate our calculations of cogeneration penetration, it is important to understand that the choice to install cogeneration in place of an existing conventional steam boiler depends on three factors, all of which are extremely site-specific and therefore difficult to model. Excess utility capacity may keep the price of electricity below its marginal cost and thus reduces the payment for energy purchased from the cogenerator. Uncertain natural gas prices and availability prevents building owners from determining whether cogeneration will be cost-effective. Finally, uncertain financing conditions such as high interest rates and short loan terms will limit any type of capital investment by building owners.

[3]Similarly, if several buildings were served by one heating system, the individual cogenerators would have interacted with the system thermal load profile rather than those of individual buildings.

[4]We also calculated the cost of heat and electric power from synthetic fuel-fired cogenerators for comparison. However, these systems were not included in the model but are discussed in the OTA report.

[5]To some extent, zero capital cost is a surrogate for lower natural gas prices since either would reduce total costs of providing cogeneration heat and power.

Analytic Techniques for Energy Planning
B. Lev, F.H. Murphy, J.A. Bloom & A.S. Gleit (Editors)

A NEW METHOD FOR ASSESSING COGENERATION POTENTIAL
Northeast Utilities' Case Study

Barry Sedlik
Director, Industrial Energy Planning
Dames & Moore
7101 Wisconsin Avenue
Suite 700
Bethesda, Maryland 20814

This paper presents a phased investigation survey approach that provides comprehensive coverage, yet focuses the level of effort on identifying customers having the highest potential for cogeneration development. This approach is based on two major elements. The first is a systematic, staged survey design, used to screen good cogeneration candidates. The second is an analytical cogeneration assessment model that processes the collected data and identifies the type, size, configuration, and economics of the cogeneration system deemed most appropriate for each candidate customer.

1. INTRODUCTION

Northeast Utilities, the electric utility serving the majority of the State of Connecticut and a portion of western Massachusetts, in October 1980 commissioned Dames & Moore to undertake a cogeneration survey of the company's large electrical demand customers. The purpose of this initial investigation was to determine the extent to which cogeneration development is technically achievable among this customer class. Of 235 customers contacted, 151 (56 percent) indicated that their facilities had thermal energy requirements sufficient to justify use of the cogeneration systems to provide needed thermal energy (primarily process steam) while producing electricity for facility use or for sale to the utility. The study concluded that approximately 200 megawatts of capacity may be economic to warrant development of cogeneration. Based on these preliminary findings, Northeast Utilities decided to execute a more comprehensive and detailed assessment of the cogeneration potential that can be expected to develop within the service area over the next 20 years. The "Phase II" study, being conducted by Dames & Moore as well, began in the spring of this year and will be completed in early 1983. This paper describes the information needs of cogeneration assessment, the assessment methdology, and interim results of the study to date. This paper details the cogeneration potential assessment process applicable to most utilities.

2. NEED FOR ASSESSMENT

Many utilities throughout the country have utilized customer provided generation (e.g., cogeneration and low head hydro) since early in this century. However, it was not until the passage of the Public Utilities Regulatory Act of 1978 (PURPA) that a concerted national effort was undertaken to encourage the development of new cogeneration and small power production projects. Previously, the economics of many such projects were unfavorable. But legislated tax credits and incentives, simplified regulatory procedures, and the promise of "avoided cost," premium rates for the sale of electricity were expected to promote new interest in reexamining project viability and identifying many new opportunities for cogeneration and small power production.

The rationale for fostering such development was based on two key factors. First, from a technical viewpoint, cogeneration is more energy efficient than the generation of electricity from large central station, oil-fired generating units. As Figure 1 indicates, a cogeneration system can produce as much as 84 percent useful energy output (electricity and thermal energy) compared to about 35 percent in central station electricity generation. It has been estimated that cogeneration, if developed to its assumed potential in the nation's industrial plants, would yield an energy savings for the country equivalent to about 300,000 barrels of oil per day by 1990. Promoters also reasoned that since the majority of the capacity would be provided by industry and third party developers, utilities would achieve some relief from the financial burden associated with construction of new central station generation facilities.

Since 1978, developments have alternatively enhanced and impaired the prospects for cogeneration development. Among these are:

- Legal court challenges to the constitutionality of PURPA (1980),
- Federal Energy Regulatory Commission rule changes (1981),
- Development of liberalized depreciation and "safe harbor" leasing (1981),
- Tightening of depreciation rules (1982),
- Impending expiration of energy tax credits (December 1982).

In addition, the deepening of the current recession and the softening of oil prices are having a general dampening effect on energy inspired capital investment.

The risk and uncertainty resulting from these factors have no doubt been major elements in dampening anticipated cogeneration and small power production over the last several years. However, it must be emphasized that the lead times associated with electric utility planning require examination of long-term (10 to 20 years) generation alternatives. From this vantage point, the experience gained in successfully executed cogeneration and small power production projects during the difficult "shakeout" period will lay the foundation for additional projects in the years ahead. The increasing momentum for cogeneration and small power production is indicated by the number of projects requesting FERC certification for qualifying status. Under PURPA, this certification is necessary to qualify for avoided cost rates and certain tax benefits. As of June of this year, FERC received requests from almost 100 prospective cogenerators representing an aggregate capacity of about 40,000 kilowatts. Of this total, 60 facilities representing 26,000 kilowatts of capacity requested certification during the first three quarters of this fiscal year. The expiration of the energy tax credits may be somewhat responsible for the surge in interest. But it is probably fair to say that cogeneration and small power production developments are perceived as technically sound and financially attractive investment opportunities, a significant achievement considering the present state of the economy.

If indeed long-term potential for cogeneration and small power production development exists, then it is in the interests of electric utilities to explore, identify, and track that potential within their service areas. While such projects may represent a small fraction of aggregate generation mix, many

FIGURE 1
COMPARISION OF FUEL UTILIZATION EFFECTIVENESS:
Electric Power Generation Only Versus Cogeneration

POWER GENERATION ONLY

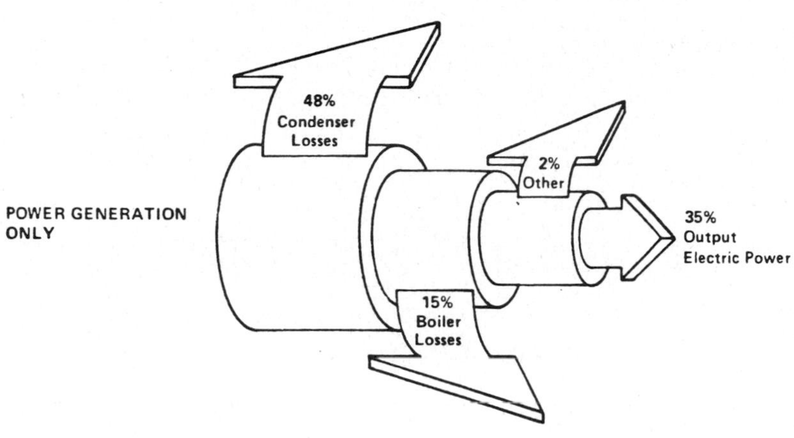

COGENERATION

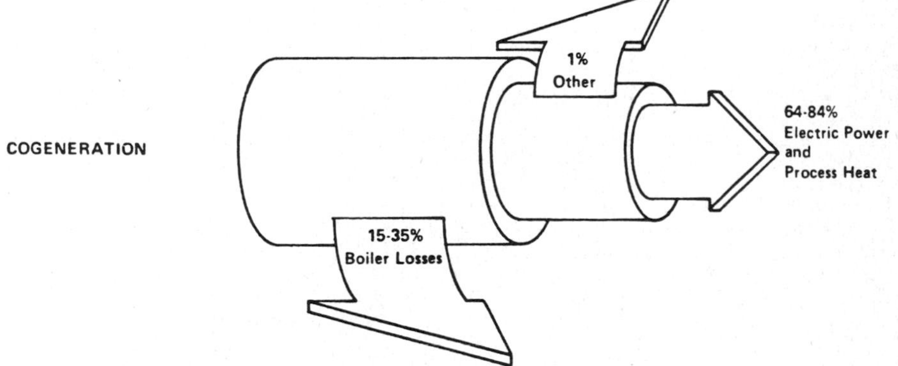

FIGURE 2

CONVENTIONAL TOPPING CYCLES

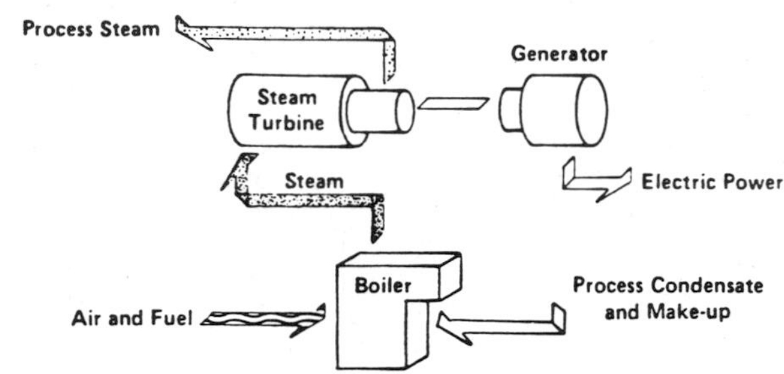

A. BACK-PRESSURE STEAM TURBINE

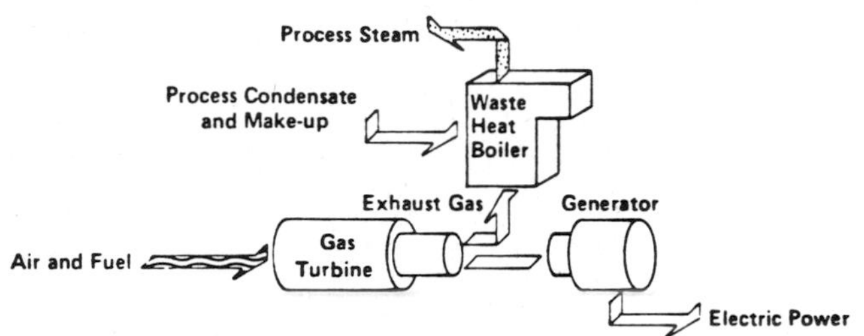

B. GAS TURBINE- WASTE HEAT BOILER

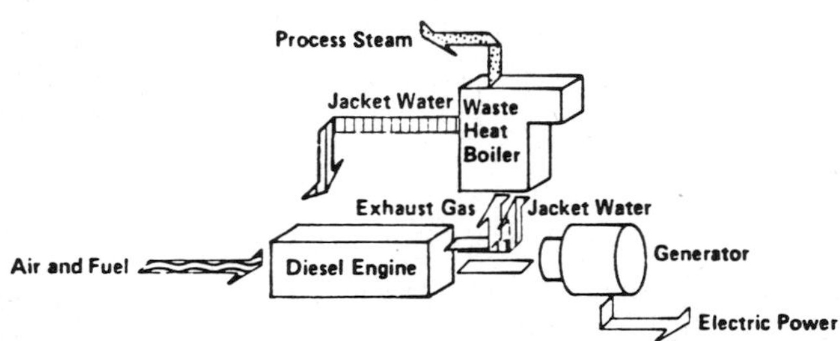

C. DIESEL - WASTE HEAT BOILER

segments of utility organization will be increasingly involved with cogeneration and small power production related matters. For example, generation planners and load forecasters must take into explicit account the impact of cogeneration and small power production development on future generation strategies, system load characteristics, and rate design. In addition, customer service departments, engineering, construction, maintenance, and accounting departments will all be involved in such projects, on a case-by-case basis. Generation dispatch will become more complex as dispatchers make provisions for the dispatchable and non-dispatchable capacity of these facilities. Senior utility management and legal staff may also be involved, as prospective cogenerators and small power producers elect to negotiate rates for long-term contracts rather than operate under available tariffs. Ultimately, utilities will need to make major policy decisions regarding financial and operational involvement in prospective cogeneration and small power production projects. Such decisions can only be made at the top echelon of utility management.

3. COGENERATION: ELEMENTS AND ALTERNATIVES

Leaving aside the matter of small power production, (the remainder of this paper focuses on cogeneration only), the level of resources that utilities will have to devote to cogeneration issues will depend on three key factors:

- Technical potential of customer facilities to support cogeneration projects,
- Economic viability of the projects,
- Decision-making processes that customers follow in choosing or rejecting cogeneration project development.

Technical potential for cogeneration is based on two key factors. First and foremost is the on-site need for thermal energy: process steam, hot water, process heat, process drying, mechanical drive, space heating and cooling. All these needs can be fulfilled with topping cycle cogeneration configurations. Several conventional topping cycle systems are illustrated in Figure 2. In each of these systems, prime movers (e.g., steam turbines, combustion turbines, diesel engines) provide mechanical shaft power required for generation of electricity with induction or synchronous generators. The exhaust steam (in the case of the steam turbine) is designed to be of sufficiently high temperature and pressure to be used for subsequent process related purposes. For combustion turbines and diesel engines, exhaust gases (and jacket cooling water in the case of diesels) are captured in a waste heat boiler to produce sufficient steam or hot water for process purposes.

Representative samples of some advanced topping cycle designs are depicted in Figure 3. The fluidized bed boiler/steam turbine configuration displayed in the diagram is noteworthy because of the operational characteristics of fluidized bed boilers (i.e., fuel flexibility, high efficiency, and low pollutant emissions). A hybrid of two conventional systems, the combined cycle, utilizing both combustion and steam turbines, offers the promise of increased overall system efficiency and operational flexibility. Finally, fuel cell cogeneration is depicted as an advanced technology slated for commercial availability in the early 1990's. The fuel cell is unique among topping cycle cogeneration systems in that electricity is produced as a consequence of chemical action rather than by mechanical means. The by-product heat of the reaction can then be used for thermal applications.

Another type of cogeneration configuration, referred to as a bottoming cycle, is

FIGURE 3

ADVANCED TOPPING CYCLES

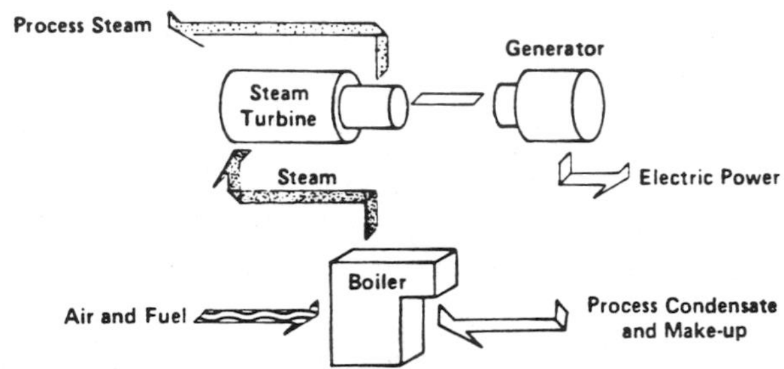

A. FLUIDIZED BED BOILER

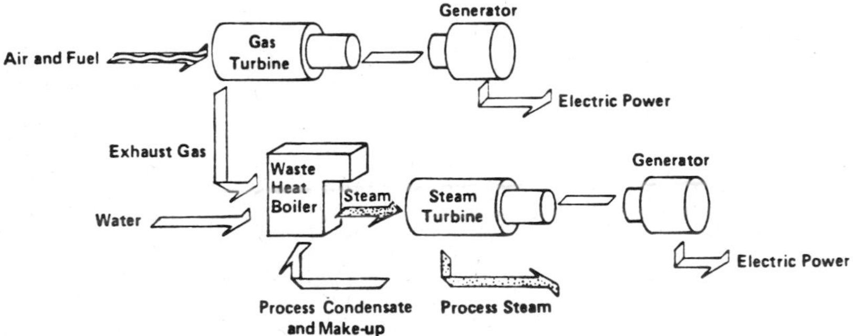

B. COMBINED CYCLE

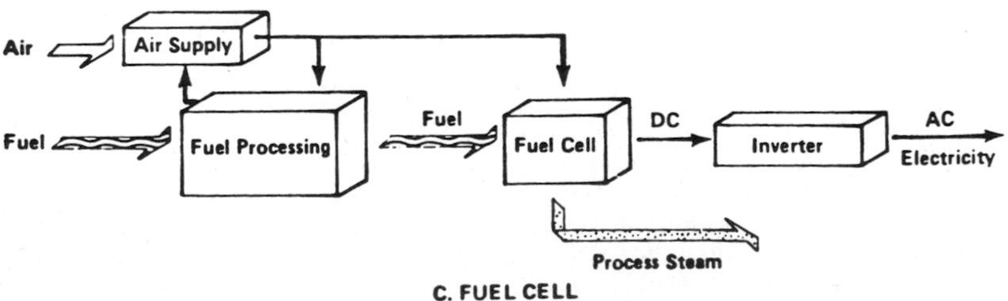

C. FUEL CELL

FIGURE 4

BOTTOMING CYCLE COGENERATION

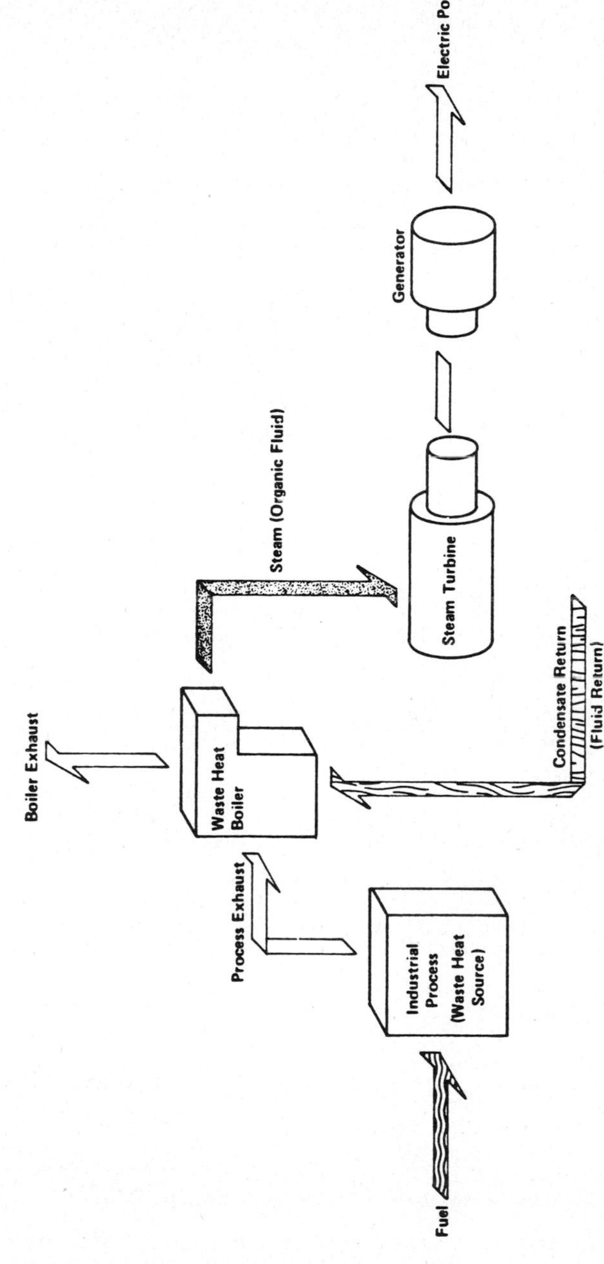

displayed in Figure 4. In this type of system, waste heat from process operations (high temperature flue gas or high temperature liquid streams) are captured in a waste heat boiler where water or an organic fluid is heated and subsequently expanded in a turbine for mechanical production of electricity.

In determining technical potential for cogeneration, the major factors are the quality (temperature and pressure), magnitude (flow rate), and duration of the facility's thermal sources. While it is conceivable that a cogeneration system could be sized to meet "trivial" thermal loads of short duration (e.g., wintertime residential space heating), serious cogeneration opportunities require year-round thermal loads at a "significant" level. Should insufficient thermal loads exist, cogeneration would not be considered technically feasible for two reasons. First, operated in an electricity-generation-only mode, the efficiency of the system deteriorates rapidly. In most instances, electricity purchased from the utility would almost always be cheaper. Second, technical efficiency rules preclude the operation of a cogeneration system in an electricity-only mode to receive the qualifying facility status necessary to be eligible for cogeneration benefits.

Finally, even if a cogeneration system could be identified to meet thermal energy needs, practical site limitations may preclude technical feasibility. Factors such as physical space, plant configuration, emission limitations, fuel availability, or noise production could each, or in combination, be sufficient to limit development.

Assuming technical feasibility is achieved, prospective cogeneration projects must also demonstrate economic feasibility. Economic feasibility is here defined as having a sufficiently short payback period or high enough return on investment to meet hurdle rates for capital expenditures. A proper economic analysis would account for the total capital cost, investment tax credits, proper accounting of depreciation, fuel costs, operation and maintenance costs, and time differential rates of sale and/or purchase of electricity. In conducting such an analysis, assumptions regarding inflation, interest rates, fuel escalation rates, and other factors must be treated explicitly. As many outside influences may affect project economics (e.g., availability of tax credits, avoided cost rates, cost of capital, etc.), the attraction of any particular project may change considerably over time. Thus projects that are evaluated as being uneconomic today but are still technically feasible could conceivably be demonstrated as having a favorable economic position when reevaluated sometime in the future.

Finally, should projects be technically and economically feasible, many barriers to successful project execution may still exist. Factors such as company policy, competitive strategy, and availability of capital are all real considerations that ultimately determine if a project will be developed.

4. METHODOLOGY

Obviously, the first step that a utility must undertake in assessing the cogeneration potential of its service area is to examine the technical cogeneration potential of its customers' facilities. Unfortunately, while a utility may have significant knowledge about its customers' electrical requirements and historical usage patterns, little information is generally maintained on nonelectrical energy usage and characteristics, the prime requisite for establishing an estimate of cogeneration potential.

The utility must decide how to collect and process such information in the most efficient and cost-effective manner. A wide range of alternatives is available. In the most rigorous case, the utility would execute engineering

FIGURE 5
COGENERATION SURVEY DESIGN

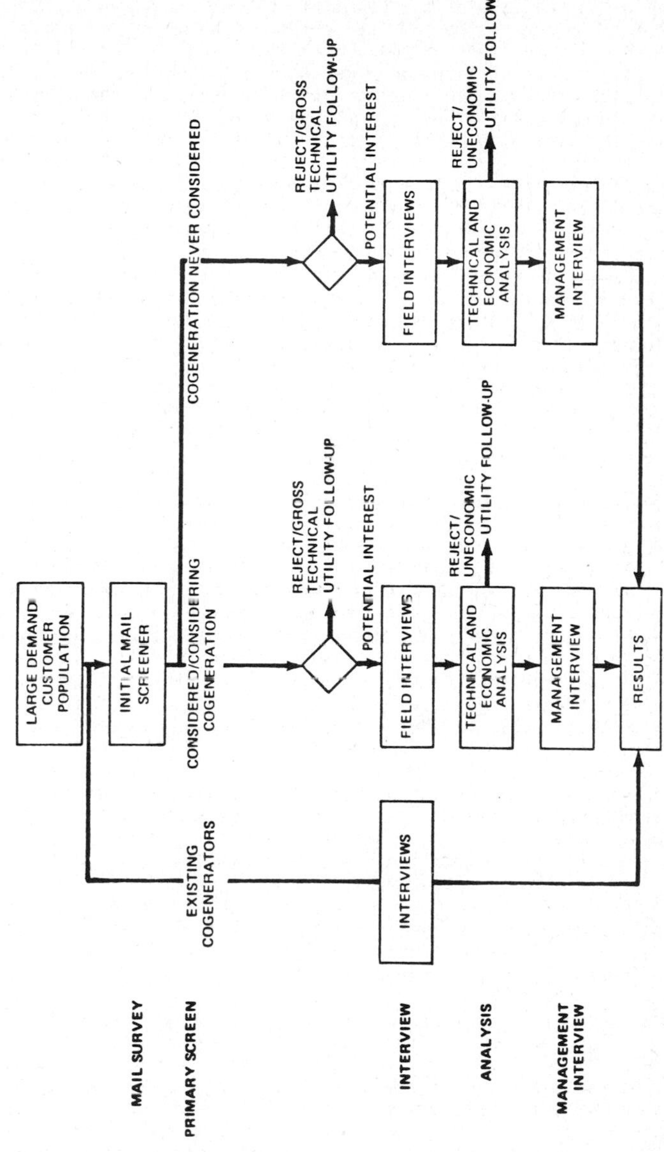

feasibility studies on a customer-by-customer basis. While this level of investigation would provide the most detailed and accurate information, the cost could quickly become prohibitive if large numbers of customers were to be examined. At the other extreme, a utility could "guess" what cogeneration potential a particular customer may have based on the type of facility (industrial, commercial, institutional) the customer has at its location. While such a procedure can provide a quick and inexpensive estimate, the site specific nature of cogeneration will cause the errors to vary in an unpredictable fashion.

In its investigation of cogeneration potential for Northeast Utilities, Dames & Moore utilized a phased investigative survey approach that provides comprehensive coverage yet focuses the level of effort on identifying customers having the highest potential for cogeneration development. This approach is based on two major elements. The first is a systematic, staged survey design, used to screen good cogeneration candidates. The second element is an analytic cogeneration assessment model that processes the collected data and identifies the type, size, configuration, and economics of the cogeneration system deemed most appropriate for each candidate customer. The survey structure and assessment model are described in more detail below.

4.1 Survey Structure

Figure 5 presents the overall Dames & Moore survey design. There are several salient features associated with this multistage approach. The three principal stages are a preliminary mail questionnaire to all large demand customers in the service area, a more detailed field investigation to collect facility data on "good" candidates, and personal interviews with those customers at the management level where cogeneration projects would be approved. A major feature, indicated on the figure, is that three major groups within the large demand customer population are segregated. The first group contains customers that are existing cogenerators. The second group consists of customers that have previously considered or are presently considering cogeneration at their facilities. The third group is the remainder of the large demand customer population, customers that have never considered cogeneration.

The mail survey is formulated to extract information from the customer in five key areas. These include:

1. Background information about the facility (e.g., number of buildings, number of employees, operating hours);

2. Energy use characteristics (e.g., fuel used, end use requirements);

3. Energy equipment characteristics (e.g., boilers, prime movers);

4. Past and present cogeneration consideration (e.g., types of systems considered, reason for accepting/rejecting);

5. Intentions and contingencies (e.g., plans for future energy use, energy conservation measures).

Other questions are asked regarding the customer's potential interest in developing a cogeneration project.

The field survey is intended to be conducted as a personal interview. The main purpose of the field survey is to collect more detailed information as follow-up to the mail survey. Particular attention is paid to developing time-of-use data so that the economics of peak and off-peak sales or use of electricity can be

FIGURE 6

ANALYTIC MODEL ORGANIZATION

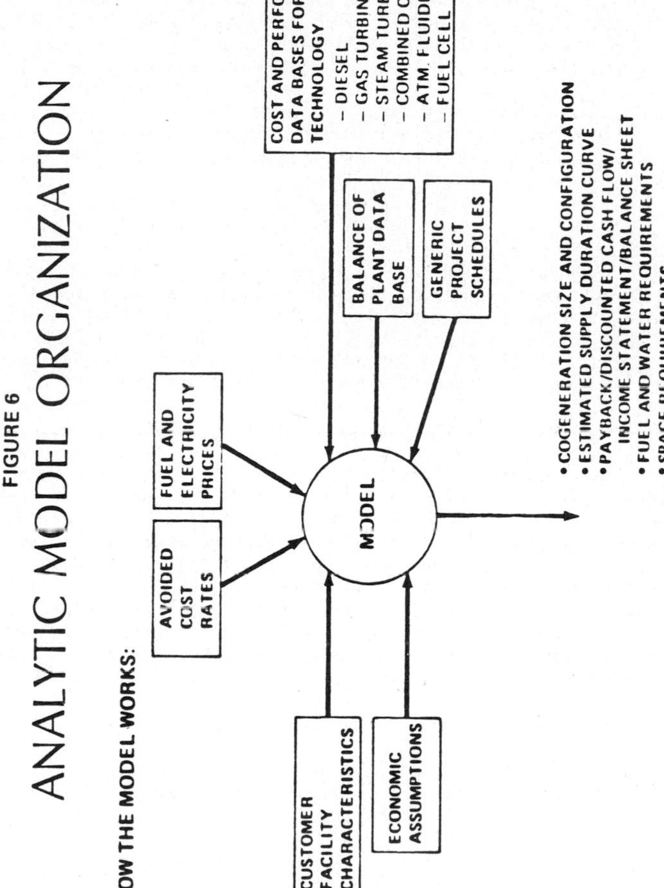

considered explicitly. More detailed information is also solicited on the customer's existing and planned energy equipment, to enable consideration of retrofit cogeneration applications.

The third stage management interview has two key purposes. First, the results of the cogeneration assessment for the customer's facility are explained to the company's (or institution's) management personnel. In discussing the technical and economic results, the steps involved in proceeding with a cogeneration project are outlined. Financial alternatives, including various project financing strategies, are also presented. The second purpose of the management interview is to solicit from the decisonmaker his attitude about the prospects for proceeding with the project and the requirements that would have to be met before such a decison could be made.

4.2 Analytic Model

The ability to estimate technical capability and economic attractiveness of a cogeneration project requires a substantial engineering investigation of operating conditions, existing physical plant, and economic criteria assumed and utilized by management. A candidate interested in assessing the cogeneration potential of his facility would normally have a rigorous engineering feasibility study performed in order to decide if it is worthwhile to proceed with a cogeneration project. Such an investigation is clearly beyond the scope of an investigation of this kind. As a consequence, it is necessary to develop an analytic approach that captures the salient features of a detailed engineering feasibility study, yet can be performed with a minimum expenditure of time and resources. Dames & Moore has developed an analytic model for this purpose. A schematic diagram of the model is presented as Figure 6. The model examines energy use, characteristics of a customer's facility (steam and thermal requirements, waste heat availability), and compares these requirements to the characteristics of available cogeneration systems tht can fulfill the requirements or utilize waste heat resources for the production of electric power. After a technical match is identified, an economic analysis is performed to indicate the return on investment and payback that such a cogeneration system would produce for its owners.

5. FINDINGS

5.1 Large Customer Characteristics

As a first step in assessing cogeneration potential, it is essential that the characteristics of the segment of the customer population believed to include the "best" candidates be defined as well as possible. Of Northeast Utilities' approximately 80,000 industrial and commercial accounts, those customers with actual or billing demand in excess of 1 megawatt were assumed to encompass most of the available cogeneration potential. Although this criterion is somewhat arbitrary, it can be justified for these specific reasons:

- It is a "well defined" population;
- Customers in this group are likely to have a high average annual demand conducive to favorable cogeneration economics;
- Northeast Utilities personnel acquainted with the customers indicate that this group is most likely to have process steam requirements.

FIGURE 7
ACCOUNTS WITH ONE MEGAWATT OR GREATER ACTUAL OR BILLING DEMAND (MAJOR STANDARD INDUSTRIAL CLASSIFICATION)
NORTHEAST UTILITIES' SERVICE AREA COGENERATION POTENTIAL STUDY

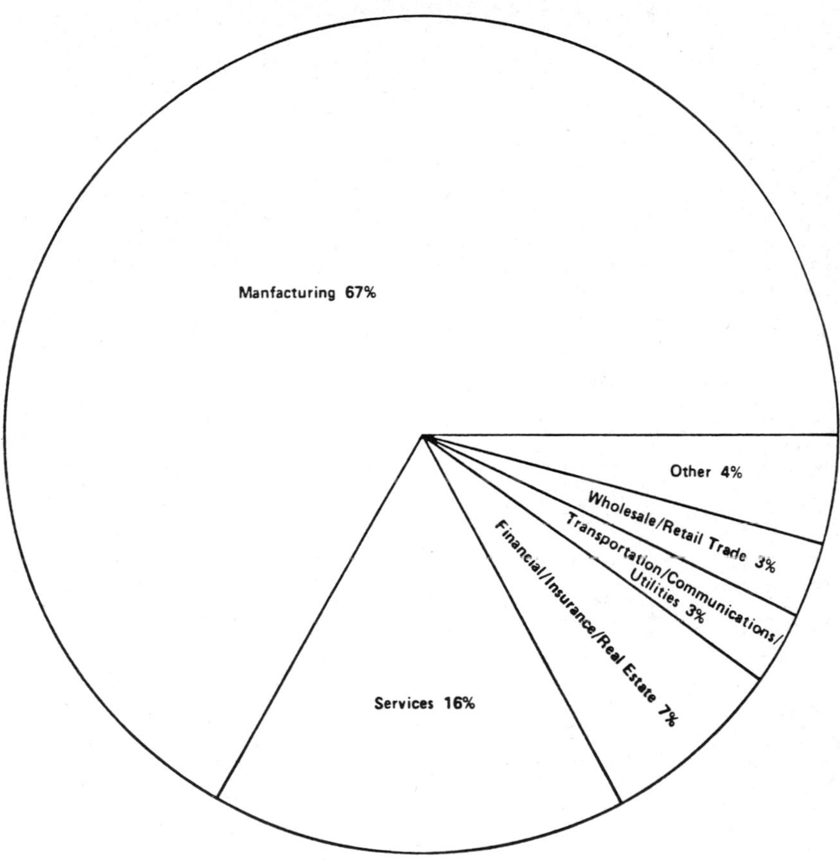

FIGURE 8
ACCOUNTS WITH ACTUAL OR BILLING DEMAND OF ONE MEGAWATT OR GREATER AS A PERCENT OF TOTAL INDUSTRIAL AND COMMERCIAL MEGAWATT-HOUR SALES
(MAJOR STANDARD INDUSTRIAL CLASSIFICATION)

NORTHEAST UTILITIES' SERVICE AREA
COGENERATION POTENTIAL STUDY

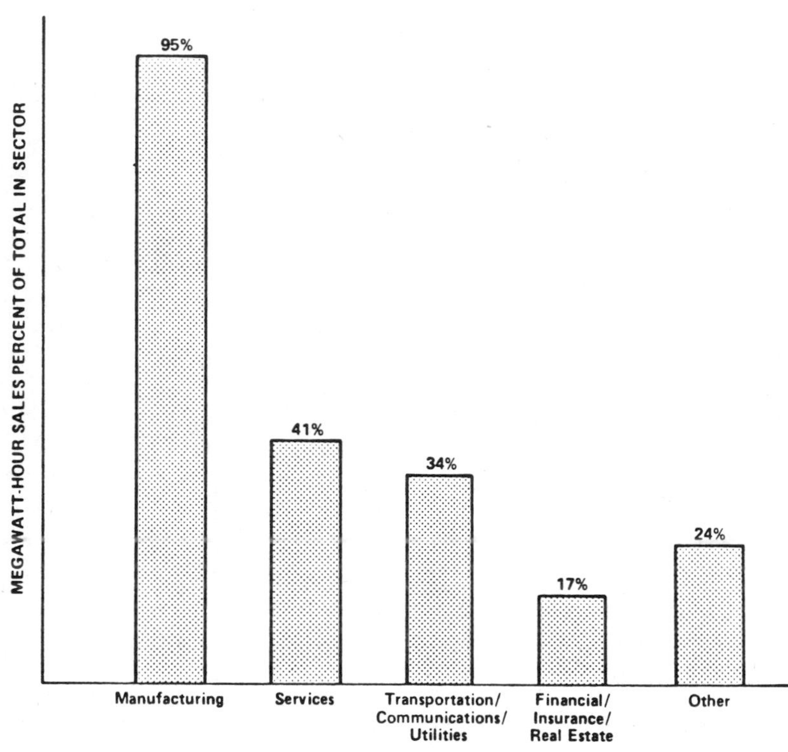

FIGURE 9

PRELIMINARY DISTRIBUTION OF TOP RANKED SYSTEMS*

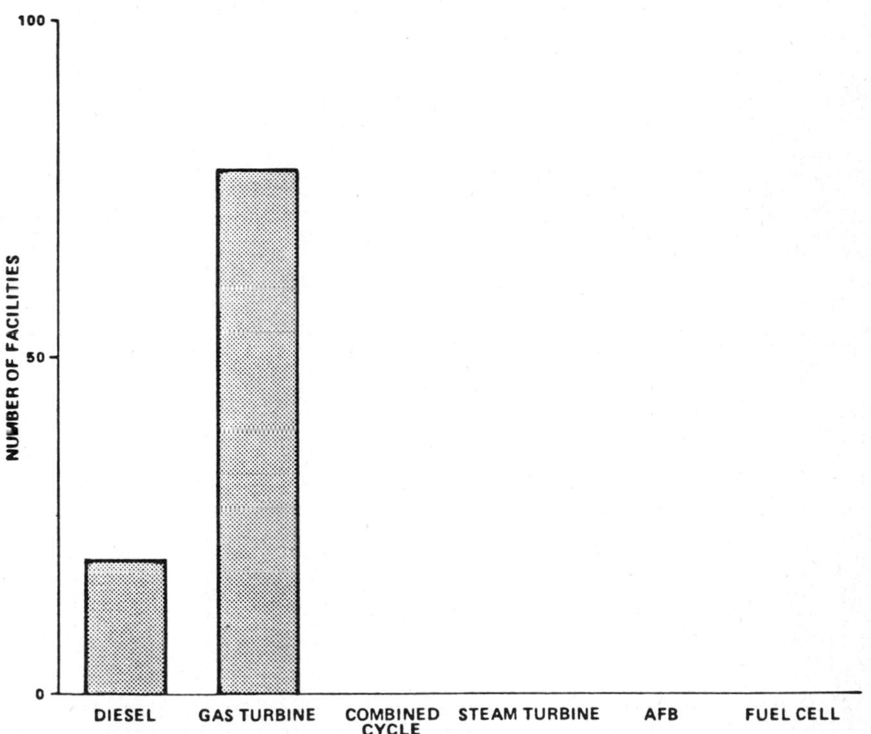

*PRELIMINARY ESTIMATES

Figure 7 depicts the mix of large customers by industry group in Northeast Utilities' service territory. Manufacturing firms account for approximately 67 percent of the total. Services make up the second largest division, with 16 percent of the total. Transportation, communication, and utilities represent 3 percent, as do wholesale and retail trade. Finance, insurance, and real estate account for 7 percent of the total accounts examined. The remaining 4 percent comprises agriculture, construction firms, and government buildings.

It is likewise instructive to note the fraction of electrical demand accounted for by each of these industrial groups (Figure 8). In the manufacturing sector, those customers with 1 megawatt actual or billing demand consume approximately 95 percent of all electrical energy in that sector. Similarly, the services, transportation/communications/utilities, financial/insurance/ real estate, and "other" large customers account for 41 percent, 34 percent, 17 percent, and 24 percent of the kilowatt-hour sales in each group, respectively.

Thus, large-demand customers dominate the manufacturing sector and represent significant fractions of the services and transportation/ communications/utilities sectors. Other industrial and commercial customers are mostly office buildings, of which large-demand users account for a relatively small fraction of total sales.

It should be mentioned that some customers are already cogenerators. Currently, 15 of Northeast Utilities' Connecticut customers provide about 15 megawatts of cogenerated electric power. Furthermore, Northeast Utilities has received inquiries from 17 customers who have expressed interest in cogeneration. Of those customers sufficiently advanced in their cogeneration planning to have already estimated system size, more than 70 megawatts in aggregate would be available if all projects were to be completed.

5.2 Preliminary Results

At this stage in the analysis process, the mail survey portion of the study has been completed and the field surveys have been distributed and returned. Of 452 mail surveys solicited from the utility's large demand customers, more than half (252) were executed. Of this number, 104 were chosen for field survey investigation. As of this time, 85 (82%) of the field surveys have been completed.

Table 1 displays the results of the mail survey screening. Of 216 mail surveys processed, 117 customers (54%) were rejected from further participation in the study. The majority of customers rejected (91) were determined to have insufficient thermal load to justify any type of cogeneration system. An additional 17 were rejected for miscellaneous technical reasons (e.g., insufficient space, anticipated change in process requirements, etc.), and 9 customer facilities were rejected for economic reasons. Of the facilities judged to have potential, the cogeneration configuration most commonly selected as most economic was the combustion turbine (see Figure 9). Diesel engines with waste heat boilers made up the balance of top selected system. Noticeably absent are combined cycles, steam turbines, atmospheric fluidized bed, and fuel cell cogeneration systems. Further investigation reveals that the high capital cost of these systems is the primary reason for their lack of success.

Preliminary results from processing the field surveys indicate that systems other than combustion turbines and diesels can be competitive. The reason is that the more detailed information available from the field surveys permits better matching of facility thermal requirements to the capabilities of the more expensive systems.

Thus, estimated return on investment improves significantly.

TABLE 1

Screening Results

Facilities Examined	216	
Facilities Rejected:		
Low thermal load	91	
Misc. Technical	17	
Economic	9	
Total Rejected	117	(54%)
Facilities with Potential	99	(46%)

6. CONCLUSIONS

Although the study of cogeneration potential in the Northeast Utilities service area is not yet complete, preliminary results indicate that sufficient potential exists to warrant the development of a strategy to accommodate future cogeneration projects.

Furthermore, the level of interest expressed by the utility's large customers indicates that where cogeneration is economic and financing can be arranged, customers are likely to proceed with cogeneration project development.

MARKET MODELING

Analytic Techniques for Energy Planning
B. Lev, F.H. Murphy, J.A. Bloom & A.S. Gleit (Editors)

ENERGY MODELLING IN SERF: THE SOCIO-ECONOMIC-RESOURCE FRAMEWORK

K.E. Hamilton
R.B. Hoffman
G.T. Sande

Structural Analysis Division
Statistics Canada
Ottawa, Canada K1A0T6

The Structural Analysis Division of Statistics Canada is engaged in the development of a Socio-Economic-Resource Framework (SERF) which permits the analysis of the flows of materials and energy from the natural resource base that are required to meet domestic and international needs.

1. INTRODUCTION

The Socio-Economic-Resource Framework (SERF) is a consistent, disaggregated set of models which, taken together with their associated data bases, can be used to simulate possible evolution paths of the Canadian economy over the long term. Emphasis is placed on modeling the physical flows of materials and energy that are required to meet human needs, and the processes that transform raw materials into finished goods. Short-term or cyclical phenomena are not captured, and the behavioral responses of economic agents are left to the model user to specify in the course of constructing a simulation.

SERF builds on the framework of the Statistics Canada Long Term Simulation Model. This earlier model was employed in studies examining Canadian energy growth possibilities [1] and the development of soft energy paths [2].

The Socio-Economic-Resource Framework is designed to meet several objectives: it is an analytical tool which may be used to develop scenarios or alternative views of the future; it is an information framework containing integrated sets of data pertaining to the socio-economic-resource system and information about relationships among components of the system; it is an interactive educational tool for the needs of policy makers; and finally it provides the means for establishing priorities for data collection and analysis.

At a very high level SERF may be viewed as a systems model of the economy with three main components. A demographic model provides the driving variables: population, households, and labor supply. The demand model measures the flows of goods and services required by the simulated population. The production model represents the material transformation processes required to convert resources into consumer goods. The details of these calculations are spread through some 24 sub-models, all linked within a common modeling framework. Constructing a simulation with SERF is typically a process of generating scenarios for simulation variables, then iteratively adjusting these scenarios in order to balance supply and demand of resources and labor, and external trade.

The bulk of this paper is concerned with the sub-models having an important bearing on energy supply and demand. We document the structural relationships in SERF using diagrams with precise meaning: boxes represent procedures, triangles stocks, circles flow variables, and hexagons ratios and other parameter types.

2. ENERGY SUPPLY AND DEMAND IN SERF

One of the prime motivations in the development of the Socio-Economic-Resource Framework is the desire to model the interaction of human populations and their needs with the resource base. The resource chosen for elaboration in this first version of SERF is energy. Because of its diversity of forms, intrinsic importance, pervasive nature, and because of the realization of the finiteness of the traditional forms of energy available in Canada, energy serves as an important and useful example of resource analysis using SERF.

The explicit modeling of the Canadian population, their stocks of goods, and the services which flow from these goods, imposes an important discipline of the exercise of examining supply and demand of energy over the next fifty years. The assumptions made about household formation, the size and type housing, the stock of heating equipment and insulation standards of this housing, the stock of appliances using energy and their efficiencies, and the number, usage, and efficiency of automobiles per household are all critical to this analysis. In a broader context, the energy-using characteristics of the industrial processes producing goods for consumers and the transportation systems required for this production also have bearing, in an essential way, on the level of energy demand.

It is equally important to measure some of the physical constraints and ramifications of the process of investing in energy supply facilities. Old facilities have finite lifetimes and declining capability. Bringing new facilities online requires significant construction lead times and a flow of goods and services associated with this construction. The process of investment itself has an impact on the resource base.

The real power of the SERF model structure lies in its imposition of consistency on the user. All components of a scenario interact to produce disequilibria of energy supply and demand. Equilibration requires explicit assumptions on the part of the user for its achievement. What is produced in this process is a consistent world view of the technological possibilities over time and the type of society employing this technology. Consistency constraints comprise a powerful test of our intuition about the future.

The remaining sections of this chapter lay out in some detail the individual components of energy consumption and supply in SERF. The elements of consumption include the residential energy demand block, the appliance model, the transportation block, and the industrial energy and use model. The design of the energy supply model is detailed. And finally there is a discussion of the modes of use of the combined energy supply/demand portions of the model in order to achieve an energy balance.

2.1 The Residential Energy Demand Model

The household model is a micro-simulation framework and related data base of the evolution of the Canadian housing stock, residential construction, and the uses of energy for space heating and hot water. It is designed to provide an analytical tool for examining a variety of energy consuming strategies involving thermal characteristics, building performance standards, fuel substitutions, and new space conditioning technologies. In common with other modules of SERF it is a simulation model, leaving the assumptions about behavior to the user. An example of the use of this model was an examination of alternative "off-oil" programs for the province of Ontario [3].

This model is distinguished from other parts of SERF in having a significant degree of regional disaggregation. This is necessitated of course by the wide

FIGURE B.1.1
HOUSING STOCK

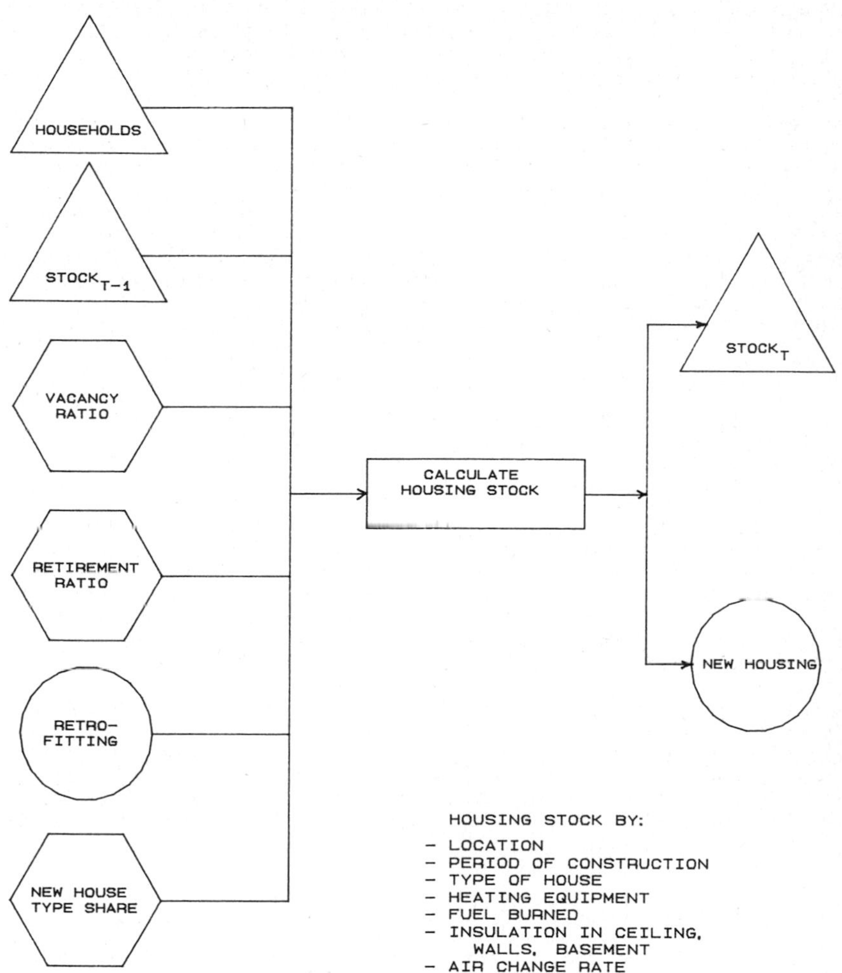

FIGURE B.1.2
HOUSEHOLD SPACE HEAT

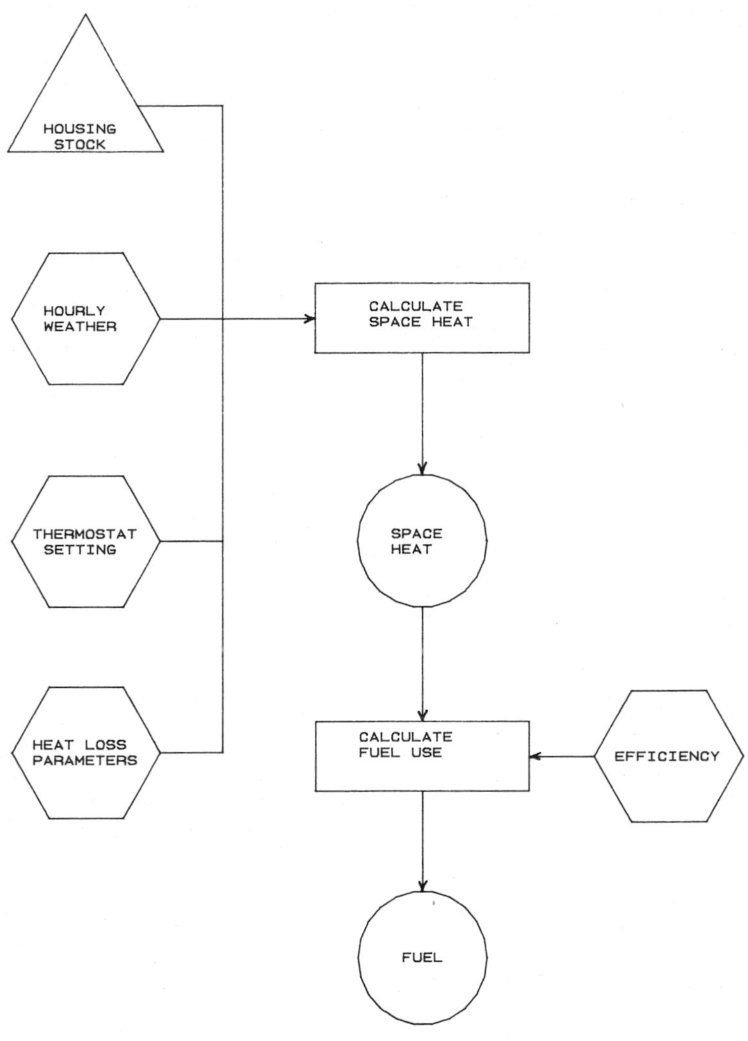

variation in weather and therefore space conditioning demands experienced from coast to coast in Canada.

Figures B.1.1 and B.1.2 give a very high level view of the housing and household energy calculations respectively. The model consists of six major blocks: the historical housing stock, demolitions, thermal retro-fitting, heating equipment retro-fitting, new housing construction, and the energy requirements calculator. The following is a brief description of each of these.

Historical Housing Stock - The starting distribution of housing stock is stratified by type, age, and heating equipment category. Housing types included are single detached, semi-detached and duplex, row housing and apartments. Heating equipment is divided into (1) water oil, (2) water gas, (3) water solid, (4) hot air oil, (5) hot air gas, (6) hot air solid, (7) electric, (8) space oil (i.e. point of use heaters), (9) space gas, and (10) space solid. Hybrid heating technologies are also permitted, such as the so-called "Saskatchewan House", heat pump-oil, heat pump-gas, heat pump-electric, heat pump-solar, gas-solar, and electric-solar. Housing of each age category and type is given a thermal archetype relating to insulation of ceilings, walls, and basement walls, and physical characteristics relating to average areas of wall, ceiling, basement wall, window, doors, and average living area.

In addition, weather data is available on a 4-hourly basis for the major geographical regions giving ambient temperatures and solar heat gain factors. Heating equipment is stratified by seasonal heating efficiences by type and fuel used.

Demolitions - The rates of demolition of existing housing are specific to the type of house and period of construction.

Thermal Retro-fit - The degree of thermal retro-fitting is simulated by using time dependent and thermal characteristic dependent propensities to upgrade the housing stock. For example, we simulate by estimating what is the probability that a particular house having R20 insulation in its ceiling will be upgraded to R28 insulation in a given period. Four heat loss areas are considered: ceiling, walls, basement, and air infiltration.

Equipment Retro-fit - Similar in concept to the simulation of thermal retro-fitting, for each period and each housing type a set of transition probabilities between equipment types is employed to calculate retro-fits; for instance the probability that a duplex will be changed from water gas heating to hot air oil heating in a given period.

New Housing - The requirement for new housing is calculated from provincial breakdowns of the Canadian population as calculated in the demographic block of SERF. Households are arrived at by applying age and sex specific probabilities that a person will be the head of a household to the population distribution. Housing is related to households through vacancy rates by housing type. The heating equipment type and thermal archetype of new housing is calculated using recent penetration rates of heating equipment and by making assumptions about future building codes.

Energy Requirements - The actual computation of energy requirements proceeds by micro-simulation of ambient weather conditions in each region applied to the simulated housing stock by type, heating equipment, and thermal characteristic. Simulation time periods as small as four hours are required to correctly calculate energy requirements in hybrid systems where, for instance, heat pumps are only effective over certain temperature ranges, or solar collectors are

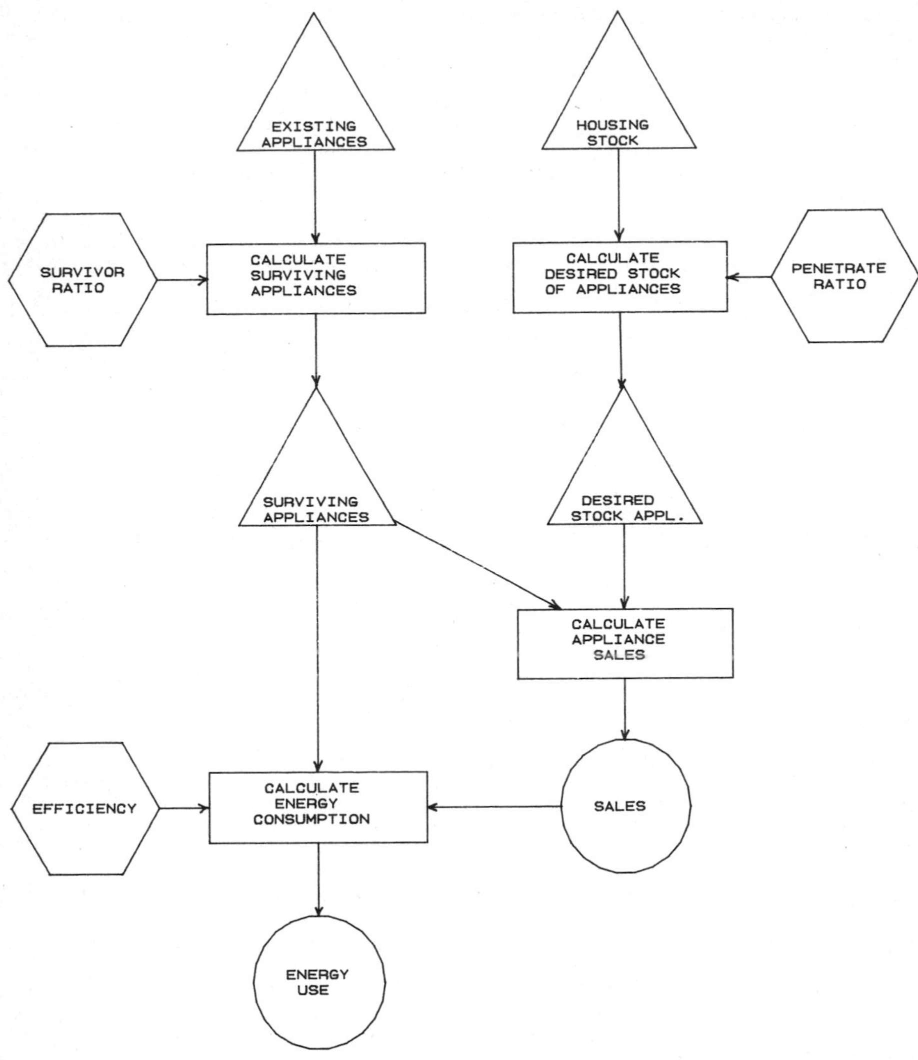
FIGURE B.2
APPLIANCE MODEL
EXISTING APPLIANCES
HOUSING STOCK
SURVIVOR RATIO
CALCULATE SURVIVING APPLIANCES
CALCULATE DESIRED STOCK OF APPLIANCES
PENETRATE RATIO
SURVIVING APPLIANCES
DESIRED STOCK APPL.
CALCULATE APPLIANCE SALES
EFFICIENCY
CALCULATE ENERGY CONSUMPTION
SALES
ENERGY USE

usable only during daylight hours.

2.2 The Appliance Model

The appliance model is designed to allow simulation of the stocks of appliances accumulating in the households of the Canadian population over the long term, and their associated energy requirements.

There are ten basic types of appliances tracked by the model: (1) electric ranges, (2) gas ranges, (3) microwave ovens, (4) refrigerators, (5) automatic washers, (6) electric dryers, (7) gas dryers, (8) dishwashers, (9) freezers, and (10) air conditioners. Together these comprise much of the non-heat energy use in homes.

Because appliance sales are naturally associated with households and not with individuals, the model builds on much the same apparatus as the Residential Energy Demand Model. In particular, the two models share the treatment of household formation from the demographic block of SERF, the same underlying historical housing stock and the same calculation of housing construction by housing type, by relating households to structures through a vacancy rate. The parts of the model unique to appliances are shown in Figure B.2.

The basic driving force in determining appliance stocks is a penetration rate stratified by appliance type and housing type. This rate is based on aggregate historical ratios of the number of appliances of each type in each type of home. One of the basic simulation variables is the projection of these rates. The consequences for the ultimate stock of appliances in Canadian households are closely tied to whether the model user simulates, for instance, that in the future every home will have a microwave oven and a dishwasher, or whether these and other appliances will remain luxury items enjoyed by some subset of homes.

It should be clear that in specifying a set of penetration rates the model user is making a statement or assumption about lifestyles in the future.

Sales of appliances will be related both to the change in stocks of appliances inherent in the other simulation variables and to the assumptions made about average lifetimes of these goods in service. Lifetimes are specified through survivorship curves by appliance type, i.e. the proportion of appliances of age T which will still be functioning, for T spanning some appropriately long time period. Appliance sales are passed to the production block of SERF as demands which must be met by the economic system, with their ultimate impact on the resource base.

Finally, starting from historical figures on appliance energy consumption per year by year of production, the user may project these figures for appliances produced in the future, creating vintage-specific energy efficiencies. The model simply sums up the energy consumption of the stocks of appliances by vintage to arrive at annual energy consumption.

2.3 The Transportation Model

In a country as large as Canada, with so widely dispersed a population, the importance of transport in the economy and its importance for energy demand, in particular, is clear. We have distinguished four categories of transport, each with its particular driving variables and characteristics. In addition, a sub-module of the transportation model calculates the required investment in infrastructure to support the transport system. A high level view of the model

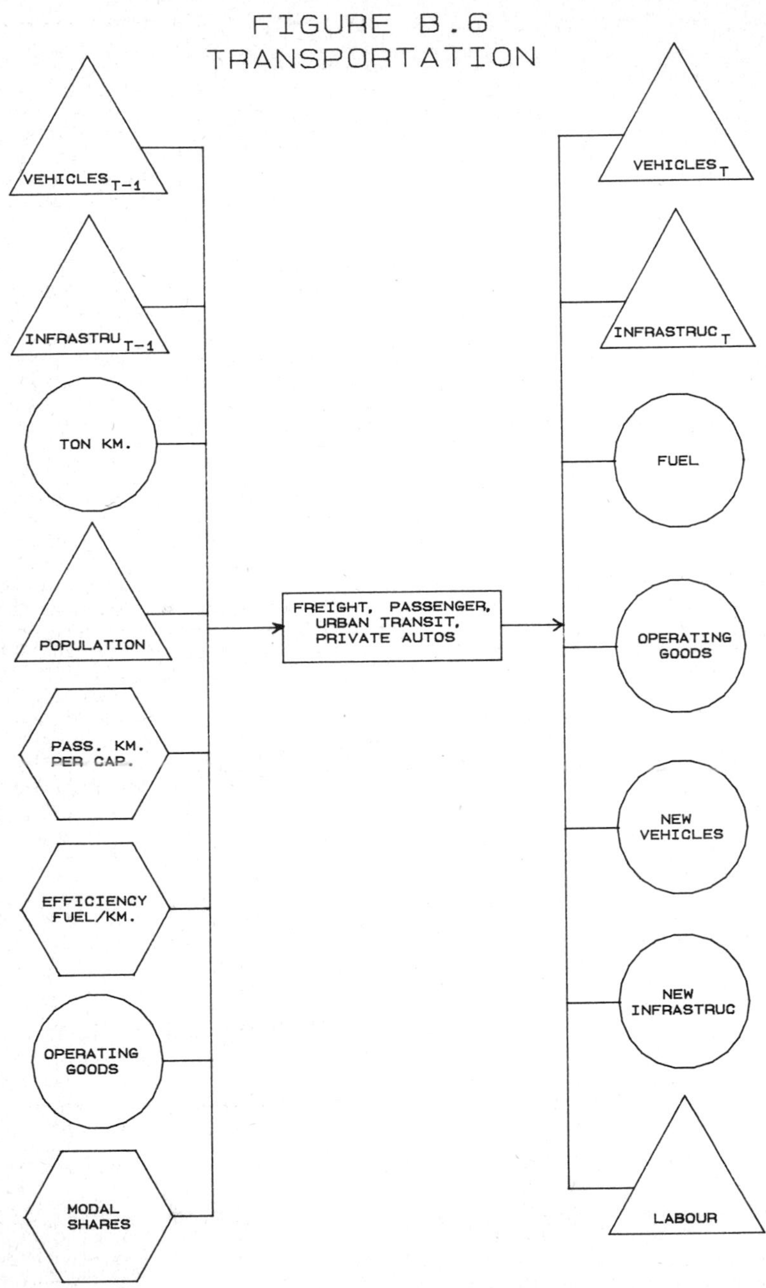
FIGURE B.6
TRANSPORTATION
VEHICLES T-1
INFRASTRU T-1
TON KM.
POPULATION
PASS. KM.
PER CAP.
EFFICIENCY
FUEL/KM.
OPERATING
GOODS
MODAL
SHARES
FREIGHT, PASSENGER,
URBAN TRANSIT,
PRIVATE AUTOS
VEHICLES T
INFRASTRUC T
FUEL
OPERATING
GOODS
NEW
VEHICLES
NEW
INFRASTRUC
LABOUR

is given in Figure B.6.

The freight transport module is essentially driven by required ton-kilometers of transport of goods by mode. This variable is decoupled from industrial production to allow maximum flexibility in simulating changing industrial structure. Coefficients of total stock of transport equipment per ton-kilometers by mode are used to calculate the required freight stock. Using variables for the average distance travelled per unit of stock, the energy efficiency by vintage (in units of energy per kilometer) and a fuel distribution, the total energy requirements are derived.

Inter-city passenger travel is calculated using the population from the demographic block, coefficients of trips per capita, and figures for average trip length. From the passenger miles so calculated, we derive passenger miles by mode (aircraft, trains, and buses) using a distribution of trip length by mode. The required stock of passenger transport equipment is calculated using coefficients of stock per passenger mile by mode. Energy requirements are derived from average distance travelled per unit of transport stock, a vintage-specific energy efficiency and the distribution of fuel types.

The stock of private automobiles is obtained by applying ownership rates to the number of households coming from the demographic block. Automobile usage is assembled from three components: commuting to work, other private auto travel, and fleet usage. By taking the labor force figures from the labor demand calculation in SERF, applying a proportion of employees commuting in autos and using figures for the average number of passengers per commuting vehicle, the number of automobiles used each working day in commuting is calculated. Total commuting kilometers comes from variables representing the average distance to work and the total number of working days per year. Total kilometers of other private automobile travel is a separate simulation variable, as is the number of autos used in fleet operations; total fleet kilometers per year is simply derived from a coefficient of average kilometers travelled in a year per fleet auto. Having arrived at total automobile kilometers travelled per year, energy usage is calculated from the usual vintage-specific vehicle efficiencies and fuel distributions. Distributions of fuels used in autos can be affected both by the characteristics of new vehicles and by retro-fitting existing ones.

Urban transit is also divided into commuting and other travel. Commuters are calculated using a simple proportion of the labor force which commutes on public transit. Other travel is derived from rates of use of public transit by the general population for purposes other than commuting. The stock of urban transit vehicles comes from ratios of stock by mode per fare population. The energy requirements for urban transit are then based on fuel usage rates per unit of stock by vintage, and split using a distribution of fuels.

Figure B.2 shows the other outputs of the transportation modules such as vehicle sales, labour required for the operation of transit systems, and the infrastructure which must be developed to support transportation. Infrastructure construction and production of new vehicles both feed demands for goods and services to the SERF production block, adding to the indirect energy requirements of transportation.

2.4 The Industrial Energy End Use Model

The philosophical basis for modeling the demand for energy in the industrial (goods producing) sector is our belief that energy is not desired per se in economic processes, but rather what are desired are the services or end uses which it provides. Thus industrial processes require heating of a particular temperature or quality, or motive power, but not gallons of oil.

So rather than representing industrial energy use in the traditional Input-Output manner of employing coefficients of fuel use per unit (constant dollar) of production, SERF is based on coefficients of energy use in Joules per unit of production. The elaboration of the relationship between energy and use, energy efficiency, and specific fuel types in the industrial sector appears in Figure C.3.

For the roughly 150 industrial sectors identified in SERF, we employ historical coefficients of the requirements for five end uses (motive power, electricity as heat, process heat < 212F, process heat between 212F and 500F, and process heat > 500F) per constant dollar of production. For many sectors these involve estimates based on aggregates; for some sectors such as farming and construction there are not even estimates. The key variables for simulating changes in energy efficiency are just these coefficients - the user's scenario for the technical possibilities for decreasing high temperature heat requirements in steel-making, for instance, is represented in changes in the end use coefficients over time, with the consequent decrease in the energy intensiveness of the industrial sector.

The relationship between end uses and fuel types is captured in a set of fuel share coefficients for each end use and industry. User scenarios for the rate of substitution of one fuel for another in, for example, the provision of high temperature process heat in the cement industry, taken together across all sectors, end uses, and fuels determine the overall extent of fuel substitution in the industrial sector. A refinement of this procedure, which we hope to introduce as data become available, will reflect the technologies transforming fuel types into end uses explicitly - this is important because the amount of natural gas which can substitute for a given amount of oil, for instance, in a particular application is technologically constrained and should be represented directly.

The product of the simulated coefficients of end use by industry and the fuel shares by end use, when multiplied by the sectoral production as calculated in SERF's Input-Output model, gives the requirements for fuels in the industrial sector over time. The essential link between technology and industrial structure on the one hand, and the resource base on the other, is therefore maintained.

2.5 Other Energy Demand

Although the bulk of demand for energy is captured in the modules described so far, there remain significant areas in which SERF does not attempt a detailed treatment. One such area is household demand for electricity used in lighting, home entertainment, and so on. Energy for lighting, space conditioning and equipment operation in the government, health, education, and service sectors is calculated using coefficients relating to the stock of structures measured in constant dollars. There are major data problems preventing any progress in developing this part of the model. It is clear that we should treat these sectors on the basis of the physical infrastructure of buildings and equipment which are employed in the course of their activities, but it is precisely these data which are the most difficult to obtain or estimate.

2.6 Energy Supply

Most energy analysts and prognosticators have their own scenarios for energy supply in the future, based on their own estimates, guesstimates, or hopes for

FIGURE C.1.1
ENERGY SUPPLY - NON OIL OR GAS

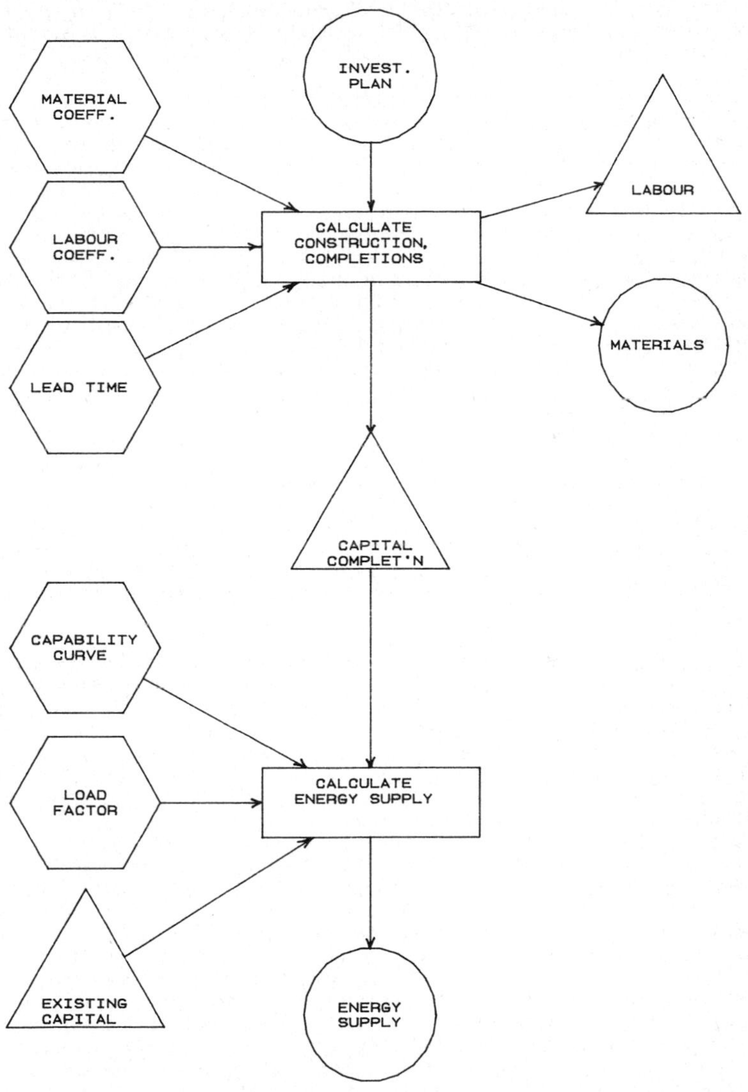

the supply possibilities which we face. What has been lacking is a tool for rigorously examining the consequences for the rest of the economy of choosing a particular energy supply development path. It was with this goal in mind that the energy supply model of SERF was designed and implemented. And, as pointed out earlier, by explicitly modeling supply and demand separately the analyst is forced to construct a consistent picture of the energy system in the context of the economy as a whole.

To date, SERF models the following energy supply technologies: conventional onshore oil, secondary oil recovery, enhanced oil recovery, offshore oil, and Arctic oil; oil sands mining and upgrading; conventional onshore gas, enhanced gas recovery, offshore gas, and Arctic gas; underground coal mining and surface mines; thermal, nuclear, and hydro-electricity; and petroleum refinery capacity. The framework will be more complete when several "soft" technologies are added, including a variety of solar and biomass options. Also lacking at present is the representation of energy transport technologies such as oil and gas pipelines, tank cars, and ice-breaking oil and LNG tankers.

The models of energy supply can in general be described as being plan driven. The major inputs are simulated additions to production capacity. Oil and gas facilities present a challenge to the modeller attempting their representation which is distinct from the other technologies. We will discuss the methodological issues for oil and gas separately.

First, though, Figure C.1.1 shows the model structure for oil sands and all other non-oil and gas facilities. The driving variable in a simulation is planned additions to production capacity measured in terms of numbers of nominal facilities representing typical facility sizes - in this manner the "lumpy" nature of capital investment is captured. Completions of energy projects are lagged by a facility-specific construction lead time. As facilities are completed their capacity is added to surviving energy capital, calculated from capability curves (a capability curve for a typical energy supply technology would start at 1.0 representing the ability to operate at rated capacity when the plant is new, then decline as the plant ages until the rated technological life is reached, when the curve drops to 0.0). Mediating between energy production capacity and actual production in any simulation time period is a load factor, which itself is a major simulation variable.

The supply model is linked to the rest of SERF in three ways. The calculated energy production is a tension variable going to one of the major reports of SERF (this will be discussed in the next section). During the reconstruction of facilities the stream of material and energy requirements is passed to the production model as a demand for goods. And finally, the labor required for construction is added into the overall model's calculation of labor demand. It should be noted that the materials, energy, and labor required for the operation of energy supply facilities is modelled in the production block.

One fundamental distinction of oil and gas production, as shown in Figure C.1.2, is in the behavior of the existing capital stock. Rather than having a capability curve and fixed technological life, individual hydrocarbon reservoirs when fully developed exhibit exponentially declining production curves as a consequence of inevitable declines in reservoir pressure and loss of contiguity of the hydrocarbon structures. The rate of decline is typically related to the rate of extraction. Rather than employing a detailed model of hydrocarbon reservoirs, we have used estimates of the aggregate rate of decline of developed reservoirs and functionally related this to the load factor for oil and gas. To capture the fact that most conventional oil wells eventually employ secondary recovery (drilling peripheral holes and pumping water into the reservoir), a lagged investment in secondary production facilities is built into the model.

FIGURE C.1.2
ENERGY SUPPLY - OIL AND GAS

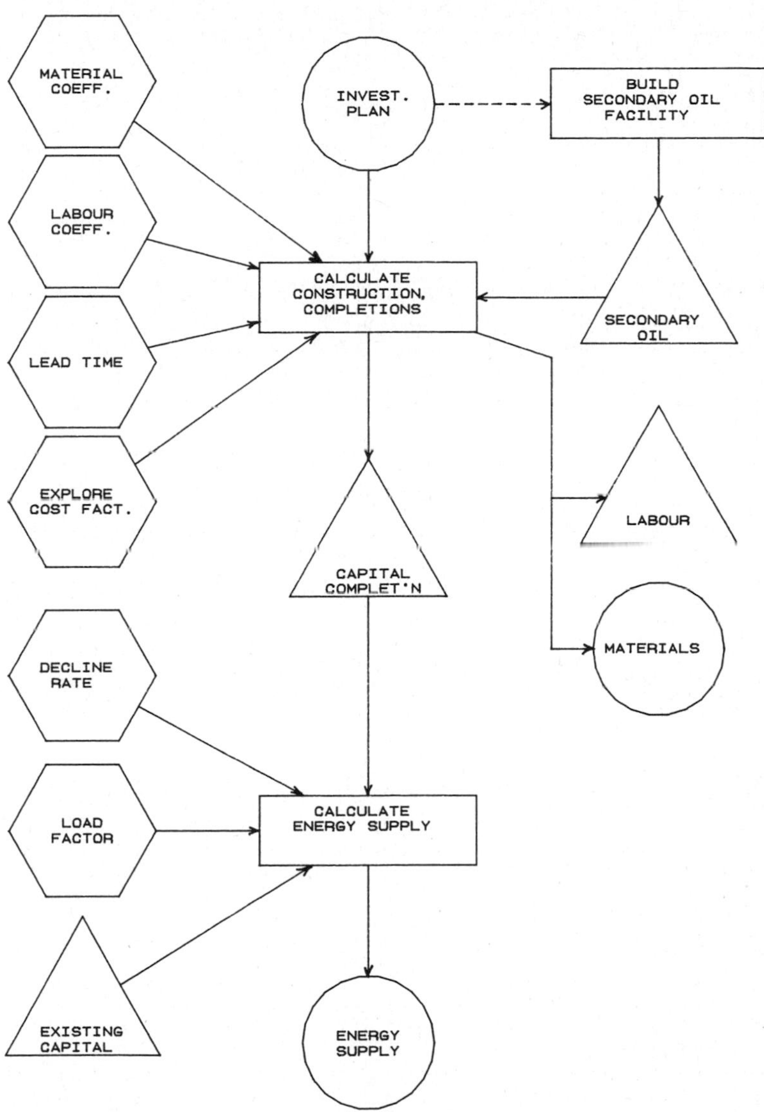

FIGURE C.3
INDUSTRIAL ENERGY END USE

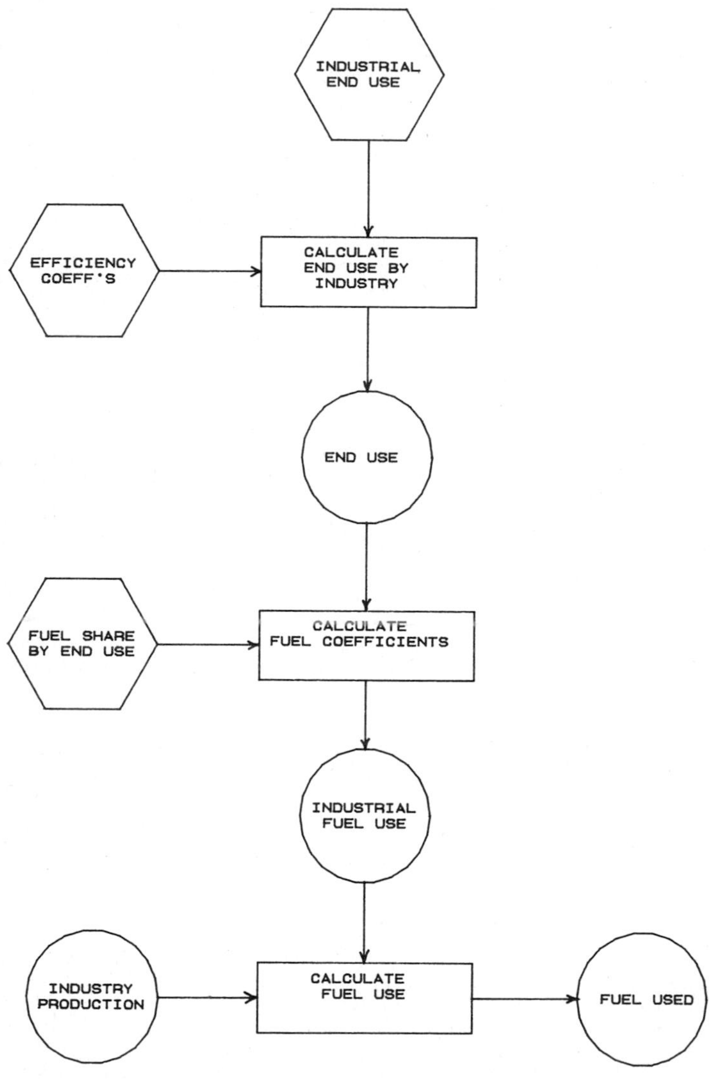

FIGURE D.4
ENERGY SUPPLY/DEMAND TENSION

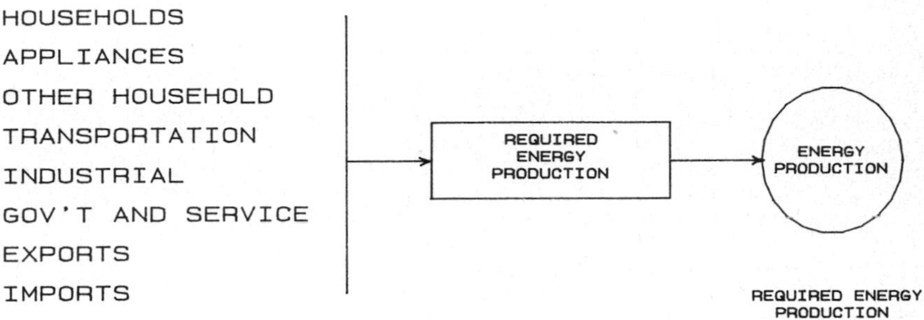

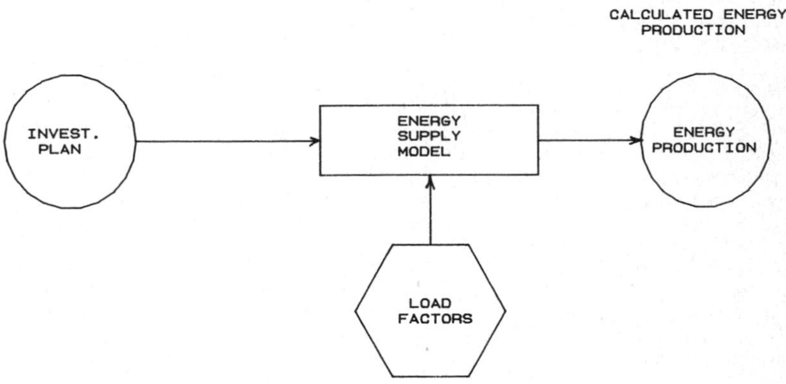

The second fundamental distinction of oil and gas production is the fact that a great deal of effort is put into exploration and development activity before a well is brought into production. In the current version of SERF we are handling this by using average numbers of holes drilled per producing well for each type of facility - the construction materials and labor for bringing new facilities online is related to this number. The user may simulate the declining drilling success rates which would be expected in a mature basin by specifying an exploration cost factor which escalates over time, proportionately increasing material and labor demand per unit of new capacity. While this is a serviceable treatment of exploration, we plan to put this portion of the model on sounder methodological grounds by developing an oil and gas exploration model based on the probabilistic methods and geological data employed by earth scientists in representing this problem.

2.7 Balancing Energy Supply and Demand

The process of constructing a complete scenario in SERF is, as the foregoing indicates, a major task. We have simplified this process where possible by producing conservative extrapolations of model variables to serve as a baseline scenario. However, the user must still make many decisions between alternate paths as they home in on a scenario which fits their expectations of the development of the Canadian economy. At the end of this process of judicious selection of simulation variables, the overall consistency of the user's scenario is tested. Nowhere is this more clearly exemplified than in the comparison of energy supply and demand.

As Figure D.4 shows, there are a great many components to energy supply and demand. In order to arrive at what the model calculates as the required energy production, scenarios must be constructed for household heating and hot water possibilities, appliance penetration, other household energy, transportation energy consumption, industrial energy consumption coefficients, energy required in government and the service sector, and finally exports and imports of energy. The calculated energy supply is, to simplify, the product of investment plans and load factors for energy facilities. Bringing the required and calculated energy production into line is an essential facet of producing a consistent scenario.

One mode of model use will likely be "demand oriented". The user would construct scenarios for the various intensity variables for energy demand, based on expectations about changing efficiencies of energy use and the mix of fuels required to meet this demand. The supply model would then be run with investment plans consistent with the required production. Because putting new energy facilities in place requires energy in turn, the model solution process would have to be iterated a couple of times in order to produce a balance.
Another basic mode of use may be "supply oriented". Here, expectations about discoveries and development of energy supplies would be the chief variables of interest. After solution of the demand portions of the model, the specified supply scenario can be examined for its adequacy to meet the required energy production. Gross shortfalls or over-supplies would force a re-examination of the assumptions going into the scenario.

In practice we expect that model users will combine elements of these strategies in constructing a consistent scenario. They will quickly discover the highly interdependent nature of the model (and the economy which it represents). Choices in one part of the model will have consequences for other parts. For instance, energy supply and demand can always be brought into line through imports and exports - but the consequences of arbitrarily high levels of imports of oil, for example, will be felt in our export industries and perhaps ultimately

Figure R.1

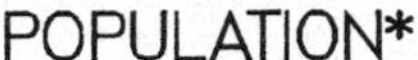

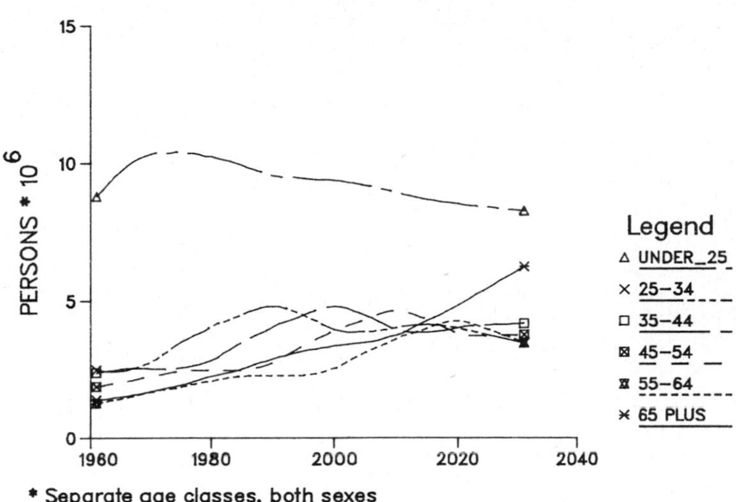

Figure R.2

POPULATION*

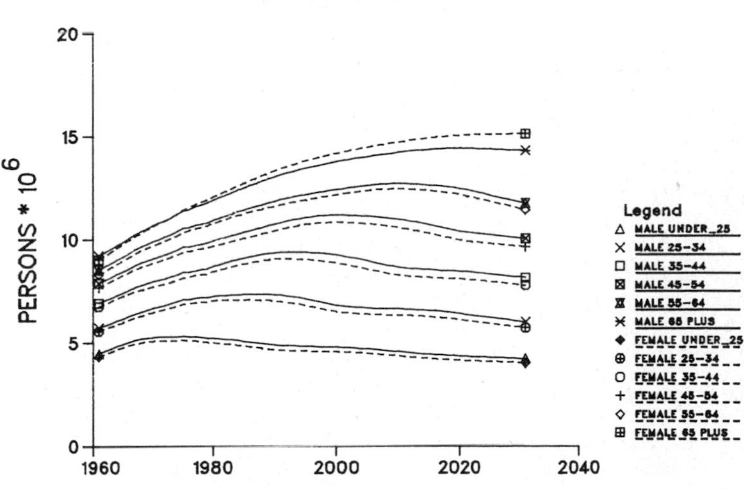

Figure R.3

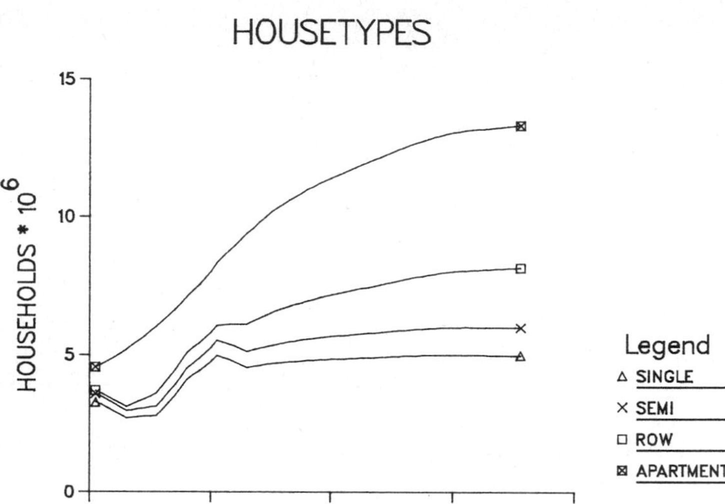

Figure R.4

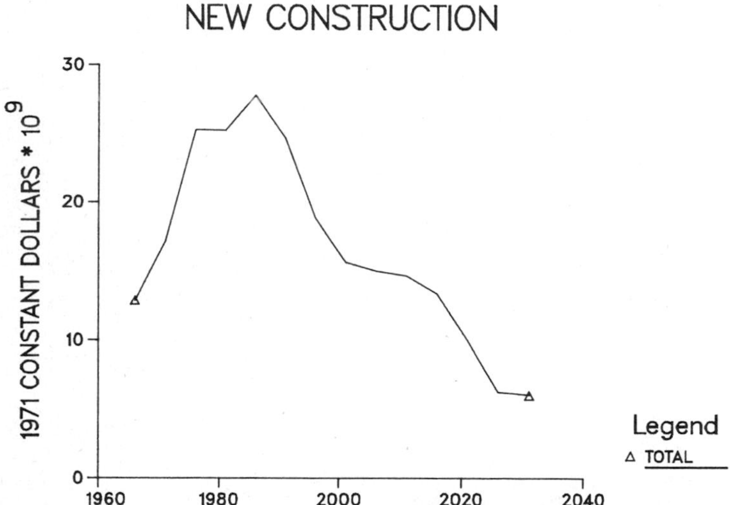

Figure R.5

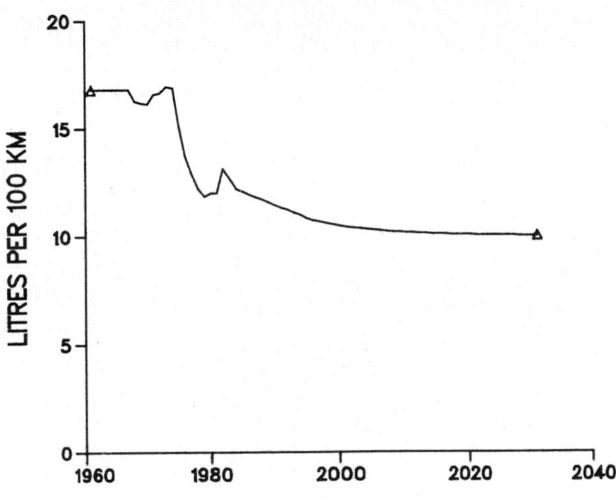

Figure R.6

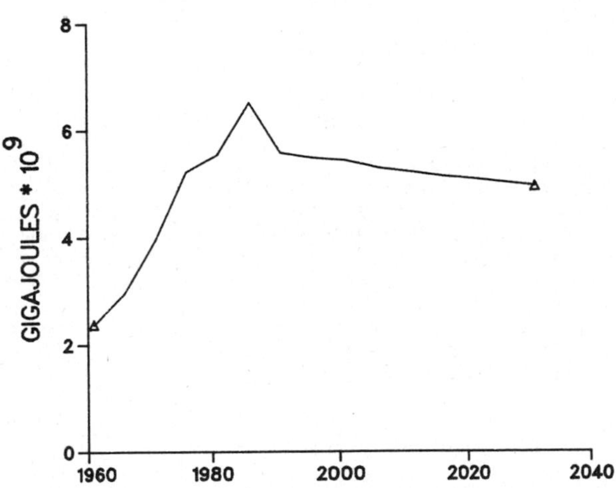

in the terms of trade, with broad-based effects on the rest of the economy.

Decoupling so many portions of the model will make the user burden high in using SERF. It is our belief, however, that this will force people to be explicit about their assumptions in producing snapshots of the future. The model will, in an understandable manner, calculate the consequences of those assumptions. This in turn should foster rational discussion of our choices for the future.

3. SELECTED RESULTS

We may illustrate the power of the SERF model by following some of the internal variables over time. The first block of the model is the demographic block. The basic data is an age-sex structured population as provided by the Census of Population with projections provided by official forecasts released by the Demography Division of Statistics Canada. A base scenario is shown in the Figure R.1. The population is far from equilibrium as can be seen by the local maxima in the numbers of persons in the various age classes excepting the elderly. The display in Figure R.2 of the cumulative age classes by sex shows that the total population is increasing. The detailed population information is used in the labor supply portion of the demographic block as well as in the food, clothing, health care, education and other components of the domestic demand block. These individuals organize themselves into households with the model reflecting this behavior through a notion of headship with associated coefficients. The number of households for a base scenario is shown in Figure R.3 as the total number of households broken out by cumulative dwelling type. Alternate scenarios are available of various dwelling-type mixes that are achievable through alternative assignments of new construction. We may easily construct the required flow of dwellings, commonly called new construction, to meet the demand and to replace those dwellings destroyed through wear out and accident. The size of the housing stock is not increasing smoothly because of the non-equilibrium population and yields erratic requirements for new construction as shown in Figure R.4. The energy consumed by the housing stock stabilizes with the size of the stock and even declines under various retrofitting scenarios.

Another illustration of the use of an age-type structured stock is provided in the transportation component of domestic demand. Considerable change in automobile efficiency has been achieved by both market and regulatory influence on automobile manufacturers. We see a major improvement in efficiency in the years 1975-1985. Figure R.5 shows the change for standard-sized gasoline automobiles with corresponding changes for other sizes and fuel types. Alternative scenarios of projected efficiencies and market penetrations are available but are not illustrated. The energy use by automobiles for a base scenario is shown in Figure R.6. We see that the reversal and decline in energy use lags the improved efficiency by years as an increasing proportion of the automobile stock is replaced by the newer fuel efficient typed. After the stock renewal, the energy consumption shows small declines resulting from further efficiency gains and some shifting to compact cars.

4. CONCLUSION

This paper has outlined, at a very high level, the structure of the energy supply and demand components of SERF. We feel that the combination of the simulation approach, disaggregation of the sectors represented, a rich data structure capturing the age and energy-using characteristics of stocks, and adherence to the physical inter-relationships of the model components, provides a robust tool for energy modelling. The inherent understandability of each component and the requirement that user assumptions be made explicit should foster useful debate of

Canadian energy policy.

REFERENCES

[1] Brooks, David B., "Zero Energy Growth for Canada", McLelland and Stewart Ltd., Toronto, Canada, 1981.

[2] Brooks, David B., Robinson, John B., and Torrie, Ralph D., "2025: Soft Energy Future for Canada", Friends of the Earth, Feb. 1983 (draft prepared for Energy Sector, Department of Energy, Mines and Resources Canada).

[3] Moll, R.H.H., Dickinson, K.H., and Hoffman, R.B., "Alternative off-oil Scenarios for Ontario" in Beyond the Energy Crisis, vol. 1, R.A. Fazzolare and C.B. Smith, eds., Pergamon Press, Oct. 1981.

Unpublished Material available from Statistics Canada

[4] Hoffman, R.B., "The Socio-Economic-Resource Framework", Structural Analysis Division working paper, April 1983.

[5] Moll, R.H.H., "User's Guide to the Statistics Canada Residential Energy Model", Structural Analysis Division working paper 81-09-01.

[6] Gribble, S.F., "The Structural Analysis Division Appliance Model", Structural Analysis Division working paper, 80-07-31.

Analytic Techniques for Energy Planning
B. Lev, F.H. Murphy, J.A. Bloom & A.S. Gleit (Editors)

AN INTRODUCTION TO THE INTERMEDIATE FUTURE FORECASTING SYSTEM

Frederic H. Murphy
Temple University
Philadelphia, Pennsylvania 19122

John Conti
Susan Shaw
Reginald Sanders

Department of Energy, Washington, D.C. 20585

IFFS has become as the tool for producing EIA energy projections in the Annual Energy Outlook. The model contains representations of all conventional supplies, energy demands and energy/economy interactions. A description of the model organization and modeling elements is provided.

1. INTRODUCTION

The Energy Information Administration has completed a new energy market model, the Intermediate Future Forecasting System (IFFS). The model will be used to study issues on energy markets. Broadly stated, the model is designed to study government policies affecting energy markets and transitions within energy markets. This paper presents an overview of IFFS. There are two important aspects to the model; how the individual sectors and energy forms are represented and how the individual pieces are combined to provide a unified representation of energy markets. This paper describes the system organization and summarizes the individual fuel market representations.

2. THE NEED FOR AN ENERGY MARKET PERSPECTIVE

Since the early 1970's, the nation has suffered several severe economic shocks because of rapid changes in energy markets. The 1973-1974 embargo, during which oil prices increased several-fold, was followed by domestic natural gas shortages in the middle 1970's. Continued Middle East instability led to a further doubling of oil prices during 1978 and 1979.

Looking back, the original energy problem of this century was the difficulty of coping with abundance. Significant oil finds had, on occasion, forced the price per barrel down to $.20. Gas reserves were continually added as a byproduct of the search for oil, and often wasted as a nuisance instead of treated as a national resource. Coal was, and still is, readily available. The major concerns of Government were to control wasteful development of oil, assist the expanding market for gas, and soften the dislocations from decreasing coal use.

By the 1950's, the picture had changed: oil started to be imported in larger and larger quantities and the Nation's gas transmission system matured. The energy concerns of the 1950's and 1960's were to protect domestic oil producers from cheap foreign oil while limiting America' dependence on imports and protecting consumers from natural gas price increases.

The regulatory machinery for oil and gas, which lasted through most of the 1970's, was put in place in this period. There was another dimension added: an awareness of the effects of energy production and consumption of the environment. The Government developed new programs to improve air and water quality. One consequence of the environmental regulations was a simultaneous increase in oil imports and decrease in coal use. Although the State and Federal governments had been regulating aspects of individual fuel markets for years, there was no comprehensive view of the program impacts. Prior to the 1973-1974 embargo there seemed to be no need. Two earlier embargoes had no serious effects on the Nation. After the 1973-1974 embargo, there was a clearly understood need for a comprehensive view of Government policy impacts and an understanding of the energy future of the Nation.

The original tools used to analyze energy markets were the Project Independence Evaluation System (PIES) and its successor, the Midterm Energy Forecasting System (MEFS). The Energy Information Administration (EIA) has replaced these models with a new model, the Intermediate Future Forecasting System (IFFS). This new model is designed to expand EIA's analytical capabilities in the 2 to 10-year time frame while actually reducing the resources required for analysis.

The purpose of policy analysis is to understand the likely consequences of a policy change. Invariably, there are losers as well as winners. The policy formulation process balances competing interests and is not fundamentally quantitative because different people weight consequences differently. The role of energy analysis is to measure the consequences so that sound decisions can be made. IFFS is an equilibrium model; it relies on economic theory to establish the relationships necessary for measuring the repercussions of a given policy change. It, therefore, falls into the class of simulation models.

An equilibrium model is one which, when solved, results in supply equalling demand at a given set of prices. The word equilibrium in this case does not mean the model treats energy markets as static and unchanging. Far from it; the model represents the changes in domestic prices, consumption, capacity utility and resource availability. Equilibrium simply means supplies equal demands under economic market forces.

3. MODEL CAPABILITIES

IFFS is designed to show trends in energy markets and their underlying causes, such as trends in oil production and imports; regional shifts in coal production and consumption; price movements in oil products, natural gas, coal and electricity; and changing financial requirements of electric utilities. That is, IFFS can illustrate the directions energy is taking in the domestic economy, highlighting problems that may arise in the future or current problems that may dissipate without requiring any action. Projections with current energy policies in place are presented in the Energy Information Administration Annual Energy Outlook (formerly part of the Annual Report to Congress).

Starting with the Annual Outlook as a baseline, representations of Government policies within IFFS may be altered and new projections made for estimating the effects of these new Government policies. As no model is capable of representing all energy-related policies, the capabilities of IFFS are best understood through examples of appropriate and inappropriate uses of the model.

One appropriate use is to estimate the effects of the Natural Gas Policy Act (NGPA) on energy markets. One can compare, for example, the impacts of deregulation versus the NGPA. Another use would be an estimation of the effects of a crude oil price change on oil imports. This would be a comparison of different market circumstances and their ramifications for the whole energy system. The model is also capable of estimating the effects of high railroad rates on the penetration of coal in energy markets. This would be an example of comparing different nonenergy policies on energy markets. A last example of an appropriate use is an estimation of the effects of a change in the rules concerning the inclusion of construction work in progress in the electric utility rate base. This issue has been under discussion within the Federal Energy Regulatory Commission. The model could be a vehicle for comparing different regulatory philosophies.

No model is appropriate for meeting all analytical needs. An example of a use for which the model is not appropriate is in issues where seasonalities are important, because the model does not contain a representation of changing oil inventories or changes of gas in storage. It is also inappropriate for estimating the immediate effects of an oil embargo because this is a disequilibrium situation and IFFS is an economic equilibrium model. Finally, it is also inappropriate for estimating the local effects of Government programs. The model has regional detail, for example, Federal regional detail on energy consumption, but the model is intended for producing estimates of national impacts and not local effects.

4. AN ABSTRACTION OF ENERGY MARKETS

To understand the workings of IFFS one needs to have a conceptual view of the energy system. Energy markets, as represented in this model, are illustrated in Figure 1. The model has a representation of energy supply, conversion and demand. The model does include some new technologies, but it emphasizes the major fuels, incorporating domestic supplies of and demands for oil, gas and coal, and imports of crude oil, refined petroleum products and natural gas. It contains a representation of the conversion activities: refineries converting crude oil into petroleum products and electric utilities taking in fossil fuels, nuclear power, hydropower, and some of the new technologies to produce electricity.

Demand is measured for natural gas, electricity, coal, distillate oil, residual oil, gasoline, jet fuel, liquified petroleum gases, petrochemical feedstocks, and other petroleum products.

Demand models translate fuel and electricity prices, the level of economic activity, and the regulations affecting consumption into estimates of demands for fuel and products. That is, they measure the levels of energy consumption plus the competition among fuels. In the residential sector, for example, coal, oil, gas, electrical resistance heat and heat pumps compete for meeting home heating needs. The demand models are organized by end-use sector as follows: residential, commercial, raw material, industrial, and transportation.

5. THE STRUCTURE OF IFFS

The Department of Energy (DOE) has used several models to study energy markets: the Brookhaven Energy Systems Optimization Model (BESOM), MEFS, the Long-Term Energy Analysis Program (LEAP), and FOSSIL2. These models represent a wide range of methodologies for modeling energy markets and they predominate in domestic energy policy analyses.

The budget cuts faced by DOE and the need for large support staffs to maintain these models have led to the closing of MEFS and LEAP. Rather than abandon longer term forecasting entirely, EIA decided to extend the forecast horizon of a model under development. IFFS was originally designed to fill the forecast gap between the EIA short-term forecasts and MEFS. The reason for developing IFFS was to have a relatively inexpensive model providing year-by-year forecasts of energy markets for the time span most relevant for policies oriented to influencing a transition from oil and gas to other conventional fuels and to conservation.

Much of what makes MEFS and LEAP too expensive to maintain is the organizational structure of EIA. EIA has had, since its inception, problems in creating an organization consistent with both meeting customer requests for analysis and being efficient in producing the analyses. Customer requests are usually for analyses that are fuel-specific, e.g., natural gas regulatory alternatives, and analyst expertise is also fuel-specific: one needs to be a student of natural gas markets with all of their institutional features to produce an adequate study. EIA is organized along fuel lines for these reasons. The current market models, however, have strong integrating model cores, requiring a team of analysts to maintain software and submodel interfaces. The massive coordination required beteween fuel divisions running supply models, demand divisions running demand models and the integrating group led to meetings regularly attended by 30 people several times per week. Producing an Annual Report consumed up to 40-50 staff years.

A good part of the problem is that each supply or demand division found it easier to test model changes by running the whole modeling system as opposed to instituting internal validation of the results beforehand. A large model must be structured to fit into the organization that supports it. In the case of EIA, the model needs to be organized along fuel lines.

IFFS consists of a central integrating procedure, an electricity market module, an oil market module, a gas market module, and a coal market module. The current operation of the model is depicted in Figure 2. The model operates iteratively to balance supply and demand for all fuels at market clearing prices. That is, the central integrating routine calls all of the modules in turn, repeating the sequence until all prices and quantities converge to an equilibrium. When called, a fuel module computes a supply/demand balance for that fuel and then returns to the integrating routine. This means, for example, that when a trial equilibrium is being determined for electricity markets, the prices of competing fuels are fixed. When each module finds a new trial equilibrium, the new prices and quantities replace previous estimates. Before initializing the next module, the integrating routine re-evaluates all demands, incorporating the effects of the most recent estimated prices of all fuels. This captures the effect of substitutable fuels on each module-specific fuel. Consequently, the most recent trial estimates of prices initialize the demand equations when the integrating routine passes the computation to a new fuel module.

Using detailed demand models each time new trial demands are needed is prohibitively expensive. A simple analytical device is used to gain operational efficiency. A single equation is used to approximate the detailed models for each of the 10 Federal Region and sector combinations. The detailed demand models are revisited after all of the fuel modules have produced a new trial solution. This means, that once a trial equilibrium is reached, it is consistent with the fuel modules and with the detailed demand models.

To summarize each of the specific fuel or energy form modules simulates the economic forces that work within that particular fuel market, while the overall integrating routine represents the linkages among the different fuel markets within the economy.

6. THE INDIVIDUAL FUEL MODULES

As part of the overall logic, the model solves for an equilibrium in each year before moving on to the next. The year-by-year nature of the solution process leads to a natural organization of the individual fuel modules. Each module simulates the operating and planning activities of firms in that business. Operating activities are the day-to-day functions such as the dispatching of existing powerplants, while planning activities involve adding capacity that will be used in later time periods. Operating decisions use only the prices of the moment, and planning decisions are made based on past and future prices. "Past" prices are either historical data or forecast years where an equilibrium has already been found. "Future" prices are extrapolations of past prices, generated within the planning component. This approach allows the model to solve one year at a time, stepping forward to solve a new year only after the solution for the previous year is complete.

When future prices are generated in planning components, they are unlikely to be the same as the prices generated by the whole model when that future year is estimated. That is, decisions are made in the planning components using information different from the model solution. The reasons for choosing this approach are two-fold. First, achieving consistency would add another dimension of complexity to the model. Second, the gains from the added effort are unclear. A perfect foresight model would lead to over optimization of planning decisions, since in reality planners do not have perfect foresight and have to plan for a range of contingencies. The model operates under the assumption that energy producers are cost minimizers. This is consistent with the conclusion that no single coal, oil, or natural gas firm represents a significant market force. Electric utilities are modeled as cost minimizers as well. Even though electric utilities are regulated monopolies, their planning models are explicitly cost minimizing. At the same time, there is no alternative theory of economic behavior that has a broad base of support.

The search of the equilibrium within each module consists of the interaction of the operations component and the demand curves. The operations component uses the existing capacity, or what is projected to be existing capacity, to meet a trial demand estimate that comes from the demand curves. This in turn produces a new set of consumer prices which are then input to the demand curves, producing new quantity estimates. The internal cycling continues until the individual fuel module converges.

Within this overall organization, a wide range of modeling techniques are used: econometric techniques and process modeling techniques. Also, some decomposition techniques simplify the operation of the models. The econometric techniques are used, for example, to determine refinery capacities and the demand estimates. For estimating refinery capacity there are time series on petroleum product prices and capacity additions for downstream units and a simple reduced-form model to project refinery capacity. In the demand models there are structural representations of various elements of demand, such as home heating.

Process models are used to simulate decisions in industries where there is enough information to do this, or it is important to capture the extra detail. For example, linear programming is used to represent refinery operations, because this is one of the standard techniques in the industry for guiding the operations of refineries. The linear program translates estimates of capacities and demands into product prices, incorporating the effects of crude quality.

Individual submodels can grow quite large. Incorporating large models directly into IFFS would result in a cumbersome system. The overall system is streamlined through a decomposition strategy. This is known as using pseudodata. A complete model is run many times, generating many solutions. In running the refinery linear program, the solutions are known as extreme points. A simple model that expresses the relationships between the inputs and outputs of the larger model is fit to the model solutions as a way of approximating the larger model. The simplified model is then incorporated into the larger system. Refineries are modeled this way. Some of the demand models are brought into the system directly because they are simple enough, but for the more complex ones, this technique is used. Finally, this approach is also used for representing oil and gas supply.

6.1 Electricity Market Module

The electricity market module is called first as an operational convenience. Electric utilities demand oil, natural gas and coal, and these estimates are needed when finding an equilibrium within the other modules. The electric utility representation, given the initial conditions that it obtains from the central module, estimates the future capacity expansion necessary for the electric utility industry and then simulates the operation of utilities. Thus equipment is purchased, scheduled, maintained, and dispatched on the basis of minimum cost.

The electricity module finds an equilibrium in electricity markets by starting with trial demands, simulating the dispatching of an inventory of powerplants to meet those demands and costing the electricity delivered. Using a combination of the new costs and previous prices, new, end-use demands for electricity are estimated, and the costing is repeated. The process continues until two successive sets of prices and quantities are within a close tolerance. Once internal convergence is achieved, the integrating module regains control and initializes the next module.

Prices, or rates, are set by an iterative computation, which includes considerations of the revenues the utilities will obtain and of the costs and constraints that they will face in financing new expansion. Because the electric utility module estimates how each class of generating equipment is dispatched (e.g., coal, nuclear, natural gas), the model derives the utility requirements for coal, petroleum products (primarily residual and distillate fuels), and natural gas.

6.2 Oil Market Module

The oil market module consists of a representation of refineries and refined product demand. Since the world price of oil is a scenario input, the costs of refining the product mix demanded determine the prices for refined products. The demands for petroleum products are the demands for the end-use sectors at the refined product prices, plus the demands from the electric utilities module. The refinery representation provides estimates of refined product prices, the utilization of existing domestic refineries, the needs for investment in new downstream refining equipment, and the total requirement for crude oil that must be supplied from domestic production or imports.

As with the utility model, the representation of refineries is based on the models used in corporate planning. In the case of refineries, this means using linear programming. As these types of models are too complex to incorporate directly, the model used is run many times and log-linear equations are fitted to the results.

Refineries consume a portion of their output and some natural gas in their operations. Thus, the natural gas requirement for the operation of refineries is provided to the central integrating module for inclusion in the gas market module. Internal convergence within the refineries module consists of balancing supply and demand, incorporating the effects of each oil product production level on every other product.

6.3 Natural Gas Market Module

The gas market module contains the oil and gas supply representation, gas demands, and a mechanism for balancing supply and demand. This module also provides the domestic oil supply estimates because oil and gas are produced by the same industry, using the same equipment. Consequently, the supply representation has to be kept as a unit in either the oil or gas modules. Since the world oil price is an input assumption, the price of crude oil to domestic producers and refiners is fixed. The gas price, however, is highly variable, making the gas module the logical place for the oil and gas supply representation.

The oil and gas supply representation simulates the amount of domestic drilling that takes place, given the prices of oil and gas and the availability of drilling equipment. This drilling is then translated into reserve additions and, subsequently, production. The fuels produced consist of crude oil, plus associated and dissolved natural gas and nonassociated natural gas. Natural gas contains natural gas liquids, and the quantity of natural gas liquids is computed as a fixed proportion of gas production. Demands for natural gas come from end-use consuming sectors and from electric utilities and refineries. The mechanism for finding a supply/demand balance is more complex than with electric utilities and oil because of the regulations on wellhead and delivered prices and the regulations on transportation costs.

6.4 Coal Market Module

Once the gas market solution has been found, the coal module is called. This module emphasizes coal supply and transportation. Supply is estimated using the Resource and Mine Costing component of the National Coal Model. Because of the importance of transportation costs in delivered coal prices, the module contains an elaborate description of regional coal movements. Rather than using fixed transportation costs, the model increases the tariffs as increasing flows create congestion.

When the coal module has converged, the central integrating procedure reevaluates the detailed demand models, returns to the electric utilities module and proceeds through the entire model again.

7. A MATHEMATICAL STATEMENT OF THE SOLUTION PROCEDURE

The problem of finding a market equilibrium is one of solving a set of simultaneous nonlinear equations. IFFS may be abstracted into a set of equations as follows:

Let $i = 1,\ldots,n$ index the fuels,

$j = 1,\ldots,m$ index the consuming sectors including the conversion activities.

p_i = price of fuel i

p = vector of prices

$S_i(p)$ = Supply of product i as a function of all fuel prices

$D_{ij}(p)$ = Demand for product i in sector j as a function of all fuel prices

Set

$$e_i(p) = \sum_j D_{ij}(p)-S_i(p).$$

Now $e_i(p)$ is known as the excess demand function for fuel i. The equilibrium problem may be stated as follows:

$$\text{find } p = (p_1,\ldots,p_n)$$

such that

$$e_1(p) = 0$$

$$\cdots$$

$$e_n(p) = 0$$

Let $(p_1^k, p_2^k,\ldots,p_n^k)$ be the trial solution from iteration k. The k+1 iteration of the algorithm proceeds as follows:

Solve

$$e_1(p_1^k, p_2^k,\ldots,p_n^k) = 0.$$

Then solve

$$e_2(p_1^{k+1}, p_2^k, p_3^k,\ldots,p_n^k) = 0$$

repeating until the last equation is solved

$$e_n(p_1^{k+1}, p_2^{k+1},\ldots,p_{n-1}^{k+1}, P_n) = 0$$

The algorithm continues until all equations are within tolerance for some p^k. In terms of IFFS, e_1 is the electricity module. Next, e_2 is the oil module, and it contains an estimate of utility oil consumption. Most importantly, e_3 is the natural gas module and two of the $D_{3j}(p)$ are the derived demand curves for natural gas in utilities and refineries. Finally, e_4 is coal. This mapping of modules to equations is not precise because each module contains more than one supply and demand curve, but this is incidental for the purposes of understanding how the model works.

The algorithm stated above is the Gauss-Seidel algorithm for solving simultaneous equations. This algorithm has the reputation for being relatively slow and has a linear convergence rate in the limit. However, it is very effective in this setting, taking eight to ten iterations in each year to reach a 1 percent convergence tolerance. The solution is efficient here because the structure of the fuel modules reduces the problem to the equivalent of solving four nonlinear equations. At the same time, the model contains thousands of equations. The equations with the greatest dependencies are solved within a fuel module, leaving relatively independent equations to be solved by the Gauss-Seidel algorithm.

8. CONCLUDING COMMENTS

IFFS provides a new approach for building energy market models. By providing a fuel market organization, the model fits more readily into the EIA organizational structure, and it is significantly faster, computationally, than MEFS and LEAP. The less structured model organization also allows for more natural formulations of the individual fuel markets.

There is more work that needs to be done to improve IFFS and other energy models. These tasks involve some of the basic, unanswered questions of economics: How should one represent expectations in structural planning models? How should one represent decision making in regulated utilities? The tasks also involve issues specific to energy markets: What is a good aggregate representation of forced outages and dispatching in electric utilities? What can be done to represent decisions of who buys what natural gas, given that price ceilings restrict what purchasers can pay? Also, more work can be done to improve the computational features of the model.

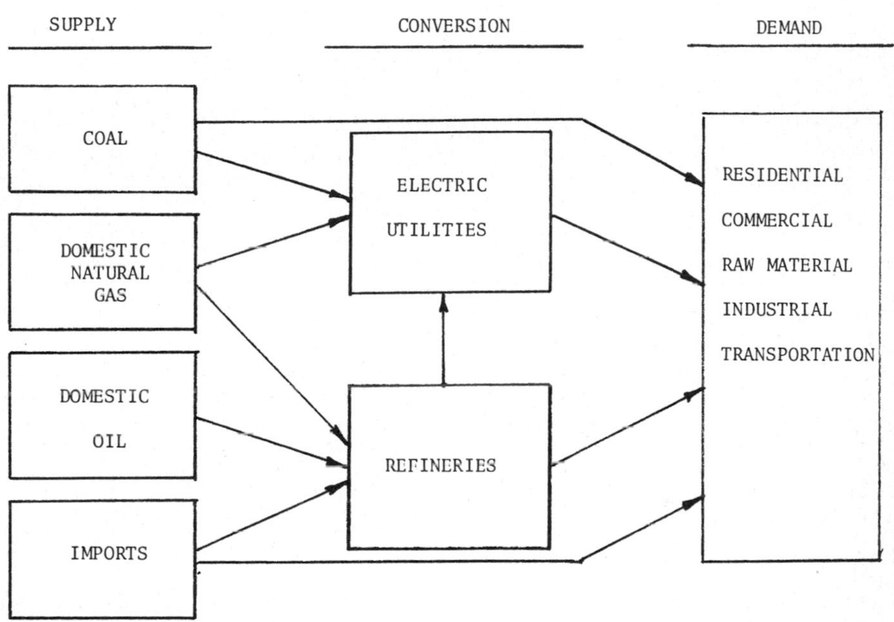

Figure 1

An Abstraction of Energy Markets

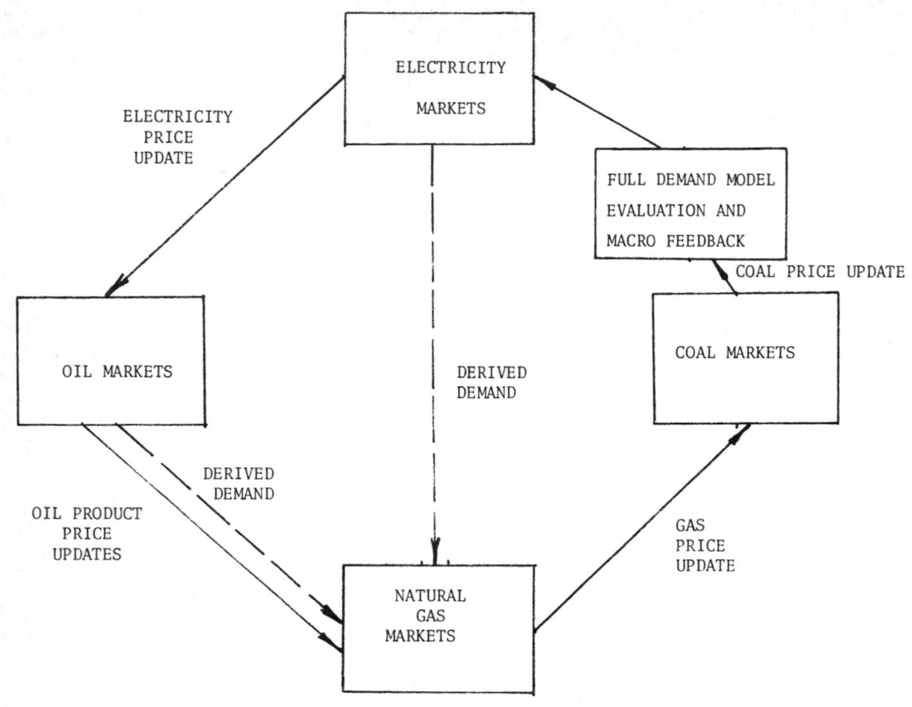

Figure 2

IFFS Organization

Analytic Techniques for Energy Planning
B. Lev, F.H. Murphy, J.A. Bloom & A.S. Gleit (Editors)

THE GAS ANALYSIS MODELING SYSTEM

Richard P. O'Neill
William G. Kurator
Barbara Mariner-Volpe
William A. Trapmann
Joan Heinkel
Ruth Stokes
Charles Mylander
Christoph Witzgall
Lambert Joel
Patsy Saunders

EIA, Washington, D.C. 20585

William R. Stewart
College of William and Mary
Williamsburg, Virgina

The Gas Analysis Modeling System (GAMS) has been developed to provide EIA with the ability to study issues associated with natural gas supply and pipeline regulatory options. GAMS represents aggregates of the major United States pipelines, domestic supply sources and end uses as well as the corresponding regulations.

1. INTRODUCTION

The natural gas market consists of four agent groups that interact with each other. They are:

- Producers: individuals and companies that search for new supplies of natural gas and sell gas to pipelines and end-users for consumption in their own operations.
- Pipeline Companies: firms that purchase supplies of gas at the wellhead, transport gas for resale to other pipeline companies to distributors or directly to consumers. These companies also consume gas as a pipeline fuel.
- Distributors: privately or publicy owned firms that purchase supplies of gas from pipelines and sell it to end-users for consumption in their own operations.
- Consumers: commercial establishments, industrial firms, electric utilities and residential dwellings that require nature gas for use as space and process heat, chemical feedstock, and boiler fuel to raise steam. Some consumers, referred to as direct sale purchasers, purchase gas directly from producers.

While the Energy Information Administration (EIA) has, in the past, produced projected estimates of the production, consumption and price of natural gas, the approach used to provide such estimates was not detailed enough to address important questions about the natural gas market. Accordingly, the EIA developed a new approach that provides a more appropriate method for representing the behavior of the above agent groups and assessing the detailed effects of deregulation and associated impacts. Based upon this new approach, a modeling system was developed, referred to in this report as the Gas Analysis Modeling System (GAMS), that spans all aspects of the natural gas market as shown in Figure 1.

Producers, disaggregated on a regional basis, undertake drilling activities involving the development and exploration of crude oil (and associated-dissolved gas) and nonassociated gas (and lease condensate). Drilling activity levels are based upon expected profitability and capital resources. The profitabiity of each type of drilling activity is represented by the net present vaue of projected revenues and expenditures of each activity. The avilability of rigs and other equipment to producers is determined by past and current revenues (net of excise taxes) at the wellhead from crude oil and natural gas production.

Every year, each type of regional activity competes for available rigs on the basis of relative profitability of prospective drilling efforts. Based upon the yields associated with finding rates, producers offer natural gas reserves (net of lease and plant fuel) to pipeline companies and other purchasers. Additional gas supplies are available from imports and synthetic natural gas.

Through a computerized simulation of future needs, pipeline companies and direct purchasers bid for reserves offered by the producers. The bid price is based upon the estimated production schedule and price of currently dedicated reserves and the estimated maximum amount and price of gas that can be marketed over the next several years. Reserves are awarded to the bidders on the basis of bid price. For price ceiling gas for which bidders are willing to bid above the ceiling, reserves are awarded according to historical market shares modified by bid prices.

Transmission and distribution of gas are simulated in a network representation of 17 interstate and intrastate pipeline systems and about 4,000 aggregated markets. Each year, pipeline companies assess supply availability and customer demand on a seasonal basis and make desisions aimed at marketing the maximal quantity of gas possible. The decisions are based primarily on producer prices, take-or-pay commitments in existing contracts, and estimated market demands. Once the gas is purchased, it is delivered to distributors (reduced by transmission losses), with demand and commodity tariffs added to the average purchase price. Prices for delivered gas included the distributors' commodity costs, the distributors' markups (which account for various operating, transmission, and storage costs plus the distributor-permitted return on investment), and demand ("hookup") charges.

Distributors deliver gas to six classes of end-use consumers: residential, commericial, electric utility (with and without alternative fuels capability), and industrial (with and without alternative fuels capability) consumers. Distributors assess demand, commodity, and user charges for each type of customer.

Estimated demand for gas is based upon historical patterns of consumption and the physical ability to switch to an alternative fuel. Response to price changes is assumed to have both an immediate effect and a lagged effect on consumption which may vary regionally and by end-user type.

Removal of price ceilings on natural gas has two effects. First, purchasers of new gas reserves are allowed to bid and pay a price based on their estimates of market-ability. Second, prices for production from currently dedicated reserves are based on escalator terms in the contract.

2. NATURAL GAS SUPPLIES

The natural gas supply forecasts used in this report are obtained from two sources: the Production of Onshore Lower-48 Oil and Gas (PROLOG) Model [1], and the Outer Continental Shelf (OCS) Model [2]. The availability of synthetic and imported gas is an exogenous estimate.

2.1. Onshore Lower-48 Reserve Additions for Natural Gas from Conventional Sources

PROLOG forecasts annual oil and natural gas exploration and production activities for the six onshore regions of the Lower-48 States depicted in Figure 2. The primary activities of these regions are exploratory and developmental drilling. Forecast values include the reserve additions from exploratory drilling. Within drilling resource constraints, the model chooses

Figure 1. Operational Data Flow of the EIA Gas Analysis Modeling System (GAMS)*

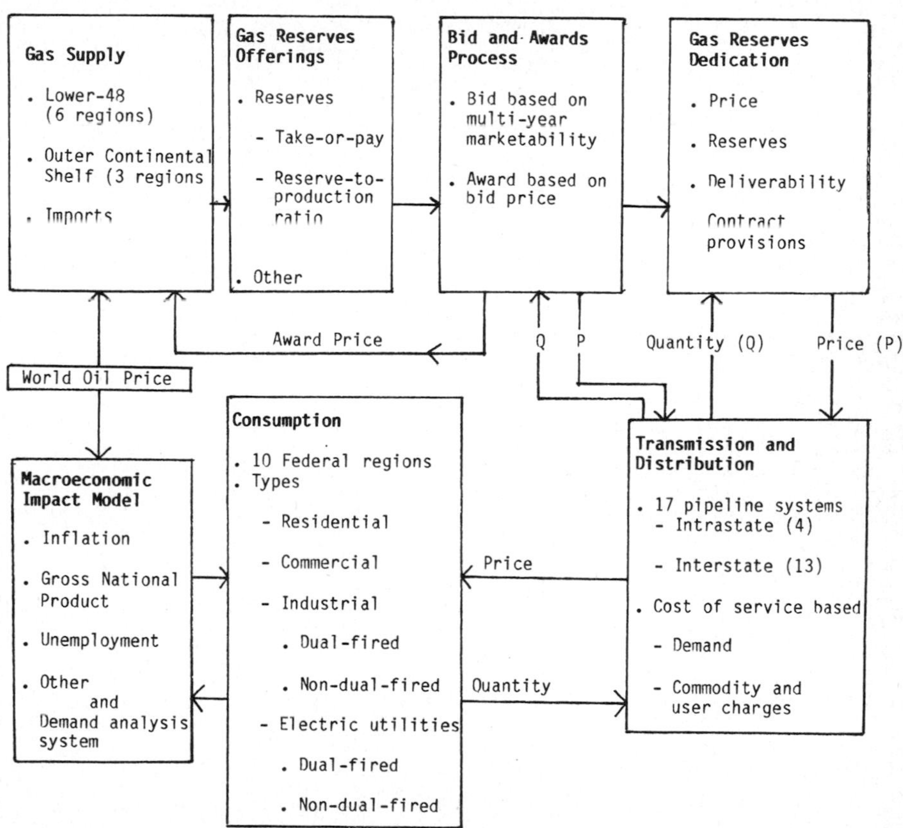

*GAMS consists of the modules shown; each box in the operational flow has an associated input, output, and operational methodology.

Figure 2. Natural Gas Supply Regions

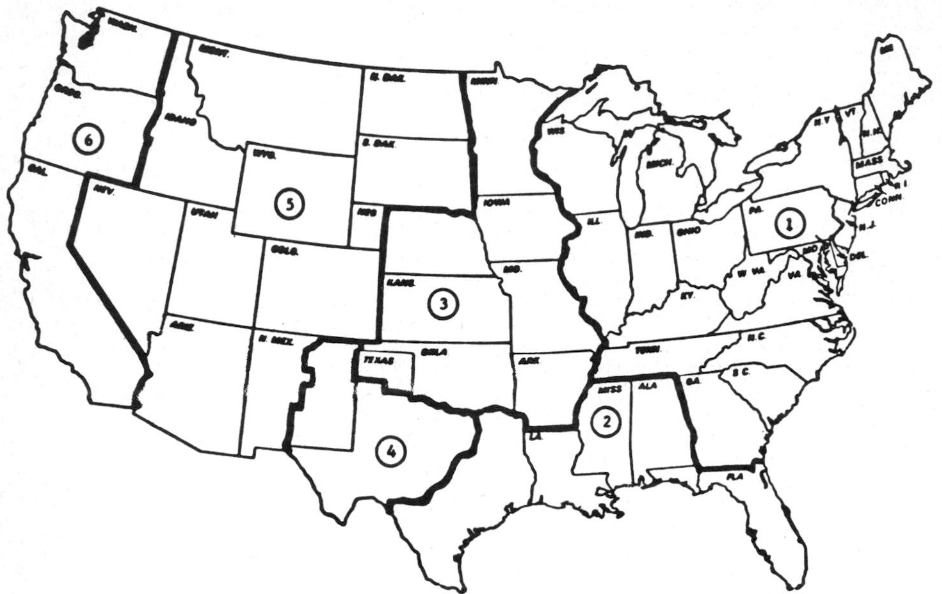

drilling activities that result in reserve additions and production on the basis of discounted present value.

Drilling activities are differentiated by category. Oil and natural gas drilling are evaluated separately for each subclass of drilling. Exploratory and developmental drilling are treated separately, with developmental drilling further subdivided by the type of reserves to be developed. The major distinction in the nature of drilling within the model lies between exploration and development: exploration yields new additions to the stock of known reserves; development determines the rate of production from the stock of known reserves.

For each year of the forecast horizon, the data transferred from PROLOG to GAMS constitute a set of projected reserve additions and projected production profiles. Production profiles generated by PROLOG are used to determine the maximum available production and to adjust the maximum available production capacity based upon subsequent developmental drilling. Annual production forecasts are determined from a range of production options based upon maximum production capacity, take-or-pay options, and the derived demands of the pipelines and distribution companies.

Figure 3 presents a schematic depiction of the PROLOG model, which steps through time in yearly intervals. For both oil and gas in each region, a range of possible footage for exploratory drilling is determined, based upon historical growth rates. The range dictates the maximum and minimum amounts of exploratory drilling that may be conducted in each region for either oil or gas. The range is divided into smaller finding ranges within each step of drilling to compute the resulting reserves added. The discounted cash flow is then calculated to evaluate the present value of these reserve additions on the basis of a generic production profile.

Developmental drilling is handled in essentially the same fashion as exploratory drilling. The range of drilling is set for both oil and gas in each region for all types of development. The range is divided into steps. For each step, the existing production profile is modified to reflect the effect of further development. Based on the new production profile, the net present value of the additional development drilling is computed using the discounted cash flow technique.

Next, net present value per foot drilled of each proposed activity is considered within a constraint on available rigs, bounds on exploratory or developmental drilling for each fuel within a region, and a short-run drilling cost curve. The choice of drilling activities is accomplished on a merit order basis by a linear program. This cycle is repeated for each year of the forecast horizon.

The rig constraint, the number of rigs and other necessary equipment available for drilling, is based upon historical relationships among wellhead revenues for oil and gas, drilling expenditures, and rig depreciation. The short-run drilling cost curve represents the change in the cost of drilling due to yearly fluctuations in drilling levels based upon historical information. Projections of unconventional gas, or gas from tight formation gas reservoirs, are based upon a study by the National Petroleum Council (NPC) [3].

Figure 3. Schematic representation of the PROLOG algorithm.

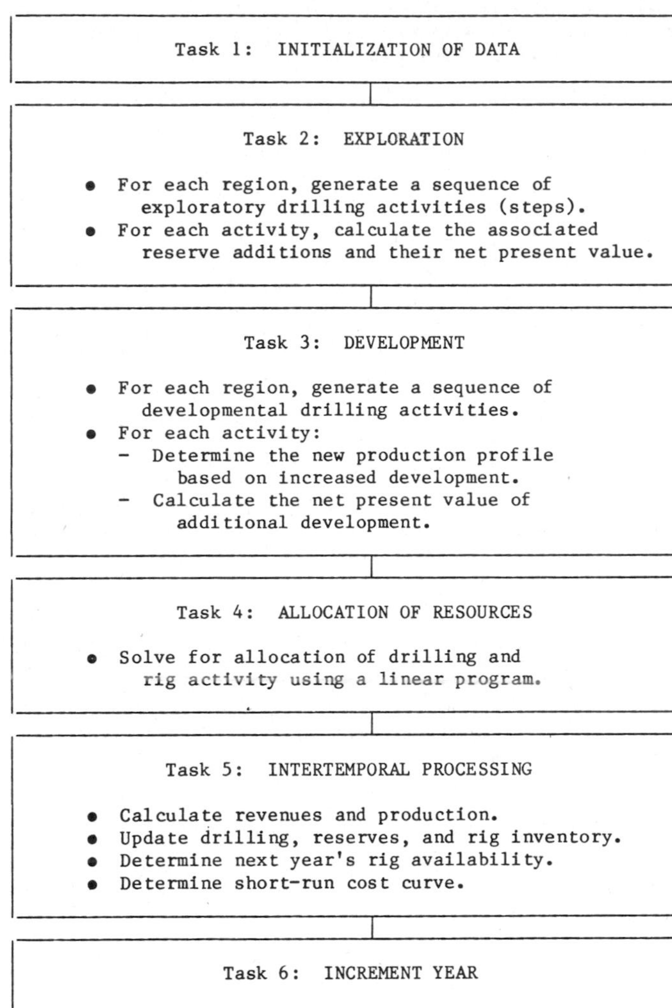

Task 1: INITIALIZATION OF DATA
Task 2: EXPLORATION
• For each region, generate a sequence of exploratory drilling activities (steps).
• For each activity, calculate the associated reserve additions and their net present value.
Task 3: DEVELOPMENT
• For each region, generate a sequence of developmental drilling activities.
• For each activity:
- Determine the new production profile based on increased development.
- Calculate the net present value of additional development.
Task 4: ALLOCATION OF RESOURCES
• Solve for allocation of drilling and rig activity using a linear program.
Task 5: INTERTEMPORAL PROCESSING
• Calculate revenues and production.
• Update drilling, reserves, and rig inventory.
• Determine next year's rig availability.
• Determine short-run cost curve.
Task 6: INCREMENT YEAR
• Let t = t+1.
• If t > forecast horizon, stop; otherwise, go to Task 2.

2.2 Outer Continental Shelf (OCS) Projections

The lag time for production from new OCS leases is 5 years or more as of the date of lease. Given the existence of the Natural Gas Policy Act (NGPA) of 1978, ceiling prices for new gas are known in constant dollars for the first half of the 1980's. Any divergence between anticipated and realized prices for the latter part of this decade can affect the behavior only in 1990, which is the last year of the forecast horizon covered by this model at this time.

OCS forecasts are generated by the OCS Model using available data on economics, offshore drilling and production, resource base, and the institutional framework (see OCS model documentation [2]). Economic data include the costs for all phases of the production process and the tax structure. The tax structure is incorporated in order to be able to account for the tax reductions generated by business expenses. The resource base is represented by a stochastic depiction of all known structures in the OCS regions. The uncertainty surrounding the resource base is dealt with by employing a Monte Carlo technique using a probabilistic representation of the resource base. The institutional framework consists mainly of the most recently announced leasing schedule from the Department of the Interior.

The projected array of new field reserve additions from the OCS Model allows production from these reserves to begin in 1986, due to the assumed 5-year lag between initial activities in a region and the beginning of production. This presents a problem for the Gulf of Mexico, but not for the Atlantic or Pacific regions, where production from these reserve additions is not initiated until the end of the decade. This gap in the forecast from 1981 through 1985 for the Gulf of Mexico is filled in the following way.

The base case forecast contains the actual 1981 level of reserve additions for the Gulf of Mexico (GOM). The methodology description for the OCS Model (OCSM) includes a procedure to develop reserve additions based on acreage leased as of 1980. These figures are used for 1982 through 1985. The completed drilling schedule requires 3 years, causing some overlap between the offline projections and the OCSM forecasts. The two sets of figures are summed for each year; one set represents reserves from acreage leased as of 1980, while the other represents reserves from new areas.

2.3. Natural Gas Reserves

The Gas Reserves Supply Table (GRST) is an accounting scheme for available supplies both dedicated and projected, and for prices on an annual basis. PROLOG and OCSM provide projected reserves throughout the remaining model time horizon. These reserve additions are adjusted annually. The price escalator routine is discussed in the Model to determine the award price for new supplies requirements. The GRST consists of "reserve blocks," and first purchasers of natural gas.

The primary item in a "reserve block" is the reserves available for sale, net of lease and plant fuel, for the current year for a particular pipeline system. About 7.5 percent of the wellhead production is "lost" to lease and plant fuel, which is an unavoidable in-kind cost incurred in the dry natural gas production process. As a well-known and therefore anticipated drain from production, the negotiations for purchases of pipeline quality gas must account for this loss during the production process. Generally, purchase negotiations are agreements for gas net of lease and plant fuel use. This procedure enables the accounting of all costs. First purchasers of natural gas contract for quantities of gas that are to be used for satisfying the demands of their customers. Information is included on the location and dedication status of the reserves. This consists of a region code for one of the six onshore regions or three offshore regions and, if dedicated, the pipeline system designation. Other information in a reserve block consists of the NGPA Title I Section and sub-category and its expected current year purchase price. Gathering charges and taxes are an additional cost to the first purchaser and are added to the wellhead price.

The three significant points in time for the gas reserve block are specified: (1) the first year of production, (2) the first year of peak production, and (3) the last year of peak production. Further information is provided that enables calculation of the rate of decline from peak production. This production profile is essential to the potential purchaser's scheduling of gas flows along a fixed capacity network and planning for future needs.

The final item in a reserve block is pipeline take-or-pay requirements. This item specifies the percentage of maximum contract volume for which a purchaser must pay, regardless of whether the gas is taken. The lower the take-or-pay value, the more flexibility a purchaser has in planning operations.

3. CONTRACT PRICE ESCALATION

Average wellhead prices of reserves are provided by pipeline group, NGPA section, and interstate or intrastate market for contracts existing in 1980 and for new contracts written in 1981 or later.

The wellhead prices are escalated over time using assumptions of contract price escalator clauses. Five types of contract clauses were used in developing these averages. Table 1 describes the various price escalator categories. The categories are mutually exclusive and collectively exhaustive. For example, a contract may contain a highest allowed regulated rate and an oil-parity clause which will take effect upon deregulation. Because contracts contain these multiple pricing provisions a hierarchy was developed, with the more volatile pricing clauses taking precedence over the others. These are listed in the order of precedence in Table 1.

3.1 Gas Supply Bid and Award

After new reserves are discovered, the producers set out to find buyers who bid for gas that has been discovered. This process is modeled by the Bid and Award Component. The supply interface with the Bid and Award Component consists of a communications loop between producers and buyers. PROLOG passes the relevant supply information to the Bid and Award Component in the Gas Reserves Supply Table format. The Bid and Award Component subsequently returns a market-clearing price (the award price) to PROLOG for use in projecting gas discoveries and developments of subsequent periods. The process simulates the market transactions for natural gas.

Table 1. Price Escalator Categories

Category	Description
Deregulation Clause, Oil Parity with No Market-Out	A redetermination clause which specifies that the deregulated price will be tied to an oil-parity value, and no market-out provision is contained in the contract which would permit the purchaser to adjust the price or terminate purchases.
Deregulation Clause, Most-Favored-Nation Clause with No Market-Out	A redetermination clause which specifies that the deregulation price will be tied to the average of other contracts and no market-out provision is contained in the contract. For this category, those contracts which had a most-favored-nation clause but were included in the oil parity category above were excluded from this category.
All Other Deregulation Clauses	This includes any contract with a deregulation clause that was not included in the above deregulation categories. This also includes contracts with oil-parity and/or most-favored-nation clauses that contain market-out options.
Highest Allowed Regulated Rate	An indefinite escalator clause which specifies that gas will be priced at highest allowable rate.
Definite Only	Fixed price contract or a contract with a specific price escalation path.

This approach is a break from the more traditional modeling approach, which views pipelines as purchasers of "spot-market" production in a given time period. Purchases of produced gas not under long-term contract are very limited. Pipelines and other first purchasers generally contract for the receipt of gas volumes over time. In essence, the pipelines contract for newly discovered reserves to be purchased over time according to specified contract terms. The long-term nature of such contracts requires the consideration of expectations in the transaction. In addition to the scheduling of gas flows along a fixed capacity network, the negotiations for the purchase require the anticipation of future discoveries. The expected availability of new supplies should and does affect the willingness of buyers to pay a particular price. In turn, the most recent price established for new reserve additions affects the price anticipated by producers over ensuing time periods.

The PROLOG component is executed to generate the Gas Reserves Supply Table, which lists discoveries of natural gas deposits over time, along with associated information characterizing these deposits. The PROLOG forecast is based upon an expected path for the price of newly discovered gas. In time periods past, the ceiling prices of new gas conformed to the formulas of the NGPA. Given the initial set of expected new gas prices, PROLOG generates a schedule of reserve additions. The information is used in the Bid and Award Module to determine the award price for gas. The new award price for gas is then used to modify the previous expected prices for new gas. The new price enters PROLOG for the next year, and the process continues for the specified time horizon.

This process approximates the market mechanism in which reserves are committed under contract according to a schedule of production and prices. Long-term contracts are negotiated with consideration of the buyers' and sellers' expectations concerning future supplies and demand. The prices realized from a current time period affect the expected price path. This new price path then influences behavior in the subsequent time period, and so the process continues. In addition to explicit approximation of the actual supply market transactions, GAMS does not allow decision makers to act with perfect knowledge. All behavior is based upon expectations that may or may not be realized. The differences between expected and realized values allow the model to represent the adjustment process, which all agents in the market must follow in the face of changing conditions.

The bidding for, and acquisition of, natural gas supply is handled within the GAMS framework by the Bidding and Award Module. The bidding module evaluates, from the point of view of each pipeline system, the current dedicated reserves and future anticipated needs. Each pipeline system makes a bid for a portion of the current year's newly discovered reserves. A bid price is the average price that a pipeline is willing to pay for new reserves. If the ceiling price of one category of gas were below this bid price, the price that the pipeline would be willing to pay for decontrolled gas would be correspondingly higher than the bid price; also, the overall average price paid would be less than or equal to the bid price. Because the majority of new reserves in years past was price-controlled gas, the decontrol price may have been quite high. To prevent extremely high values, based solely on the system's ability (as opposed to its willingness) to pay, the decontrol price is now capped at 130 percent of the projected price of No. 2 fuel oil. Thus, the awards routine evaluates bids from the producer's point of view and enters into contracts with pipeline systems for the current year's reserves based upon the bids of all pipeline systems.

The bidding routine uses a dynamic programming approach to determine a bid price for new gas reserves. The bid price is the decision variable. The quantity of reserves controlled by a pipeline system and the average price for production from the reserves are called "state variables" because these variables describe the state of the system at any point in time. The bid price determines an expected fraction of new reserves to be captured. The bidding routine establishes a series of bids based on different expected prices. The function that specifies the fraction of expected new reserves returns different values depending upon what the system expects the overall average acquisition price of new reserves to be. The higher this expected price, the lower the fraction of reserves will be for a given bid price. The awards routine uses the bids of each pipeline to establish an overall average price, the actual bid price, and the actual fraction of reserves allocated to each pipeline. In this way, it brings the quantity of new reserves demanded into line with the actual quantity of reserves available.

The awards routine uses the bid price and the desired quantities to allocate the gas reserves. After realigning the bid prices and desired quantities, the awards routine allocates the controlled reserves to each pipeline according to the actual fraction of existing reserves, and allocates decontrolled gas to each pipeline according to bid price with the higher bidders receiving proportionately more than the lower bidders. The decontrol price is the lower of 130 percent of the projected No. 2 fuel oil price and the average price the pipelines would be willing to pay for decontrolled gas based on rolled-in gas. The higher a pipeline system bids, the larger the share of newly discovered reserves it captures.

The bidding routine is based upon the assumption that a pipeline system, which bids for newly discovered reserves, seeks to maximize the amount of gas it can purchase and resell over the planning horizon. The lower it can keep the cost of purchased gas, the larger the share of the end-use market it captures. The bidding routine is executed for each pipeline system, independent of other pipeline systems. The decision variable is the price bid for newly offered gas reserves. The bid price determines the portion of new gas reserves awarded to a pipeline system and the average production price of new reserves. The price paid for new reserves will affect the price the pipeline system must charge its customers in future years. The pipeline system "rolls in" the price of new reserves; i.e., it passes an average gas production price on to its customers.

A pipeline system is assumed to be concerned with controlling the average price of all new gas reserves contracted for in a given year. Likewise, a pipeline system is concerned that gas be sold in bundles, such that the price of gas not be subject to changes in the control of the wellhead price; by selling gas in bundles the average price of the bundle, including controlled gas, stays at the agreed price. Based upon the average bid price of all pipeline systems, the reserves available in the current year are awarded to a pipeline system contingent upon observing the following principles:

- The average price of new reserves must not exceed the average bid price.
- The quantity of reserves must not exceed the expected quantity.
- Reserves in price-controlled categories must be assigned using a market share formula that allocates shares based upon a prespecified percentage and the prices bid by pipeline systems.

The amount of gas resold in one year by a pipeline system is the minimum amount of gas that can be produced from reserves dedicated to the pipeline, and the amount of gas demanded by a pipeline system's gas consumers combined with net transactions with other pipeline systems and imports.

4. NATURAL GAS TRANSMISSION AND DISTRIBUTION

Transmission and distribution of natural gas is simulated by a network of nodes representing pipeline companies, distributors, and end-use markets, and links of "arcs" representing sales relationships. This network is divided into pipeline systems. A pipeline system is a prespecified group of purchasers that includes pipeline companies, distributors associated with pipelines, and markets acting as a single unit in their bidding for available reserves.

The network is divided into 17 pipeline systems, each of which represents a group of purchasers. These pipeline systems transmit gas to the end-user markets directly or indirectly from producers (that is, sales for resale) and from distributors that link the indirect market sales with the pipelines. Each node in the base network is in a single pipeline system. Each distributor in a system has one designated primary supplier, the pipeline or the distributor, identified by Form FERC-50 baseline data as the source of greatest domestic supply volume. All other supplies to the distributor are aggregated.

The "primary supply" relationship is specified by an arc in the pipeline system and the supplier and customer nodes, i.e., the structure of a pipeline system is fixed by the initial data. Thus, an underlying assumption of the model is that the transmission and distribution system can be represented by classifying resale supply contracts involving distributors into two basic types, "committed" and "optimal," such that all supplies that flow on "primary" or system arcs are optimal, whereas those that flow on other or "secondary" arcs are take-or-pay. Figure 4 presents a sample two-pipeline system network. A distributor providing primary supply to another in a particular system may also furnish part of the aggregate take-or-pay supply to a distributor in the network of a different system.

For a pipeline system that has more than one pipeline, a pipeline system "root node" is created as a surrogate for aggregate producers (the "wellhead"). The root is defined as the primary bidder on behalf of other pipeline nodes in the pipeline system.

Links or "arcs" in these systems, as in the base network, represent gas supply relationships; they may also represent direct physical conduits, such as pipes, but not in all cases. Market nodes, which appear explicitly in the system, represent user sectors. A residential node, for instance, represents all of the residential customers of a particular distributor in a given state. Thus, a distributor may have up to six customers, representing (in curtailment priority order) the residential, commercial, electric utility, industrial, electric utility with dual capability and industrial with dual fuel capability sectors. The latter two are sometimes referred to as "fuel switchers" because they can readily use residual oil instead of gas, in response to price differences. Market sector nodes are each served by a single supplier.

The root node (or the single pipeline node in systems that have only one pipeline) is the system interface to the wellhead and is sometimes called the "pipegate." The intermediary distributor nodes are collectively called the "city gate," and the markets are called the "burner-tip."

The model first sets up initial conditions for the iterated annual operation of the market. That is, inconsistencies and omissions in the supporting data are reconciled to yield an overall consistent pattern of demands, prices, and flows, along with status of reserves, take-or-pay commitments, and storage requirements throughout the network.

At the start of each ensuing year, the status of reserves and currently available wellhead supply for each pipeline system is determined by query to the bid and awards model. Secondary flows and costs are combined and posted to pipeline system nodes. Node storage quantities for heating season withdrawal are assigned by reference to the difference between summer and winter demand in the previous year. Pipelines and distributors set tariff and demand rates based on estimates of current (forthcoming) year customer demand (derived from simple escalations of previous year demand). Finally, parameters for the calculation of demand are updated.

Thus the stage is set for clearance of the markets for each system in the summer, delivery of gas to customers and injection of storage gas, followed by winter (heating season) withdrawal from storage, market clearance and delivery of gas, after which annual market summary bookkeeping and reporting are done. A second interaction with the bid and award model occurs at this point, this time to report to that model drawdown of reserves in satisfaction of market demand.

At year end, prices and quantity flows are updated on the secondary arcs based mainly on the change in primary (system) prices for the year. Updating transmission tariffs (from pipelines) completes the determination of starting conditions for the next model year.

The direct interactions between pipeline systems can occur at the start of a year when secondary inflow to nodes is accumulated, because this committed supply will affect net system demand in the clearance of markets. Indirect interactions occur at the end of the year when the system prices affect secondary flow for the following year.

4.1 Network Construction

The Form FERC-50, "Alternate Fuel Demand Due to Natural Gas Deficiencies," is the major source of information that was used to create the gas market transmission and distribution network. FERC-50 was designed to collect the data necessary to support efforts pursuant to the Department of Energy's (DOE) responsibility for equitable allocation of natural gas and related products among all regions of the United States, all sectors of the natural gas industry, and all users. All interstate and intrastate pipeline companies, municipalities, and other suppliers of natural gas to end-users were required to complete the form. Completed FERC-50 forms provide the information on volume of gas purchased from each source, nature of suppliers (interstate, intrastate, imports, or producer) and total volume of gas delivered monthly to end-use customers and number of customers by customer category (residential, commercial, industrial, electric utility, and other) and by State.

Monthly end-use sales by customer category were processed to determine load factors and heating season factors. Another data source used extensively was Form FERC-2, "Annual Report of Natural Gas Companies." Among other information, FERC-2 reported average prices of gas sold for resale to each company, and average prices of direct sales by pipelines to end-users, i.e., "Field and Main Line Industrial Sales," as well as distribution sales to other end-users.

The base network is a collection of points or nodes, and links between nodes called arcs. The nodes represent natural market entities, such as pipeline companies, distributors, and conceptually, end-use market sectors. The arcs represent transitional or supply relationships between the entities. The initial set of 48 pipeline nodes consists of one node for each actual or aggregate pipeline company plus one for each multipipeline system.

Figure 4. Diagram of a Sample Distribution Network with Two Pipeline Systems

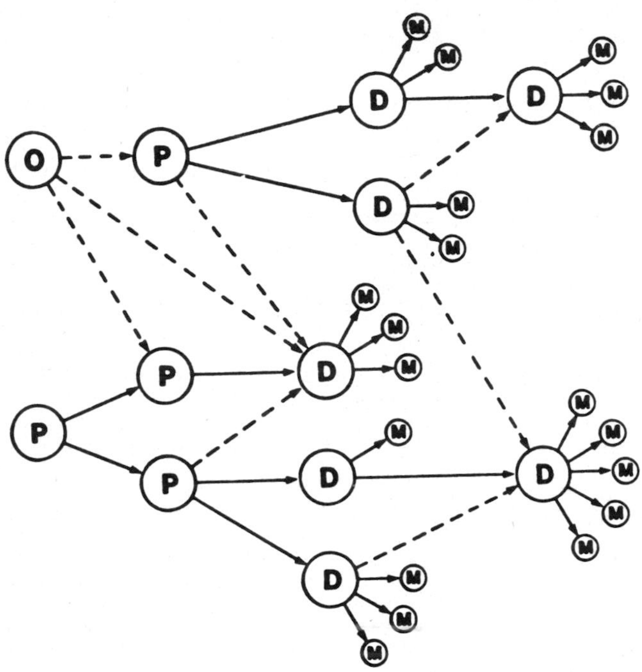

Key: P, pipeline companies; D, distributors; O, imports; M, market sectors; solid arrows, primary or system supply arcs; broken arrows, secondary or "committed" supply arcs.

Given this set of pipeline nodes, the network is augmented using data from the Form FERC-50 Supply File to identify other nodes, which are then added to the network. In the Supply File, every respondent (pipeline or distributor) identifies each source of supply by its 5-digit identification number and by gas volume. For each respondent, a node is generated and added to the node list (becoming a potential qualifying supply source in a subsequent pass) if one or more of its supply sources is currently listed. At present, two complete passes are made through the Supply File, creating and adding nodes according to the specified rule.

After making two passes through the Supply File and adding appropriate nodes to the node list, a third pass is made to create the arcs of the network. Typically, each respondent reports several supply sources. The arc generation procedure depends upon whether or not nodes exist which correspond to the respondent and to one or more sources on the node list. If there are nodes corresponding to both the respondent and the source on the node list, an arc is created with origin at the source node and destination at the respondent node. If the respondent is on the list and the source node is not (i.e., the respondent has at least one source on the list and at least one source not on the list), an arc is then created with a base node origin and destination equal to the respondent node. When the State location of the respondent's end-use sales is later identified, the origin of this arc will become the generic intrastate pipeline which serves that State. If the respondent is not on the list, all supplies to that respondent are then aggregated and associated with an arc from the appropriate generic intrastate pipeline origin to a generic node in the State indicated by the leading two digits of the 5-digit identification number of the respondent.

After the Supply File is read, the FERC-50 End-Use Sales File is used to establish markets for each node in the network. Each FERC-50 respondent reports the following information for each State in which there were end-use sales: monthly and total volumes, and average number of customers category, i.e., residential, commercial, industrial, electric utility, and "other." Sales reported as "other" include sales to public facilities, e.g., schools and hospitals. As each end-use sales record is read, the following data transformations are made:

- All "other" sales are aggregated with commercial sales and are not distinguished subsequently.
- Industrial and electric utility sales above a threshold volume, as reported on the FERC-50, are split into two markets, one of which has the capability of switching to alternate fuels.

The data transformations described above lead to a maximum of six markets per State for each respondent: residential, commercial, electric utility, industrial, electric utilities with alternate fuel capability, and industrial with alternative fuel capability. The end-use markets are assumed to have priority in the order listed above, whereas residential customers are the last to be curtailed during supply shortages.

Input to the network specifies the storage capacity available at pipelines and distributors. Gas stored in the summer and completely withdrawn in the winter is assumed to be used by distributors or pipelines in an attempt to balance seasonal flow. Therefore, market entities annually estimate current storage requirements as half of the difference between winter and summer demand of their customers in the previous year, adjusted for losses.

Market sector nodes carry preset parameters describing consumption patterns. These data were generated using FERC-50 monthly end-use sales data for the period April 1980 through March 1981. A "heating factor" and a "load factor" were calculated for each user category (residential, commercial, utility, industrial, and other) per FERC-50 respondent. The heating factors are used to represent seasonability of demand; the load factors are used in a rate-setting routine. The heating factor is defined as end-use sales to a market sector from October through March divided by the total end-use sales (April through March) to that market sector. Roughly speaking, the heating factor is the ratio of winter consumption to total consumption. The monthly load factor is the peak monthly end-use sales divided by the average monthly end-use sales during the reporting period April through March. A transformation from monthly load factors to daily load factors (multiplying by 1.5) is performed when the load factors are used for rate setting.

Prior to first-year simulation, adjustments are made to the initial ("base year") gas quantity flows and prices in the pipeline system networks in order to reconcile inconsistencies in baseline data from disparate sources and account for distribution losses and unrecorded sales or purchases. For flows, a material balance or flow conservation condition is imposed on the activity for the year at each node. In that way, with transmission losses taken into account, total outflow is equal to total inflow, and flows in the direction of markets are all positive. "Inflow" at root pipeline nodes is wellhead production, "outflow" at market nodes is consumption.

The balances are achieved by allowing for market distribution losses up to 10 percent of deliveries and then, if necessary, by pro-rata increases in the recorded demand at the markets. The values for transmission loss from pipelines are determined by the average mileage of transported gas in each pipeline zone on those supply arcs for which specific values have not been preset by input. These values are not altered in adjusting the base-year flow. In this process, corrections are made to the loss factors for delivery from distributors and their market nodes and are considered permanent. The adjusted market loss factors are fixed throughout the subsequent simulation.

4.2 Tariffs

The (seasonal and annual) transaction prices in each pipeline system have three components: a purchase gas charge, a transmission or distribution tariff or "commodity" surcharge, and a fixed or "demand" charge. The commodity charge is the average "bottom line" price, i.e., a net acquisition cost per unit volume of all supplies to the seller, and is the same for all system customers of the seller. The surcharge (which, by convention, is labeled "transmission tariff" when the seller is a pipeline and "distribution tariff" when the seller is a distributor) represents recovery of the seller's operational expenses, permitted return on investment, transmission and storage losses, and "interzonal rate differentials"; thus, the surcharge varies among customers. The demand charge is a fixed charge, representing typically the cost of maintaining the capability of delivering an estimated peak-day volume of gas to the buyer. Initial formulations for the markups are derived from baseline data by regression models and adjusted in the base year as described below. In subsequent years, they are increased by fixed inflation factors. Markups for committed supply transactions are fixed fractions (currently 10 percent) of the purchase gas charge. Note that in a price path from the wellhead to the burner-tip, each reseller's acquisition cost is the average net cost per unit volume, i.e., adding committed supply and subtracting committed sales; the price paid at a market reflects all markups in the path.

4.3 Tariff Calibration

Several types of price data are used to make the network operational. For sales from interstate pipelines to distributors, prices are taken directly from the average annual prices reported by the pipelines in the Form FERC-2 for each recipient of "Sales for Resale." Should FERC-50 report a transaction that is not reported in FERC-2, the weighted average price of a pipeline's sales is used. For interstate pipeline direct sales, the base-year price is taken from the FERC-2 as the average annual price reported by State for "Field and Main Line Industrial Sales."

For direct sales by intrastate pipelines, prices are the "Resale Prices" reported in the 1980 Gas Facts, State average prices are representative of city-gate prices. The reported prices are used directly in 12 States. These States all have substantial intrastate markets that would be reflected in the reported prices. For all other States, the prices are averaged over the aforementioned 12 States and used for sales from generic intrastate pipelines to distributors.

The remaining resale prices are those for sales from one distributor to another. No source of price data on these transactions has yet been found. The procedure used to calculate prices for these sales follows. First, the network nodes are ordered so that if node A preceded node B, the longest path from a root node to node A would be shorter, i.e., it would have fewer arcs than the longest path from a root node to node B. Proceeding through the network ordered in this way, the prices, which are paid for supplies by node A and increased by some markup. The markup currently used is 10 percent. Available data on sales from distributors to user markets consist of State averages by market sector from the 1981 Natural Gas Annual (NGA).

Price adjustment for the base-year networks reconciles State/market sector data from the Energy Information Administration's 1980 NaturalGas Annual, with prices compiled from pipeline reserve purchases.

Price adjustment is a two-stage process. First, a pipe-gate price is determined by averaging retrogressively from the distributor customers of the pipelines, using given estimates of transmission tariff demand charges and commodity surcharges. These latter tariffs are then adjusted so that they will reproduce the pipeline pipe-gate purchase price. Burner-tip prices are then propagated through the network to the markets, using surcharges derived from the model by Guldmann [5]. Finally, the surcharges are adjusted by the ratio of average observed prices on a State/market sector to the average State/sector price calculated above.

Setting rates by pipelines requires an estimate of the expected sales volume and the number of customers, in order to convert fixed charges to per-unit tariffs. Estimates are substantially based on census projections.

4.4 Market Clearing

Using the Gas Reserves Supply Table (GRST), production capability is determined from the parameters of the production profiles; reserves are drawn down by pipelines using committed supplies followed by the cheapest available gas. The resulting average price enters the market clearance calculations; the available supply is then delivered to markets.

As noted previously, base-year (1980) demand is given in Form FERC-50. For each subsequent year and for each market, there is a demand curve which is based on current prices, previous year price and demand, plus other parameters.

Market clearance is, in principle, the solution of pairs of simultaneous equations. The simulated process is slightly more complicated in that each demand quantity at the wellhead results from accumulating demands from the markets backward through a pipeline system, accounting for distribution/transmission losses, transfers in and out of storage, and intersystem sales (those systems that are treated as take-or-pay) along the way. Prices start at the wellhead and are "marked up" as they move forward through the system to the burner-tip market.

In the event of a shortfall in supply, flows to all distributors in a pipeline system network are reduced by a common factor. Market curtailments are then represented by fulfilling market demands in priority order until supply is exhausted, by distributors with the end-use customers.

After summer and winter market clearing, the market quantities and prices are combined to yield annual values in each pipeline system. The annual prices are used to update committed quantities in the base network. Demand parameters are further updated, and the annual process is then iterated, starting with aggregation of the committed quantities for pipeline system nodes, rate setting, and determination of available reserve supply blocks.

Structural attributes of the pipeline systems are fixed after base-year initialization. Customer relationships, storage capacities, and transmission or distribution loss factors are not altered. Moveover, in the base network, the "market shares" of take-or-pay gas furnished by all suppliers to a distributor are constant over time. Import supplies are also fixed throughout a simulation.

Storage occurs in the summer, with a total drawdown in the winter; the fraction of storage capacity employed each year is determined by half of the difference between winter and summer consumption in the previous year. Storage costs are calculated as a constant fraction (currently 0.25 percent) of the commodity cost of the stored gas. Although the model structure allows storage at all nonmarket nodes, storage is currently used only at pipeline nodes. Each year, transmission and distribution tariffs are increased by a fixed inflation factor which is currently 2 percent.

A portion of natural gas consumption by utilities and industrial users is subject to alternate fuel capability. Switching is "automatically" triggered by prices equal to residual fuel oil prices multiplied by preset market-specific factors. For markets lacking alternate fuel capability, there are demand cutoffs determined by other (larger) market-specific multiples.

5. NATURAL GAS DEMAND MARKET

This section describes the determination of the demand for natural gas used in the Gas Analysis Modeling System (GAMS). In general, the set of demand models used to produce the 1982 Annual Energy Outlook (AEO) was used to produced the estimate of natural gas demand; however the additional regional detail required by the 10 Federal regions for the demand quantities and switching levels required additional adjustments. The 1982 AEO incorporated updates to the major assumptions concerning the world oil price, macroeconomic variables, and base period data in order to produce the natural gas demand forecast contained in this report. This section describes the updating procedure used, the changes in assumptions, and the methodology for reducing the complete set of energy demand functions into a simpler version of natural gas demands for use in GAMS.

Estimates of energy demand for all purchased fuels include estimates for distillate fuel oil, residual fuel oil, natural gas, other petroleum products, and coal. Because this report emphasizes the demand for natural gas, much of the detail provided by these models was not needed. Therefore, a much simpler, reduced form version of the models was developed to represent the natural gas portion of demand. This reduced form version involves calculating a set of parameters, which characterize the demand curve for natural gas. The form of this relationship is:

$$\ln(Q'_{t,i}/Q^{o}_{t,i}) = B_i(\ln(P'_{t,i}/P^{o}_{t,i}) + C_i \ln(Q'_{t-1,i}/Q^{o}_{t-1,i}) \quad (1)$$

where Q^o and P^o represent the base quantities and prices, respectively, and Q' and P' represent the simulation (or values to be solved for) quantities and prices, respectively, for year t and sector i per region. Since this model is log-linear, B_i represents the short-term price elasticity of demand, and C_i represents a lag term that determines the long-run (B/1-C) price elasticity of demand.

The adjusted base quantities and prices were taken from the 1982 AEO. They represent the outputs of the models described above, and are adjusted for the changed assumptions previously discussed.

To obtain B and C, a series of Demand Analysis System (DAS) simulations over the 1980 to 1995 period was completed. In each simulation, the price path is perturbed by a constant percent; own elasticities are then computed between the base quantity price pair and the "perturbed case" pair. B_i is the own price elasticity of demand with respect to fuel price i, calculated for each year. Because the elasticities grow over time at a decreasing rate, the 1995 elasticities are assumed to represent the long-term elasticity, and the expression $B_i/(1-C_i)$ is used to solve for C_i.

This methodology for determining the reduced form price and lag coefficients assumes that:

- the short-run elasticity is constant;
- the impact of a price increase in time period t is greatest in time period t and decreases thereafter; and
- all lagged effects of a price increase have occurred approximately after 15 years.

A system for automating these calculations has been implemented to allow recalibration and its reflection of different price or macro assumptions.

REFERENCES

[1] Energy Information Administration, U.S. Department of Energy. Production of Onshore Lower-48 Oil and Gas Model Methodology and Data Description, DOE/EIA-0345. Washington, D.C., June 1982.

[2] Energy Information Administration, U.S. Department of Energy. Outer-Continental Shelf (OCS) Oil and Gas Supply Model, Volume I - Model Summary and Methodology Description, DOE/EIA-Draft. Washington, D.C., April 1982.

[3] National Petroleum Council, Unconventional Gas Sources, Washington, D.C., December 1980.

[4] American Gas Association, Department of Statistics, Gas Facts: 1980 Data, Arlington, Virginia, 1981.

[5] Guldmann, J.M. "A Procedure for Calculating Rates of a Typical Fuel Gas Distribution Company." Model developed under contract with the National Bureau of Standard, Work Order #NB8INAAH5 127, October 1981.

Analytic Techniques for Energy Planning
B. Lev, F.H. Murphy, J.A. Bloom & A.S. Gleit (Editors)

A MODEL FOR PLANNING INVESTMENTS IN THE ENERGY SECTOR IN THE MEDIUM RANGE

Nissan Levin
Faculty of Management, Tel Aviv University
Tel-Aviv, Israel

Asher Tishler
Faculty of Management, Tel Aviv University
Tel-Aviv, Israel

Jacob Zahavi
Faculty of Management, Tel Aviv University, Tel Aviv, Israel

A time-step equilibrium model is described for planning investments in the energy sector in the medium range (10-15 years). The model can be applied to energy systems which are price takers in the world energy market, with no energy resources of their own, for which the variation in the refining cost as a function of the quantity produced can be ignored. The basic equilibrium model has been extended in several directions to respond to uncertainties in the fuel prices and the quantity demanded of electricity, considering the impact of the rising energy prices on the GNP and others, and some of these extensions are discussed. Finally, we describe an application of the equilibrium model for a realistic system.

1. INTRODUCTION

The 1973 energy crisis has brought about the development of large scale national energy models as a means to set up energy priorities and evaluate alternative energy options. Of these models, equilibrium models have gained increased popularity since they provide a comprehensive framework to combine the behavioral description of the demand side and the engineering representation of the supply activities. Typically, the demand side of an equilibrium model is represented by a set of econometrically-estimated demand functions, whereas the supply side is represented by activities, with the objective function being, usually, but not necessarily, the minimization of the total cost involved. To name some of these models--the PIES model [9], the Brookhaven Illinois model [3], the SRI Gulf model [5], the Hudson-Jorgenson energy model ([12, 13]), and others. In addition, other energy models have also been developed, but they are not equilibrium models, such as the Brookhaven BESOM and TESOM models ([6, 11, 16]), the PILOT model [7], the OMER model [15] and others.

By and large, most of the energy equilibrium models mentioned above are rather complicated, requiring large amount of input data and long processing times. In this paper we describe an alternative equilibrium model, developed initially to model the energy sector in the state of Israel, which is much easier to manipulate than any of the other energy models, yet it describes the energy sector in enough detail to allow its use for evaluating alternative policy options and supporting a whole range of decision making issues. In building the model we took cognizance of the particular conditions of the Israeli energy sector:

a. It is an economy which is a price taker in the world energy market. Hence the prices of primary energy resources facing the economy are constant, regardless of the quantity consumed, and depend only on the international primary energy prices and the transportation and refining costs.

b. The country has no fuel resources of its own, thus confining the supply side of the equilibrium model to modelling only the conversion process of the primary energy resources into secondary energy resources (electricity, liquid fuels, etc.).

c. Moreover, the total cost incurred in developing and generating electrical power is significantly higher than the total cost incurred in the refining sector. Thus, the variation of the refining cost as a function of the quantity demanded for liquid fuels can actually be ignored. This assumption confines the supply side even further to modelling the conversion process of the primary energy resources (oil, coal, nuclear energy, etc.) to electricity.

As a result of these conditions, only the end-use prices and the quantity determined of electricity are determined by the equilibrium mechanism. Given the electricity prices, the quantity demanded of the other types of energy (e.g., liquid fuels) are determined based on their demand functions. While these assumptions simplify the equilibrium model, they hold true for many of the smaller countries and most of the developing countries, thus, rendering this model a most useful tool for supporting energy-related decisions.

The equilibrium model itself consists of three components - the demand model, the supply model and the price model, integrated together by an equilibrium mechanism to yield the end-use prices and quantity demanded of electricity by the various sectors of the economy. We now proceed to describe these components in more detail. In the second section we formulated the dynamic equilibrium model in the electricity sector and its time-step equivalent; in the third section we extend the electricity model to encompass the entire energy sector; in the fourth section we describe some important extensions of the basic equilibrium model; in the fifth section we describe an implementation of the equilibrium model to the Israeli energy sector; and in the sixth section we conclude our discussion with a short summary.

2. THE EQUILIBRIUM MODEL COMPONENTS

We initiate our discussion by describing the basic components of the electricity equilibrium model.

2.1 The Demand Model

The role of the demand model in an electricity equilibrium model is to estimate the demand function for electricity by the various sectors of the economy. One of the most common demand functions, also used in our study, is the log-linear, or the Cobb-Douglas function, defined by:

$$q_D(t) = Ay_t^{\alpha}\, p_D^{\beta}(t) \tag{1}$$

where

$q_D(t)$: the quantity demanded of electricity by all sectors at year t

$p_D(t)$: the demand price of electricity at year t

y_t : the GNP at year t

α : income elasticity of demand

β : the price elasticity of demand

A : a given constant

α and β are estimated by the demand model; $p_D(t)$ is determined endogenously by the equilibrium model as described below; A is determined by the initial conditions; and finally y_t is calculated using the formula:

$$y_t = y_o \prod_{k=t_o+1}^{t} (1+\delta_k) \tag{2}$$

where

y_o : the GNP at the base year t_o

δ_k : the rate of increase in the GNP in the year k

It should be noted that in order to express the variability in the electricity consumption of various segments of the economy, one has to first estimate a separate electricity demand function for each sector of the economy and then combine the results to yield the aggregate demand function for the whole economy. Methods to estimate demand functions have been discussed widely in the literature (see for example the survey by Taylor [29]) and will not be discussed here.

2.2 The Supply Model

The role of the supply model in the electricity equilibrium is to find the optimal expansion program of the power system over time to meet the predicted demand for load (MW) and energy (MWH) as defined by the system's load duration curve (LDC). Assuming no economies of scale in the variable and capital costs, and ignoring the set up cost to bring the generating units on line, the dynamic capacity expansion problem can be formulated as follows:

$$\underset{x,z}{\text{Min}}\ TC = \sum_{t=1}^{T} \left[\sum_{i=1}^{n} a_t c_{it} x_{it} + \eta^{t-1} \sum_{i=1}^{n} \sum_{j=o}^{t} b_{ijt}\, Q_{ijt} \right] \tag{3}$$

subject to

$$x_{it} \geq 0 \qquad i=1,\ldots,n \qquad t=1,\ldots,T \tag{4}$$

$$0 \leq z_{ijt} \leq x_{ij} \quad i=1,\dots,n \quad j=0,\dots,T \quad t=j+1,\dots,T \tag{5}$$

$$\sum_{i=1}^{n} \sum_{j=0}^{t} z_{ijt} \cdot \theta_{ijt} \geq L_t^m \quad t=1,\dots,T \tag{6}$$

$$Q_{ijt} = \int_{D_{ijt}}^{D_{ijt}+z_{ijt} \cdot \theta_{ijt}} g_t(x)dx \quad i=1,\dots,n \; j=0,\dots,t, \; t=1,\dots,T \tag{7}$$

$$D_{ijt} = \sum_{e=1}^{n} \sum_{k=o}^{t} z_{ekt} \cdot \theta_{ekt} \quad i=1,\dots,n \quad j=0,\dots,t \quad t=1,\dots,T \tag{8}$$

where only units for which $m_{ekt} < m_{ijt}$ are taking part in the double summation

$$Q_{ijt} \leq \overline{Q}_{ij} \quad \text{for all limited energy plants} \tag{9}$$

where

- T : number of years in the planning horizon
- t : index for years within the planning horizon, $t=0,\dots,T$ with $t=0$ being the base year
- n : number of unit types (existing and new) in the planning horizon
- x_{it} : installed capacity of unit type i introduced into the system at year t (MW)
- c_{it} : fixed cost for unit type i vintage t ($/MW)
- b_{ijt} : variable cost of unit type i vintage j at year t (MWH)
- Q_{ijt} : energy output of unit type i, vintage j at year t (MWH)
- $\overline{Q}_{ij}$: the energy production capability for LEP (limited-energy plant) type i vintage j (MWH)
- z_{ijt} : the utilization (or operable capacity) of unit type i vintage j at year t (MW)
- θ_{ijt} : availability factor of unit type i vintage j at year t
- η : the discount rate
- $a_t \stackrel{\Delta}{=} \sum_{k=t}^{T} \eta^{k-1}$: the discount coefficient

$L_t(\tau)$: the LDC at year t (MW)

L_t^m : the peak demand for power at year t (MW)

$g_t(x)$: the inverse LDC (hours)

m_{ijt} : the merit order position of unit type i, vintage j at year t

D_{ijt} : the loading point of unit type i, vintage j at period t (MW)

$\overline{TC}$: the total discounted costs ($)

In the optimization model (3)-(9):

(4) is the non-negativity constraint;

(5) implies that the operable capacity of unit type i vintage j at year t cannot exceed its installed capacity;

(6) is the peak demand constraint;

(7) defines the energy output of unit type i vintage j at year t (i.e., this is the area under the LDC for year t over the loading interval of the unit);

(8) defines the loading point of unit type i vintage j at year t, under the merit order procedure;

(9) is the energy production capability constraint for the LEPs.

We note that if we define x_{it} and z_{ijt} as available capacities, and c_{it} as the fixed cost for an available MW, then it is possible to omit the factor θ_{ijt} (or equivalently, assume it is equal to 1).

Clearly, because of (7), the objective function (3) includes nonlinear elements, rendering the optimization model (3)-(9) a nonlinear programming model. The decision variables are the installed capacities x_{it} and the operable capacities z_{ijt}. Or, equivalently, we can regard Q_{ijt}'s as the decision variables, in which case x_{it} and z_{ijt} are determined by (7) and (9).

2.3 The Price Model

The electricity price is the driving force leading to the equilibrium solution. The role of the price model in the electricity equilibrium model is to determine the end-use price of electricity to the various sectors, for the expansion program given by the supply model. A variety of methods have been devised to determine the end-use electricity prices in energy models, including marginal cost pricing [9] and the fair-rate-of-return criterion [14]. In this study, the electricity supply prices are based on the average production cost of electricity, a method which has been generally accepted by public service commissions as a basis for setting up electricity prices [1]. Within this framework, commissions have allowed the utilities wide latitude to determine the structure of their rates to particular group of customers. This option is provided in our model by allowing the power utility to use a different mark-up factor for each sector. Denoting the total cost of providing electricity at a given year by TC (for simplicity we omit the time index t) and the corresponding electricity output by Q (both are determined by the supply model), the average production cost is given by TC/Q and the price of electricity for sector k, p_k, is defined by:

$$p_k = U_k(\frac{TC}{Q}) \tag{10}$$

where $U_k(\cdot)$ is a scalar-valued, positive and monotonically increasing function. Using the mark-up approach, p_k is given by:

$$p_k = \mu_k \cdot (\frac{TC}{Q}) \tag{11}$$

where μ_k is the mark-up factor for sector k.

Clearly, $\mu_k < 1$ implies that sector k enjoys a subsidy for each KWH it consumes; $\mu_k > 1$ implies that a tax is levied on each KWH consumed by sector k. The total revenue for the utility with this price scheme is given by

$$R = \sum_k p_k \cdot Q_k \tag{12}$$

where Q_k is the consumption of electricity by sector k and the profit margin for the utility, μ, is given by:

$$\mu = \frac{R}{TC} \tag{13}$$

$\mu=1$ implies zero profits for the utility; $\mu>1$ implies positive profits; $\mu<1$ implies negative profits to be covered, perhaps, by subsidies from the government.

2.4 The Dynamic Equilibrium Model

Denoting by $p_S(Q_S)$ the supply price of electricity for the quantity produced Q_S and by $Q_D = f(p_D)$ the quantity demanded of electricity at price p_D, then at equilibrium there exists:

$$Q_D = Q_S \text{ and } p_D = p_S$$

for each year in the planning horizon or alternatively

$$f(U(\frac{TC}{Q_s})) = Q_s \tag{14}$$

Thus, the dynamic equilibrium model for the electricity sector is defined by (3) - (9) with the following additional conditions:

(a) The maximum load L_t^m depends on the quantity of electrical energy produced and the LDC.

(b) The inverse LDC, $g_t(x)$ depends on the quantity of electrical energy produced and the manner in which the LDC is updated to respond to changes in prices.

(c) Condition (14) must hold for each year in the planning horizon, where the total electricity output at each year t is given by $\sum_{i=1}^{n} \sum_{j=0}^{t} Q_{ijt}$.

Three procedures have been used in our study to update the LDC as a result of a change in the relative prices of electricity: scaling, shifting, and combined scaling and shifting.

In scaling, the LDC is scaled upwards or downwards by a constant amount S, yielding:

$$L^P(\tau) = S\, L^O(\tau) \qquad S \in [\tilde{S}, \infty] \tag{15}$$

where:

$L^P(\tau)$: the LDC after the price change,

$L^O(\tau)$: the LDC prior to the price change

$\tilde{S}$: the minimal possible value of S (see [20] for precise definition).

An upward scaling (S > 1) is exhibited in Figure 1.

In shifting, the LDC shifts upwards or downwards by an amount K, yielding:

$$L^P(\tau) = L^O(\tau) + K \qquad K \in [\tilde{K}, \infty] \tag{16}$$

where $\tilde{K}$ is the minimal possible value of K (see [20] for precise definition). An upwards shifting (K > 0) is also exhibited in Figure 1. Finally, these two procedures can be applied together to yield a combined scaling and shifting of the LDC, i.e.;

$$L^P(\tau) = S\, L^O(\tau) + K\ .$$

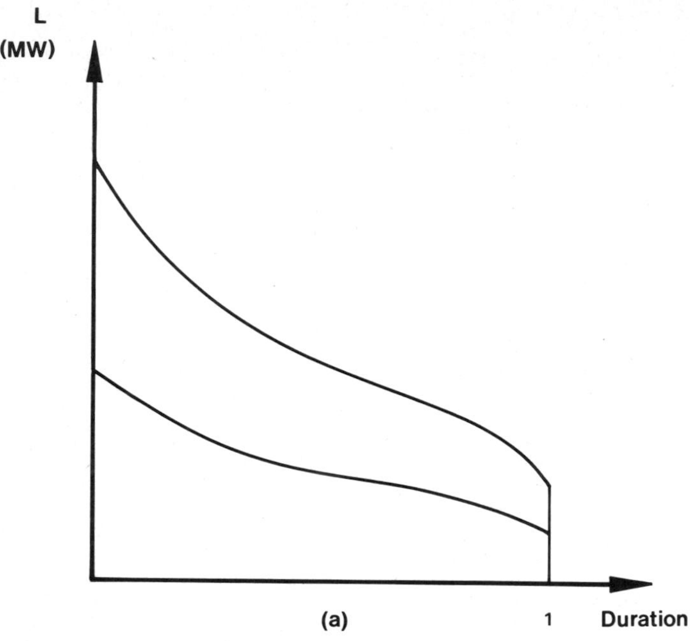

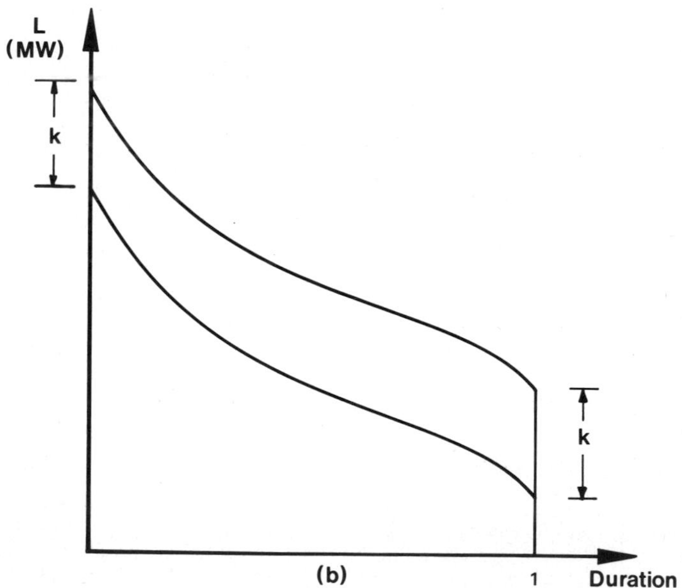

Figure 1.

2.5 The Time-Step Approach

It is not difficult to see that the dynamic equilibrium model formulated above is a very complicated problem to solve, if at all possible. Consequently, we have used a time-step approach to find the equilibrium solution, by solving the problem as a series of related one-year problems, with the equilibrium solution for a given year constituting the input for the equilibrium problem of the following year until the planning horizon is covered. With this approach, the one-year equilibrium problem becomes the core of the equilibrium solution [20]. For any target year t, we initiate the calculation by solving the supply model (3)-(9) for T=1 to find the optimal mix of units to meet the demand for load and energy during that year as given by the LDC. (The one-year capacity expansion problems are formulated and solved in [17], [18]). Given the mark-up factors, the total cost of power generation is then translated into end-use prices of electricity to the various sectors. The prices are then substituted in the electricity demand functions to calculate the aggregate quantity demanded of electricity. If the quantity of electricity demanded is equal to the quantity supplied, an equilibrium solution is achieved, and the calculation procedure proceeds to the following year. Otherwise, the LDC is updated using scaling, shifting or combined scaling and shifting, in order to equate the electrical energy supplied to the electrical energy demanded and the procedure is repeated again until convergence occurs ([21],[22]).

3. THE TIME-STEP EQUILIBRIUM MODEL FOR THE ENERGY SECTOR

Using the basic assumptions of section 1, the extension of the time-step electricity equilibrium model to cover the entire energy sector is done rather easily [23]. The demand model in the enlarged model consists of a set of demand functions, one for each energy type and each sector of the economy. Generalizing the Cobb-Douglas demand function of section 2.1 for several energy services and several sectors, we obtain:

$$q_{ij}(t) = A_{ij}\, y_i^{a_{ij}^{o}}(t) \prod_k p_{ik}^{a_{ij}^{k}}(t) \tag{17}$$

where

i	:	index for consuming sector
j	:	index for energy type
t	:	index for time period
$q_{ij}(t)$	:	the demand for energy type j by sector i at period t
$y_i(t)$	:	the output of sector i at period t
$p_{ik}(t)$	:	the price of energy type k facing sector i at period t

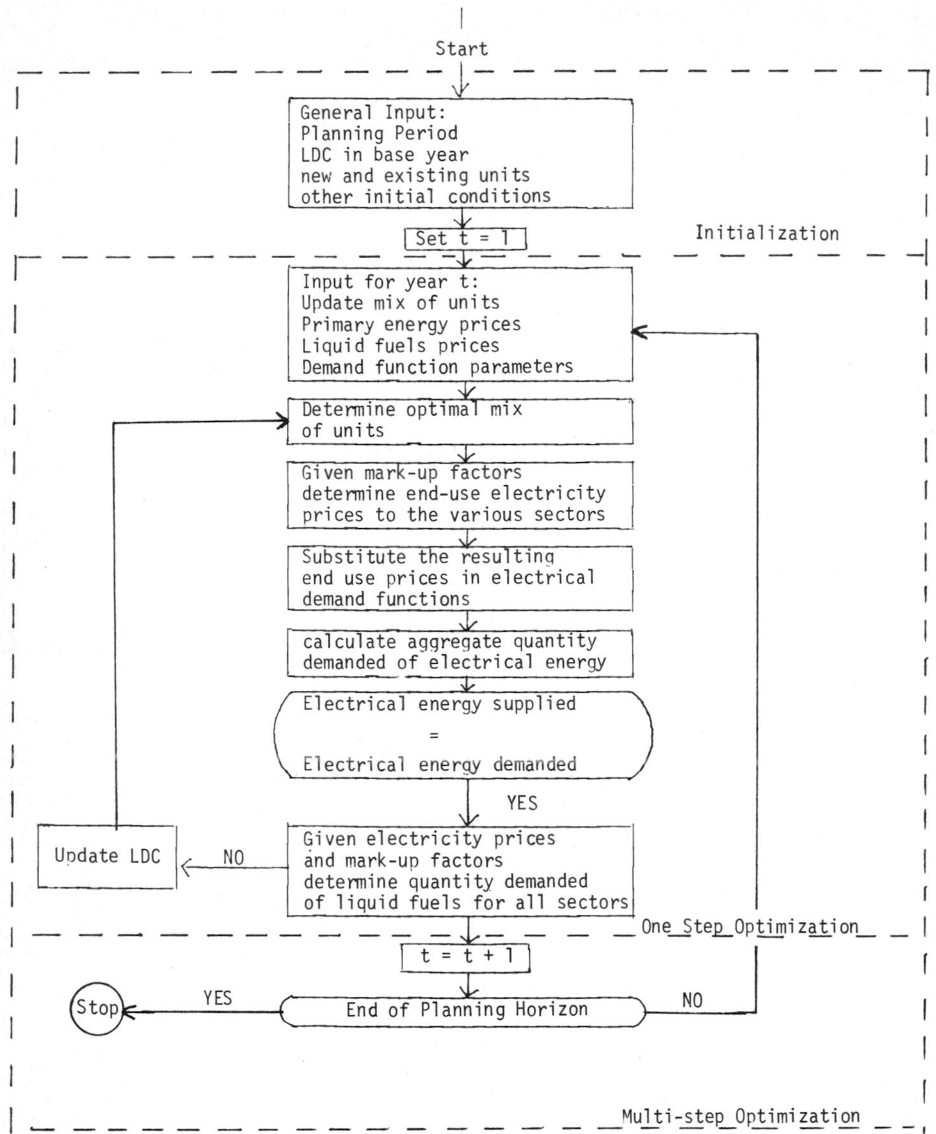

Figure 2. Flow Chart of General Energy Model

a_{ij}^{o} : the income elasticity of demand for energy type j by sector i

a_{ij}^{k} : the price elasticity of demand for energy types j and k by sector i

A_{ij} : a given constant

The supply function of electricity is determined in exactly the same way as in the electricity equilibrium model. However, the supply functions of the other types of energy are assumed to be infinitely elastic implying an infinite supply of energy for the given energy price.

Finally, the end-use price for each energy type and each sector is also determined by using the mark-up approach, i.e.,

$$p_{ij}(t) = \mu_{ij}(t)\ p_j(t) \tag{18}$$

where

$p_{ij}(t)$: the end-use price of energy type j for sector i at year t

$\mu_{ij}(t)$: the mark-up factor for energy type j sector i at year t

$p_j(t)$: the price of energy type j at year t, determined endogenously by the equilibrium model (using (11)) for electricity, and exogenously, based on the international energy price, transportation cost and refining costs, for the other types of energy.

As in the electricity model, the equilibrium solution is obtained in an iterative manner, as described graphically in Figure 2.

4. EXTENSIONS OF THE EQUILIBRIUM MODEL

The basic equilibrium model described above has been extended in several directions. It is beyond the scope of this paper to describe these extensions in detail. Instead, we summarize here only the important features of these extensions, referring the interested reader to our other publications on these topics.

4.1 Equilibrium Solution for Given Utility Profit Margin

In the basic model described above, it was assumed that the mark-up factors for all sectors and all types of energy are known. Alternatively, we extended the model to the case where the profit margin of the utility (determined by (13)) is given, as are the mark-up factors for all the other sectors, except the residential sector. The problem then is to find the mark-up factor for the residential sector that yields the required profit margin for the utility [23]. Typically, the mark-up factor for the industrial sector is less than 1, implying that the other sectors, primarily the residential sector, have to pay more for each KWH they consume to attain the required profit margin for the electrical utility. Among the rest, this provision in the equilibrium model allows one to examine how various taxation policies and pricing schemes affect energy consumption and investment programs.

4.2 Uniqueness and Existence Conditions

Because of the relative simplicity of the equilibrium model, we were able to find conditions under which the equilibrium solution exists and is unique for a variety of constraints regarding the mix of units in the target year and updating procedures of the LDC ([20], [22]). These conditions have important practical implications because they determine the range of values for the input parameters and/or the properties of the input data (e.g., the demand function) for which the equilibrium solution exists and is unique, and thus provide more confidence in using the model for supporting decision making problems.

4.3 Deriving Conditions Under Which the Time Step Solution and the Dynamic Model Solution Coincide

As discussed above, the time step approach offers computational benefits over the dynamic approach, since each period is dealt with separately. The main obstacle with this approach is that it cannot account for future developments in determining present investment decisions, thus yielding solutions that might not be optimal in the dynamic case. Consequently, we have derived conditions under which the time-step model yields solutions which are effectively the same as those obtained by the dynamic model [24]. These conditions pertain to two basic cases. In the first case, it is assumed that all present generation technologies are available for erection in the first year of the planning horizon, allowing only for new technologies to become available in the middle of the planning horizon [e.g., nuclear units). In the second case, it is assumed that some of the more advanced technologies occupying low merit order locations, will not be available for erection at the beginning of the planning horizon because of lead time constraints. In addition, we also derived bounds on the rate of increase of the power demand that yields a time-step solution that is equal to the dynamic model solution. Basically, these conditions imply that in case the demand for power exhibits sufficient increase over the years, requiring additional new capacity at each year, the time-step model solution and the dynamic-model solution coincide. Clearly, these conditions, usually met in countries with large electrification rates, such as the developing countries, enhance the usefulness of the equilibrium mode for evaluating energy options.

4.4 The Effect of Energy Prices on the GNP

So far we have assumed that the outputs of the various sectors are not affected by the energy prices, which in effect means that the equilibrium model provides only partial equilibrium solutions. To relax this assumption, without having to solve the energy model together with a macro-economic model as done, for example, in [3], we offer an approximate approach, similar in spirit to the one described in [10], to account for the impact of energy prices on the GNP.
Let $U^o = F(\underline{E}^o, \underline{p}^o)$ denote the production function corresponding to international primary energy prices $\underline{p}^o$ and primary energy consumption $\underline{E}^o$ ($\underline{p}^o$ and $\underline{E}^o$ are vectors). Since the primary energy resources are imported, we have:

$$GNP^o = U^o - (\underline{p}^o)' \cdot \underline{E}^o$$

where the prime denotes a transposed vector (i.e., a row vector).

Now, assuming the primary energy prices have changed from $\underline{p}^o$ to $\underline{p}^1$ (say at the next period), then it can be shown (see [23]) that the GNP corresponding to $\underline{p}^1$ can be approximated by [23]:

$$GNP^1 = GNP^o - (\underline{E}^1)' \cdot (\underline{p}^1 - \underline{p}^o) \tag{19}$$

implying that the change in the GNP is equal to $(\underline{E}^1)' \cdot (\underline{p}^1 - \underline{p}^o)$. Clearly, if $\underline{p}^1 > \underline{p}^o$, there is a net loss in the GNP. Since the demand for primary energy resources by the electric utilities is not known in advance but is given by the equilibrium model, we obtain the equilibrium solution for any given target year using a three-stage approach:

Stage 1. For the current energy price $\underline{p}^o$ and the corresponding GNP^o, solve the equilibrium model to find the end-use electricity price and the total quantity demanded of the primary energy resources $(\underline{E}^o)$.

Stage 2. For the predicted energy price $\underline{p}^1$, in the next period, solve the equilibrium model for the end-use electricity prices and the primary energy consumption $\underline{E}^1$, using GNP^o and $\underline{p}^1$.

Stage 3. Compute $GNP^1 = GNP^o - (\underline{E}^1)' \cdot (\underline{p}^1 - \underline{p}^o)$. Solve the equilibrium model using GNP^1 and $\underline{p}^1$. This solution gives the desired results.

While this approach requires solving the equilibrium model three times for each year, it results in better estimation of the end-use prices and quantity demanded of electricity.

4.5 Incorporating the Uncertainty in the Prices of Primary Energy Resources

The increasing variability in the prices of the primary energy prices, especially of crude oil, that we have recently witnessed has increased the role of the fuel prices in shaping up energy policy. For this end, we extended the electricity equilibrium model to explicitly account for the uncertainty in the primary energy prices, using two approaches [25]:

(a) seeking the primary energy prices that minimize the loss incurred by the deviation of the fuel prices that actually materialized in the target year from the energy prices used in the planning process;

(b) devising several mechanisms that can also be implemented in the short run to equilibriate the supply and the demand in the target year.

To formulate the problem, we let the price vector of the primary energy resources be a random variable $\underline{B} = (B_1, B_2, \ldots, B_n)$, with joint probability density function (PDF) $f_B(\cdot)$. We also let $\underline{b}^o$ be the one realization of $\underline{B}$ used by the power utility to find the equilibrium solution at the target year, $\underline{b}$ the realization of the primary energy prices that actually materialized in the target year, and p^o and $\bar{p}$ the end-use electricity price for the price realization $\underline{b}^o$ and $\underline{b}$, respectively. Typically, $\underline{b}^o \neq \underline{b}$, implying $p^o \neq \bar{p}$, and thus a loss or a penalty is incurred, the magnitude of which depends on the deviation of the actually-materialized price b from the planned-for price b^o. Let $\psi(b^o, b)$ denote the loss incurred, and $\psi(b^o)$ the expected value of $\psi(b^o, B)$, i.e.,

$$\psi(b^o) = E_B(\psi(b^o, B)) \tag{20}$$

In the first approach mentioned above we seek the input price vector b* that minimizes the expected cost incurred, i.e.,

$$\psi(b^*) = \underset{b^o}{\text{Min}}\ (\psi(b^o) \tag{21}$$

To find the minimizing energy input prices, one has to define the loss function explicitly. One possibility is to define the loss incurred in terms of the loss in consumer surplus plus the loss in producer's output. Assuming the demand for electricity in the target year is to be met by new units only, we obtain the interesting result that the input price b^o that minimizes the expected loss in the social welfare is given by:

$$b_i^* = E(B_i) \qquad i = 1, 2, \ldots, n$$

i.e., minimum loss results when we use the expected values of the primary energy prices, predicted for the target year, as input to the equilibrium model regardless of the PDF involved. Clearly, it is easier to predict the expected fuel prices than it is to find their joint probability distribution.

In the second method, we attain the equilibrium in the target year by letting both the end-use price of electricity and the quantity supplied of electricity to vary in response to the actually-materialized energy prices, until a new equilibrium is reached. The basic idea behind this approach is that the primary energy prices are more or less known a year or two prior to the target year, so that the utility can still take some measures to equilibriate the demand and the supply. Obviously, these measures should be of short term nature such as adding gas turbines (in the case of excess demand) for which the installation period is relatively short, or utilizing the generating units at partial capacity (in the case of excess supply). Using these mechanisms to bridge the gap between the supply and the demand, we investigate the condition under which the system will converge to a new equilibrium. In particular, it is shown that if the aggregate demand function for electricity is of the form $f(p) = ap^{\beta}$ (e.g., equation (1)), where $-1 < \beta < 0$, the system will indeed converge to a new equilibrium solution which does not only exist, but is also unique, with an end-use price $\tilde{p}$ which is different than the end-use prices p^o and $\bar{p}$ discussed above. Clearly, given the new end-use price $\tilde{p}$ we can plug it in the loss functions discussed above to assess the magnitude of the damage incurred.

4.6 Incorporating the Uncertainty in the Quantity Demanded of Electricity

As another development, we extended the electricity equilibrium model to also account for the uncertainty in the quantity demanded of electricity for both an additive and multiplicative disturbance [19]. Assuming the demand function f(p) is subject to a random disturbance V, then under additive disturbance, the demand function f(p,V) is of the form:

$$f(p,V) = f(p) + V, \ E(V) = 0 \tag{22}$$

and under multiplicative disturbance

$$f(p,V) = V \cdot f(p), \ E(V) = 1 \tag{23}$$

For both types of disturbances, we use the scaling procedure discussed above (see Figure 1) to equate the area under the LDC to the quantity demanded of electricity.

Clearly, in the stochastic case, the quantity demanded of electricity experienced in reality is in general different than the planned-for energy output, resulting again in an imbalance between the supply and the demand for electricity. Consequently, the consumers will experience a loss in consumers surplus and the producers a loss in revenues, the magnitude of which depends on the demand function f(p,V), the LDC, the supply structure and the equilibrium mechanism. We thus seek the end-use electricity price p^0, the generating unit capacities x_i^0, i=1,..., n, and the electricity output Q^0 that minimize the expected loss incurred, or alternatively, that maximize the social benefits. Two approaches are discussed to address the uncertainty issue. In the first, we seek the electricity output and prices prior to the resolution of demand uncertainty; in the second, we seek the output and prices after the demand uncertainty is resolved. The results, reported in [19], constitute a generalization of the results obtained previously by several authors ([2], [4], [8], [26], [30]) to the case of multiple technologies and temporal distribution of demand.

4.7 Validating the Model

Finally, following the approach taken by the Energy Modeling Form (EMF), we validated our model by comparing its results to the results of two other energy models, run on the same data base: the OMER model [15], which is basically a modification of the PILOT model [7] to allow for modelling the supply side in more detail, and the ETA-Macro model of Alan Manne [27]. Clearly, such a validation is a pre-condition to using the model to support the decision making process. Indeed, this comparison has led to a few modifications of the equilibrium model, including the development of the procedure to account for the impact of the energy prices on the GNP, as discussed above (see section 4.4).

5. IMPLEMENTATION

To conclude our discussion, we now describe an application of the time-step equilibrium model to the Israeli energy system. To implement the model, we have divided the economy into four major sectors - the electric utilities (i=1), the residential sectors (i=2), the industrial, commercial and agricultural sector (i=3), and the public sector (i=4); and have divided the energy sector into six

TABLE 1

Cross and Own Price Elasticities

Sector	Demand for	Electricity	Coal	Fuel Oil	Diesel Oil	Gasoline
	Electricity	-.5	0	0	.1	0
	Coal	0	0	0	0	0
Residential	Fuel Oil	0	0	0	0	0
	Diesel Oil	.2	0	0	-0.3	.05
	Gasoline	0	0	0	.1	-0.6
	Electricity	-.75	.05	.15	.15	0
	Coal	.2	-1.0	.4	.3	0
Industrial	Fuel Oil	.2	.1	-1.0	.4	0
	Diesel Oil	.3	.05	.3	-1.0	.2
	Gasoline	0	0	0	.5	-1.0

TABLE 2

Equilibrium Solution in the Electricity Sector

	Energy Produced (10^9KWH)	Total* Cost (10^9 $)	Equil.* Price ($/MWH)	Max Load (MW)	Additional Installed Capacity (MW)				
					Nuclear	Coal	Fuel Oil	Diesel Oil	Total
1983	18.1	1.179	65.08	3112.	0	0	0	0	0
1984	17.9	1.192	66.63	3073.	0	0	0	0	0
1985	17.7	1.205	68.22	3034.	0	0	0	0	0
1986	17.4	1.213	69.87	2984.	0	0	0	0	0
1987	17.4	1.223	70.14	2995.	0	161.	0	0	161.
1988	18.6	1.285	69.07	3196.	0	400.	0	0	400.
1989	19.7	1.359	68.97	3385.	0	311.	0	0	311.
1990	20.8	1.439	69.08	3578.	0	305.	0	15.	320.
1991	22.1	1.521	68.96	3790.	0	368.	0	46.	415.
1992	23.3	1.610	68.98	4010.	0	373.	0	47.	420.
1993	24.7	1.704	69.07	4240.	0	390.	0	49.	439.
1994	26.1	1.805	69.24	4480.	0	408	0	50.	458.
1995	28.5	1.864	65.35	4902.	897.	0	0	75.	972.
1996	30.5	1.956	64.05	5248.	566.	0	0	65.	630.
1997	33.3	2.026	60.77	5728.	1023.	0	0	99.	1122.
1998	36.2	2.105	58.07	6229.	1041.	0	0	84.	1125.
1999	38.7	2.216	57.29	6648.	609.	0	0	73.	682.
2000	41.9	2.310	55.11	7203.	1088.	0	0	251.	1339.
2001	44.2	2.415	54.70	7588.	654.	0	0	58.	622.
2002	46.5	2.526	54.34	7988.	585.	0	0	60.	645.
2003	48.9	2.643	54.03	8406.	612.	0	0	62.	675.
2004	51.5	2.766	53.75	8841.	648.	0	0	65.	712.
2005	54.1	2.895	53.51	9297.	682.	0	0	68.	749.
2006	56.9	3.030	53.27	9773	734.	0	0	71.	805.
2007	59.8	3.172	53.06	10271.	772.	0	0	76.	849.
2008	62.8	3.320	52.87	10792.	815.	0	0	82.	896.
2009	66.0	3.476	52.69	11337.	862.	0	0	87.	949.
2010	69.3	3.639	52.52	11907.	911.	0	0	153.	1064.

*1980 prices

types of energy services: electricity (j=1), coal (j=2), nuclear energy (j=3), fuel oil (j=4), diesel oil (j=5), and gasoline (j=6). Further disaggregation to sectors and additional types of energy are possible, but do not seem to be necessary.

The detailed description of all inputs to the model and the output results are found in Levin et al ([20], [21]). Here, we present only a brief summary of these details.

5.1 Demand Input

The demand functions of the four sectors for the six types of energy at year t are given by equations (17). The end-use prices of energy type j for sector i are determined by (18) where $p_j(t)$ is the price of energy type j at year t relative to the base year; i.e., $P_j(t_0) = 1$ for all j at the base year (1980). All μ_{ij}, the mark-up factors for sector i and energy type j, are known. The output of sector i at year t, $y_i(t)$, is calculated by assuming the same rate of increase (δ) in the output of all sectors (δ is 5% per year for 1983-2000 and 4% per year for 2001-2010). The income elasticity of the demand for energy is assumed to be unitary for i = 2, 3, 4 and j = 1, ..., 6. The own and cross price elasticities, a^k_{ij}, in the demand equations are described in Table 1. These values are based on econometric estimations of the energy demand functions in Israel, as well as elasticities reported in the literature (see [28], [29]). Price elasticities for the public sector (i = 4) are assumed to be zero. Nuclear energy is consumed only by the electricity sector and is determined solely from the optimal mix algorithm. The LDC is updated by scaling, starting with the actual LDC of 1977.

5.2 Supply Input

The planning horizon extends from 1983 through 2010. The existing system in 1983 contains 30 existing units, all are required to operate at future years, at their rated capacities. New units to satisfy increasing demand in the planning horizon consist of four types - nuclear, coal-fired, oil-fired and gas turbine units.

In the results reported in Tables 2-4, we assumed a moderate change in the real prices of primary energy resources, i.e., an escalation rate of 2.5% per year for coal and 5% per year for liquid fuels. The real price of nuclear fuel is unchanged over the planning horizon. The computations were made for time-step of one year.

Finally, we require that at any point in time, gas turbine capacity will constitute at least 10% of the total installed capacity. This operational constraint is required since gas turbines, due to their short start-up and shut-down time, are essential to satisfy peak demand for power.

5.3 Results

Tables 2-4 summarize the results for the case where all mark-up factors are known and equal to 1.0. Table 2 describes the supply side of the equilibrium solution over time. Because of the lead time constraints (1988 for coal-fired units and 1995 for nuclear units) only coal-fired units (and some gas turbines) are added to the system during the period 1988-1994, whereas from 1995 on, as nuclear technology becomes available, only nuclear units are added to the system. Note that by and large, the average production cost of electricity, and thus the equilibrium end-use prices, declines over the years, due to the increased share

Table 3

1994 Energy Balance Table

Sector	Electricity (GWH)	Coal (10^3 ton)	Fuel Oil (10^3 ton)	Diesel Oil (10^3 ton)	Gasoline (10^3 ton)
Electricity	0	5445	400	9	0
Residential	6790	0	0	114	641
Industrial	15426	733	852	1469	415
Public	3858	0	0	219	183
Total	26074	6178	1251	1810	1238

Table 4

The Use of Primary Energy in Electricity Production

Year	Nuclear Energy	Coal (GWH)	Fuel Oil (GWH)	Diesel Oil (GWH)
1983	0	8769	9308	34
1984	0	8769	9081	35
1985	0	8769	8850	37
1986	0	8769	8558	38
1987	0	9851	7543	34
1988	0	12510	6064	28
1989	0	14486	5190	23
1990	0	16303	4499	22
1991	0	18345	3690	23
1992	0	20303	3010	24
1993	0	22262	2388	26
1994	0	24227	1820	27
1995	5108	22413	974	30
1996	8329	21414	769	32
1997	14152	18839	312	35
1998	20080	16037	94	38
1999	23541	15025	81	40
2000	29583	12291	0	44
2001	32599	11513	0	46
2002	35639	10801	0	48
2003	38738	10128	0	51
2004	41934	9466	0	54
2005	45225	8822	0	56
2006	48682	8136	0	59
2007	52249	7465	0	62
2008	55948	6793	0	65
2009	59794	6114	0	69
2010	63788	5437	0	72

TABLE 5

The Effect of Energy Prices on GNP

	Energy Prices Do Not Affect GNP						Energy Prices Affect GNP					
	1985	1990	1995	2000	2005	2010	1985	1990	1995	2000	2005	1010
GNP (index, 1980 is 100)	128	163	208	265	323	393	126	158	198	248	297	353
Total energy consumption (MTOE*)	10.2	12.6	16.0	20.8	25.4	31.1	10.0	12.2	15.2	29.5	23.4	28.
Electricity consumption (10^9 KWH)	16.0	21.6	30.0	44.8	59.0	77.2	15.8	20.8	28.5	41.9	54.1	69.
Crude oil consumption (MTOE)	7.7	7.7	7.9	8.7	9.5	10.5	7.6	7.5	7.6	8.1	8.8	9.
C oal consumption (MTOE)	2.3	4.5	6.1	4.0	3.4	2.9	2.2	4.3	5.8	3.7	3.2	2.
Nuclear energy consumption (MTOE)	0.0	0.0	1.2	7.1	11.2	16.1	0.0	0.0	1.1	6.7	10.2	14.

*MTOE - million ton oil equivalent.

of coal, and later on of nuclear units, in satisfying customer demand.

Table 3 describes the demand side of the equilibrium solution for one year in the planning horizon (1994). Since no nuclear technology is available at that year, no entry is provided in Table 3 for nuclear fuel. Clearly, under equilibrium, the total requirements for electrical energy by all sectors is equal, except for some minor rounding errors, to the total electrical energy supplied, as given in Table 2.

The production of electricity (1 GWH = 1000 MWH) using nuclear energy, coal, fuel oil and diesel oil is given in Table 4. We note in Table 4 the diminishing role of oil-fired units in satisfying future electricity demand as compared to the increasing role of coal-fired units, at least until the year 1995. From that year on, nuclear technology becomes available and coal requirements start to decline. Fuel oil consumption reduces to zero from 1999 on, as all oil-fired units are retired by that year, and no more new units are erected. Diesel oil consumption, on the other hand, fluctuates only slightly throughout the period because of the 10% minimum level constraint on the gas turbine capacity.

The direct effect of energy prices on GNP is presented in Table 5. As is expected, the rate of growth of all types of energy is somewhat slower when the GNP responds to the increase in the real price of primary energy.

6. SUMMARY

In this paper we presented a time-step approach to find the end-use prices and quantity demanded of energy over time for an economy which consists of several types of primary and secondary energy and several major consuming sectors. The model can be applied to energy systems which are price takers in the world energy market. The model produces the output results efficiently and inexpensively, as is demonstrated using a practical example. An entire run of the energy model over the 28-year planning horizon (1983-2010), with 30 existing units, needed about 30 CPU seconds on a CDC 6600 COMPUTER (including compilation time).

While the model is relatively simple, it can be applied to a wide variety of energy systems, especially of the smaller countries, thus rendering it an important tool to assess alternative energy policies and support the decision making process in the energy field.

REFERENCES

[1] M. M. Bridger, W. G. Manning and J. P. Acton, Peak Load Pricing, Cambridge, MA: Ballinger Publishing Company, 1978.

[2] G. Brown and M. B. Johnson, "Public Utility Pricing and Output Under Risk," American Economic Review, Vol. 59, pp. 119-128, 1969.

[3] C. W. Bullard and A. V. Sebald, "A Model for Analyzing Energy Impact of Technolgical Change," presented at the Summer Computer Simulation Conference, San Francisco, 1975.

[4] D. W. Carlton, "Peak Load Pricing with Stochastic Demand," American Economic Review, Vol. 67, pp. 1006-1010, 1977.

[5] E. Cazalet, Generalized Equilibrium Modeling - The Methodology of the SRI-GULF Model, SRI, Draft Report to the Federal Energy Administration, 1977.

[6] E. A. Cherniavsky, Brookhaven Energy System Optimization Model, BNL # 19569, Upton, New York, 1974.

[7] T. G. Connolly, G. B. Danzig and S. C. Parish, The Stanford PILOT Energy/Economic Model, Technical Report SOL 77-19, Stanford Systems Optimization Laboratory, Stanford University, 1977.

[8] M. A. Crew and P. K. Kleindorfer, "Peak Load Pricing With a Diverse Technology," The Bell Journal of Economics, Vol. 7, pp. 207-223, 1976.

[9] Federal Energy Administration, Project Independence Report, U. S. Government Printing Office, Washington, D.C., 1974.

[10] W. W. Hogan and A. S. Manne, "Energy-Economy Interactions: The Fable of the Elephant and the Rabbit?" in Advance in the Economics of Energy and Resources, R. S. Pindyck, ed., Vol. 1, JAI Press, 1979.

[11] K. C. Hoffman, A Linear Programming Model of the Nation's Energy System, BNL, ESAG-4, Upton, New York, 1973.

[12] E. A. Hudson and D. W. Jorgenson, U.S. Economic Growth 1975-2000, Data Resources, Inc.: Cambridge, MA.

[13] D. W. Jorgenson and E. A. Hudson, "U.S. Energy Policy and Economic Growth 1975-2000," The Bell Journal of Economics and Management Science, Vol. 5, pp. 461-514, 1974.

[14] P. L. Joskow and M. L. Baughman, "The Future of the U.S. Nuclear Energy Industry," The Bell Journal of Economics, Vol. 7, pp. 3-32, 1976.

[15] R. Karni, A. Breiner and M. Avriel, "Energy-Economic Planning in Israel: The OMER Study," Perspectives on Resource Policy Modeling: Energy and Minerals, R. Amit and M. Avriel eds., Mallinger Publishing Company, Cambridge, MA., 1982.

[16] A. S. Kydes and J. Rabinoiwtz, "The Time-Stepped Energy System Optimization Model (TESOM) - Overview and Special Features," BNL, Upton, New York, August 1979.

[17] N. Levin and J. Zahavi, "Optimal Mix Algorithms With Existing Units," to appear in the IEEE Transactions on Power Apparatus and Systems.

[18] N. Levin and J. Zahavi, "Optimal Mix-Algorithms With Limited-Energy Plants," to appear in the IEEE Transactions on Power Apparatus and Systems.

[19] N. Levin and J. Zahavi, "Electricity Equilibrium Models With Stochastic Demand," Department of Decision Systems, School of Business, University of Southern California, 1983.

[20] N. Levin, A. Tishler, and J. Zahavi, "An Electrical Energy Equilibrium Model - The Static Case," Research Report 29/80, The Israel Institute of Business Research, Faculty of Management, Tel Aviv University, June, 1980.

[21] N. Levin, A. Tishler and J. Zahavi, "An Electrical Energy Equilibrium Model - The Dynamic Case," Research Report 30/80, the Israel Institute of Business Research, Faculty of Management, Tel Aviv University, June 1980.

[22] N. Levin, A. Tishler and J. Zahavi, "A Time-Step Equilibrium Model for the Electricity Sector," in Perspectives on Resource Policy Modeling: Energy and Minerals, R. Amit and M. Avriel, eds., Cambridge, MA., Ballinger Publishing Company, 1982.

[23] N. Levin, A. Tishler and J. Zahavi, "A Time-Step Equiibrium Model for the Energy Sector," Department of Decision Systems, School of Business, University of Southern California, 1982.

[24] N. Levin, A. Tishler and J. Zahavi, "Time-Step vs. Dynamic Optimization of Generation-Capacity-Expansion Programs of Power Systems," to appear in Operations Research.

[25] N. Levin, A. Tishler and J. Zahavi, "Electricity Equilibrium Models With Stochastic Fuel Prices," Department of Decision Systems, School of Business, University of Southern California, 1982.

[26] S. C. Littlechild, "A State Preference Approach to Public Utility Pricing and Investment Under Risk," The Bell Journal of Economics, Vol. 3, pp. 340-345, 1972.

[27] A. S. Manne, "ETA-MACRO: A Model of Energy-Economy Interactions," Presented at ORSA/TIMS Meeting, San Francisco.

[28] R. S. Pindyck, The Structure of World Energy Demand, Cambridge, MA., MIT Press, 1979.

[29] L. D. Taylor, "The Demand for Electricity: A Survey," The Bell Journal of Economics, Vol. 6, pp. 74-110, 1975.

[30] M. L. Vissher, "Welfare Maximizing Prize and Output With Stochastic Demand: Comment," American Economic Review, Vol. 63, pp. 224-229, 1973.

POLICY MODELING BY TENRAC

Analytic Techniques for Energy Planning
B. Lev, F.H. Murphy, J.A. Bloom & A.S. Gleit (Editors)

STATE ENERGY MODELING AND PLANNING: THE CURRENT TEXAS EXPERIENCE

Robert L. Kieschnick, Jr.

Texas Energy and Natural Resources
Advisory Council
200 East 18th St.
Austin, Texas 78701

This paper presents an overview of the modeling, forecasting, and planning activities of the Texas Energy and National Resources Advisory Council. It also presents the design and structure of the different modeling systems, of which the following paper presents descriptions of different components.

1. INTRODUCTION AND OVERVIEW

The purpose of this paper is to present a summary of the modeling activities conducted by the Texas Energy and Natural Resources Advisory Council (TENRAC). TENRAC is an independent state agency directed by a council comprised of the major political figures of Texas government with either energy or natural resource concerns. Its primary roles are to assist in the development of energy and natural resource policies for the state and to represent the state's interest in these policy areas in national discussions. Because of such responsibilities, the state has sought to develop several analytical tools for the analysis of different policy options and their consequences, as well as to forecast the path of critical energy and energy related variables (e.g. domestic production of crude oil).

The modeling efforts of TENRAC are being conducted under the Texas Energy Policy Project. As a result the paper will first discuss the nature and background of this project before presenting a description of each of the major modeling "systems" being developed under the auspices of this project. There are five major modeling systems being developed, each focused upon a particular market. They are: (1) the Natural Gas Policy Analysis System (NGPAS), (2) the Petroleum Sector Policy Analysis System (PSPAS), (3) the Electric Utility Policy Analysis System (EUPAS), (4) the Energy Demand Policy Analysis System (EDPAS), and (5) the Coal Market Policy Analysis System (CMPAS).

2. THE TEXAS ENERGY POLICY PROJECT

The Texas Energy Policy Project (TEPP) has its origins in the Texas National Energy Modeling Project. The Texas National Energy Modeling Project (TNEMP) represented an effort by Texas through the Texas Energy Advisory Council (predecessor to TENRAC) to transfer and evaluate the Project Independence Evaluation System (PIES), or the Midterm Energy Forecasting System (MEFS) as it became later known.

Upon completion of TNEMP, the National Advisory Board to the project recommended that Texas engage in the development of energy modeling which paid particularly attention to the regional effects of national energy policy. As a result of that and other recommendations, the Texas Energy Policy Project (TEPP) was born as the umbrella for funding of energy modeling by the state.

The project began first with an extensive identification of the type of issues, both current and foreseeable, for which a model might assist in the analysis.

The set of issues identified were then mapped into a set of information requirements (e.g. Texas crude oil production), and finally into a set of modeling systems. This work and its associated work plan was then submitted to the National Advisory Board for comments and approval.

The fact that issues were used to guide model development at the start probably had a major effect upon the project as a whole, from the choice of systems to develop to their detailed implementation. Another factor that was important to the overall project was that of maintaining regional detail in all the modeling work.

However, these factors were mitigated by the requirement that when possible the project was to develop needed models from already existing models with similar coverage. This was not always possible, but in those cases where it was, the decision imposed additional design constraints. The idea behind the requirement was to both lower the cost of developing needed models and to assure the operationality of those that were. Experience, however, produced mixed results on both counts.

With these and other considerations in mind, five modeling systems were agreed upon for development under TEPP. Each took on a partial equilibrium viewpoint of analysis for rather broad terrains. The first three focused upon a particular fuel (e.g. the Natural Gas Policy Analysis System focused upon the natural gas market). The last two focused upon energy consumption and the critical energy conversion industry, the electric power industry (see figure 1; solid lines indicate work completed and dotted lines work underway). The following discussion provides a brief description of each of these systems.

3. THE NATURAL GAS POLICY ANALYSIS SYSTEM

The Natural Gas Policy System (NGPAS) presently comprises two major modeling components, but will be expanded to comprise other components when fully developed. The first modeling component of the NGPAS is the TENRAC Oil and Gas Supply Model (OGSM). The second modeling component is the Gas Pipeline Competition Model (GPCM).

The OGSM is based upon an oil and gas supply model originally developed by Mathtech, Inc. for the Electric Power Research Institute (EPRI). In a conceptual sense the model consists of two components; an onshore oil and gas supply model, and an offshore oil and gas supply model. Both components forecast an expected path, under certain assumptions, for exploratory drilling, reserve additions, and production by National Petroleum Council province. Reserves are added in accordance with a cumulative discovery function and a computed risk return index, which represents a valuation of additional increments of exploratory drilling. Production is then determined using maximum efficient recovery curves. The primary exogenous variables are the expected price path for crude oil and natural gas.

The field price of domestically produced natural gas is determined, along with other variables, in the GPCM. The GPCM is a nonlinear programming model of the natural gas pipeline industry. The model represents the competition between pipelines for incremental supplies of natural gas in the field market and the sales of gas to distributors and mainline industrial customers in the city gate market.

In its present form the NGPAS represents the integration of the OGSM and the GPCM, with the GPCM containing an embedded set of demand curves for distributor and mainline industrial demand for natural gas. As such, the system is able to

FIGURE 1.

I. NATURAL GAS POLICY ANALYSIS SYSTEM

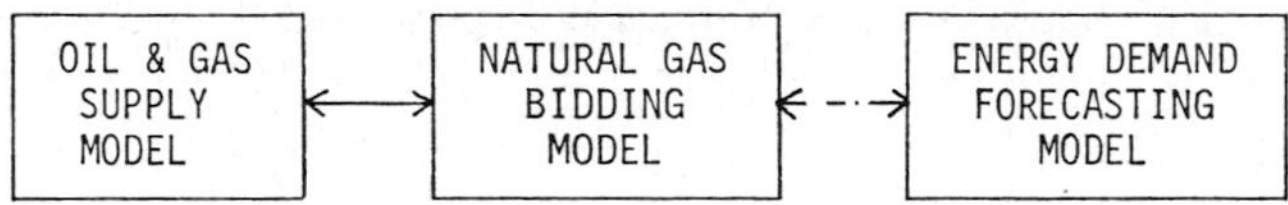

II. PETROLEUM SECTOR POLICY ANALYSIS SYSTEM

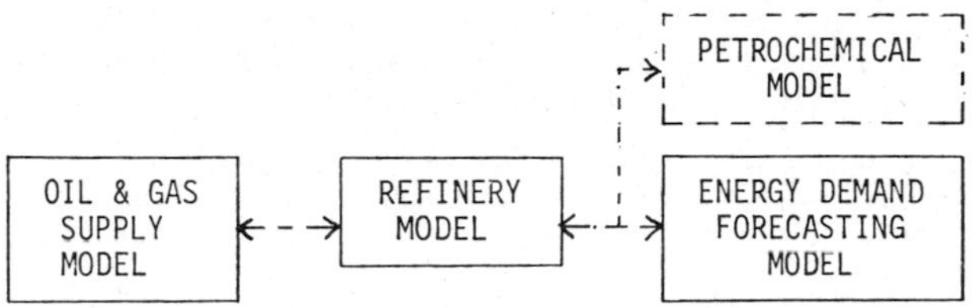

III. ELECTRIC UTILITY POLICY ANALYSIS SYSTEM

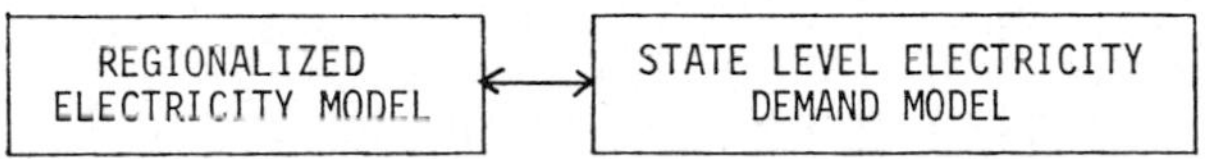

IV. ENERGY DEMAND POLICY ANALYSIS SYSTEMS

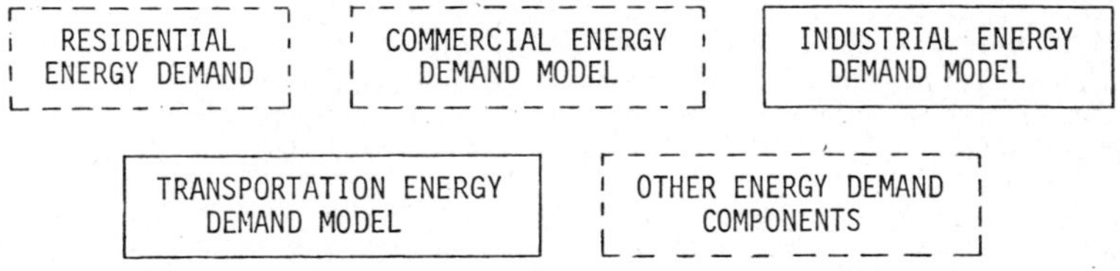

V. COAL MARKET POLICY ANALYSIS SYSTEM

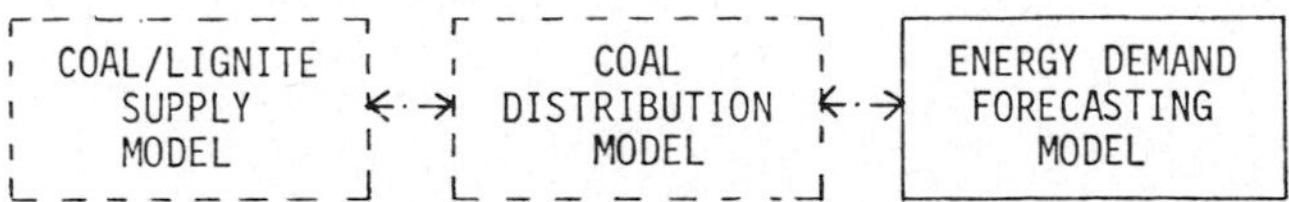

compute prices and pipeline takes which directly incorporate demand considerations in model solutions. In future work, the demand characteristics will come from an multi-fuel demand model which will provide demand information for the other fuel market modeling systems. In addition, GASNET, a natural gas transmission model, will be incorporated into the system in order to provide better information on pipeline capacity and investment.

4. THE PETROLEUM SECTOR POLICY ANALYSIS SYSTEM

The Petroleum Sector Policy Analysis System (PSPAS) is not presently integrated, but the component models for first stage integration have been completed. They are the TENRAC Oil and Gas Supply Model (OGSM), the TENRAC Refinery Model (TRM), and the Energy Demand Forecasting Model. In the first stage of integration, the OGSM and the TRM will be integrated, with information on quantities demanded of various refined products coming from the Energy Demand Forecasting Model and other sources in a recursive manner. In subsequent stages of development, the system will incorporate a petrochemical industry model.

As the OGSM was described earlier, attention will turn to the TRM. The TRM is a multi-region, multi-product and multi-time period linear programming model of the refinery industry. The model determines the cost minimizing path of refinery investment and operation given supplies of crude oil by type (e.g. high sulfur crude) and the quantities demanded of various refined products. The model is unique in that it views the industry at a more aggregate level than most refinery models, which either do not capture process choice, or do so at the level of an individual refinery.

The Energy Demand Forecasting Model is the multi-fuel demand model mentioned above in the natural gas model discussion. This model is being developed by EPRI and will provide information on the demand for various fuels by sector for each state. Its design is particularly well suited for integration within various modeling systems.

5. THE ELECTRIC UTILITY POLICY ANALYSIS SYSTEM

The Electric Utility Policy Analysis System (EUPAS) consists of two models and is presently operational. The first model is an updated version of the well known Regionalized Electricity Model (REM), developed by Dr. Martin Baughman. Given the demand for electricity, REM produces information on the fuel choice and the operating and financial characteristics of electric utilities by electric reliability region.

The second model is the State Level Electricity Demand Model (SLED) developed at Oak Ridge National Laboratory (ORNL). The present version in use is a revised version of the original model by EPRI. The model produces estimates of the quantity of electricity demand given a path for the average cost of electricity by region.

The system integration work was funded recently by EPRI and made available to TENRAC. Further systems work is anticipated to focus upon parameter and data refinements.

6. THE ENERGY DEMAND POLICY ANALYSIS SYSTEMS

The Energy Demand Policy Analysis Systems (EDPAS) is less a set of integrated models than a collection of stand alone models. Further, as with the EUPAS, the models used are ones originally developed by other entities. In this case, most of the models used were originally developed at the Oak Ridge National Laboratory (ORNL). In particular, they are: (1) the Oak Ridge Residential Model, (2) the Oak Ridge Commerical Model, (3) the Oak Ridge Industrial Model, and (4) the Oak Ridge Transportation Model. As these models have been described in detail elsewhere, we will not do so here.

Each of these models have been, or will be used by TENRAC to perform detailed analysis of end use demand for energy by a particular sector. In order to do so, TENRAC is making minor revisions and updating each of the models. As more experience is gained with their use, additional modifications will be made (e.g. adding vintage capital stock model to the residential model). In addition, each model will be used to enhance or guide revision of the Energy Demand Forecasting System described earlier. In this sense, there is a loose connection between the models in this "system".

7. THE COAL MARKET POLICY ANALYSIS SYSTEM

The last system, the Coal Market Policy Analysis System (CMPAS), is scheduled for development next year. When developed it will comprise three models: (1) the Coal/Lignite Supply Model, (2) the Coal Distribution Model, and (3) the Energy Demand Forecasting Model. The Energy Demand Forecasting Model is the same as discussed earlier. The Coal Distribution Model will probably build upon an already existing model (of which there are several). Whether to base the Coal/Lignite Supply Model on existing work or to start anew is presently an open question.

8. SUMMARY AND CONCLUSIONS

The present discussion has not attempted to chronicle the history of energy modeling in Texas, but rather to present a picture of the current and anticipated modeling efforts by the state. While the primary impetus for the State of Texas to fund such modeling efforts was due to their uses as tools to aid energy policy analysis and evaluation, they will also be used to assist in the generation of an outlook report for the state, as required by law. The performance of this latter function should critically promote the maintanence and enhancement of the modeling systems described.

There are several conclusions that arise from the Texas experience with energy modeling that will be relevant to others contemplating similar activities, particularly other states. First, energy modeling, and particularly for policy analysis, is expensive and increases almost exponentially with the number of information requirements placed upon any given model or modeling system.

Second, there is a dynamic tension between the information requirements that decision makers impose, the data that exist to enable the modeler to design a system that satisfies them, and model complexity. Each of these are important dimensions to address in model design and development, in fact the perceived success of the modeling efforts may turn upon decisions along these lines, but they are extremely difficult to explicitly elucidate much less separate. Therefore care is suggested when addressing these issues.

And third, often too much attention is paid to model development and too little to model maintenance and enhancement, particularly with the money and personnel requirements to perform these ongoing tasks. This fact is manifest in a number of dimensions, from needing to develop the experience of personnel with the use of a particular model or modeling system to the cost of continually updating the database and parameters of the existing modeling system. There are few entities that have obtained the benefits that, say, the American Gas Association has because of their continued commitment to maintenance and enhancement of a modeling system that they have developed. Too often models die quiet deaths of neglect after a tremendous amount of time and resources have gone into them for just a few runs or a single report.

Analytic Techniques for Energy Planning
B. Lev, F.H. Murphy, J.A. Bloom & A.S. Gleit (Editors)

AN OVERVIEW OF THE TENRAC OIL AND GAS SUPPLY MODEL

Robert Ciliano
William Hery

Mathtech, Inc.
P.O. Box 2392
Princeton, New Jersey 08055

This paper describes the structure of the TENRAC Oil and Gas Supply Model, a deterministic simulation of the exploration for and production of crude oil and natural gas. The model is intended primarily as a tool to examine the impact of existing and proposed regulatory and legislative policies (e.g., NGPA, Windfall Profit Tax) under different economic scenarios.

1. INTRODUCTION

The following sections describe the structure and technical characteristics of the Oil and Gas Supply Modeling (OGSM) system developed by MATHTECH, Inc. for the Texas Energy and Natural Resources Advisory Council (TENRAC). The model represents the most detailed, regionally disaggregated assessment of oil and gas field supply attempted to date and is based upon concepts and modeling techniques earlier developed by MATHTECH in projects for the American Gas Association (AGA), Energy Information Administration (EIA) and Electric Power Research Institute (EPRI).

The OGSM is intended primarily as a tool for integrative policy analysis which permits the user to explicitly examine the impacts of the Natural Gas Policy Act, Windfall Profit Tax and other existing legislative and regulatory policies on gas and oil supply response. Moreover, it provides the user with a framework in which to perform sensitivity analyses with respect to prospective future changes in these policy initiatives.

2. MODEL STRUCTURE

OGSM is a deterministic simulation of the processes of exploring for, developing and producing crude oil and natural gas at the industry aggregate level. For each year in the simulation period, the levels of exploratory effort, new discoveries, extensions and revisions, and production are estimated for each of ten onshore and three offshore regions on the basis of prevailing economic/financial and geologic conditions, and (for natural gas) feedback from the marketplace (as modeled by the TENRAC natural gas bidding model, GPCM). The lag structure and implicit capital/materiel constraints built into the model (and described in sections 8 and 9) ensure that unrealistically dramatic changes in the level and regional allocation of effort do not occur.

Figure 1 shows the inter-relationships among the major (sub-) models, with solid lines indicating information flows within the simulation year and dashed lines indicating information flows to the subsequent year. The function of each of these models is as follows:

- The Geology Model estimates the new discoveries and extensions and revisions resulting from the "next" increment of exploratory drilling in a region; it also estimates the average depth of exploratory and development wells each year.

Figure 1

Crude Oil and Natural Gas Field Supply Evaluation System
Structural Overview

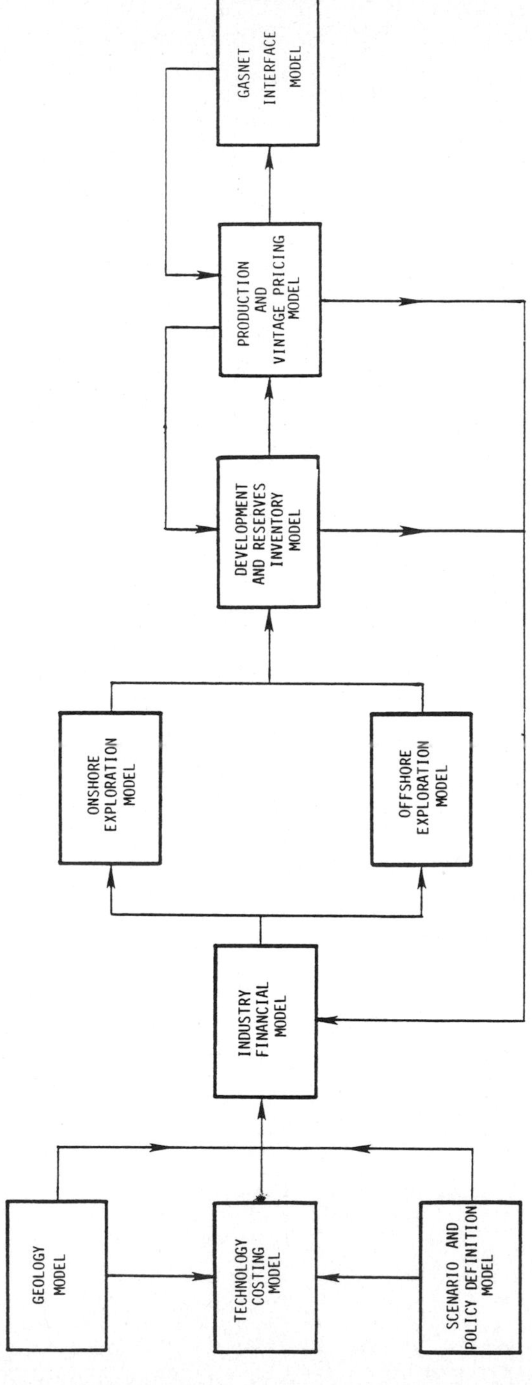

Figure 2

U.S. Geological Survey - National Petroleum Council
Future Petroleum Provinces of the United States

Regional Boundaries: Region 1 – Alaska and Hawaii, except North Slope. Region 2 – Pacific Coast States; Region 2A – Pacific Ocean, except Alaska; Region 3 – Western Rocky Mountains; Region 4 – Eastern Rocky Mountains; Region 5 – West Texas and Eastern New Mexico; Region 6 – Western Gulf Basin; Region 6A – Gulf of Mexico; Region 7 – Midcontinent; Region 8 – Michigan Basin; Region 9 – Eastern Interior; Region 10 – Appalachians; Region 11 – Atlantic Coast; Region 11A – Atlantic Ocean.

Source: NPC, *Future Petroleum Provinces of the United States* (July 1970) – with slight modification.

- The Technology Costing Model estimates the exploration, development and production costs for the current year.
- The Industry Financial Model computes the financial decision-making variables: the expected net present value (for offshore regions) and the "risk-return index" (for onshore regions).
- The Onshore Exploration and Offshore Exploration Models use this information to select the level, regional allocation and directionality (oil versus gas) of exploratory drilling.
- The Development and Reserves Inventory Model books new reserves and extensions and revisions expected from each year's exploration activity; it also computes net proven reserves at the end of each year.
- The Production Model computes the production available from existing and new (simulated) reserves.
- The GPCM Interface passes information to and from TENRAC's Natural Gas Bidding Model (GPCM). OGSM can be run without GPCM, in which case it assumes that all gas is purchased at the prices input by the user.

Subsequent sections describe these models in greater detail.

3. REGIONALITY

The model developed for TENRAC is highly disaggregate in terms of its level of regional detail. Major USGS/NPC Provinces are explicitly represented. Additionally, activity within individual basins situated in Provinces 5, 6, and 6A which contain one or more Texas Railroad Commission Districts, or parts thereof, is also modeled. Figure 2 shows the USGS/NPC regions maintained within the system.

4. METHODOLOGIES UTILIZED

Among the quantitative modeling techniques used in developing the system are:

- geostatistical analysis (e.g., expected discoveries as a function of exploratory activity are based upon statistically derived "finding rate functions").
- engineering cost analysis (e.g., costs of exploration, development, delineation and production have been derived from a variety of secondary sources and costing models).
- econometrics (e.g., the onshore level and regional allocation of exploratory activity is modeled as an econometrically derived function of a "risk-return index" of investment attractiveness).
- economic decision analysis (e.g., regional and hydrocarbon-specific direction of exploratory activity is based on an economic decision analysis framework).
- nonlinear optimization (e.g., offshore exploratory activity is modeled using nonlinear optimization with a "short term" finding rate function to reflect the "lumpiness" of the structure-specific prospect base offshore).

Figure 3

Generic Cumulative Discovery Function

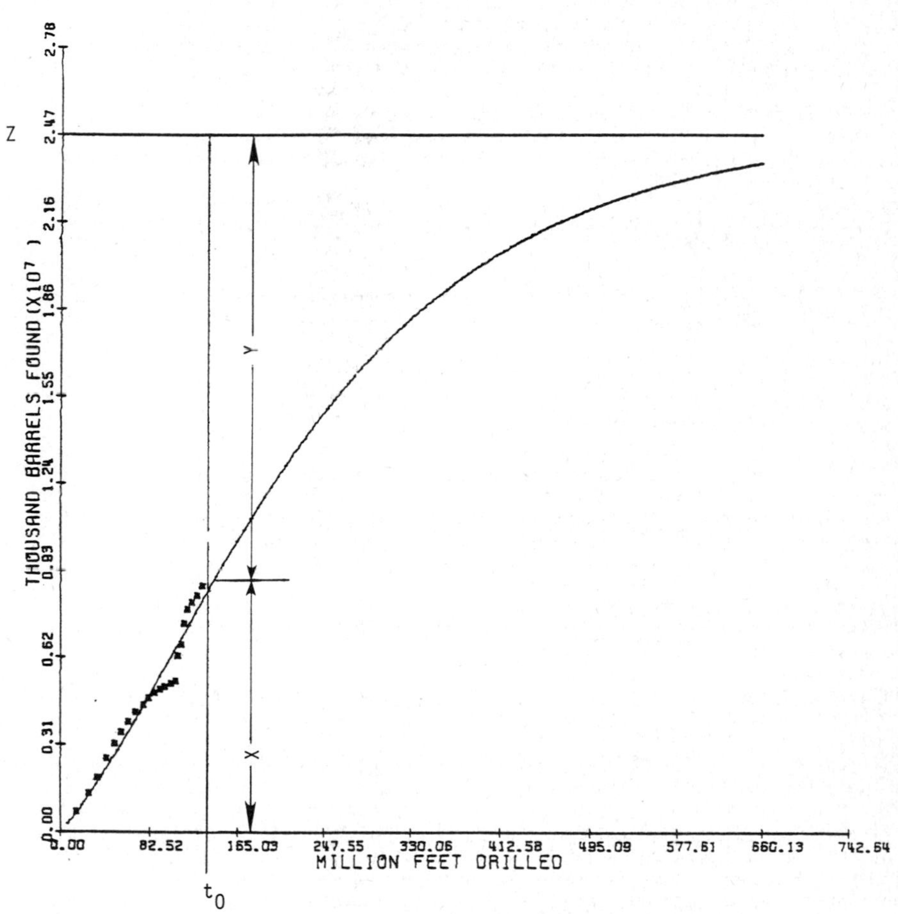

Key

X = cumulative production to date, plus current estimate of measured, indicated and inferred reserves

Y = ultimately discoverable, recoverable resources residing in as yet unexplored areas

Z = total ultimately discoverable, recoverable resource

- deterministic simulation (e.g., oil and gas industry behavior is simulated over a user-specified planning horizon. "Deterministic" denotes that no Monte Carlo procedures are used and that for a given set of user inputs, the system outputs are uniquely determined).

The role of these methods will be discussed more fully in subsequent sections which describe the modeling of exploration, development and production.

5. GEOLOGY MODEL

The Geology Model has three primary functions:

- to estimate the total reserve additions resulting from an increment of exploratory drilling;
- to estimate the growth in reserves over time through extensions and revisions; and
- to estimate the average depth of exploratory and developmental drilling in each year.

The estimation of reserve additions as a function of exploratory drilling is done via the cumulative discovery function (CDF), which relates cumulative discoveries (from some fixed point in time) to cumulative drilling (since that same point in time). The function form used for the CDF is

$$y = A(1-\exp(-Bx)) + (L-A)\,(1-\exp(-Dx)), \tag{1}$$

where x is cumulative drilling, y is cumulative discoveries, L is an a priori estimate of the ultimately discoverable, recoverable resources, and A, B, and D are parameters to be estimated.

This form was chosen because it forces the cumulative discoveries to asymptotically approach L, and it allows an initial "slow start" (typical in a frontier region), followed by an increasing rate of discovery and then a period of decline. Note that the finding rate often used in oil and gas models is simply the derivative of the CDF; if A=0, then the first term drops out and the derived finding rate is a simple exponential decline.

This functional form is related to the form introduced by Arps and Roberts [1] to estimate the number of fields discovered as a function of the number of wildcat wells drilled. They use the relationship $F=A(1-\exp(BW))$, where F is cumulative fields, W is cumulative wildcats, and A and B are constants; different values of B are derived for "random drilling in trend areas" and "drilling on geological or geophysical leads". The two-term form used here can be thought of as a combination of the "random" and "leads" terms, with one term (the "leads" term, corresponding to the smaller of B and D) becoming dominant as drilling proceeds and the geology and geophysics of the region become better understood.

The parameters A, B and D were estimated from historic drilling and discovery data for each region. The estimates were based on a least squares fit of the function to the historical data using a grid search on B and D, and a closed form derivation of A for fixed B and D.

For the TENRAC model, the estimate of ultimate discoverable, recoverable resource was taken from USGS Circular 860. Three scenarios (low, mid and high) are presented there; correspondingly, three CDF's were estimated for each region.

The graph in Figure 3 shows a sample CDF, along with the historic data and ultimate recoverable resource used to estimate its parameters. For the sake of clarity, one of the poorest fitting regions was selected.

The growth of reserves through extensions and revisions is modeled as a set of fixed growth factors, with different factors being used for oil and gas. These factors are estimated from the AGA "back-cast" tables, which show the growth over time in estimated ultimate recovery by year of discovery and by state or substate region.

The average well depth by region is computed by interpolation from forecasts by the National Petroleum Council of average well depth in each region as a function of cumulative drilling in that region.

6. TECHNOLOGY COSTING MODEL

The Technology Costing Model estimates the cost of exploration, development and production for each simulation year. Exploration and development costs are computed on a per well basis, are region specific and are a function of average well depth.

Exploration and development costs are estimated in several subcategories (direct drilling and equipping, geological and geophysical, land and lease acquisition, etc., as shown in Figure 4) and aggregate costs are computed. Using data published in the American Petroleum Institute's annual Joint Association Survey, equations approximating each of these costs as a function of drilling depth were estimated by regression analysis. In each case, linear, log-log and log-linear models were fitted to the data and the best outcomes were selected. Figure 5 shows two graphs typical of the results obtained.

All costs were initially estimated from 1980 data and inflated to 1981 dollars (the units used throughout OGSM). Real cost growth factors are supplied by the user.

7. INDUSTRY FINANCIAL MODEL

The Industry Financial Model is used to evaluate the financial attractiveness of each increment of exploratory drilling; this information is then used by the Exploration Models to estimate the level of exploration.

In practice, onshore and offshore exploration decisions are made with very different financial criteria and constraints. The cost of an exploratory well offshore is literally an order of magnitude greater than a typical onshore well; and a significantly larger discovery is typically required to justify the cost of a production platform, gathering lines, etc. Furthermore, very larget "up front" bonuses are paid for the right to explore offshore tracts, and the availability of these tracts is a function of changeable government policy, not pure economics. For these reasons, offshore exploration is typically done by major oil companies with exploration programs large enough for the "expected return" to be a good approximation to the actual return (the law of large numbers) without a need to consider the riskiness of a single venture. Onshore exploration, however, is usually done by smaller operators who must balance the amount at risk in a venture with its expected return. The Industry Financial Model reflects this difference in the financial computations done for the onshore and offshore regions.

For an exploratory venture in the offshore regions, the current average depth of

Figure 4

JAS Cost Categories of Estimated Expenditures* for
U.S. Oil and Gas Exploration, Development and Production

(1.) Exploration Costs

a. Drilling Equipping Exploratory Wells**
b. Acquiring Undeveloped Acreage
c. Lease Rentals and Expense for Carrying Leases
d. Geological and Geophysical
e. Contributions Toward Test Wells
f. Land Department, Leasing, & Scouting
g. Other (including Direct Overhead)
h. Total Exploration

(2.) Development Costs

a. Drilling & Equipping Development Wells**
b. Lease Equipment
c. Improved Recovery Programs
d. Other (including Direct Overhead)
e. Total Development

(3.) Production Costs

a. Production Expenditures (including Direct Overhead)
b. Production or Severance Taxes
c. Ad Valorem Taxes
d. Total Production

(4.) G&A Overhead Not Reported Elsewhere

a. Allocated to Exploration
b. Allocated to Development
c. Allocated to Production
d. Total G&A Overhead

(5.) Drilling & Production Platforms**

---

* Exclusive of federal, state, and local income taxes; payments of interest; payments for the retirement of debt; and payments to owners as return on investment.

**For 1969 and prior, instructions for the JAS "Section II" specified that expenditures for drilling and production platforms be assigned to item 1.a. (Drilling and Equipping Exploratory Wells) or item 2.a. (Drilling and Equipping Development Wells).

Figure 5

Direct Exploratory Well Drilling and Equipping Costs as a Function of Well Depth

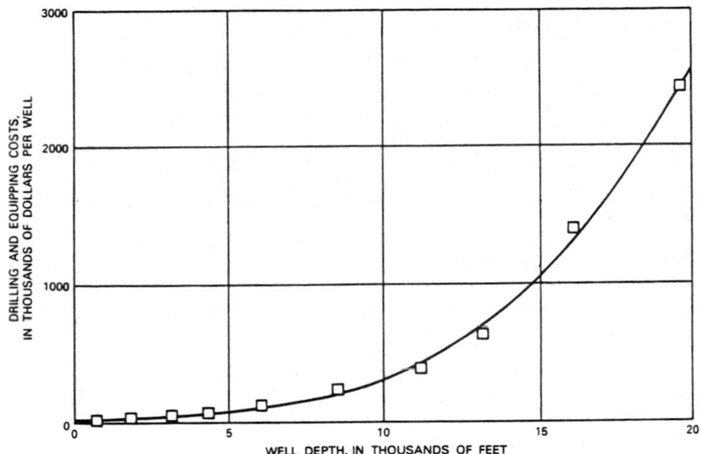

Total Exploration Cost per Exploratory Well as a Function of Direct Drilling Cost per Well*

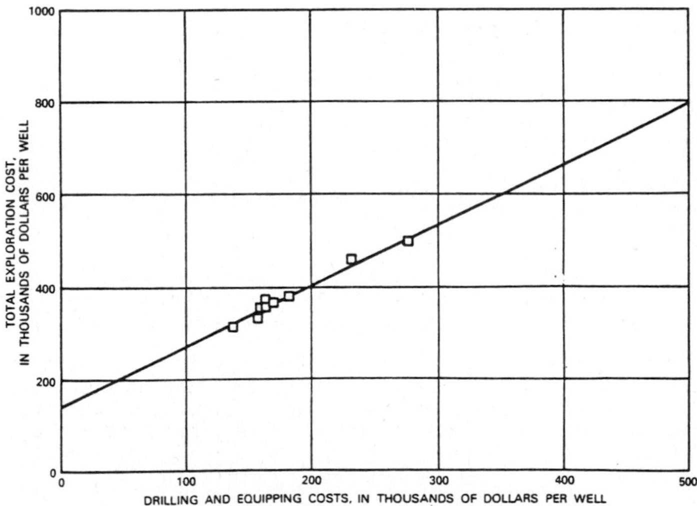

*minus cost of acquiring undeveloped acreage

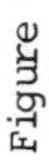

Figure 6

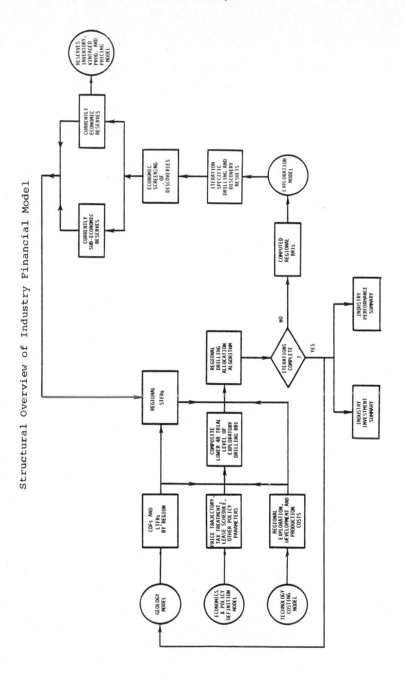

Structural Overview of Industry Financial Model

Figure 7

Structural Overview of Onshore Exploration Model

(1 of 2)

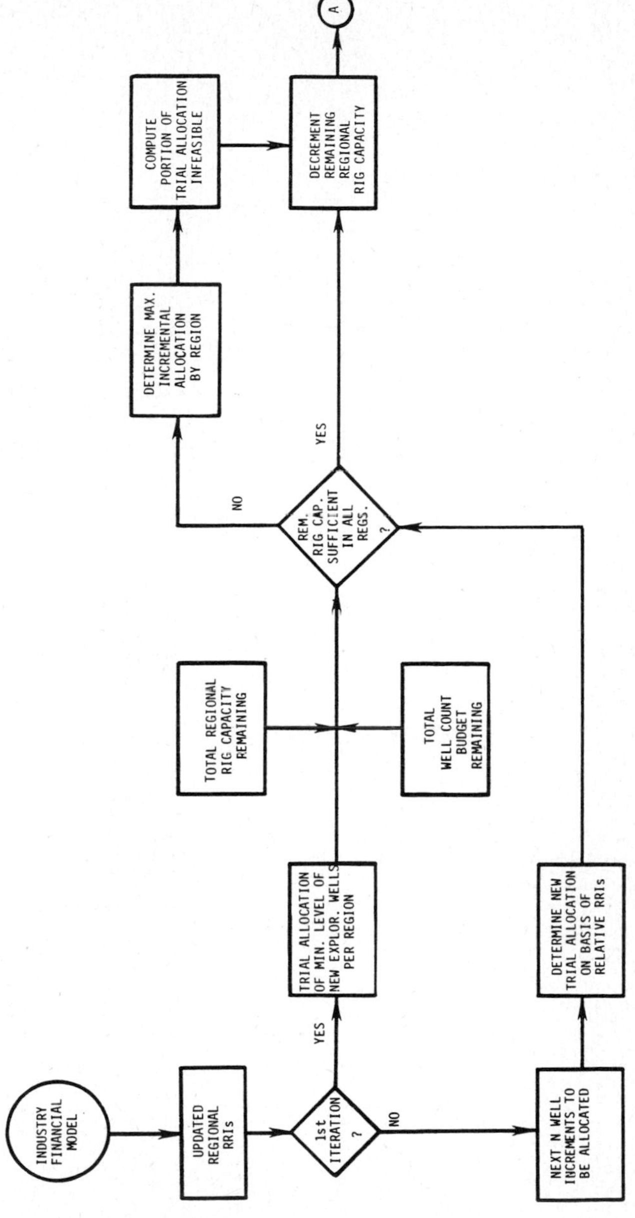

Figure 7 (2 of 2)

Structural Overview of Onshore Exploration Model

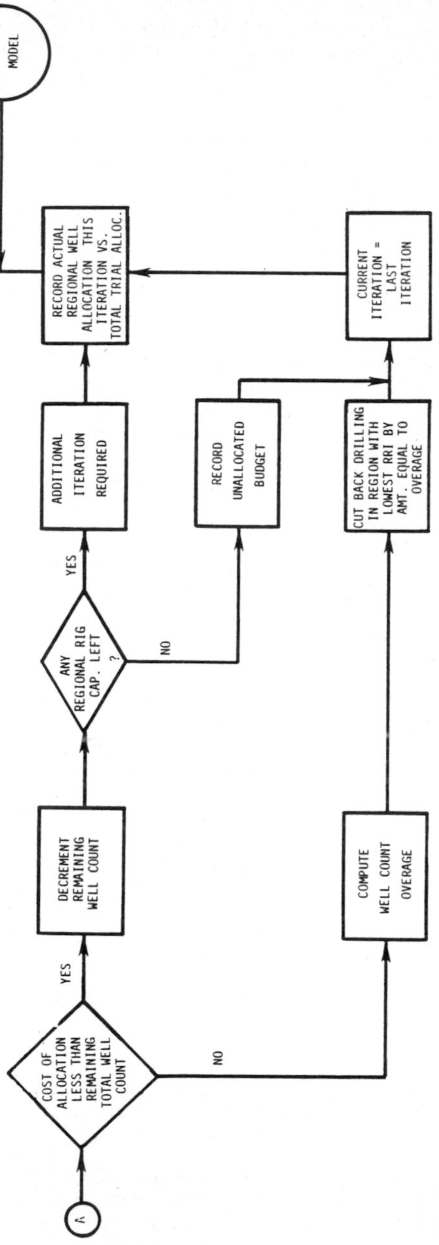

A

COST OF ALLOCATION LESS THAN REMAINING TOTAL WELL COUNT

YES

DECREMENT REMAINING WELL COUNT

ANY REGIONAL RIG CAP. LEFT ?

YES

ADDITIONAL ITERATION REQUIRED

RECORD ACTUAL REGIONAL WELL ALLOCATION THIS ITERATION VS. TOTAL TRIAL ALLOC.

RECORD REGIONAL AMTS OF OIL AND GAS RESOURCES FOUND

INDUSTRY FINANCIAL MODEL

GEOLOGY MODEL

NO

RECORD UNALLOCATED BUDGET

NO

COMPUTE WELL COUNT OVERAGE

CUT BACK DRILLING IN REGION WITH LOWEST RRI BY AMT. EQUAL TO OVERAGE

CURRENT ITERATION = LAST ITERATION

drilling is used to estimate the expected outlays required each year, expected discovery size, and expected revenues each year. Using user-supplied economic and financial variables (corporate discount rate, inflation rate, tax rate, real cost growth rate, etc.), the annual cash flow and expected net present value of the venture is computed.

For an exploratory venture in an onshore region, the expected net present value is again computed. In addition, the total cost of the venture is computed, as well as their ratio called the risk return index (RRI). The index will be used in the Onshore Exploration Model in a regression equation as a predictor of exploration activity level. This particular function of risk and return was selected from several candidates because the regression equations based on it were found to be the best predictor of national exploratory drilling. Figure 6 provides a simplified overview of this recursive algorithm.

8. ONSHORE EXPLORATION MODEL

The Onshore Exploration Model estimates the national level of exploration, its allocation to regions, and how much is directed towards oil versus gas within each region. This is done in a series of steps using the risk return index (from the Industry Financial Model) and national and regional constraints on exploration growth, exploration decline and directionality. Figure 7 is a flow chart of this process.

First, the expected national number of exploratory wells is estimated by a regression equation from the number of wells in the prior year and the two prior years' observed RRI; this value is also constrained by a user-supplied maximum growth rate.

Next, region and direction specific maximum decline rates are used to allocate a portion of the national total wells to regions and directionality. The remaining wells are then allocated iteratively, in "bundles" of N at each iteration, where N is typically set to 50 for production runs and 1000 for testing purposes (in order to save computer cost).

At the start of each iteration, the expected RRI for exploratory wells in the next set of N is computed for each region, and the N wells are then allocated to each region with positive RRI (and which has not yet surpassed its user supplied regional growth constraint, which corresponds to the implicit capital and materiel constraint) in proportion to each region's RRI. Within each region, there are two directionality constraints (derived from historical data) on the minimum fraction of the exploratory wells in that region directed towards oil and gas exploration; these constraints are used to allocate part of the region's portion of the N wells to oil and gas. The remaining wells in the region are allocated to oil and gas in proportion to the oil and gas specific RRI's in the region.

This iterating continues until either the national expected number of exploratory wells has been allocated, or each region has a non-positive RRI or has readied its growth constraint.

The use of a relatively small value of N enables the model to respond to the region-specific declining attractiveness of exploration (due to the decreased finding rate coupled with the constancy of prices and costs within a simulation year) over the course of the year.

Figure 8

Optimal Sequencing of Resource Acreage Partitions

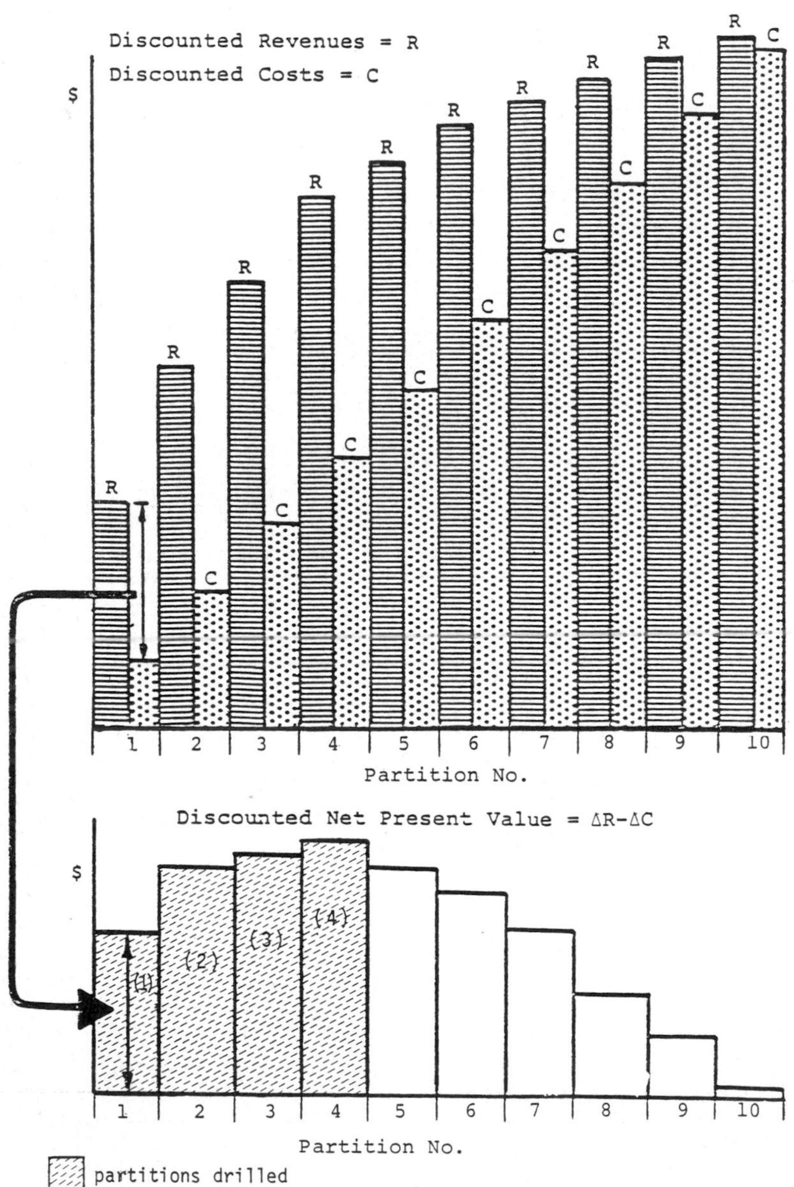

Figure 9
Typical Hydrocarbon Depletion Function

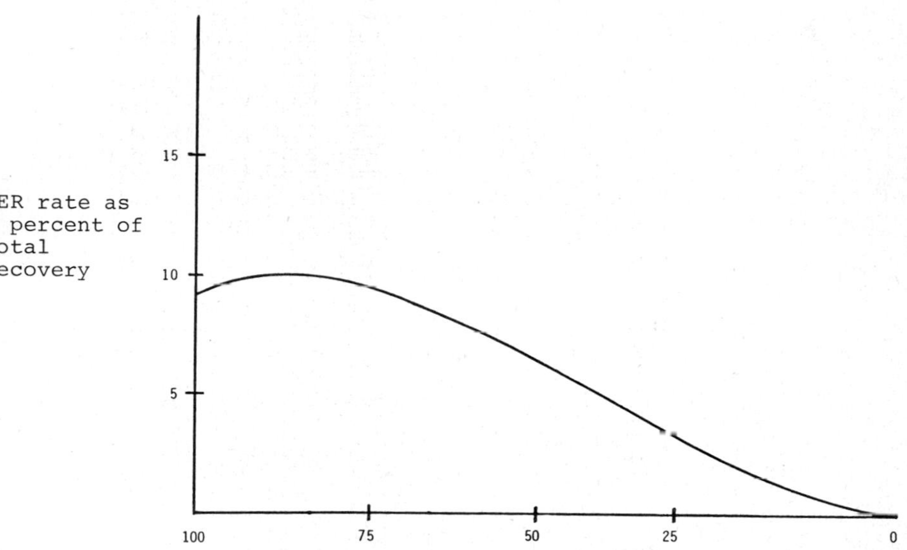

9. OFFSHORE EXPLORATION MODEL

The Offshore Exploration Model estimates the level of oil and gas drilling in each of the three offshore regions (Pacific, Gulf and Atlantic).

A major constraint in offshore exploration is the amount of acreage available for leasing in a year. In each offshore region each year, the available acreage is broken down into 10 partitions (of equal size). This breakdown is assumed to place the most attractive ten percent of the acreage in partition 1, the next most attractive in partition 2, etc. (based on an adjusted version of the CDF). The Industry Financial Model is used to sequentially evaluate each of these partitions as if directed toward gas or oil, and select the optimal directionality. If both expected net present values are negative at some iteration, the process stops and all additional acreage is deemed unattractive in the current year. In addition, drilling rig availability constraints can stop this process prematurely. These constraints are supplied by the user as either a vector of annual rig availability, or as an initial value with the annual expected capacity expansion estimated by the model on the basis of demand. Figure 8 illustrates the acreage partitioning.

10. DEVELOPMENT AND RESERVES INVENTORY MODEL

This model estimates the new reserves and extensions and revisions resulting from the resources discovered in the Exploration Models; total net proven reserves at the end of each year are also computed.
The extensions and revisions to the simulated discoveries are estimated from the oil and gas extension factors computed in the Geology Model. Extensions and revisions to the existing (pre-simulation) reserves are estimated from E&R factors adjusted to ensure conformity with exogenous estimates of inferred reserves.

Net proven reserves at the end of a year are computed as the prior year's proven reserves plus new discoveries plus extensions and revisions less production (as computed in the Production Model).

11. PRODUCTION MODEL

The Production Model computes production from both new (i.e., simulated) reserves and existing reserves.

Production from new reserves is estimated from region and hydrocarbon-specific "maximum efficient recovery" (MER) curves. Each MER curve gives the maximum annual production rate as a function of the fraction of recoverable reserves produced to date. These functions are derived analytically from the maximum production rate (as a function of time) which is constant for an interval, then declines exponentially. The advantage of the MER is that it allows the Production Model to estimate the maximum production rate at any point in time, even if the maximum production level has not been maintained to date. A typical MER is illustrated in Figure 9.

New gas reserves are maintained in the model by vintage (year of discovery) and region, and the MER curves are applied to each vintage individually. Pointers for the cumulative fraction produced are maintained for each vintage and region.

Production from existing non-associated natural gas reserves is derived from estimates published by the Department of Energy.

Production from existing oil and associated gas reserves is estimated from the existing reserves base and reserves to production ratio.

Figure 10 describes the "bookkeeping" framework within which the Development and Reserves Inventory Model and the Production Model work.

12. GPCM INTERFACE

The GPCM Interface sets up the inputs required by GPCM and uses the results of GPCM to adjust data in the OGSM.

More specifically, it sets up arrays of maximum production available, NGPA ceiling price, and producer's minimum acceptable price for each natural gas category and region used by GPCM. The prices estimated by GPCM for new gas are used to adjust the price expectations in the supply model, and the excess supplies of natural gas (if any) are used to adjust the MER pointers to indicate that the maximum production level was not achieved. As mentioned above, when the OGSM is run without GPCM, the interface assumes that all gas is taken and the price bid for new gas is precisely the expected price input by the user.

13. SCENARIO DEFINITION

The user defines the scenario for a particular run by supplying the following information:

- wellhead price trajectories
- corporate discount rate
- inflation rate
- real cost growth rate
- tax structure
  --corporate income tax
  --windfall profit tax
  --investment tax credit
- OCS leasing schedule
- NGPA controlled gas prices
- geologic scenario

14. OUTPUTS

OGSM provides the user with a selection of optional reports ranging from a brief overview of each year's exploration activity to a full set of detailed reports running several hundred pages in length. These formatted reports include reports on:

- model inputs
- regional exploration and discoveries
- production and cash flow streams resulting from each year's exploration
- offshore acreage accepted and average bonus per acre offered

Figure 10

Structure of the Reserves Inventory, Production Vintaging and Pricing Model

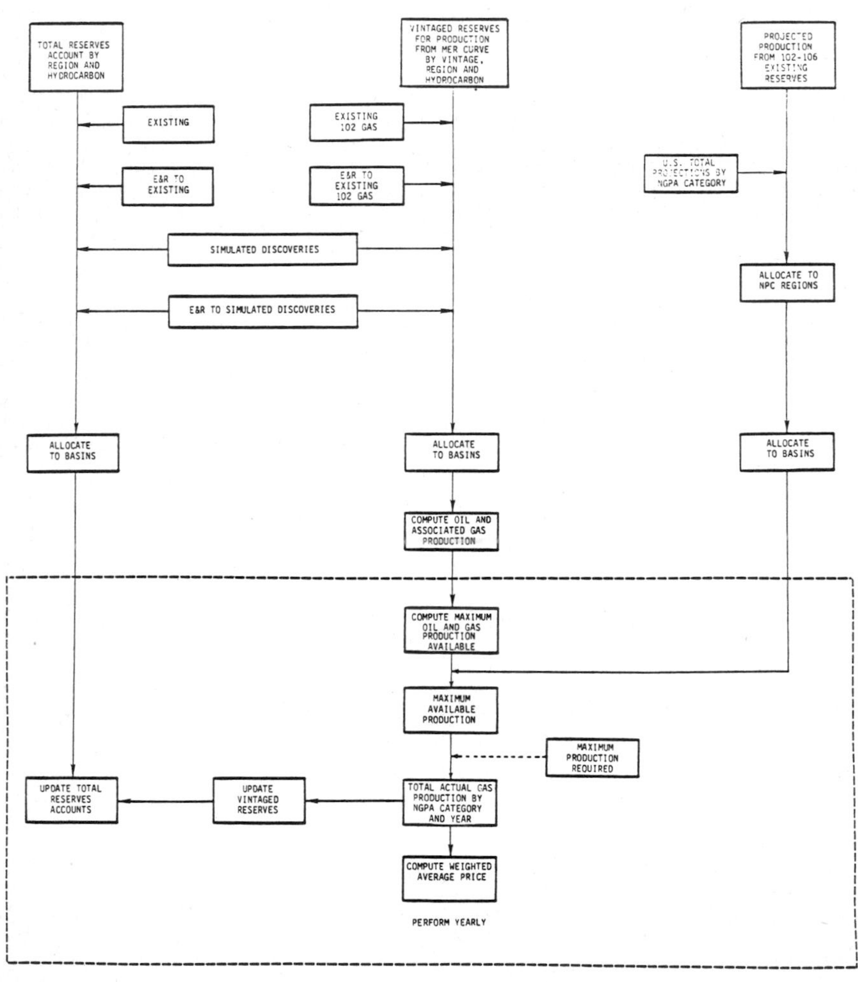

- natural gas and crude oil production by region, year and NGPA category (for gas)

- regional and annual reserves accounting

- natural gas and crude oil wellhead prices by region, year and NGPA category (for gas)

- regional and annual weighted average (across NGPA category) wellhead price of natural gas

15. IMPLEMENTATION

Portions of the Geology, Technology Costing and Industry Financial Models (namely those portions which estimate equations) are essentially preprocessors which are only used to set up input files for OGSM, but most of what has been described above is part of a single integrated program. This program is currently implemented in FORTRAN IV on both the Texas A&M Amdahl computer system and the Princeton University IBM 3083 computer system.

REFERENCE

[1] Arps, J.J., and T.G. Roberts. "Economics of Drilling for Cretaceous Oil on East Flank of Denver - Julesburg Basin," Bulletin of the American Association of Petroleum Geologists, Volume 42, No. 11, pp. 2549-2566, November 1958.

Analytic Techniques for Energy Planning
B. Lev, F.H. Murphy, J.A. Bloom & A.S. Gleit (Editors)

THE TENRAC GAS PIPELINE COMPETITION MODEL

Robert E. Brooks, Ph.D.

RBA Consultants
4209 Santa Monica Blvd., Ste 201
Los Angeles, California 90029

This paper presents a mathematical programming model developed to forecast competition for incremental natural gas supplies among interstate and intrastate pipelines. The model consists of explicit representations of the largest interstate and intrastate pipelines, their supply sources, derived demands, interconnections, financial conditions, and reserve cushions. The model is primarily intended as a tool to examine the effects of alternative natural gas policies on the price and availability of natural gas to different regions.

1. INTRODUCTION

One of the primary concerns of gas producing and consuming states such as Texas and Louisiana, is the effect of the Natural Gas Policy Act of 1978 or other deregulation plans on competition for new gas supplies between interstate pipelines primarily serving customers outside these states and intrastate pipelines serving customers within them. Interstate pipelines have been viewed as having a distinct advantage in this competition, because many of them have cushions of lowcost gas to which they may be able to add higher priced deregulated gas without substantially reducing demand. Intrastate pipelines, on the other hand, have less cushion and service industrial customers with higher price elasticities of demand and, thus, may be unable to pay the higher prices for new gas demanded by gas producers who can also sell their gas to the interstate pipelines.

To estimate the shares of new gas which the various interstate and intrastate pipelines may get, we have developed a computerized mathematical model which explicitly represents these pipelines, their purchase and sales options, their regulatory constraints, and their assumed behavior in the gas market.

2. GENERAL DESCRIPTION OF MODEL

The Gas Pipeline Competition Model (GPCM) consists of six basic components:

1) a network model which identifies each pipeline's supply areas, demand regions, and pipeline interconnects;

2) a pricing model which calculates pipeline weighted average cost of gas and wholesale prices based on field prices, dedicated supplies of old gas, and transportation markups;

3) non-linear price-sensitive demand curves for each sector and region;

4) a supply model interface for getting new gas supplies available each year and an old gas supply model for dedicated old gas supplies;

5) an objective function consisting of a weighted average of producer and pipeline profits and excess demand penalties;

6) a mechanism for updating model parameters for each simulation year based on an extensive historical data base and previous year results.

Figure 1 shows a simplified model of natural gas markets. In this model, gas is purchased by pipelines (represented by circles) in various producing regions (triangles) or from other pipelines and delivered to various demand regions (squares) where it is sold to distributors, industrial customers, or other customers. Prices paid by the pipelines for various categories of gas are rolled in to get an average supply cost for each pipeline. This is known as the WACOG (weighted average cost of gas). To this value, a markup is added which accounts for the pipeline's fixed and variable costs and a fair return on its equity.

Regional sectoral demand is assumed to be price sensitive. Increased prices tend to reduce demand. Supply is considered to be inelastic in the short run. Both new and old gas prices are assumed to be no greater than the maximums allowed by NGPA until deregulation at which time they are assumed to be limited only by the market. Gas production is constrained to a maximum level for each category in each region as projected by the TENRAC Oil and Gas Supply Model.

Pipelines are assumed to own dedicated supplies (cushion gas) in regulated categories which are not available to other pipelines except indirectly through interpipeline sales.

Pipelines are assumed to compete for available new gas in order to acquire sufficient supplies to meet their customers' needs while maximizing pipeline return-on-equity i.e. profits.

The factors described above comprise the qualitative model. These basic features are given a quantitative structure through a computerized mathematical model consisting of a linked series of linear programs. Each linear program is solved for estimates of quantities and prices of gas purchased and sold by over 160 inter- and intra-state pipelines in various regions of the United States.

Projections of sales and purchases for each forecast year are used to help compute parameters which define the model's specifications for the following year. In this way, the model steps through each year of the forecast horizon.

The final result is a projection of the relative positions of the various pipelines with respect to quantities of new gas acquired in competition with others, sales to distributors and end-users, equilibrium prices when supply is sufficient to clear the markets, and curtailments when supplies are short. These results will, in general, be different for scenarios with different Federal policies regarding wellhead price ceilings and deregulation plans. The GPCM model is a tool designed for analysts to use in the comparison of such alternative policies.

3. GPCM MODEL STRUCTURE

GPCM is a multi-year model solved as a linked series of mathematical programming problems, one problem for each year. Figure 2 shows the model's program control sequence in flowchart form.

From top to bottom, the system first obtains user selections and parameters to establish a scenario to run. This includes selection of a particular set of supply assumptions and demand forecasts previously stored by the system, the

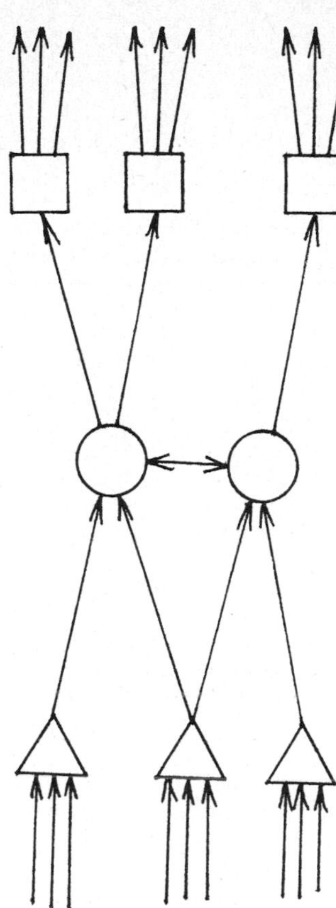

Figure 1. Network Model of Gas Markets

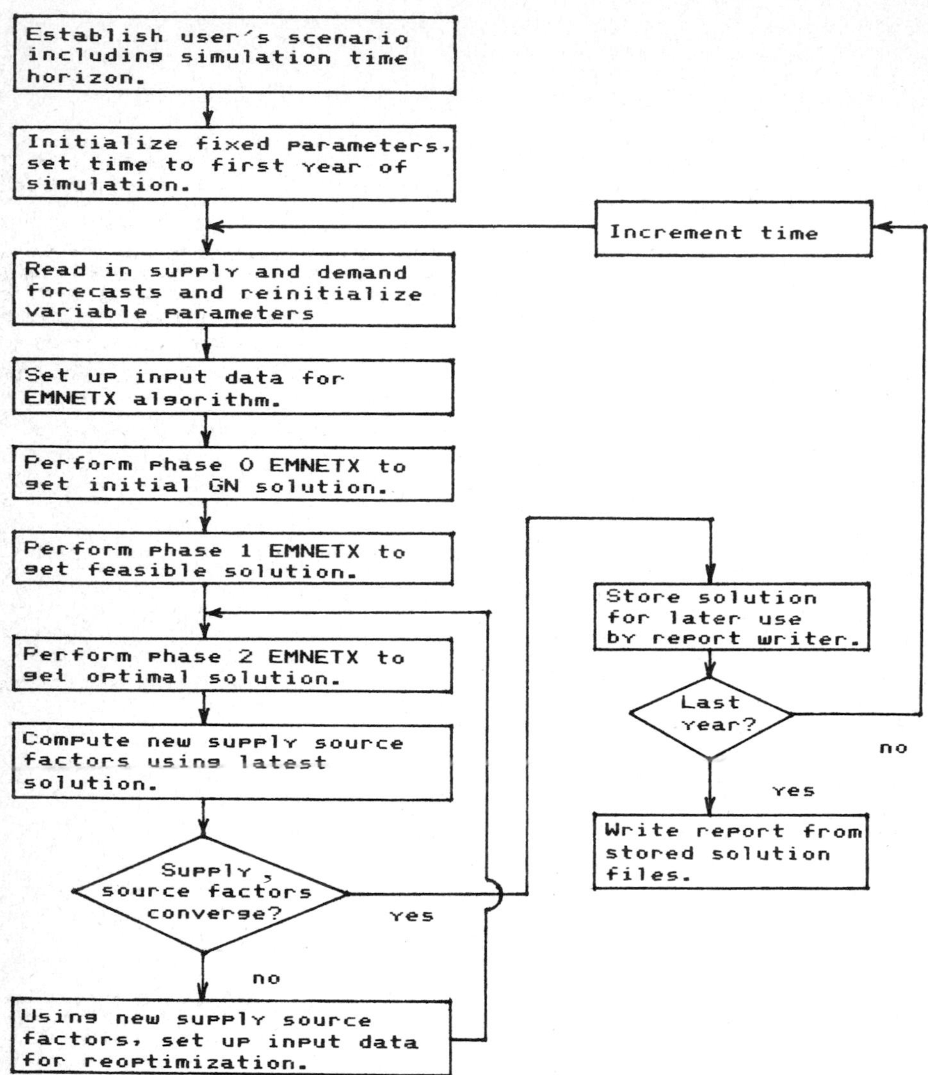

Figure 2. GPCM System Flow Chart

definition of a simulation time horizon, deregulation strategy, wellhead price ceiling structure, and so on. The computer model then uses these values in combination with the pipeline physical, financial, and transactions database to initialize its fixed parameters and set the simulation to year one.

For each consecutive simulation year, the model then carries out a sequence of operations aimed at computing forecasts of pipeline purchases of old and new gas supplies from each region, sales to pipelines and distributors, and the prices for each of these transactions.

The first step in these calculations is to retrieve previously computed supply and demand forecasts for the year and to reinitialize the model's variable parameters. These values, along with those of the fixed parameters, are then used to set up the data structure which defines the physical and financial constraints of the pipelines and their behavior under supply and demand market conditions for each year. This annual model is solved by the use of a program called EMNETX.

EMNETX first solves a "phase 0" subproblem for the values of pipeline purchases and sales ignoring the weighted average cost of gas (WACOG) equations which link wellhead prices to wholesale prices. This subproblem has a network structure whose solution can be computed very quickly by the generalized network algorithm contained in EMNETX. Next "phase 1" and "phase 2" procedures in EMNETX are used to compute supply and demand prices and transactions (purchases and sales) for the complete model with WACOG constraints. Demand prices are computed using new and old gas field prices and preliminary estimates for transaction volumes from the model database. These are called "supply source factors". If the WACOGs computed, using preliminary estimates for supply source factors, are not sufficiently close to the WACOGs computed using forecast volumes and prices from the model, then the new volumes and prices are used to calculate new estimates for supply source factors and the revised model is run through EMNETX phase 2 again (reoptimization).

This process is continued until convergence between the estimated and computed WACOGs is achieved. When this occurs, the solution is stored for later use by the GPCM report writer and to compute new estimates of the variable parameters for the next year's simulation. This continues until the final year of the forecast has been simulated.

4. THE GPCM ANNUAL MODEL - MATHEMATICAL DESCRIPTION

The following is a list of symbols and definitions used in the mathematical description of the GPCM to follow:

Subscripts;

i : pipeline company

m : demand region

n : demand sector

j : supply region

k : gas category

l : pipeline company

h : grid index

Variables;

XD_{imn} : pipeline i sales in region m to sector n

ED_{imn} : unsatisfied demand in region m, sector n served by pipeline i

XX_{il} : deliveries by pipeline i to pipeline l

XS_{ijk} : purchases by pipeline i in region j of type k gas

PD_{imn} : wholesale price of gas delivered by pipeline i to sector n in region m

PX_i : weighted average cost of gas for pipeline i

PS_{jk} : price paid by pipelines for new gas in region j of category k

Z^h_{imn} : grid variable used in demand function approximations

ES_{jk} : unsold available supply of type k gas in region j

R_{imn} : unit profit on gas sold by pipeline i in region m to sector n

$D_{imn}()$: demand function for sector n in region m served by pipeline i

SD_i : excess unmarketable supply for pipeline i

Constants;

r_i : regulated before tax return per unit of gas for pipeline i

q_{imn} : unit "cost of service" less supply cost and return for pipeline i to region m, sector n

w_n :excess demand penalty in sector n

a_{ijk} : estimated fraction of pipeline i's total supply bought from producers in region j of type k new gas

b_{ijk} : estimated fraction of pipeline i's total supply bought from producers in region j of type k old gas

c_{il} : estimated fraction of pipeline i's total supply bought from pipeline l

p^c_k : ceiling price on type k gas

p^o_{jk} : minimum price for type k gas in region j

d^h_{imn} : demand at price p^h of approximated demand function

p^h : h^{th} price in approximated demand function

e_i : overall efficiency of gas handling by pipeline i

s_{jk} : maximum supply available in region j of gas type k

g^s_{ijk} : supply of type k old gas dedicated to pipeline i in region j

g^x_{li} : supply of gas dedicated to pipeline i by pipeline l

g^d_{imn} : supply of gas dedicated by pipeline i to region m, sector n

N_j : regional competition factor

v_{li} : markup on sale from pipeline l to pipeline i

u : penalty on unmarketable pipeline supplies

The annual GPCM model serves two basic, related purposes: it forecasts the amounts of new gas which pipelines are able to win from producers in competition with other pipelines and it computes a set of transaction quantities and prices which either clear the market for gas or allocate gas, according to NGPA guidelines when markets cannot be cleared and excess demand occurs. These two functions are highly interrelated since the demand curves facing a pipeline and its desire to maximize its profits will determine the amount of new gas it will want to acquire from producers at the going field-market price. This price will be determined by overall demand conditions in the country during the forecast year, by the amount of available new supplies, and by wellhead price ceilings imposed by NGPA or other user scenarios.

The exact form of this model is highly non-linear and cannot be efficiently solved using sophisticated network oriented linear programming codes alone. By using linear approximations to this problem, we can make use of these powerful methods as will be discussed below.

The exact non-linear mathematical program describing the GPCM annual model is given as follows:

maximize:
$$\sum_{imn} R_{imn}XD_{imn} + \sum_{ijk} Nj(PS_{jk} - p^o_{jk})(XS_{ijk} - g^s_{ijk}) - u\Sigma_i SD_i - \sum_{imn} w_n ED_{imn} \qquad (1a)$$

subject to:
$$PD_{imn} = PX_i + q_{imn} + R_{imn} \qquad (1b)$$

$$(\sum_{jk} XS_{ijk} + \sum_{l} XX_{li})PX_i = \sum_{jk} ((XS_{ijk} - g^s_{ijk})PS_{jk} + g^s_{ijk}p^s_{ijk}) + \sum_{l} XX_{li} \; (PX_l + v_{li}) \qquad (1c)$$

$$XD_{imn} + ED_{imn} = D_{imn}\;(PD_{imn}) \qquad (1d)$$

$$\sum_{i} XS_{ijk} + ES_{jk} = s_{jk} \qquad (1e)$$

$$e_i(\sum_{jk} XS_{ijk} + \sum_{l} XX_{li}) = \sum_{mn} XD_{imn} + \sum_{l} XX_{il} + SD_i \qquad (1f)$$

$$R_{imn} = r_i \text{ (regulated sales only)} \qquad (1g)$$

$$PS_{jk} \le P^c_k \qquad (1h)$$

$$PS_{jk} \ge p^o_{jk} \qquad (1i)$$

$$XS_{ijk} \geq g^s_{ijk} \tag{1j}$$

$$XX_{li} \geq g^x_{li} \tag{1k}$$

$$XD_{imn} \geq g^d_{imn} \tag{1l}$$

All variables except R_{imn} are non-negative.

4.1 Objective Function (1a)

This model contains a non-linear objective function which is really the sum of four objectives with different weights. The first objective is to maximize pipeline profits. This term is the sum over all pipeline sales to distributors and direct customers of quantity times unit profit. Note that R_{imn} is a variable for unregulated sales to mainline industrial customers, but constant for regulated sales to distributors.

The second objective is producer profits, measured as the difference between sales price and cost of gas at the well head times quantity sold, summed over all pipelines, regions, and categories of gas. This term is weighted with a competition factor related to how many companies buy gas in the region. The more the competition for supplies, the higher the factor and the greater the push for higher wellhead prices.

The third objective is to eliminate unmarketable supplies by having pipelines sell to other pipelines or refuse to buy high priced gas which will not be marketable to their distributor or mainline customer.

The final objective is to minimize curtailments, in particular to high priority customers. Weights are assigned to each sector and region in order to assure allocation of gas in order of priority class in times of shortage.

Even though this formulation is a single objective mathematical program, selection of appropriate values for u and w_n will result in a representation equivalent in essence to a multiple objective "goal programming" model. The user can select the values of these weights to simulate a variety of different conditions or to "tune" the model to historical conditions.

4.2 Constraints (1b-1l)

The constraint set for this model consists of a number of linear and non-linear expressions. Some of these non-linear constraints can be shown to be convex within the region of interest, i.e. for non-negative values of all variables (except R_{imn}), while others are non-convex (e.g. the demand functions).

Equation (1b) defines the wholesale price variables PD_{imn}. These prices are equal to the pipeline's weighted average cost of gas (WACOG) plus cost of transportation and handling and profit per unit sold. For regulated sales the unit profits are given by (1g) whereas those for unregulated sales are determined by supply and demand conditions facing the pipeline.

WACOGs are computed using non-linear equations (1c). On the left side of the equations, the WACOGs (PX_i) are multiplied by total gas purchases by pipeline i from all sources. This represents the total gas available to pipeline i for sale to others. The right side represents total cost of all gas bought by pipeline i. The three rhs terms are: cost of new contrast gas from producers, cost of old contract gas from producers, and cost of all gas from other pipelines. The WACOG is then the rhs divided by the lhs multiplier of PX_i.

Demand for gas is represented in equation (1d). Demand as a function of price is equal to deliveries plus excess demand. Note that the ED_{imn} are similar to slack variables except that they have non-zero coefficients in the objective function. These variables are required in order to allow for reallocation of gas in periods of shortage.

Equation (1e) defines the supply equations for each region and gas category. These say that the sum of quantities of gas delivered to all pipelines must not be greater than total supply (production capacity) in each region for each gas type. ES_{jk} measures the amount of gas taken and is a slack variable with no cost in the objective function.

Equation (1f) is the material balance constraint for each pipeline. The amount of gas received times the pipeline efficiency of gas handling (e_i) is on the lhs. This must equal the amount sold to distributors, pipelines, and others, plus the unmarketable gas of pipeline i on the rhs of the equation.

Wellhead price ceilings are represented by constraints (1h). These can be from NGPA or from other proposals as desired by the model's user. Lower limits on wellhead prices represent the least price which producers will accept for their gas (equation 1g).

Dedicated contracts are represented in (1j) - (1l). These are dedicated volumes from producers to pipelines, pipelines to pipelines, and pipelines to wholesale customers, respectively. Take-or-pay clauses are assumed to be binding on the pipelines. The SD_i variables measure quantities of gas which pipelines are forced to buy which they can't market, and thus situations where they might be tempted to break their take-or-pay contracts.

5. LINEARIZATION OF THE GPCM ANNUAL MODEL

In order to solve this model efficiently, the non-linearities in both the objective function and constraints must be eliminated. Two different approaches are necessary: the WACOG and objective function non-linearities are handled by linearizing and relinearizing until convergence is achieved whereas the demand functions are handled by piecewise linearization and separable programming.

5.1 Linearization of WACOG Constraints

There are several ways to go about linear approximations to the WACOG constraints. One which has worked well in practice is to use estimates of the variables XS and XX to convert the constraints into linear equations relating WACOG's (PX_i) to wellhead prices (PS_{jk}). A cyclical or iterative procedure is used to adjust the estimates of XS and XX to forecast model solutions for XS and XX until successive solutions for the PX_i are within the convergence tolerance preset in the program (1%).

Mathematically, we define the parameters:

$$a_{ijk} = (XS^o_{ijk} - g^s_{ijk})/(\sum_i XS^o_{ijk} + \sum_i XX^o_{li}) \qquad (2a)$$

$$b_{ijk} = g^s_{ijk} /(\sum_i XS^o_{ijk} + \sum_i XX^o_{li}) \qquad (2b)$$

$$c_{il} = XX^s_{li} / (\sum_i XS^o_{ijk} + \sum_i XX^o_{li}) \tag{2c}$$

where the superscript o refers to estimates from historical data or previous cycles (iterations) of the model. Dividing through by the total supply expression on the lhs of (1c) and using (2a) - (2c), the linearized WACOG equations become:

$$PX_i = \sum_{jk} (a_{ijk} PS_{jk} + b_{ijk} P^s_{ijk}) + \sum_l c_{il} (PX_l + v_{li}) \tag{3}$$

5.2 Objective Function Linearization

The two quadratic terms in the objective function are linearized as follows. The $R_{imn} XD_{imn}$ is reexpressed in a simple Taylor's series expansion to first-order. This is written as:

$$R_{imn} XD_{imn} = R^o_{imn} XD^o_{imn} + (R_{imn} - R^o_{imn}) XD^o_{imn} + (XD_{imn} - XD^o_{imn}) R^o_{imn} + \dots$$

$$= R^o_{imn} XD_{imn} + XD^o_{imn} R_{imn} + \text{constant terms} + \text{2nd order terms} \tag{4}$$

Therefore, we can replace the $R_{imn} XD_{imn}$ term in the objective function with this linear approximation. As we cycle through the relinearization and reoptimization procedure discussed above for the WACOG constraints, we also adjust the values of R^o_{imn} and XD^o_{imn}. When the PX_i have converged, it will be found that R_{imn} and XD_{imn} will also have converged, since demand is driven by the PX_i.

The second quadratic terms in the objective function are handled somewhat differently. First, the supply equation (1e) is used to convert the terms as follows:

$$\sum_{ijk} (PS_{jk} - p^o_{jk})(XS_{ijk} - g^s_{ijk}) = \sum_{jk} (PS_{jk} - p^o_{jk}) \sum_i (XS_{ijk} - g^s_{ijk}) \tag{5a}$$

$$= \sum_{jk} (PS_{jk} - g^o_{jk})(s_{jk} - \sum_i g^s_{ijk} - ES_{jk}) \tag{5b}$$

$$= \sum_{jk} (s_{jk} - \sum_i g^s_{ijk}) PS_{jk} - \sum_{jk} (PS_{jk} - p^o_{jk}) ES_{jk}$$

$$+ \text{constant terms} \tag{5c}$$

This is approximated as in the previous case by using an estimate for PS_{jk} in the second term, i.e.:

$$\sum_{ijk} (PS_{jk} - p^o_{jk})(XS_{ijk} - g^s_{ijk}) = \sum_{jk} (s_{jk} - \sum_i g^s_{ijk}) PS_{jk} - \sum_{jk} (PS^o_{jk} - p^o_{jk}) ES_{jk} \tag{5d}$$

5.3 Demand Function Approximations

The demand functions used in this model are assumed to be continuously non-increasing as shown in Figure 3.

Such functions can be approximated by piecewise linear (polygonal) functions as shown in Figure 4.

This new function can be explicitly described as:

$$D_{imn}(PD_{imn}) = d^o_{imn} + \sum_{h=1}^{H} \Delta d^h_{imn} Z^h_{imn} \tag{5}$$

where

$$PD_{imn} = \sum_{h=1}^{H} \Delta p^h_{imn} Z^h_{imn} + p^o \tag{6}$$

and where

$$D_{imn} \leq Z^h_{imn} \leq 1 \tag{7}$$

and, finally, where the values of Z^h_{imn} are restricted so that if any Z^h_{imn} is greater than zero then all Z with smaller h are equal to one and if any Z_{imn} is less than one, all Z with greater h are equal to zero. This is known as a sequential basis entry criterion. In (5) - (7), H is the number of grid points in the polygonal approximation. In the model, H is five. In the model also, p^o is equal to \$1.00/mcf and all the Δp^h_{imn} are equal to \$1.25. This gives an effective range of \$1.00 - \$7.25 for average wholesale prices during the 1981 to 1990 period, expressed in constant 1980 dollars.

5.4 Summary of Linearized Model

The mathematical form of the linearized model is:

maximize:

$$\sum_{imn} R^o_{imn} XD_{imn} + \sum_{imn} XD^o_{imn} R_{imn} + \sum_{jk} N_j (s_{jk} - \sum_i g^s_{ijk}) PS_{jk} -$$

$$\sum_{jk} N_j (PS^o_{jk} - P^o_{jk}) ES_{jk} - u \sum_i SD_i - \sum_{imn} w_n ED_{imn} \tag{8a}$$

subject to:

$$DP_{imn} \quad : \sum_{h=1}^{H} \Delta p^h_{imn} Z^h_{imn} - PX_i - R_{imn} = p^o_{imn} + q_{imn} \tag{8b}$$

$$CG_i \quad : PX_i - \sum_{jk} a_{ijk} PS_{jk} - \sum_l c_{il} PX_l = \sum_{jk} b_{ijk} p^s_{ijk} + \sum_l c_{il} v_{li} \tag{8c}$$

$$DF_{imn} \quad : XD_{imn} + ED_{imn} - \sum_{h=1}^{H} \Delta d^h_{imn} Z^h_{imn} = d^o_{imn} \tag{8d}$$

$$SG_{jk} \quad : \sum_i XS_{ijk} + ES_{jk} = s_{jk} \tag{8e}$$

$$MB_i \quad : e_i(\sum_{jk} XS_{ijk} + \sum_l XX_{li}) - \sum_{mn} XD_{imn} - \sum_l XX_{il} - SD_i = o \tag{8f}$$

$$R_{imn} = r_i \quad \text{(regulated sales only)} \tag{8g}$$

$$PS_{jk} \leq p^c_{jk} \tag{8h}$$

$$PS_{jk} \geq p^o_{jk} \tag{8i}$$

$$XS_{ijk} \geq g^s_{ijk} \tag{8j}$$

$$XX_{li} \geq g^x_{li} \tag{8k}$$

$$XD_{imn} \geq g^d_{imn} \tag{8l}$$

$$Z^h_{imn} \leq 1 \tag{8m}$$

All variables except R_{imn} are non-negative and the sequential basis entry criterion is applied to each set of Z's. The codes to the left of each constraint are the names associated with that row in the constraint matrix.

This model is solved as follows:

1) Begin by establishing estimated values for a_{ijk}, b_{ijk}, and c_{li}; R^o_{imn}, XD^o_{imn}, and PS^o_{jk}.

2) Solve the linear model.

3) Recompute a_{ijk}, b_{ijk}, and c_{li} using (2a) - (2c) and values for XS_{ijk} and XX_{li} from the solution to the linear model.

4) Substitute these parameters in the linear model and use solution values to estimate new R^o_{imn}, XD^o_{imn}, and PS^o_{jk} as well.

5) Resolve the linear system.

6) Compare values of PX_i from the last two cycles of the linear model. If they differ by less than 1% for all i, STOP. Otherwise, go to step 3.

In practice, it has been found that convergence of this procedure is usually obtained in 3 to 6 cycles (iterations). Performance of the procedure is enhanced by using an advanced starting basis to begin each reoptimization, namely the final basis of the previous cycle. Special procedures have been developed to keep this basis feasible with the new problem even when constraint coefficients and right hand sides have been changed. Specifically, two sets of PX_i and PS_{jk} variables are used along with two sets of coefficients a_{ijk}, b_{ijk}, and c_{li}. The second set are called companion variables and coefficients. At each reoptimization, only the companion coefficients are changed, i.e., the set which was not changed in the previous cycle. At each cycle, the "old" variables are given large negative values in the objective function (for maximization) so that they are driven out of the basis to their lower bounds (which are set to zero for this cycle) and the "new" variables (their companions) are allowed to enter the basis with their new coefficients. This procedure makes unnecessary the time-consuming task of having to achieve feasibility in the new cycle before driving toward optimality. Similarly, rather than actually changing the right hand side coefficients of the CG_i constraints, a new variable is added to the problem with coefficients equal to the negative of the right hand side changes, upper bound of unity, and large positive cost so that it will be naturally driven to its upper bound in the reoptimization. This has the same effect as changing the right hand side, but without the pain of having to get back to feasibility first.

6. SIZE OF THE MODEL

The model currently utilized for GPCM has 537 equations and 3160 variables. Because much of the model is a network, it is logical to try to partition the problem into that which has a generalized network structure and that which does not. In doing so, it is easy to show that only the CG_i constraints and the PX_i and PS_{ik} variables do not have the network form. Or, to put it another way, if these constraints and variables are set aside, the remainder of the problem does have the form of a generalized network, namely, all remaining variables appear in at most two of the remaining equations.

Thus the model can be partitioned into a generalized network part containing 510 equations and 2696 variables and a non-network component consisting of 27 side constraints and 464 side variables. Because this problem has such a large generalized network component, greater speed of solution can be obtained by using a special purpose linear programming code which takes advantage of the network structure. Such a code has been developed by Richard McBride of the University of Southern California. This code, called EMNET for embedded network code, has been enhanced to include a separable programming capability for the linearized demand functions and a reoptimization capability for the procedure described in the last section (for specifics regarding this code see [2]).

7. GPCM MULTI-YEAR MODEL PARAMETER EVOLUTION

Certain parameters in the GPCM are assumed to be constant from year to year whereas others change due to the results from previous years. The primary fixed parameters are pipeline efficiencies (e_i), excess demand penalties (w_n), and the unmarketable supply penalty (u).

Pipeline efficiencies are estimated prior to the running of GPCM based on 1981 gas account statistics of the pipelines. The equation is:

$$e_i = 1 - (L_i + FU_i)/ Q_i \tag{9}$$

where L_i is the amount of gas lost in transmission, distribution, and storage; FU_i is the amount of fuel used in compressor stations; and Q_i is total gas purchased in the base year by the pipeline.

Excess demand and unmarketable supply penalties are currently hardwired in the program. They are set to values such that the higher the priority for a particular demand sector, the higher the penalty for excess demand in that sector. The unmarketable supply penalty is set equal to the highest excess demand penalty.

Variable parameters in the model include price markups, supply source factors, available supplies (maximum production capacity), pipeline cushions of dedicated gas, and demand function coefficients.

7.1 Price Markups

Markups on wholesale sales can be divided into two components: the cost component and the profit or return on capital. In the case of unregulated sales, the return on capital is a function of the existing supply and demand conditions. For regulated sales, it is determined as a reasonable return on the pipeline's capital, or rate base.

Initial year (1981) values for these parameters are obtained by:

$$q_0 = (C_0 + A_0 + I_0 + N_0 + D_0)/\ Q_0 \quad (10)$$

$$r_0 = (kR_0\ /(1-T))/\ Q_0 \quad (11)$$

where pipeline, region, and sector subscripts have been dropped for simplification of presentation and where:

q_0 = unit cost of transporting gas

r_0 = unit profit for transporting gas

C_0 = total transportation cost

A_0 = administrative cost

I_0 = interest expense

N_0 = taxes other than income taxes

D_0 = depreciation

Q_0 = annual sales volume

k = equity rate of return

R_0 = rate base

T = effective income tax rate

Values for q and r in subsequent years are computed based on functional relationships among these financial variables and assumptions about growth rates in capital plant. Such relationships have been estimated by Guldmann for the U.S. Department of Energy [1]. They are as follows:

$$C_t = 0.00316787\ Q_t^{0.949361} M_t^{0.4435929} \quad (12)$$

$$A_t = 653402 + 0.05327069\ Q_t \quad (13)$$

In addition, we assume that interest, non-income taxes, and depreciation increase proportionally to rate base growth as follows:

$$I_t = (1+y)^t I_0 \quad (14)$$

$$N_t = (1+y)^t N_0 \quad (15)$$

$$D_t = (1+y)^t D_0 \quad (16)$$

$$R_t = (1+y)^t R_0 \quad (17)$$

In the above, t refers to year t after the base year (1981), M to total pipeline mileage, and y to annual growth rate in pipeline rate base. M and y are computed separately for each pipeline based on historical statistics and then remain fixed throughout the simulation. A ceiling of 10.4% per annum growth is allowed for all pipelines. This is the average growth for the past three years.

Using these relationships we can compute a formula for incremental change in q and r, respectively. These are:

$$\Delta q_t = \frac{y(I_{t-1} + N_{t-1} + D_{t-1})}{Q_{t-1}} - \frac{(0.050639\ C_t + 653402 + I_t + N_t + D_t)\Delta Q_t}{Q_{t-1}} \qquad (18)$$

$$\Delta r_t = \frac{kR_{t-1}/(1-T)}{Q_{t-1}} \quad (y-(1-y)\frac{\Delta Q_t}{Q_{t-1}}) \qquad (19)$$

7.2 Supply Source Factors

These have been discussed earlier in the paper. For the first cycle of each year, the final values of XS_{ijk} and XX_{il} from the previous year are used to compute these factors. For the first year (1981) historical values for these variables are used.

7.3 Regional Gas Production Capacities

These values for s_{jk} are calculated using the TENRAC Oil and Gas Supply Model. Future values for these numbers depend on feedback from GPCM to the OGSM in the form of actual production taken or not (excess supplies) and field prices paid for new gas supplies. These prices will affect price expectations in the OGSM and thus the trajectory of future investment in oil and gas exploration and, ultimately, future gas production.

7.4 Cushions of Dedicated Gas

Initial year values for the g^s_{ijk} and g^x_{il} parameters are computed based on the deliverability of gas from 1981-1999 as given in DOE's <u>Gas Supplies of Interstate Pipelines</u>. Each pipeline's deliverability profile is adjusted to actual 1981 field and pipeline purchases and then apportioned to regions according to 1979 Form 2 reports of the pipelines and to gas categories according to DOE estimates of old gas production by category in the Two Market Study [3]. Values for intrastate companies are not available from primary sources, but are estimates based on the average deliverability profile of the interstate pipelines.

As the model computes the results of competition for new gas reserves, the amounts dedicated to each pipeline change from year to year. Additional reserves and future production from those reserves are allocated based on the assumption that the amounts of new production won by each pipeline in a given year reflect the same percentages of new reserves won by those pipelines.

If we let f^{t-z}_{jk} represent an index of production for year t of gas first produced in year z in region j of type k such that $f^0_{jk} = 1$ and f^n_{jk} is the fraction of first year production available in year n, then we can compute the total production cushion available to pipeline i in year t as:

$$g^{s,t}_{ijk} = g^{s,0}_{ijk} + \sum_{z=1}^{t-1} f^{t-z}_{jk} \quad XS^z_{ijk} \qquad (20)$$

where $g^{s,0}_{ijk}$ is the initial dedicated production described earlier. In GPCM, the f^t_{jk} factors are computed using Maximum Efficient Recovery (MER) curves from the TENRAC Oil and Gas Supply Model (OGSM).

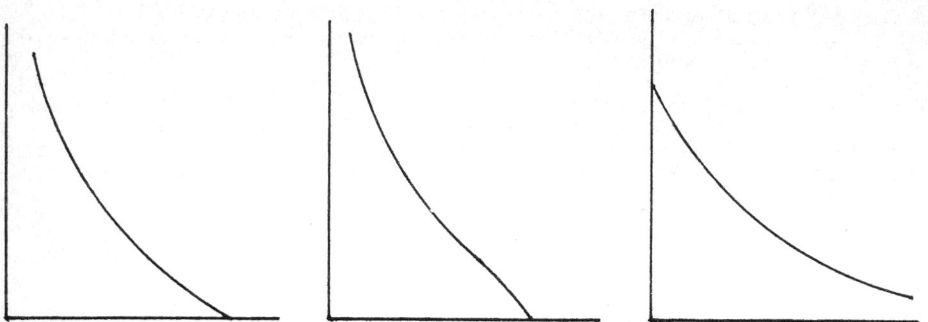

Figure 3. Acceptable Forms for the Demand Function

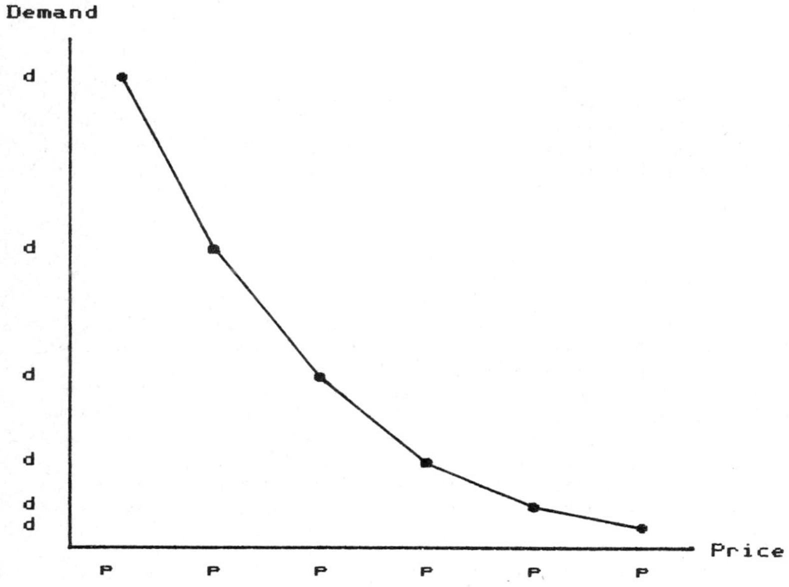

Figure 4. Polygonal Approximation to Convex Demand Function

considered to be a rejection of the entire block of reserves which that production represents. In OGSM this reserves block becomes available for sale in the next year of simulation.

The average price of dedicated reserves produced in the forecast is computed in a similar fashion. In GPCM we assume there are contract escalation clauses which cause the price of old gas to rise over time. The rate of this increase is a user input called "alpha". The equation for average price is given by:

$$P^{s,t}_{ijk} = (1+alpha)^t \, P^{s,0}_{ijk} \, g^{s,0}_{ijk} / g^{s,t}_{ijk} + \sum_{z=1}^{t-1} (1+alpha)^{t-z} \, PS^z_{jk} \, f^{t-z}_{jk} \, XS^z_{ijk} / g^{s,t}_{ijk} \qquad (21)$$

In (21) the individual price terms, when multiplied by the price escalation factor, are not allowed to go higher than the ceiling prices p^c_{jk}. These ceiling prices are set by NGPA or by the user at the beginning of each simulation.

7.5 Demand Functions

In the GPCM system there is a demand function generator which the user employs to establish alternative demand forecasts. This generator uses elasticities of demand within each price interval P^h described previously along with the 1981 volumes and prices delivered to distributors and mainline customers to generate demand curves for the base year. Future demand curves are generated using a user-supplied expected annual growth rate in demand which is applied to the entire base year demand function. In this way, each pipeline is faced with a demand curve normalized to its own market in the base year and alternative future demand possibilities are available to the model's users at TENRAC.

8. MODEL PERFORMANCE

Preliminary results from the model as programmed in FORTRAN IV and run on the Texas A & M Amdahl V6 computer show that the system can be solved efficiently and within reasonable bounds on execution time and cost. As mentioned above, each year's forecast can usually be completed within three to six cycles (reoptimizations). This usually takes between 3,000 and 4,000 pivots of the EMNETX program. Average execution time per year of simulation appears to be between 60 and 90 cpu seconds. This includes the OGSM supply forecast, setting up the annual problem, solving it, readjusting parameters for reoptimization, and writing the solution out to files for later use by the GPCM report writer. Overnight rates at Texas A & M are such that a 10 year simulation costs between $90 and $135.

Results from simulation of NGPA and alternative deregulation scenarios have been published in another paper recently prepared by TENRAC [4].

REFERENCES

[1] Guldmann, Jean-Michael, "Pipeline Modelling - Task 2", Letter Report to National Bureau of Standards and U.S. Department of Energy.

[2] McBride, Richard D., "Solving Embedded Generalized Network Problems", University of Southern California, Graduate School of Business, July 1982.

[3] U.S. Department of Energy, "Two Market Analysis of Natural Gas Decontrol, Appendix A", November 1981.

[4] Brooks, Robert E., Hery, William, Kieschnick, Robert, "An Examination of Potential Natural Gas Pipeline Bidding Behavior," TENRAC, July, 1983.

ADDITIONAL READING

1. Brooks, Robert E., "System Documentation Report: GASNET2 Natural Gas Pipeline Model, Version 2", prepared for Texas Energy and Natural Resources Advisory Council, August 1982.

2. MathTech, Inc., "System Documentation Report: Crude Oil and Natural Gas Supply", prepared for Texas Energy and Natural Resources Advisory Council, August 1982.

Analytic Techniques for Energy Planning
B. Lev, F.H. Murphy, J.A. Bloom & A.S. Gleit (Editors)
© Elsevier Science Publishers B.V. (North-Holland), 1984

AN INVESTMENT MODEL FOR THE U.S. GULF COAST REFINING/PETROCHEMICAL COMPLEX FOR POLICY ANALYSIS

Vicky C. Langston
7700 Old Springhouse Road
McLean, Virginia 22102

This paper presents a multi-period, multi-region, multi-product, multi-process linear programming model developed to analyze investment decisions under conditions which change the relative cost of delivered products such as imposition of an import fee on U.S. refineries, increased U.S. domestic supply or increased product demand in the U.S.

1. INTRODUCTION

Several factors suggest that government energy policies, such as import fees, must be more carefully evaluated in terms of their impact on refining costs in addition to macroeconomic supply and demand responses. They include:

- regional concentration of industry;
- vertical integration and economic dependency of companies;
- integration with an uncertain world market;
- technical constraints on operations; and
- depressed markets.

A multi-period, multi-region, multi-product, multi-process linear programming model is developed to analyze investment decisions under conditions which alter the relative cost of delivering refined products to markets. Examples of these conditions are imposition of an import fee on U.S. refineries, increased U.S. domestic crude supply, or increased product demands in the U.S.

The discussion is divided into four sections: the model, base case forecasts, the results, and concluding remarks.

2. THE MODEL

The model incorporates detailed technical information about production processes and products in order to predict efficient utilization among refining centers over time for given regional crude availability, product demands, and refining costs. The model combines refineries and primary petrochemical plants into three regional centers -- the U.S. Gulf Coast, the Eastern U.S., and Europe including the Caribbean Islands. These centers compete for investment dollars and markets in the Eastern U.S., the Southwest U.S., and Europe by minimizing the total discounted costs of delivered products.

Key features of the model are that it identifies:

- crude quality;
- specific process units which have operating flexibility;

. expansion, replacement, retirement, and retrofit investments;

. activities in three regional refining centers;

. product demands in three regional markets;

. three time periods representing the next 15 years.

Each refinery is a unique grouping of processing units which receive crude or intermediate products and produce the marketed products we know as gasolines, home heating oils, jet fuels, residual fuels, engine oils, etc. A petrochemical plant receives liquids extracted from natural gas (LPG) or intermediate refined products and produces basic petrochemicals which are further processed into products, such as plastics, fabrics, rubber, and detergents.

The model identifies 12 productive units and 21 distinct processes (linear activities) which utilize the plant and equipment. A flow diagram of a refining center is presented in Figure 1.

One of the key features of the model is the distinction in crude quality which results in seven distinct crudes. The crudes are grouped into three generic classifications to assign the appropriate distillation unit. Each crude, however, produces a slightly different product slate, which will affect its relative value to the refineries. In general, the U.S. crudes are lighter than their foreign counterpart; that is, they produce relatively more straight-run naphtha and gas oil.

The ethylene plant activities are developed similarly. The hydrotreating and additive activities represent different feedstocks processed in a unit which could not be distinguished at the level of aggregation. The catalytic reforming and cracking activities provide operating variability in a unit with one feedstock. These activities allow the refinery a gasoline-middle distillate trade-off with existing equipment.

The objective of the mathematical model is to minimize total discounted costs over all regions and time periods subject to:

. supply restrictions;

. material balances;

. technical input-output relationships;

. product specifications;

. product demand requirements;

. relative costs.

The supply restrictions are given in Equations 1-4. Equation 1 restricts crude purchases to the forecasted available supply. Equation 2 is an import quota on U.S. refiners assumed to be 8.0 million b/d. Equations 3 and 4 identify available LPG supplies which can be purchased by the U.S. and European refineries separately.

Equations 5-7 are the material balance equations which are distinguished by three product classifications: raw materials, intermediate products, and final products. Gasoline, middle distillate fuels, and products are produced by blending selected intermediate products.

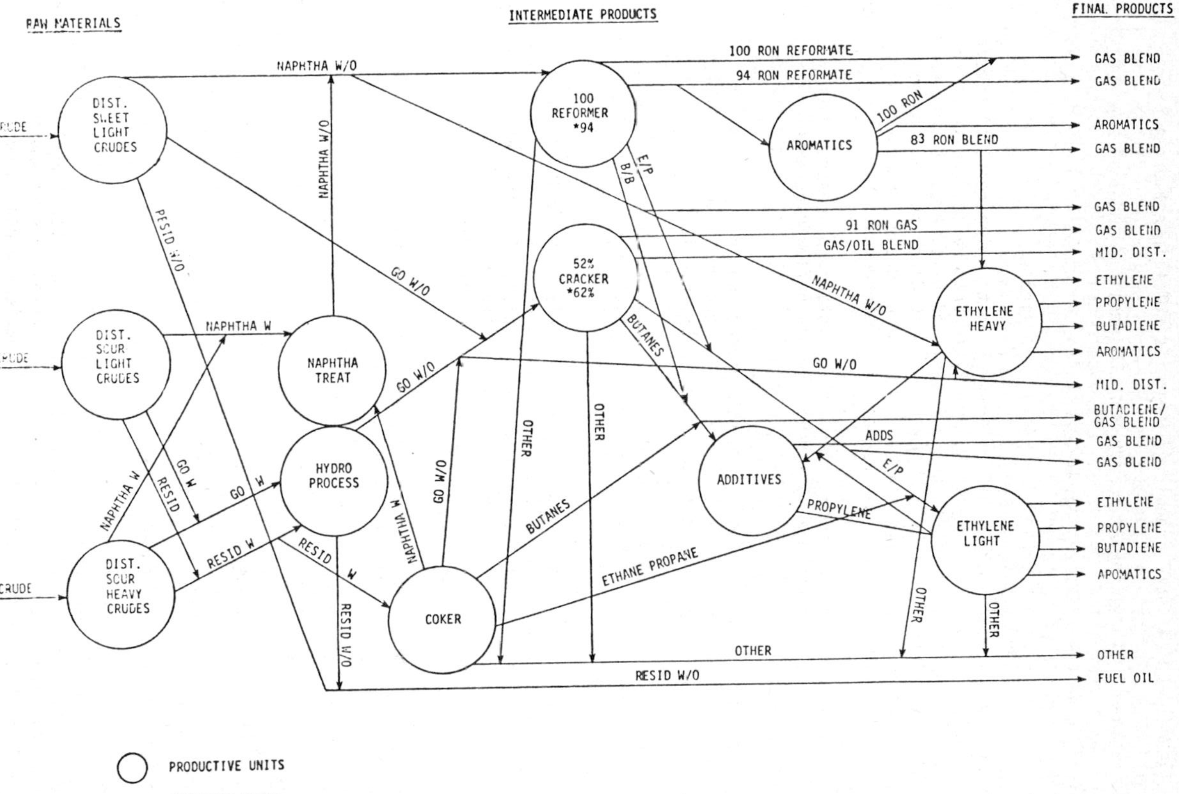

Figure 1. Flow Diagram of a Refining Center

Gasoline is the only marketed product with explicit quality specifications. A minimum octane requirement and maximum Reid vapor pressure requirement are specified in Equations 8 and 9. The octane requirement determines the efficiency of gasoline as a combustible fuel, and Reid vapor pressure (RVP) controls the volatility of gasoline. Gasoline is assumed to be unleaded with at least a 91 RON and RVP no greater than 17.8

Equation 10 accounts for capacity accumulation. The utilization of a unit can be no greater than existing capacity plus net investment (new construction minus retired capacity). The B matrix assigns processes to productive units. Equation 11 restricts the retrofitting of existing sweet, light distillation; sour, light distillation; and light feed ethylene capacity to capacity which would not retire during the forecast period. This, in fact, is equipment less than 10 years old with a retirement factor of 1/25 per year.

The refineries are required to supply minimum regional market demands in Equations 12-13. High transportation costs, however, may make shipping prohibitive under ordinary conditions. There are no shipments among the refining centers. Therefore, intermediate products, such as naphtha, cannot be produced at one center and further processed at another center.

The costs to the refineries are identified in Equations 14-18. There are four categories of costs: crude and LPG purchases (which are refiners' acquisition costs), operating costs, product shipping costs, and capital costs. Capital costs are annualized using a capital recovery factor σ which spreads the cost of construction over the economic life of the equipment which is assumed to be 20 years. Costs are discounted over time using δ_t. The interest rate ρ is assumed to be 15%.

3. KEY FORECASTS

Key forecasts in the base case are crude supplies, product demands, cost differentials, and the retirement schedule for capacity. Each of these will be discussed briefly.

3.1 Crude Supplies

Forecasted supplies for each of the seven crudes in the model indicate that total potential supply is relatively constant over the next 15 years. However, in both the U.S. and the world, potential heavy crude supplies will be growing while potential sweet light supplies will be declining. Potential world heavy crude supplies increase 55%. Although U.S. heavy crude potential increases, total U.S. supplies, including lighter crude oil, are forecast to decline by 1.4 million b/d by the mid-1990s.

A $3.00-$4.00/barrel price differential between African sweet crude and World Heav crude is forecasted; however, the price differential between Mid-east sour light crude and World Heavy crude is only $1.00/barrel. U.S. crudes are priced slightly below comparable foreign crudes. The FOB price of crude is forecasted to increase between 7-8% per year in the first period, 7.5-8.0% per year in the second period, and about 9% per year in the third period. Underlying annual inflation rates are assumed to be 7%, 8%, and 8%, respectively. The resulting nominal refiners' acquisition costs, which include transportation charges, are $40-$43/barrel in the first period, $59-$62/barrel in the second period, and $90-$95/barrel in the third period.

3.2 Product Demands

Petrochemical are forecasted to be the dominant growth market in all markets. Demand for butanes/butadiene, propylene, and aromatics increases over 60% between 1980 and 1995; ethylene demand increases 50%-60%.

In the eastern U.S. market, demand for all refined products will be down. Gasoline demand will have the most precipitous decline, 1.95 million b/d, which is roughly one-half of 1980 consumption. Refined products demand in the smaller southwest U.S. market is not expected to decline as significantly. In Europe, gasoline demand is forecasted to increase about 25% (677 mb/d). Fuels demand, on the other hand, is forecasted to decline almost 40% below 1980 consumption (1.42 million b/d).

In Europe the refined product barrel will be getting lighter; in the U.S. the product barrel will be getting heavier, as illustrated in product demand forecasts in Figure 2.

3.3 Cost Differentials

It is forecasted that Europe will be the cheapest location for construction in all time periods. There is about a 1% cost differential between the Gulf Coast and Europe over the forecast horizon. In the first time period, 1983-1987, the cost differential between the Eastern U.S. and Europe is about 16%; this gap closes to 6% in the subsequent periods.

Construction costs in the Gulf Coast are forecast to increase 8-10% annually (1-2% in real dollars). This means, for example, that a coker, one of the most expensive units ($3,600/barrel in 1980), would cost $5,290/barrel in 1983-1987, $8,519/barrel in 1988-1992, and $13,720/barrel in 1993-1997.

Fuel cost is one of the largest components of operating cost. The 1980 fuel cost was estimated to be $3.00/mmBTU in the Gulf Coast, $3.76/mmBTU in the Eastern U.S., and $4.55/MMBTU in Europe. Fuel cost in the Gulf is expected to rise rapidly causing operating costs to rise.

In the first period, the operating cost for most units in the Gulf Coast is about 12% below the cost in Europe. Only the most energy-intensive processes, low severity catalytic cracking and additives processing had higher operating costs in the Gulf Coast. The Gulf Coast operating costs are 10% and 24% higher than Europe's costs in the second and third periods, respectively. Costs in the Eastern U.S. are between Gulf Coast and European costs.

3.4 Equipment Retirement

The current retirement rule in the model retires the 1980 capacity of each unit at 1/25 per year. For Europe, this is about three large refineries (769 mb/d of distillation capacity). In the Gulf Coast and Eastern U.S., one large refinery each is retired (273 mb/d and 245 mb/d of distillation capacity). Europe and the Gulf Coast annually lose about 1.5 ethylene plants (1.5 billion lbs/year).

4. RESULTS

The principal implications of the study for the next 15 years for the refining industry are:

- selective withdrawal of refining capacity resulting in the likely exit of firms from the market;

- a decrease in the relative share of Mid-east crude in the world market at current price differentials;

- a decrease in the price of gasoline relative to other refined products, resulting in price instability until a new equilibrium is reached; and

- a substantial negative impact on U.S. refining, especially petrochemical production if the U.S. imposes an import fee.

These will be further discussed.

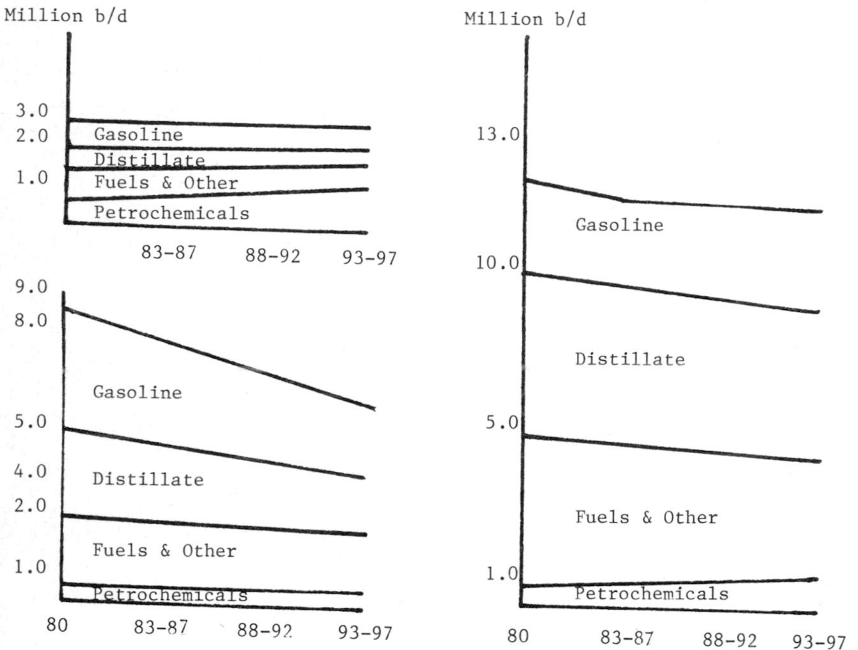

Regional Product Demand Projections

Figure 2

4.1 Capacity and Industry Structure

The next 15 years will be a period of selective withdrawal of refining capacity in the U.S. and Europe, regardless of any threat from Mid-east, Mexican or Canadian exports. Figure 3 shows crude throughputs in the U.S. under the two scenarios. In both cases, production is substantially below the 1980 nameplate distillation capacity which was in excess of 6.0 million b/d in each region.

By the mid-1990s, the U.S. refineries operate only 50-60% of nameplate 1980 distillation capacity. Europe's position is only slightly better at 66% of 1980 capacity. An import fee reduces U.S. operations another 8% as refining capacity, which supplies Eastern U.S. fuels markets and the Gulf Coast petrochemicals market, moves to Europe to avoid the tax.

Over the next 15 years gasoline producing units in Europe, heavy feed ethylene plants and retrofitted sour light distillation units will be major capacity expansion projects. On the Gulf Coast catalytic cracker, coker, and light feed ethylene plant construction projects just about keep pace with retirements. The Eastern U.S. reduces capacity across the board, with the exception of heavy feed ethylene capacity, to no more than 50% of 1980 nameplate capacity.

On the Gulf Coast and in Europe, two important processing reconfigurations evolve:

1) the catalytic cracker becomes the primary unit for gasoline production;

2) the heavy feed ethylene plant becomes the primary unit for petrochemicals production.

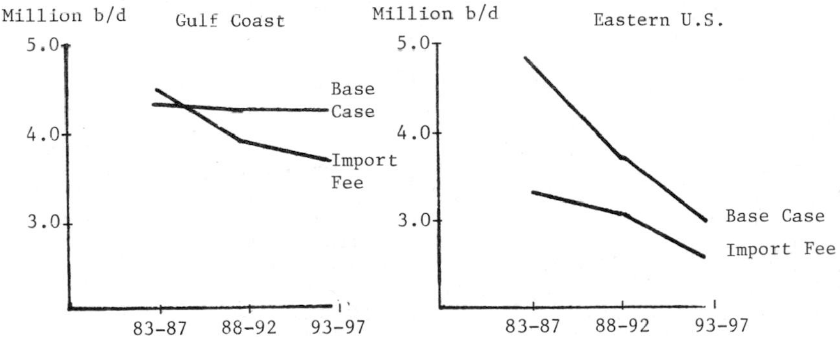

Crude Throughputs

Figure 3

The refineries fully utilize the catalytic crackers which provide a 12% yield gain and the flexibility of both a 91 RON gasoline blend and distillate blend as output. With low gasoline demand, all refineries use the low severity cracking process which produces 54% gasoline and 36% distillate along with other products. The U.S. Gulf Coast, particularly, relies heavily on cracker gasoline as a gasoline blending base rather than on reformates.

The increase in European gasoline demand forces Europe to double its catalytic cracking capacity, aromatics units, and additives units. The expansion is necessary to realign the refineries for gasoline production.

The naphtha, which formerly went to the reformer for octane upgrading, increasingly goes to the ethylene plant. In the base case, naphtha is the primary feedstock for petrochemical production in all regions over the forecast horizon. Consequently, at all the refining centers, the maximum amount of light feed to heavy feed retrofitting occurs in the first period.

Accompanying the decrease in capacity will be a withdrawal of firms from the market place. On the Gulf Coast, 2.7 million b/d of distillation capacity will be exiting the market. That is equivalent to the capacity of the Top 4 companies. Old or inefficient equipment will be the first to go. Which companies replace capacity and which companies permanently shrink will depend on overall efficiency in the market place.

Although the Gulf Coast receives about 80% of the investment dollars spent in the U.S., the reduced activity will have a depressing effect on local economies in the concentrated areas of Houston-Galveston Bay, Port Arthur-Orange, and Baton Rouge-New Orleans.

With large investments throughout the production to market stream, integrated companies will likely be survivors because they will be able to withstand short-run pricing wars and dislocations. International companies will be better situated to handle any scenario. Companies with larger domestic crude supplies should also fare better, particularly under an import fee. Therefore, without government protection, small non-integrated refineries are likely to be nonexistent in a few years, with the exception of those producing specialty products or those serving an isolated market.

4.2 Mid-east Crude Prices and the World Market

In the base case, U.S. refineries (Eastern U.S. only) purchase less than 1.0 million b/d of Mid-east light crude. There is only a $2.00/barrel discount on the price of African crude. In the first period, less than 50% of the available Mid-east light supplies are purchased; that percentage falls to 20% by the last period. To minimize costs, the refineries purchase the growing volumes of slightly cheaper world heavy crude to refine with domestic and African light crudes. Mid-east crude is used only to supplement increased demand. The results suggest that the premium crudes should receive premiums in the long-run. Mid-east crude is used only to supplement increased demand.

Sensitivity tests, however, suggested that the world market is very sensitive to small relative price changes. A $1.00/barrel reduction in the relative price of Mid-east crude almost doubled purchases in the first period and maintained at least a 70% production rate in the subsequent periods. In the short-run, this pricing scheme displaces primarily African crude. Over the long-run heavy crude production is most affected.

The most significant effect of increased Mid-east light crude in the crude mix at the refineries is the impact on the coker. If Mid-east light crude replaces African crudes, then Europe needs about three times more capacity. The coker is one of the most expensive processing units. In addition, the heavy crude retrofitting is not needed.

Given the relative prices in the base case, the crude import mix suggests that the ARAMCO partners and other companies with Mid-east crude will need to look for other markets. Also, those companies with heavy crude slates will be profitable only if heavy crudes are discounted at least $1.00/barrel against the FOB Saudi light price.

4.3 Product Prices

The gasoline market could be an unstable market in the U.S. commensurate with the forecasted decline in the gasoline demand in the base case, Gulf Coast gasoline production falls almost 50% by 1990 before recovering to just under 70% of 1980 production in the mid-1990s. If there is recovery in gasoline demand, however, the Gulf Coast gasoline production could be 20% higher than in 1980 by the mid-1990s.

In addition, gasoline prices historically have carried a large share of refining costs. Gasoline prices have been as high as 150% of the cost of crude. The base case results suggest that in the future the marginal cost of gasoline and middle distillates will be roughly equivalent at around 120% of the cost of crude.

Consequently, gasoline price wars are possible as profit margins are redistributed to other products by the integrated refineries with or without reductions in crude prices. In recent spot markets, distillate prices have been above gasoline prices and, at the gasoline pump, diesel fuel is priced above regular unleaded gasoline.

4.4 An Import Fee

Energy taxes have been a major item on the budget agenda. A federal gasoline tax has already been passed. The import fee is a partial tax on U.S. refiners' acquisition cost of imported crude and U.S. markets' acquisition costs of select identifiable refined products. Although the model does not incorporate price effects on available crude supply or product demand, the model is useful for analyzing how and why industry will restructure itself to avoid the additional cost. The key word is partial and any import fee is a partial tax with respect to the world market.

The model suggests that refining capacity, which supplies the U.S. fuels and petrochemical markets, will relocate in Europe to avoid the tax. As Figure 3 indicates, the Eastern U.S. refineries could lose 1.5 million b/d of base case crude throughput. This loss is primarily in imported fuel oils and sitillates in the first period. The Gulf Coast crude throughput eventually falls below 4.0 million b/d; refined fuels production, however, is relatively unhurt. The most significant impact on the Gulf Coast, as shown in Figure 4, and one which may have been overlooked, is the loss of 50% of the potential ethylene production in the mid-1990s resulting from the increased dependence on naphtha as a feedstock.

An import fee reduces base case crude imports by 2.0 million b/d. Most of this reduction is accounted for by product imports. However, the import fee, which raises the cost of imports to $45-$48/barrel, makes 850 mb/d of U.S. heavy crude (priced at $42.19/barrel) attractive to U.S. refineries. Consequently, revenues from the fee are only $6.0 billion annually for the first five years. In subsequent years revenues are less than $5.0 billion annually as crude imports fall below 3.0 million b/d.

The marginal value of domestic crude rises by just over $5.00/barrel; however, several forecasts suggest that no new domestic supplies would be available to the refineries in this study over the forecast horizon. At the same time, the import fee adds about $.12/gallon to the marginal cost of gasoline and $.04/lb. to the marginal cost of ethylene at the refinery gate.

An import fee on all refined products increases revenues and improves operating conditions in the Eastern U.S.; however, potential Gulf Coast petrochemical capacity migrates to Europe. Because of the increasing use of naphtha as a petrochemical feedstock resulting from the decline in gasoline demand and the increasing breadth of the petrochemical market, a subsidy or raw material exemption may be necessary to retain petrochemical production in the U.S. With the additional threat of Canadian and Mexican supplies (not included in this model) the impact of an import fee on U.S. petrochemical production must be carefully evaluated.

5. CONCLUSIONS

The case study of an import fee on crude oil, gasoline, and middle distillate imports is an enlightening example of the impacts of tax exemptions and tax avoidance by industry under partial taxes.

There are valuable uses of the model and results other than a policy case study tool:

- the model provides a dynamic outlook for a key sector in regional economies;
- with the regional outlook and additional off-model analysis, future problems, such as refinery natural gas requirement or a possible independent refiner-integrated refiner war as markets shrink, may be identified;
- the results, such as shadow values, also provide insights into the role of the refineries in the recent relative price wars in crude and gasoline markets;
- the processing utilization outlook assesses technology requirements and adequacy of existing capacity and extends the investment profile beyond a single company or plant to the industry.

The focus of this research has been to develop an industry model which could provide regional detail, process unit detail and product detail. The additional dimension of time and investment decision rules required a significant reduction in the technical detail found in larger static models, especially company-specific models, in order to develop a reasonable model with conceptual and computational integrity. Consequently, the model is a companion to the plant/company-specific model, not a replacement. In addition, the model needs to be integrated with price sensitive crude supply and product demand models to provide the technical rationalization and integration of market conditions.

There are several improvements, which would expand the size of the model and require additional parameter estimation from sparse data, but should be addressed in future research to improve the model's applicability in planning and policy analysis. They include:

- additional crude processing vectors specific to Europe;
- explicit risk aversion rules to capture extreme price sensitivity;
- additional investment possibilities, such as retrofitting for energy cost savings and discretionary retirement; and
- additional regional detail separating Texas and Louisiana.

Despite this list of improvements, the results do illustrate general trends and the order of magnitude of impacts of various forecasted conditions in petroleum markets on refineries.

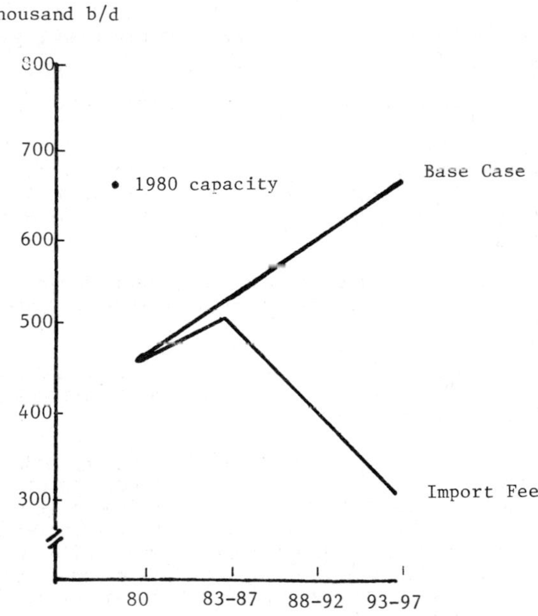

Gulf Cost Ethylene Production
Figure 4

SUMMARY OF THE MODEL

SETS

R	Refining Centers
RU	U. S. Refining Centers
RE	European Refining Centers
CR	Raw Materials - Crude
CRU	U. S. Crudes
CRF	Foreign Crudes
CI	Intermediate Products
CIP	Purchased Intermediate Products
CIF	Intermediate Final Products
CF	Final Products
CFCI	Product Blending Combinations
CF91	91 RON Gasoline
M	Markets
MU	U. S. Markets
Q	Quality Specifications
U	Productive Units
UR	Retrofit Combinations
P	Processes
T	Time Periods

PARAMETERS		Units of Measure
f_{ct}	Available Crude Supply	mb/d
g_t	Imposed Quota	mb/d
f'_t	LPG Available to the U. S.	mb/d
f''_t	LPG Available to Europe	mb/d
a	Technical Coefficients	
q_c	Blending Component Qualities	
Q_c	Gasoline Specifications	
b	Capacity Utilization	
k_{ur}	Base Year Capacity	mb/d
$s_{ur\tau}$	Retired Capacity	mb/d
d_{cmrt}	Market Demand Final Product	mb/d
d^1_{cmrt}	Market Demand Intermediate Final Product	mb/d
n^{cr}_{crt}	Crude Acquisition Cost	\$/b
n^{cI}_{crt}	LPG Acquisition Cost	\$/b
n^{p}_{prt}	Process Unit Operating Cost	\$/b
n^{B}_{crt}	Blending Cost	\$/b
n^{x}_{crmt}	Product Shipping Cost	\$/b
$n^{u}_{ur\tau}$	Capital Cost	\$/b of daily capacity

VARIABLES		Units of Measure
Y_{crt}	Crude Purchase	mb/d
Y^1_{crt}	LPG Purchase	mb/d
Z_{prt}	Process Level	mb/d
$W_{cc'rt}$	Blending Level	mb/d
X_{crmt}	Final Product Shipment	mb/d
X'_{crmt}	Intermediate Final Product Shipment	mb/d
$h_{ur\tau}$	Capacity Expansion	mb/d
ϕ^c_t	Crude and LPG Purchases	\$/yr
ϕ^p_t	Operating Costs	\$/yr
ϕ^x_t	Product Shipping Costs	\$/yr
ϕ^k_t	Capital Costs	\$/yr

EQUATIONS

Raw Material Availability

--Crude Purchases

1 $$\sum_{r\epsilon R} y_{crt} \leq f_{ct} \qquad c\epsilon CR,\ t\epsilon T$$

--Foreign Crude Purchases: U. S.

2 $$\sum_{c\epsilon CRF} \sum_{r\epsilon RU} y_{crt} \leq g_t \qquad t\epsilon T$$

--LPG Purchases: U. S.

3 $$\sum_{r\epsilon RU} y^1_{crt}\Big|_{c\epsilon CIP} \leq f'_t \qquad t\epsilon T$$

--LPG Purchases: Europe

4 $$y^1_{crt}\Big|_{c\epsilon CIP, r\epsilon RE} \leq f''_t \qquad t\epsilon T$$

Balance Equations

--Raw Materials

5 $$\sum_{p\epsilon P} a_{pc}\, z_{prt} \leq y_{crt} \qquad c\epsilon CR,\ r\epsilon R,\ t\epsilon T$$

--Intermediate Products

6 $$\sum_{p\epsilon P} a_{pc} z_{prt} - \sum_{c'\epsilon CF} w_{cc'rt}\Big|_{cc'\epsilon CFCI} + y_{crt}\Big|_{c\epsilon CIP} \leq \sum_{m\epsilon M} x_{cmrt}\Big|_{c\epsilon CIF} \qquad c\epsilon CI,\ r\epsilon R,\ t\epsilon T$$

--Final Products

7 $$\sum_{p\epsilon P} a_{pc}\, z_{prt} + \sum_{c'\epsilon CI} w_{cc'rt}\Big|_{(c,c')\epsilon CFCI} \geq \sum_{m\epsilon M} x_{cmrt} \qquad c\epsilon CF,\ r\epsilon R,\ t\epsilon T$$

Product Quality Specifications

--Gasoline Octane

8 $$\sum_{c'\epsilon CI} (q^1_{c'} - Q^1_c)\, w_{cc'rt}\Big|_{(c,c')\epsilon CFCI} \geq 0 \qquad c\epsilon CF91,\ r\epsilon R,\ t\epsilon T$$

--Gasoline Reid Vapor Pressure

9 $\sum_{c' \in CI} (q^2_{c'} - Q^2_c) \; w_{cc'rt}\Big|_{(c,c')\in CFCI} \leq 0$ $\quad c\in CF91,\ r\in R,\ t\in T$

Capital Accumulation

10 $\sum_{p\in P} b_{up}\, z_{prt} \leq k_{ur} + \sum_{\tau}\Big|_{\tau\leq t} - (h_{ur\tau} - s_{ur\tau})$ $\quad u\in U,\ r\in R,\ t\in T$

11 $\sum_{\tau} h_{ur\tau}\Big|_{(uu)\in UR} \leq k_{u'r}\Big|_{(uu')\in UR} - \sum_{\tau} s_{u'r\tau}\Big|_{(uu')\in UR}$ $\quad u\in U,\ r\in R$

Market Demand

--Final Products

12 $\sum_{r\in R} x_{cmrt} \geq d_{cmt}$ $\quad c\in CF,\ m\in M,\ t\in T$

--Intermediate/Final Products

13 $\sum_{r\in R} X^1_{cmrt} \geq d_{cmrt}$ $\quad c\in CIF,\ m\in M,\ t\in T$

Objective Function

(3.13) $\text{MINIMIZE} = \sum_{t\in T} \delta_t \; (\phi^c_t + \phi^p_t + \phi^x_t + \phi^k_t)$

--Crude and LPG Purchases

(3.13a) $\phi^c_t = 365\,(\sum_{r\in R}\sum_{c\in CR} \eta^{cr}_{crt}\, y_{crt} + \sum_{r\in R}\sum_{c\in CIP} \eta^{cI}_{crt}\, y_{crt})$ $\quad t\in T$

--Operating Costs

(3.13b) $\phi^p_t = 365\,(\sum_{r\in R}\sum_{p\in P} \eta^{p}_{prt}\, z_{prt} + \sum_{c\in CF} \eta^{B}_{crt_{c\in CI}}\, w_{cc'rt}\Big|_{(c,c')\in CFCI})$ $\quad t\in T$

--Product Shipping Costs

(3.13c) $\phi^x_t = 365\,[\sum_{r\in R}\sum_{m\in M} (\sum_{c\in CF} \eta^{x}_{cmrt}\, x_{cmrt} + \sum_{c\in CIF} \eta^{x}_{cmrt}\, x^1_{cmrt})]$ $\quad t\in T$

--Capital Costs

(3.13d) $$\phi_t^k = \sigma \sum_{\tau | \tau \leq t \varepsilon T} \sum_{r \varepsilon R} \sum_{u \varepsilon U} \eta_{ur\tau}^{u} h_{ur\tau} \qquad t \varepsilon T$$

where

(3.1) $$\sigma = \frac{\rho}{1-(1+\rho)-\ell}$$

(3.2) $$\delta_t = [(1+\rho)^{-\omega_t}] \ \theta$$

Non-negatives

$y \ y^1 \ z \ w \ h \ x \ x^1$